Social Competence
in Children

Social Competence in Children

Margaret Semrud-Clikeman
Michigan State University,
East Lansing, Michigan, USA

Margaret Semrud-Clikeman Ph.D.
Departments of Psychology and Psychiatry
Michigan State University,
East Lansing, Michigan, USA

ISBN-13: 978-0-387-71365-6   e-ISBN-13: 978-0-387-71366-3

Library of Congress Control Number: 2007925373

Printed on acid-free paper.

Printed in the United States of America.

9 8 7 6 5 4 3 2 1

springeronline.com

This book is dedicated to my family. I learned my social skills and resiliency from my mother, Margaret Semrud, and father, Ray Semrud. I learned how to work with people, deal with conflict and love from my siblings: David Semrud, Karen Cameron, Kathy Peterson, Richard Semrud, Laurie Semrud, and Amy Steva. There is no way I can ever repay all of the love and support I have received from my family to pursue my dreams.

Contents

About the Author

MARGARET SEMRUD-CLIKEMAN, Ph.D., received her doctorate from the University of Georgia in 1990. She completed an internship and postdoctoral fellowship at the Massachusetts General Hospital/Harvard Medical school and received a post-doctoral neuroscience fellowship at MGH from NIH to study neuropsychological and brain morphology in children with ADHD. Her dissertation was awarded the Outstanding Dissertation of the Year Award from the Orton Dyslexia Society. She has authored four books and numerous articles and continues her research interests in the areas of ADHD and brain morphology using functional and structural MRI scans. She is currently working on research in ADHD, 18q-syndrome, and nonverbal learning disabilities. With Dr. Plizska at UTHSCSA, Margaret was awarded an NIH grant to study the effects of stimulant medication on neuropsychological functioning. Dr. Semrud-Clikeman and her students have developed a social competence intervention that has been successfully piloted at UT. Dr. Semrud-Clikeman was recently awarded the 1999 Early Career Contributions award from the National Academy of Neuropsychology. She has published more than 30 articles, 40 chapters and 3 books. Dr. Semrud-Clikeman is currently a professor at Michigan State University with a joint appointment in Psychology and Psychiatry.

Preface

This book is meant to provide information about social competence in children for clinical practitioners and school professionals. It is also meant to serve as a resource for parents who are searching for answers as to why their child may be experiencing social difficulties. In this vein, I have provided case illustrations to illustrate the struggles and successes that children with various disorders experience. These illustrations are combinations of cases drawn from my experience over the past 30 years with children with and without developmental challenges. I believe that these composites help the reader to put a real face on the difficulties that can be present when a child has difficulty making and keeping friends. It was surprising to me to find, in many cases, very little empirical evidence or information about social competence many of the disorders provided in this book.

This book is organized to provide a developmental framework for our understanding of social competence at various ages. It begins with a discussion of the theories of what social competence is and then proceeds to discuss how children who are typically developing progress through various stages as they grow and experience. These chapters are based in transactional theory in that the environment plays a role in the development of these skills as well as the biological contributions the child brings to his/her experiences. I believe it is crucial to understand how social competence develops in a typically developing child before attempting to appreciate how social competence is problematic in a child with a disorder. In addition, the familial and school contributions to social understanding are crucial aspects for development of social competence and are discussed in this book.

The second part of this book provides social competence information for various disorders ranging from the more commonly experienced childhood difficulties such as attention deficit hyperactivity disorder and learning disabilities to more rare disorders such as childhood cancer and genetic disorders. Some of the areas have been well researched (i.e., ADHD, LD, internalizing disorders) while others have very little information about social competence (genetic disorders, TBI, etc.). This book was designed to provide information that is empirically validated as well as to provide clinical insight into the development of social competence that may be not as well studied in the field.

Interventions are also provided within the context of each chapter. In cases where there is empirical validation of these interventions, the text provides note of this validation. In other cases where the work appears clinically valid but has not been validated at this time, the book indicates this finding and provides cautions about the need for such corroboration. It is important not only to understand these disorders from a social and emotional standpoint, but also to recognize the need for development of appropriate interventions.

Schools are at the forefront for working with children with social competence disorders and yet teachers may not be fully prepared for assisting with such development. Clinicians, school psychologists, and school counselors are at a crucial juncture to provide assistance to parents, teacher, and children. This book was intended to provide a blueprint for these clinicians in understanding the areas of concern as well as providing an overview of possible interventions.

Families are also very important in the socialization process and much of the literature indicates that the child learns social interactions from his/her parents. It is important to provide families with support for learning how to work with children experiencing this difficulty. It is also very important to recognize that parents may also have social understanding deficits and may need not only support but ongoing teaching of skills for themselves. For children with some disorders, the heritability index is quite substantial and parents may have a similar disorder as their child. In this case, providing instruction that does not take these problems into account may backfire and actually cause the parent to be reluctant to pursue assistance for their child and themselves.

In closing, writing of this book helped me to understand the areas of research that are still open for further empirical study. It also brought home to me how important social understanding is for normal child development and the resulting success in life for emotional and social fulfillment. Having worked with children with these difficulties and seen the toll that it takes on them and their parents really brings home the importance of developing interventions that can help these children adjust. While this book has taught me a great deal, it has also been difficult as I have needed to pull together literature from various sources and consolidate this information into, hopefully, a coherent whole. I would like to acknowledge the help that I have obtained from my editor, Judy Jones, throughout this project. I would also like to acknowledge all of the children with whom I have worked who have enriched my life as well as provided me the privilege of knowing them. I would further like to acknowledge my graduate students who have assisted me in the development of our intervention program and have allowed me to teach them and learn from them in this area. The list is long but I would like to acknowledge Jenifer Walkowiak, Laura Guli, Kimberly Glass, Mary Kay Corlett, and Allison Wilkinson and their tireless efforts to work with children with special needs.

1

Social Competence in Children

The [socially] competent individual is one who is able to make use of environmental and personal resources to achieve good developmental outcome (Waters & Sroufe, 1983, p. 81).

It's a rainy day and the children have been unable to go out for recess and so are quite restive. Maggie comes running into my office very upset and talking a mile a minute. I can hear laughter coming from her classroom that is across the hall. Maggie proceeds to tell me that her "friends" told her it was raining cats and dogs and she started to cry because she was afraid the animals would get hurt falling from the sky. She also tells me that when she said that, her "friends" started to laugh at her and she doesn't know why.

Maggie has significant difficulties with social relationships and many of these problems stem from her difficulty with idioms, sarcasm, and humor. Her social competence is limited, and while she knows something is wrong, she is never sure just what. It makes it quite difficult for her to change her behavior when she doesn't really understand social interactions.

There is sufficient empirical evidence that links social competence to mental and physical health (Spitzberg, 2003). It has been linked to such varied disorders as anxiety, cardiovascular disease, juvenile delinquency, and substance abuse, to name a few (Ewart et al., 1991; Fydrich et al., 1998; Renwick & Emler, 1991; Segrin, 1998). Good social competence is valued by organizations and employers and leads to higher success financially and in careers (O'Neil et al., 1997). Recent estimates indicate that between 7 and 10% of the population has difficulties with social interaction skills and may be considered socially incompetent (Hecht & Wittchen, 1988). Approximately one-fifth of the populations in epidemiological study have been found to show loneliness, anxiety, and shyness (Segrin, 1998; Segrin & Flora, 2000).

Social competence is an ability to take another's perspective concerning a situation and to learn from past experience and apply that learning to the ever-changing social landscape. The ability to respond flexibly and appropriately defines a person's ability to handle the social challenges that are presented to us all. Social competence is the foundation upon which expectations for future interactions with others are built and upon which children develop perceptions of their own behavior. Social experiences are intimately connected to emotional competence. It is rare that social competence is present without appropriate emotional functioning also present.

The concept of social competence frequently encompasses additional constructs such as social skills, social communication, and interpersonal communication. Social skills assume that these are behaviors that are repeatable and goal-directed (Spitzberg, 2003). Social interaction assumes that the goal can be accomplished through interaction with another person using language and nonverbal communication. These skills are also thought to be goal-directed. In addition to behaviors, social competence requires correct perception of the social interaction. This perception also encompasses motivation and knowledge on how to perform the skill. Without appropriate perception the motivation and ability to do the skill will not result in socially appropriate actions. Similarly without motivation, the skill will not be performed.

Social experience rests on the foundation of parent–child and peer relationships and is important in the later development of prosocial behaviors. Attachment of an infant to the mother is important for the development of later social competence (Greenberg et al., 1993; Speltz et al., 1999; van IJzendoorn, 1997). This attachment helps the infant to learn that the world is predictable and trustworthy or in less healthy instances that it is capricious and cruel. The foundation of the attachment bond allows the child to venture out from his/her mother to try new experiences and new interactions. Thus, the child brings a set of biologically determined aspects (or temperament) to the environment and the environment works on these aspects to modify and adjust to the biology. In turn the child's temperament also influences the environment. Dodge (1986) conceptualizes social competence as an interaction between the environment and a set of biologically determined abilities. These biologically determined abilities may partially account for social difficulties frequently experienced by children with developmental disorders.

In addition to biological determinants, one must also consider the context for understanding social interactions. Spitzberg (2003) conceptualizes context as incorporating the following aspects: culture, time, relationship, situation, and function. Culture includes the beliefs and values that are part of a generation and a group identity. These beliefs and values provide the texture for how behaviors are learned and passed on to the next generation. Time is how things are learned in sequence. Culture plays a part in how things are learned and when they are learned. Aspects such as how close you stand to someone when you talk with them, the intensity or volume of your voice, and touching are all culture and time bound. Some cultures are "in your face" with talking and touching while others discourage such behaviors. For example, coming from a Nordic tradition space and voice volume were taught to me at an early age as well as a stoic response to emotion. Working in an environment with people from differing cultures was an adjustment for me to make as they talked louder and stood closer to me than I had been used to and I was uncomfortable with these differences. It is important to recognize the importance of culture in defining the relationships and nonverbal communication skills that are present in a social interaction.

Relationships also differ within context. Social communication between husband and wives, brothers and sisters, friends, and other relationships vary depending on the social interaction. Skills valued in one relationship are not appropriate in another. The situation in which the interaction takes place is also important. Situations differ in type varying from casual to intimate and formal to informal. Behaviors in one setting are not appropriate in another—the inability to be flexible depending on the context often contributes to social competence difficulties. Finally the function is important. Spitzberg (2003) states "communication *does* rather than just *is*" (p. 96). He uses the example that assertive behavior may be appropriate in one situation but not when trying to obtain something else such as affection or comfort.

When behaviors do not match the context and the child does not understand this mismatch, the child or adult often has difficulties relating to others. The example cited early in this chapter was of a child who literally translates language and reacts inappropriately to this miscommunication. It is not uncommon for these children to have difficulties with their peers and they are very often evaluated and found to have one or more psychiatric diagnoses. The following section discusses one way of understanding social difficulties.

Voeller's Clusters

Voeller (1994) hypothesizes three clusters of problematic behavior that often lead to impairment in social competence. These clusters include a group with aggressive and hostile behavior, a perceptual deficits subgroup, and a group who has difficulty with self-regulation. Children with aggressive and hostile behavior are those whose acting out behaviors negatively influence their ability to form relationships. Behaviors often seen with these children include butting into games, difficulty waiting for their turn, and becoming nasty when thwarted. Their peers reject these children frequently. The most common diagnosis for these children is oppositional defiant disorder or conduct disorder. Children who are aggressive have been hypothesized to have deficiencies with social information processing and often employ inappropriate social problem-solving strategies. For those with aggressive difficulties, it has been shown that they will search for fewer facts in a social situation and pay more attention to the aggressive social interaction present in an interaction than those children who are less aggressive (Crick & Dodge, 1994; Gouze, 1987).

The second diagnostic cluster consists of children who do not perceive their environment appropriately and who interpret interpersonal interactions inaccurately. These children have difficulty reading social cues, facial expressions, and body gestures. The most common diagnosis is pervasive developmental disorder, Asperger's disorder, and/or nonverbal learning disabilities. The final diagnostic cluster includes those children who have classic difficulties in executive functioning. Some children in this group may be diagnosed with attention deficit hyperactivity disorder (ADHD) while many may simply be seen as disorganized and flighty. Emerging evidence suggests that the last two diagnostic clusters are not exclusive and there may be overlap between these two types. Children with social perceptual difficulties may also show problems with executive functioning (Carlson & Moses, 2001; Hala et al., 2003).

Models of Social Competence

Crick and Dodge (1994) proposed a social information-processing model for understanding social competence. There are six steps in this model that are important in processing of social interactions—difficulty at any step in these skills generally translates into problems relating to others. The six steps are:

1. Encoding of relevant stimuli—the child must pay attention to non-verbal and verbal social cues both obvious and covert.
2. Interpretation of the cues—the child must understand what has happened as well as the cause and intent underlying the interaction.
3. Goals are established—the child determines what he/she wants from the interaction and how to put forth an understanding.
4. Representation of the situation is developed—the child needs to compare the experience to previous situations and recall his/her reaction to those situations as well as what was the result of the interactions.
5. Selection of possible responses—responses are chosen based upon the perception of the event and skills in the child's repertoire.
6. The child acts and the success of the act is evaluated.

Figure 1.1 shows the relationship between perception, interpretation, and response. As one can see from Figure 1.1, facial expressions, body

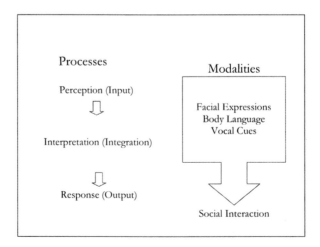

Figure 1.1 A model for social perception. Used with permission from Dr. Laura Guli

language, and vocal cues provide information about the success of these skills—with inaccurate perception these modalities do not provide the feedback needed to perform appropriately socially.

Maggie had difficulty at stage one—encoding of the relevant stimuli—and at stage two—interpretation of the cues. These misinterpretations colored her response as well as the reaction of others to her behavior. An integral part of social competence is the importance of emotions in these skills. Emotions can and do impact processing at each and all of these levels. As Maggie became more and more upset, she was less able to calmly assess what was happening, and perhaps change her responses. Social competence involves the child's ability to adapt to a dynamic environment and to assess when the behaviors chosen have been effective (Saarni, 1999). Maggie had difficulty with this skill due to faulty encoding.

Crick and Dodge (1994) have used their model to describe the behavior of aggressive children and adolescents. For these children, deficits in the ability to process information both cognitively and socially lowered their ability to adapt their behavior appropriately when faced with everyday frustrations. In this model, aggression is seen as a way to solve social problems (Pakaslahti, 2000).

Social situations provide a great deal of information at one time. What one selects to "pay attention" to helps to narrow the stimulus field as well as what aspects are selected that are most salient to that particular person. For an aggressive person, the stimuli selected are often different from those selected by a nonagressive person. Crick and Dodge (1994) suggest that children who are aggressive have difficulty processing information and often employ aggressive problem-solving strategies. This processing of information relies on the child's past memory of previous experiences. These memories involve emotional and physiological components that in turn influence how the child/adolescent responds in the current scenario (Huesmann & Eron, 1989). Thus, the child's past learning and social experiences come into play in his/her interpretation of the current event (Crick & Dodge, 1994; Huesmann & Eron, 1989). Additional variables include temperament and maturation (Pakaslahti, 2000). Further discussion of these areas will be provided in the chapter on oppositional behavior/conduct disorder.

Another way to conceptualize social competence is to consider underlying constructs. Cavell et al. (2003) suggest a three-tiered model. The most advanced level is called social adjustment. Social adjustment is where the child is developmentally on target for achieving appropriate social goals. This level reflects how well the child meets the expectations of parents, teachers, and society. Most children achieve this level without problems but when difficulties arise the child is often seen as "different" and may be socially rejected or isolated from his/her peers. The next level is social performance or how well the child performs in social situations. This level incorporates the child's style in interactions, the efficiency of the style, and what situations may be problematic for the child. The most basic level is social skills or the specific abilities the child uses within a social situation. This level includes how the child responds to the situation as well as how the situation is encoded.

Cavell et al. (2003) incorporate the Crick and Dodge model into the social skills level of their constructs.

The theory of mind model is another conceptualization of social competence and processing. This hypothesis (Baron-Cohen et al., 2000) suggests that difficulties in children with autism are a result of impairment in the ability to understand mental states as a method for interpreting and predicting the behavior of the child or of other people's behavior (Joseph & Tager-Flusberg, 2004). The ability to represent the world and to understand that this representation of the world may not be the same for each individual begins at about age 4. It is thought that limited self-awareness and other awareness significantly limits social interactions that are reciprocal (Tager-Flusberg, 1999). A difficulty in establishing a representation of "reality" for the individual with autism has been found related to problems with conversational ability (Capps et al., 1998) and poor social functioning (Frith et al., 1994). Difficulty with language skills likely impacts the ability of children with autism to communicate their ideas. There is not, however, a direct line between the child's ability to understand the other's perspective and improvement in social competence and/or social language. When direct training has been provided to establish attributions of other's feelings and thoughts, improvement in social competence or language has not been also observed (Hadwin et al., 1997; Ozonoff & Miller, 1995).

Many aspects of the theory of mind are also contained in Dodge and Crick's (1990) theory. Faulty encoding (Dodge & Crick, 1990) would appear to be synonymous with the social perceptual skills discussed by Joseph and Tager-Flusberg (2004). These are skills that allow the child to understand what the other is feeling and saying. Thus, social competence requires several different elements to be learned in order to understand the relationship between attribution of meaning, nonverbal cues, and perspective taking.

Elements of Social Competence

A key element for social competence appears to be facility with language and the ability to have a conversation. Garfield et al. (2001) suggest that the ability to understand the world from another's point of view is dependent on both language acquisition and a child's growing social understanding that is developed through conversation and interaction with others. These authors do not believe that language skills and social ability can be separated and are jointly required for the development of social competence. Similarly Bruner (1998) suggests that children give meaning to what people do in relationship to their ability to learn language as well as accepted social practices within the culture.

Language is socially obtained and parents and teachers provide models and scaffolding for the child to learn (Vygotsky, 1986). The knowledge the child develops about social interactions is often verbally mediated. The scripts that are developed to aid the child in understanding their own affective experience and that of others are also socially mediated (Saarni, 1999). The beliefs, desires, and needs are all expressed through language and play into the attribution of social exchanges and appropriate behavior is subsequently taught (Leanh & Frye, 1999).

A study by Joseph and Tager-Flusberg (2004) controlled for language difficulties and found that social perceptual abilities (interpreting facial expressions, gestures, and voice prosody) were related to difficulties in social reciprocity. A social exchange requires fast processing of these social perceptual skills that serve as a means for making judgments about the intention of the speaker and interpretation of the accompanying nonverbal cues. In children with difficulties in social communication, these social perceptual aspects become important for appropriate interactions. When language skills are intact, the child is more able to interpret social exchanges. However, when language skills are intact and are inconsistent with nonverbal cues, the child will rely on the language cues rather than the more subtle facial expression, voice prosody, or intent of the speaker. The difficulty that Maggie had in interpreting idiomatic speech was related to problems with understanding subtleties in language as well as a misinterpretation of the intent of the speaker.

Another of the key elements of social competence has been found to be the ability to accurately send and receive emotional messages (Halberstadt et al., 2001). Social competence incorporates emotional competence and vice versa. A necessary skill to develop rewarding friendships and relationships includes the ability to infer the emotional states of others. Understanding the emotional state of the other person in the situation requires encoding nonverbal cues including facial expressions, prosody, and gestures.

An early skill that has been found to be important for the development of additional social ability is the ability to understand and recognize facial expressions appropriately. These expressions allow the child to understand the other's mood, reaction to their behavior and to adapt accordingly (Singh et al., 1998). These skills develop early and have been found to be already present in the preschool years (Nowicki & Mitchell, 1998).

Additional skills involved in social competence include the ability to learn, to take another's perspective, to manage one's behavior, and the ability to work cooperatively with others (Vaughn & Haager, 1994). These skills are consistent with the neuropsychological term executive functions. Executive functions consist of abilities that allow the child to evaluate his/her behavior, assess its appropriateness, and make changes if required (Damasio, 2001). They include working memory (the ability to hold information in mind while solving a problem) and cognitive flexibility. Executive functions allow for problem solving be effective as the child uses situations that have previously occurred and applies learning and flexibility to solving and/or understanding what is occurring. Thus, social problem solving involves the executive functions of working memory and cognitive flexibility.

Two components that are closely related to executive functioning have been hypothesized to be involved in social interactions: problem orientation and problem solving skills (Shewchuck et al., 2000). Problem orientation includes the schemas the child has formed from past experience as well as his/her attributions for how the social world works. Included in this orientation are the attributions the child makes for other's behavior as well as his/her sense of his/her own ability and self-esteem (Chang & D'Zurilla, 1996). Problem-solving skills are the strategies that are used to solve the problem or to understand the situation and to arrive at the most adaptive solution (Ciarrochi et al., 2003).

A link between mental health and problem orientation has been empirically supported. Effective problem orientation has been linked to low incidences of depression, suicidality, health problems, and with positive coping strategies (Chang & D'Zurilla, 1996; Ciarrochi et al, 2003). Good performance on executive function tasks such as concept formation, problem-solving skills, and cognitive flexibility have also been linked to effective problem orientation (Shewchuk et al., 2000). Children who are typically developing acquire these skills fairly readily and are able to adapt them to changing expectations. Direct teaching of the skills is generally not required, and if difficulties present themselves, a short corrective experience seems to be sufficient to change behavior.

Perspective taking is another skill important for social competence. Very young children see the world as revolving around them. As they develop, they begin to realize that others may not see an action or a situation in the same way as they do. The development of perspective taking is crucial for more mature social relationships to form. The ability to utilize increasing amounts of information as well as to simultaneously process information is a necessary prerequisite for perspective taking. These skills appear approximately by age 10 and continue to develop into adolescence. Most children develop the ability to analyze other's viewpoints and as they mature become able to step back from the situation and analyze it objectively (Woolfolk, 2004). This skill is very important for a child/adolescent to utilize adult cues and suggestions for changing behavior (Berk, 2002). Without this underlying foundation, it becomes very difficult for children to understand how their actions affect others and to change their behavior accordingly.

Perspective taking also requires the child to understand another's desires and beliefs. Emerging research indicates that a child understands another person's desires prior to understanding their beliefs (Wellman & Liu, 2004). A meta-analytic study indicated that a child can correctly judge a person's desires before beliefs. Moreover, it was found that children first learn to judge that two people have differing views and then develop the ability to understand how the person's action follows from their belief (Wellman et al., 2001).

Saarni (1999) suggests that in order for a child to develop self-efficacy, they need to establish an understanding of social transactions as well as establishing one's identity through successfully negotiating social interchanges. Success in this area requires the ability to apply past knowledge and experiences appropriately to a situation at hand. Saarni (1999) suggest the following eight skills for emotional competence that also appear necessary for adequate social competence:

1. Awareness of your emotional state and motivations.
2. The ability to understand the other person's emotion from nonverbal cues.
3. The ability to use emotional language.
4. Empathy.

5. Understanding that external and internal expressions may not be concurrent.
6. Coping with distressing emotions.
7. Understanding that relationships are intimately related to how one negotiates emotional communication.
8. Emotional self-efficacy.

These skills are described as emotional competence and while Saarni (1999) correctly identifies that emotional and social competence cannot be separated, it is important to note that several of these topics are very important in social competence. The ability to express one's feelings as well as be aware of one's and the other's feelings is a cornerstone for social competence. In addition, the ability to communicate feelings and desires is highly important for appropriate social exchanges. Finally it is very important for the person to not only develop emotional self-efficacy but to also develop social efficacy—the ability to deal with situations that arise and to change one's behavior depending on the environment. Moreover, social efficacy also assumes that one is open to learning new ways of interacting when the old ones don't work and that one is able and motivated to do so. Thus interpersonal reasoning and emotional understanding are closely related topics. Interpersonal reasoning refers to the child's ability to understand their relationship with others as well as being aware of how they think about themselves. Emotional understanding is the ability to recognize emotions of himself/herself and others as well as to interpret context (Welsh and Bierman, 2003).

Summary and Conclusions

Although the concept of social competence is understood by the clinician and the lay public, the definitions for social competence are problematic. Embedded within this term one must consider culture, relationships, timing, perception (encoding), integration, and the behaviors involved in social relationships. Motivation, knowledge, and the ability to complete the skills are also important constructs for understanding social communication. In addition, emotional competence enters into our understanding of social functioning and the two abilities overlap. I do not believe that one can have emotional competence without social competence and vice versa.

In addition to defining social competence, it is also important to understand how to assess this ability. The use of observations, self-report rating scales, behavioral rating scales, and direct measures of social understanding are useful tools for first evaluating where the child/adolescent functions. In addition to these measures, clinical interviews are very important to provide a window into the child or adolescent's level of functioning as well as the parent's ability to model and teach the child. As indicated earlier, the parent–child relationship sets the foundation upon which social competence is built. To further understand this construct, it is important to briefly discuss the developmental issues that are present at each stage for the development of social competence. The following chapter will provide a brief overview of development from a social competence stance.

2

Development of Social Competence in Children

Social competence develops over time. Tasks that are crucial for mastery of social skills emerge at various points on the developmental continuum and build on previously learned skills and knowledge. Thus, a breakdown at certain points in the continuum will have a ripple effect on subsequent development. As the child learns appropriate social skills, emotional maturation also occurs. These parallel developmental tasks of social and emotional competence again emphasize the importance of addressing both abilities to understand either one. Social interactions are often defined as communication with underlying emotional components (Halberstadt et al., 2001). When these two competences do not develop in concert, the child often has difficulty with many aspects of his/her environment. Although some researchers emphasize the relationship between social and emotional competence (Saarni, 1999), others do not explicitly discuss this interdependence when describing either or both variables (Denham, et al., 2004).

The following sections will review the development of social (as well as emotional competence) during specific period of childhood. The discussion will include infancy and preschool, middle childhood (ages 6–12), and adolescence (13–18). The major issues that children at these ages face will be reviewed as well as the contributions of parenting, ethnicity, and school environments to developing social competence. Biological issues such as temperament and emotional regulation will also be addressed as well as issues of aggression, prosocial behavior, and inhibition.

Infancy

In infancy children learn to understand their world through sensory input (vision, hearing, and touch) and how to acquire things that they need. Initially the child is happy to have anyone touch him/her but gradually the infant learns to associate a particular voice, touch, smell, and face to someone who is important—the mother, father, or other caretaker. This association is the first social experience of the child. At 9–14 months of age the child is able to follow another person's gaze, to act differentially to objects depending on how their caretaker reacts to it whether positively or negatively, and to become upset when not granted their desires (Wellman et al., 2004). Infants begin to understand that when their caregiver looks at an object with a smile that it is a desired object and the infant will reach for it spontaneously (Phillips et al., 2002). Moreover, it was found that the development of this social cognition related well to the later ability to understand another person's perspective when the child reaches 3 and 4 years of age.

These initial experiences pave the way for later understanding and begin the development of perspective taking. It is through these interactions that preschoolers begin to develop the "theory of mind" construct where they begin to understand that others may have differing thoughts and beliefs from themselves. Toddlers and preschoolers begin to understand that emotions and desires are internal and based on the other's experience and that language can communicate these feelings ("he is mad") to others (Carpenter et al., 1998).

Temperament Contributions

Temperament is a construct that describes a person's biological responses to the environment. Issues such as soothability, rhythmicity, sociability, and arousal make up this construct. Sociability contributes to social competence. These are children that prefer the presence of others and value interactions with others compared to being alone. Most children also seek out the attention of others. Babies left to themselves for periods of time will cry and seek out attention from the caretaker. Related to the concepts of sociability and attention is that of responsivity. Responsivity means that the infant or preschooler responds to the other person. In turn this responsivity means that the other person will again approach the infant. When a child does not respond to others by smiling, gurgling, or liking to be touched, there is a good chance the infant will not be approached as frequently, and thus not develop the skills required to interact with others even at a basic level. Overarousal or underarousal often complicates the approach and response of others to the infant. For this reason the child may have too intense of reactions to others or seem not to react at all. Rhythmicity refers to the child's ability to modify his/her responses to the environment. Sleep schedules, feeding, and other types of activities generally have a rhythm to them. A child with problems in rhythmicity may have difficulty sleeping or eating on a schedule. For the infant the mother often accommodates her schedule to the child's.

As the child grows to approximately 6–8 months of age the infant will seek out other activities and be content to leave the mother within sight for periods of time. If a child is high in sociability, the child's demands on the mother may be excessive and result in pushing away or encouraging less interaction unless the mother has a similar temperament. Similarly if the child is low in sociability, he/she may not wish for as much interaction and may actually find social interaction aversive and seek to reduce it through crying or other distress. When there is a mismatch between the mother's temperament and the child's, problems arise and frustration can arise for both participants. Crucial to this experience is the finding that these difficulties later translate into problems with adjustment and peer relationships (Buss & Plomin, 1984).

Self-regulatory ability increases in importance as the infant matures into a preschooler. Children who are unable to regulate their emotions often experience difficulty with acting out and frequently show problems with social competence (Diener & Kim, 2003). Eisenberg and Fabes (1992) suggest that children who are high on negative emotionality but who develop good abilities for self-regulation generally develop adequate prosocial behaviors. However, those children who are high on negative emotionality and low on self-regulation frequently experience very difficult development both socially and emotionally. These children are also not seen as desirable playmates due to tantruming, whining, and/or aggressive behaviors associated with negative emotions and poor self-regulation.

Attachment

Ainsworth (1979) has distinguished three types of attachment style in infants. The first is the secure infant who does not become upset when the mother leaves and greets her warmly when she returns. The avoidant infant complains when the mother leaves and then ignores her when she returns. Finally the resistant infant is angry when the mother leaves and returns. Buss and Plomin (1984) suggest that children with moderate sociability and emotionality are generally securely attached infants. They further hypothesize that avoidant infants are unsociable and low in emotion while resistant infants are emotional. Some researchers dispute the relationship between attachment and temperament (Sroufe, 1982) while others support such a relationship (Buss & Plomin, 1984)—further study is required in this area.

A recent study of the relationship between attachment, temperament, and theory of mind found that early mother–child relationships do contribute to the ability to develop understanding of another's point of view. Symons & Clark (2000) evaluated children at age 2 and again at age 5. These children and their mothers were assessed as to attachment security and maternal sensitivity as well as an understanding of unexpected identities and object locations. Findings were that maternal sensitivity and emotional distress at age 2 predicted how successful the child would be on a perspective taking task (the theory of mind task) at age 5 where an unexpected occurrence happened. Children with mothers with low sensitivity and who were high on emotional distress performed much more poorly than those with mothers who had average levels of sensitivity and the child showed typical levels of emotionality.

Rubin et al. (1998) found that young boys with poor self-regulation who had mothers who were demanding often showed behaviors that were characterized by tantrums, acting out, and destructive aggression. Children who are resistant and who have a parent who is dominant and demanding frequently develop anger (Matthews et al., 1996) while those whose parent is supportive develop empathy and appropriate social functioning (Zhou et al., 2002). In this way, the mother's temperament interacts with the child's temperament. When there is a goodness of fit between mother and child, social competence appears to develop more smoothly. When the mother's difficulty compounds the child's problems, then the child develops coping behaviors that are not helpful to his/her social development.

While many have studied infant attachment, there is emerging evidence that the mother's attachment also has an effect on social competence. When a mother experiences separation anxiety from her child, higher levels of depression, low self-esteem, and low self-efficacy have been identified in that mother (Hock & Schirtzinger, 1992). Moreover, such maternal separation anxiety has been linked to infants also showing high levels of separation anxiety as well as a pattern of insecure attachment or an avoiding of developing attachments at all (McBride & Belsky, 1988; Stifter et al., 1993). In this manner the mother's attachment impacts how the child responds socially to her and others. In addition, the mother's depression and feelings of insecurity are transferred to her child with resulting behavioral difficulties most frequently seen.

Although a full exposition of the attachment literature is beyond the intent of this book, the interested reader is referred to the work of Ainsworth, Stroufe, and Buss and Plomin for further information. Attachment likely plays a role in the infant's ability to develop and/or desire attachments to others. Erikson's theory (Erikson, 1980) suggests that the main task of infants is to develop trust with others followed by autonomy and then initiative. These basic tasks underlie the child's ability to function socially as well as to have the confidence to approach others. When the mother's psychopathology interferes with attachment or when the child's temperament is more difficult, problems arise not only in the parent–child relationship but also in the child's later ability to form social bonds.

Preschoolers

The tasks a preschooler needs to master involve the ability to manage their emotions with others particularly peer groups and to meet social expectations of society at large. Prior to this point, the most important people in the preschooler's life have been his/her parents, and extended family, daycare providers, and possibly some peer involvement. Once the child becomes a preschooler, additional requirements are generally placed on the child to adapt to preschool teacher expectations as well as peer group requirements. The preschooler needs to learn how to play with others and this requires the skills of conflict management, assertiveness, sharing, and emotional regulation. As the child becomes more adept at managing his/her own emotional response, peer relationships become smoother. Such management assumes that the child is able to evaluate his/her own need states as well as generate alternatives for behavior and select appropriately.

Denham et al. (2004) suggest that the first step in this development is the recognition of what emotion is being experienced and then the recognition of how others are responding to the child. Moreover, the child must access previously learned rules of behavior and select the most appropriate alternative. In order to accomplish all of these tasks within a short period of time, the preschooler needs to be able to process information smoothly and quickly and to use the environmental context to modify his/her behavior.

In the preschool years management of these emotions is an important aspect of socialization. Children who are unable to adjust their reactions are often not selected for play and may be rejected outright by their peers. A child must not only be able to recognize what is the appropriate action to take, he/she must also be able to modulate the emotional state well enough to be able to take that action. A child who is intense in responding to situations and will cry or have a tantrum will be unable to use skills that he/she may know due to difficulty with emotional regulation.

Preschoolers often require additional structure and support in order to regulate their emotions. Caretakers will provide limit setting as well as identifying the emotion the child is expressing and often suggesting a solution to the problem. Parents will also often attempt to be proactive and structure the environment as well as limit the experiences and stimulation a child has at certain times or when in a certain mood or emotional state. This type of behavior management is particularly important for children with difficult temperaments or those who become easily overwhelmed. These coping skills are eventually applied to similar situations as the child matures and understands the consequences of his/her actions and emotions. Finally the child begins to understand how his/her ability to modulate their emotions affects feelings as well as the ability to interact with others. In this manner their ability to manage situations improves and the child is able to choose appropriate reactions to varying environments (Denham et al., 2004). During this transitional time, instances of intense emotional outbursts such as tantrums and crying decrease.

These issues are very important because several studies have found that the social behaviors shown by preschoolers are predictive of behavior in early and middle childhood (Diener & Kim, 2003; Eisenberg et al., 1997; Ladd & Price, 1987). Aggression and withdrawal in preschoolers has been found to be related to expression of these behaviors at a later time. Children who are aggressive or withdrawn tend to be rejected by peers and to have more feelings of loneliness and self-esteem than children with good social competence (Hymel et al., 1993).

Emerging evidence indicates a gender difference in development of social competence. Diener and Kim (2003) evaluated 110 preschool children and their mothers using observations, parent and teacher report over a 5-month period. Findings indicated that boys were significantly higher on externalizing behavior measures while girls were significantly higher on prosocial behavior ratings. No gender differences were found between genders on social withdrawal measures. Results for measures of social competence found a significant relationship between temperament ratings and self-regulation as well as a relationship to the mother's positive support during classroom observations. Moreover, externalizing behavior in girls was found to be associated with poorer self-regulation and higher levels of activity. Social withdrawal in girls is related to lower levels of maternal positive support. For boys social competence was significantly related to self-regulation as well as maternal separation anxiety. The boys' prosocial behaviors were related to good self-regulation, lower levels of anger with externalizing behaviors related to poor self-regulation and high levels of reported maternal anger. Social withdrawal in boys was related to greater maternal separation anxiety.

The findings of the above study are important because they indicate differences in genders as young as 24 months of age in the development of social competence. They also highlight the importance of the mother's ability to separate from the child and the child's evolving social competence. Moreover, teacher and mother reports indicate the importance of developing self-regulation as a major step in succeeding in an academic environment apart from educational attainment. Similarly kindergarten teachers have repeatedly endorsed the importance of the behaviors of the ability to take turns, follow directions, to not disrupt the class, and to be empathic to other children's feelings as more important than a knowledge of colors, shapes, letters, and numbers (Diener & Kim, 2003). The study also underlines the need for children who have high emotionality to develop better emotional regulation skills. Promoting these skills appears to be an important tool particularly for the child to learn problem solving when faced with negative emotions and developing appropriate coping strategies (Bronson, 2000).

Biological Contributions

Effective self-regulation has also been studied from a biological standpoint. Individual differences in individual sensitivity to environmental stimuli have been demonstrated to be important for understanding arousal and activation (Blair, 2003). Kagan (1994) found a relationship between behavioral inhibition (shyness) and sensitivity to arousal. This neural circuitry has been called the BAS/BIS system. The Behavioral Activation System (BAS) is believed to underlie withdrawal while the Behavioral Inhibition System (BIS) is related to personality and psychopathology (Quay, 1993). Approach–withdrawal tendencies shape cortical representations of their experiences which feedback to motivational and attentional systems over time. These tendencies are active in shaping the child's development both socially and cognitively as well as in the development of psychopathology (Blair, 2002; Rothbart & Ahadi, 1994).

The BAS/BIS system has been found to be related to neural activity in the prefrontal cortex with approach behavior and positive affect associated with the left prefrontal cortex and the right prefrontal cortex associated with withdrawal and negative affect (Davidson, 1994; Tomarken et al., 1992). Blair (2003) studied the effect of approach (BIS) and withdrawal (BAS) tendencies in young children through parent report and teacher-reported adaptive behavior within the classroom. He hypothesized the sensitivity to incentive and threat is central to self-regulation and is likely regulated through prefrontal systems. In addition to parent and teacher report, Blair (2003) examined cardiac vagal tone and the ability to suppress vagal tone (vagal suppression), which has been found to be related to emotionality and emotional regulation/approach behavior in children (Porges, 1998). Those with higher levels of approach behavior (BIS) generally show higher levels of vagal suppression while those with less ability to suppress reaction to the environment often show lower levels of approach and higher levels of withdrawal (BAS).

Kagan et al. (1984) have suggested that a key temperament characteristic of children who are shy is that of behavioral inhibition toward the unfamiliar or the tendency to withdraw from new situations. These children show a greater degree of stress when placed in novel and unfamiliar environments and learning/social experiences. In addition, these children show higher high rates and more cardiac reactivity than children who are not inhibited (Snidman et al., 1995). When children who show higher inhibitory characteristics are placed in novel situations they often respond with distress and experience an approach–avoidance conflict, wanting to play with other children and being fearful to do so (Rubin, 1993). They also show lower social competence and often possess lower levels of reciprocity or empathy (Bohlin et al., 2000). Frequently children with inhibition toward the unfamiliar show social isolation (Thorell et al., 2004). It has also been found that behavioral inhibition is more noticeable for these children in unfamiliar settings while their behaviors do not differ from other children when in familiar surroundings (Aspendorpf, 1993).

In addition to temperament characteristics, executive inhibition plays a role in social competence particularly in preschool and elementary children. Executive inhibition is the ability to inhibit or stop responding and to inhibit distractibility (Barkley, 1997). Nigg et al. (2000) found that good inhibitory skills in kindergarten children predicted excellent social competence skills 2 years later. For children with poor executive inhibition, problems in social relationships appear to be related to rejection by their peers due to low ability to recognize other's wishes and problems with evaluating the emotional reaction of their peers (Henker & Whalen, 1999).

Thorell et al. (2004) suggest that the behavioral inhibition system is related to inhibition to the familiar while effortful control is related to executive inhibition. Effortful control is thought to be related to frontal lobe functioning while inhibition to the familiar is hypothesized to be related to the limbic system (Rothbart et al., 1994). These two systems interact with inhibition to the unfamiliar motivating executive inhibition allowing for the child to evaluate novel situations (Nigg, 2001). In turn these systems are reciprocal and may be important for self-regulation (Thorell et al., 2004). These two inhibitory processes have been found to be significantly predictive when measured at age 5 and then again at age 8 (Thorell et al., 2004). Children with high levels of both types of inhibition at age 5 were found to have an increased risk for developing social withdrawal and social anxiety by age 8. Furthermore, those children with low levels of both types of inhibition are at risk for developing hyperactive behavior but do not develop social anxiety difficulties.

Relationships with Teachers

Teachers also function as attachment figures and research has indicated the children who are securely attached to their preschool teacher also appear to be readily able to explore their physical and social environments more appropriately (Pianta, 1998). Moreover, preschoolers who form a conflictual teacher relationship seem to have difficulty forming adequate social relationships and also have problems with learning while those who are dependent have significant problems forming peer relationships (Pianta et al., 1995). These relationships also appear to be stable and continue into the elementary school years (Hamre & Pianta, 2001).

In free play, teachers interact a significant amount of time with the children and have been found to interact a similar amount of time as they do for cognitive learning (Bronson et al., 1995; Moulton et al., 1999). Most children have been found to interact approximately 11% of the time with teachers during free play (Vliestra, 1981). Those who spend more time interacting with teachers, tend to have more problematic behaviors and tend to be more frequently rejected by peers (Coie et al., 1990). Moreover, children who are shy also garner more teacher interactions and also have poorer social relationships (Pianta et al., 1995). Participating appropriately in social play with the teacher develops the ability to converse appropriately and share and is a predictor variable for peer acceptance in early childhood (Coplan & Rubin, 1998).

Coplan and Prakash (2003) sought to evaluate the social and emotional characteristics of children who frequently interacted with teachers. They based their study on findings from Sroufe et al. (1983) that children with insecure parental attachment tended to receive more teacher-initiated contact than those who were securely attached. Children who were more aggressive or shy/anxious tended to have more contact with teachers but the initiator of this contact has not been studied. Coplan and Prakash (2003) studied 135 children ranging in age from 33 to 66 months who were attending preschools. These children were observed during indoor free play and teacher ratings were also obtained. Findings indicated the presence of two different types of groups. The first group initiated or solicited teacher attention and the second group received teacher initiation. The children who frequently initiated contact were rated by teachers as more aggressive and engaged in more physical play. These children were also found to be more social, outgoing, and active than their peers and initiated more contact with their peers which was also more frequently rejected (Coie & Dodge, 1998). Thus, Coplan and Prakash (2003) suggested that these children turned to the teacher for attention and social interaction since they were more frequently rejected by their peers.

The groups of children that received more teacher attention but did not initiate these contacts were found to engage in solitary and passive play and were rated as more anxious than their counterparts. Teachers appeared to respond to behavioral and affective cues of the shy child and initiated contact to soothe these children. Moreover, teachers also appeared to perceive these children as more dependent on them than others in the classroom. In addition, children who did not fall into either of these two groups were found to not only be more socially facile but also have academic skills and better behavioral control.

Peer Relationships in Early Childhood

Peer relationships also appear to be influenced by emotional understanding and quality of play. Girls who are preschoolers who use high levels of pretend play were found to have high levels of emotional regulation and competence while boys with high levels of pretend play showed good emotional understanding and appropriate play that was physical in nature (Lindsey & Colwell, 2003). Similarly the ability to understand the perspective of another child at the preschool level has been found to be positively related to social skills ratings by teachers (Cassidy et al., 2003). Moreover, when language abilities were parceled out of this equation, perception of peer's understanding continued to significantly discriminate the groups.

Further study has found that preschoolers who show good emotional regulation have better social competence. Moreover, those who show positive affect often experience higher peer status and good teacher ratings as far as friendliness and aggression while those with negative affect are rated more poorly and have troublesome peer relationships (Denham et al., 2004). In addition, preschoolers who understand emotion appear to have higher peer status and those who perceive their peers as angry when no anger is present often have poor social behaviors (Barth & Bastiani, 1997).

Children as young as 3 years of age show affective reciprocity and higher levels of affection with friends than with siblings (Volling et al., 1997). A young child is also more sympathetic to a friend's problem than that of a nonfriend and will suggest solutions (Rose & Asher, 1999). In addition, preschoolers by the age of 4 are readily able to share positive interactions and to talk about their feelings and play (Brown et al., 1996). Children at the preschool level who are able to engage in more complex play were found to have better social competence and were more socially accepted (Cillessen & Belmore, 2004).

Cultural differences have been found to relate to differences in peer relationships. Korean-American preschoolers were found to participate in less social pretend play than Caucasian children (Farver et al., 1995). Differences in perception of positive peer interactions have been found in samples of African-American preschoolers also with those who were more aggressive showing higher levels of social acceptance (Fantuzzo et al., 1998). Further study is needed in this area.

Gender differences are also present. Solitary-passive play for preschool girls but not boys has been linked to lower social acceptance (Hart et al., 1993). Moreover prosocial behavior is related to social acceptance only for girls not for boys. For boys physical play was linked to higher social acceptance while withdrawn behavior was related to poorer peer relationships (Cillesen & Bellmore, 2004). These gender differences vary in the preschool years with mixed gender peer relationships accepted by younger preschoolers and same gender peer relationships valued by older preschoolers. These developmental shifts have only been recently studied and far more investigation is needed in this area.

Summary and Conclusion

Thus, for the infant, toddler, and preschooler, social understanding and competence are underlaid by issues of attachment to parent and teacher as well as temperamental issues. The ability to regulate one's behavior, feelings, and perception becomes important for the development of social relationships. Similarly, the ability to attach appropriately to the parent and later to the teacher is predictive of peer relationships and the ability to become socially competent. Gender and cultural differences have not been well studied and further work is sorely needed in these areas. The preschooler must master not only the ability to attach and then separate from the mother (or main caretaker) but also his/her regulation of behavior and emotions and begin understanding another person's perspective. Moreover, physiological differences may underlie some of the abilities to master these skills and need to be taken into consideration during development. Of utmost importance is the finding that early skill development translates into later functioning in the early and middle school years and likely into high school and adulthood. The following section explores developmental issues in social competence for the child in elementary school.

The Development of Social Competence in Middle Childhood

During the elementary and middle school years, the child's main focus changes from the family to the school and peers become more important for socialization. Additional factors that continue to be important are emotional regulation and sociability—two temperamental variables that have been described earlier. These skills may be the foundation for beginning a friendship (Fonzi et al., 1997; Wang et al., 2002) while social skills and shared interest are important for continuing the friendship. The ability to regulate one's emotions is likely important for peer acceptance because a child who can control emotional reactions will be able to understand other variables present in the situation and not become overwhelmed by their emotional state (Rydell et al., 2003). Children who become very upset or even very happy have more difficulty understanding the situation and using problem-solving strategies to relate more effectively with their peers (Denham et al., 1990). Blair (2002) suggests that the necessary brain structures for developing these problem-solving strategies develop during middle childhood and are directly related to developing social competence as well as academic skills. She further suggests that further study is needed in this area and that curricula in the schools need to provide instruction on how to develop these problem-solving skills also termed "executive functions."

Basic social skills become more important at this age also. The ability to take turns, to listen to the other speaker, and to nonverbally show comprehension have been linked to popularity and peer acceptance (Black & Hazen, 1990; Zsolani, 2002). Conversational ability appears to play a very important part in social interactions. Children who are successful socially are found to be able to communicate clearly and to be responsive to the other speaker (Burleson et al., 1986). Entry into the peer group is another important skill. Children who can successfully enter the conversation and integrate their behavior with the ongoing activity or conversation succeed more readily in these interactions than those who attempt to interrupt, disagree, or talk about themselves (Putallaz & Wasserman, 1990).

Characteristics that appear to be important for social competence include a sense of humor, being entertaining, handling teasing, and enjoying playing (Asher & Williams, 1987). In a study of summer camp relationships, children who were shy, had trouble talking, were easily angered, and couldn't manage any playful teasing were often not accepted by peers and either actively avoided or socially isolated (Parker & Seal, 1996). Interviews with children have indicated that a child who argues or frequently disagrees is not someone with whom they would like to be friends (Smollar & Youniss, 1982).

Although disagreements are viewed negatively by most children at this age, conflict inevitably arises. Children in middle childhood can distinguish between arguments that are minor or major and understand how to resolve the problem (Parker & Gottman, 1989). Disagreements are generally around violation of rules or about a shared activity. Gossip becomes more important and again revolves around someone who violated the rules of the group. Parker and Gottman (1989) suggest that this gossip not only allows for inclusion into a group, it provides a vehicle for disseminating the rules of the peer group.

Conflict also distinguishes between friends and nonfriends. Differences have also been found whether the interaction is in an enclosed space or with fewer limitations for movement. More conflict is found between friends than between nonfriends but the conflict more often serves to solidify the relationship and to preserve the bond through prosocial and problem-solving strategies (Hartup et al., 1988). In smaller spaces the conflict is generally more intense possibly because there are fewer choices than available within a larger setting (Hartup et al., 1993). An important developmental task is the ability to negotiate a solution, to compromise when appropriate, and to disengage when the conflict threatens the relationship (Hartup et al., 1988). Children who are unable to negotiate or to disengage generally are less accepted by peers and show poorer social competence (Putallaz & Sheppard, 1990).

Aggressive behavior is negatively related to peer acceptance. When boys engage in pretend fights, the boy who becomes thwarted and then aggressive is most frequently socially rejected. Moreover, these children are found to view these interactions as being hostile and have difficulty understanding the pretend nature of the play (Dodge & Frame, 1992). In addition, these children have been found to underestimate their aggressive behavior and to overestimate their social skills (Kupersmidt et al., 1990). Rose and Asher (1999) studied fourth and fifth graders and found that children who believed that revenge was appropriate or believed the aggression is a good means for managing conflict had fewer and poorer friendships. These findings are present for both boys and girls although the type of aggression may vary from physical to verbal (Grotpeter & Crick, 1996).

Thus, important skills such as negotiating, conflict resolution, and compromise develop during this period. Managing emotional behavior appropriately as well as being able to describe feelings and thoughts become more important and are related to socially competent skills. How do children acquire these skills and what types of peer relationships and parenting styles can assist with this development? The following section describes parenting variables and styles that have been linked to social competence in the middle childhood.

Interpersonal Perception

The ability to understand who you are in relation to another is an important developmental task for middle childhood and throughout life. Cillessen and Bellmore (2004) suggest that a child's understanding of self and peers is an important influence in entering a peer group, emotional regulation, and in resolving of conflict. Accuracy in perception of how a child is seen generally involves children aged 6 and up (Malloy et al., 1996). Using Piagetian stages of social perspective taking, a child before age 6 would not be expected to understand how others view him/her. However, Smith and Delfosse (1980) found that children at age 4 are able to accurately identify friends of themselves and others.

Studies have found that children who are less popular tend to also be poor at accurately rating themselves through the eyes of another child (Kurdek & Krile, 1982). Findings have also been present that indicate that rejected children overestimate their acceptance, average children underestimate this acceptance, and neglected children underestimate their social skills (Patterson et al., 1990) while rejected children's ratings have also been found to negatively correlate with their teacher's ratings of their ability (Cillessen & Bellmore, 1999). Emerging research indicates that girls may be more accurate in their interpersonal perception of themselves and their peers than boys (Bellmore & Cillessen, 2004).

The ability to form perceptions of others that are accurate is an important skill for social competence. These skills appear to be consistent with the concept of executive functions—that is the ability to evaluate a behavior and change your responses based on additional information. Executive functions are believed to be a function of the anterior portion of the brain that matures during middle childhood through early adulthood (Teeter & Semrud-Clikeman, 1997). Previous experiences and generalizing these experiences to novel situations is part of executive functions and plays a role in interpersonal perspective taking. Relationships with other children allow them to acquire these skills and to adapt to changing circumstances. Children who are rejected or socially isolated do not have the experiences to profit from this learning and often are at a disadvantage in changing their behaviors (Cillessen & Bellmore, 2003). As discussed in Chapter 1, if the child experiences difficulty in encoding social interactions, it is likely he/she will have problems interacting effectively with peers. Similarly, a child's self-perception is related to the child's ability to interact with peers (Crick & Dodge, 1994).

There are few studies that evaluate ethnic differences in social perception. One of the few was conducted by Glanville and Nowicki (2002) and studied the ability of elementary children to identify facial expression of African-American and European-American subjects. Although the ability to read faces differing in ethnicity did not differ by the child's ethnicity, the child's social competence was more related to accurately identifying the facial expression within the child's same ethnic group than his/her score for outside the ethnic group.

Parenting Aspects Related to Social Competence

Parke et al. (2004) suggest that parents shape the timing of entry into peer relationships as well as how frequently these interactions occur. In addition to a one-way interaction, Hart et al. (1997) suggest a bidirectional influence with parent's affecting the child's peer relationships and the child's peer relationships in turn shaping the parent–child relationship. Parke et al. (2004) suggest three different pathways for these influences—parent–child interaction, parent advice concerning peer relationships, and parents' regulation of peer activities.

Parent interactional styles are related to peer relationships with warm styles related to positive outcomes and negative styles or authoritarian styles to poor social outcomes (Parke & O'Neill, 1997). Furthermore, positive maternal interaction style and sensitivity to the child have also been linked to social competence. Conversely, overcontrolling maternal behavior or negative affect has been found related to poor peer acceptance and lower social skills (McDowell & Parke, 2000; Olsen et al., 2002). The gender of the parent also appears to affect social competence. Fathers who were more directive tended to have children with lower social competence ratings and had more of an effect than that of mothers who were equally directive (McDowell et al., 2003).

Similar to the attachment research cited above, the parent–child attachment style has been linked to peer outcomes with infants having a secure attachment showing better-developed competence in peer relationships (Sroufe et al., 1993). Insecurely attached children have been found to have hostile perceptions of another person's intentions (Parke et al., 2004). Moreover, perceived rejection of the caretaker by the child is related to the child later linking hostile intent to his/her peers (Cassidy et al., 1996).

These findings have been replicated in studies with various cultures. For example, Chen et al. (1998) found that family relationships including parental warmth and monitoring were related to child misconduct in a similar manner for Asian as was found for American children. Moreover, Chen and Rubin (1994) found a link between childhood aggression and peer rejection to negative and punitive parenting practices while authoritative parenting was related to peer acceptance. These findings were also present in a study of Russian children (Hart et al., 2000). Similarly, parents that provided more peer contacts for Chinese, Russian, and American children had children who were more accepted by peers. There were no studies found that compared children with

African-American, Hispanic, or Native American parents with peer acceptance. Further study is certainly needed in these areas.

In addition to the parent–child interaction, basic skills in relationships are learned within the parent–child bond. The ability to manage affect and to solve problems are acquired in these early relationships and subsequently applied to later peer relationships. Skills such as emotional encoding and emotional understanding are related to peer competence and these skills are developed within the family setting and later transferred to peer interactions (Denham, 1998). The ability and/or willingness to process emotions by the parent for the child has been linked to a child's awareness and understanding of other's emotions as well as developing constructive methods for coping with intense emotions (Denham, 1998; Eisenberg & Fabes, 1992).

Similar to the section on infants and preschooler, attentional regulation is important for social competence. These processes allow for the child to organize his/her experience and to manage the level of emotional arousal (Rothbart & Bates, 1998). Wilson (1999) suggests that the ability to self-regulate a child's attention is a cornerstone for emotional and cognitive responses and indirectly influence social competence.

Parents may directly influence the child's peer relationship through the advice that is offered about the child's interactions with friends. For younger children the advice may center on appropriate behaviors and entry into social groups. As the child develops, parents turn from telling how to do something to encouraging the child to think about the consequences of his/her behavior (Mounts, 2000). For less-skilled children, this evolution in parent advice giving may not occur as remediation of skills continues to be paramount. Thus, these children often do not learn to solve their own problems and continue to be dependent on the parent for peer relationships.

The final method that parents influence peer relationships at this age is through managing their child's social lives (Parke et al., 2004). Such monitoring has been found to be important for the development of appropriate social relationships with little monitoring present for children who later develop delinquent and antisocial behaviors (Patterson & Stouthammer-Loeber, 1984). Dishion (1990) studied discipline style and level of monitoring and supervision. Findings indicated that inconsistent and punitive discipline coupled with low levels of supervision was related to rejection by the child's peers due to poor behavioral control. Moreover, an authoritative parenting style resulted in the need for less monitoring and less susceptibility to peer pressure (O'Neil et al., 2001).

Parents who provided one or more situations where the child interacted with peers outside of the school environment had children who had more friendships and who were rated as more socially adept (Kerns et al., 1998). Moreover, parents who initiated several after-school peer contacts had children who were rated higher on prosocial behavior and participated in more social interaction during school hours (Ladd & Hart, 1992). These informal peer contacts appear to have positive outcomes for children both in and out of school. Formal peer contacts have also been found to be important for children's development of social competence. Those children enrolled in formal peer activities have been found to have better perspective-taking skills (Bryant, 1995) and fewer externalizing behaviors and higher grades while those with few outlets showed poorer outcomes (Pettit et al., 1997).

Parent Variables

In addition to directly influencing the child's peer relationships, the number of social interactions the parent has with other adults also influences the child's social competence (Parke et al., 2004). This finding may be partially explained by the opportunity of the children to play with the children of the parent's friends. Cochran et al. (1990) found that more than one-third of a young child's peer relationships may be through the parent's social contacts. A parent's friendship network was found related to the child's social competence (Parke et al., 2004). The happier the parent was with his/her friendships, the more positive the perception of the child by peers. It was also found that the parental social relationships were related to the child's social competence. Fathers who did not enjoy social interactions with friends were more likely to have a child who was disliked by peers and was aggressive. Mothers who were socially isolated also had children who avoided friendships and were withdrawn. These findings strongly suggest that the parent influences the child not just by what he/she says and provides but also by what the child observes as to the parent's own social relationships and comfort with these interactions.

Parental stress is a variable that has also been linked to the child's social competence. When stress is multiplicative and there are several sources of stress, the resulting social competence of the child appears to be compromised (Sameroff et al., 1998; Shaw & Emery, 1988). For families with very limited income, children have been found to have fewer friendships, more social isolation, and fewer opportunities for peer companionship (Patterson et al., 1991). Moreover, stressed parents have been found to be more hostile and less nurturing and disruptions in parenting are common. These difficulties have been related to poor peer relations including fewer close relationships and less perceived support (Brody & Flor, 1997; Conger et al., 1995).

Similar to the findings about stress affecting parenting and social competence, studies have found that poverty and single parenthood also affect the child's resulting social skills (Bates et al., 2003). Children with more highly rated social skills and fewer behavioral problems had better parenting, higher academic skills, and lower poverty rates compared to those with poorer social skills. Academic skills were related to social competence, as was stability of school. It is likely that the children from lower socioeconomic status who had a stable home and school were provided the time and skills to develop friendships and knowledge compared to children who moved around a lot and who had more stresses at home.

Peer Groups

The second socializing force for children in elementary and middle school ages is that of the peer group. One of the main developmental tasks for children at this age group is that of understanding social relationships and developing social competence. Integration in the classroom plays an important part in a child's development. At these ages the child begins to spend an increasing amount of time outside their home and away from their parents (McHale et al., 2003).

Being accepted by peer groups has been linked to the development of a healthy self-concept as well as academic success (Hart et al., 2003). Boys tend to play more physical games including chase and ball games while girls play more verbal games (Pellegrini et al., 2002). The ability of both boys and girls in this study to play these games was linked to later adjustment in school. Play is an important part of friendship in middle childhood and most games at this age are formal and rule-governed. The ability to internalize these rules and comply with them is thought to be a cornerstone in social competence (Samter, 2003).

The ability to take the perspective of another in understanding thoughts and emotions has been linked to positive social interaction skills as well as to good language ability (Bosacki & Astington, 1999). Recognizing that others have thoughts and ideas separate from one is an important task for children and is related to how the child interacts with his/her peers. While a child is able to understand another child's point of view during this period of development, he/she cannot accomplish this task while in the middle of a situation (Samter, 2003). Moreover, a child is not able to see himself or herself from the other child's point of view. Therefore, friends are defined as another child who can help or do things with them (Haslet & Samter, 1997).

Middle childhood is also a time where peer approval becomes increasingly more important and the desire to belong and be accepted becomes paramount (Parker & Gottman, 1989). Samter (2003) suggests that these friendships are the foundation for acculturation of society's values and morays. Children at this age may appear more self-conscious about having friends and are more worried about being accepted. Friendships also change in structure at this age and the number of friendships increases as well as the stability of these friendships. In preschool and kindergarten, children will often switch friendships by the day or even by the hour. In elementary and middle school, these friendships become more stable and the word "best friend" begins to appear. Intimacy and confiding in the friend become more important than just "doing something." In addition, many of the friendships at this age have endured for more than one year and shared knowledge between these friends has increased—children at this age know their friends better than those who are younger (Berndt et al., 1986; Ladd & Emerson, 1984).

Friendships at this age tend to be gender specific with the friendships of girls found to be exclusive and in two-somes while boys are inclusive and group-oriented (Samter, 2003; Thorne, 1986). Girls have been found to spend more time talking to each other compared to boys with turn-taking in the conversation to be present as well as agreeing with the speaker (Leaper, 1994; Raffaelli & Duckett, 1989). In contrast, boys tend to set up a social pecking order in their interactions and tend to be more competitive than girls (Thorne, 1986).

Although these differences exist between boy and girl friendships, there is kindness, caring, and support present for both genders. Boys and girls show interest in friends and the need to be appropriate in social environments (Maccoby & Jacklin, 1987). Responsivity to the other, understanding the perspective of the other and interest in group and individual activities are similar across genders. Older children tend to provide more prosocial solutions that were effective than boys who are younger. Moreover, boys who are well accepted by their peers also provide more prosocial responses and view aggression as less acceptable for solving peer conflicts (Mayeux & Cillessen, 2003).

Thus, the movement from parallel to cooperative play and then to emotional support and interaction occurs in peer relationships during middle childhood. Differences are present in gender-specific friendships but there are also several similarities present. The relationship of appropriate peer relationships to academic competence appears to be an important piece of development and underscores the need for developing socially appropriate behaviors for later developmental success. These peer relationships improve, deepen, and become more intimate in adolescence and young adulthood.

Adolescence and Young Adulthood

Social ability in adolescence and young adulthood changes and expectations for friendships also change. The adolescent is able to remove himself/herself from the situation and objectively view what is occurring. This development allows the adolescent to look at the situation as if he/she were a neutral observer. The ability to take this perspective allows the adolescent to understand the other person's beliefs and motivations and to change behavior accordingly. In addition, the adolescent no longer believes that the friend sees a situation in the same manner that he/she does. These abilities coincide with the brain development that allows for abstract thinking and abstraction.

The ability to understand the emotional state of another has been linked to social competence and has been termed "psychological pragmatics" (Nelson et al., 2000). Psychological pragmatics is defined as a dynamic knowledge that includes the self-perception, emotions, and thoughts that change during social encounters. These schemas basically inform the individual about his/her behaviors in the past and what alternatives are available to cope with the current situation. In addition, cultural values and societal standards interact with these mental states and inform behaviors and thoughts during a social encounter consistent with the early learning of the child (Bosacki, 2003).

Self-evaluation is an important process during adolescence and includes one's self-esteem, perceived attractiveness, and perceived social ability. The ability to seek out support from peers and parents as well as teachers has been found to assist adolescents with adjustment with peers most instrumental in modulating social adjustment to transitions. Adolescents who perceive themselves as able to make and keep friends are less vulnerable to stress in academic and school-related areas (Fenzel, 2000). Similarly, adolescents who are not socially skilled have been found to have lower self-worth and to also experience significant feelings of stress academically and in school-related environments. Moreover, parent support was not found to ameliorate these difficulties socially but providing support academically for these students (Fenzel, 2000; Grolnick et al., 1999).

Adolescents who are better able to understand another's perspective in understanding themselves and a situation have been found to show fewer behavioral and emotional problems than those who are unable to objectively view themselves (Lenhart & Rabiner, 1995). Moreover, these adolescents have also been found to show more advanced problem-solving skills that are also related to improved competence both socially and academically. Pellegrini (1985) evaluated the relationship between social competence and academic intelligence and found that children who have good reasoning skills appear to be better at modulating their social conduct and utilizing the social context to their advantage.

Landsheer et al. (1998) found that popularity was negatively related to success in the challenging academic fields of mathematics and physics. In this same study, students who excelled in English were not rated as low socially as those excelling in physics. It is not clear whether students who have social difficulties are more likely to chose subjects that require less emotional and social engagement. This is an interesting area of study and begs the question of which comes first—less interest in social interaction or talent in an area that is intellectually challenging but possibly more socially isolated.

Peers

Friendship evolves from a relationship founded on mutual interests to one that is based on intimate sharing and mutual support. Adolescents continue the move from the family as the main level of emotional support to that of close friends. Samter (2003) suggests that the main task of adolescence is to establish peer relationships that allow the person to learn more about himself/herself through sharing and support of another. This validation of one's view of oneself and the support that is received from the friendship provides the foundation for identity and self-esteem.

There may be differences between girls and boys as to the relationship of social competence and time of adolescence. Boys have been found to have more problems and less social competence in early adolescence with fewer problems present and better social competence in mid-adolescence (Forehand et al., 1991). In contrast, girls had a relatively easier adjustment in early adolescence but experienced a drop in self-esteem and social ability in mid-adolescence. Thus, girls and boys may differ in the developmental needs depending on the stage of adolescence that is present.

Empathy and concern for others begins to emerge in preadolescence and blossoms during the adolescent phase of development (Buhrmester & Furman, 1986). The idea of a "best friend" becomes more and more important during this time and research has indicated that by the age of 13 most adolescents report that best friends must put the friend's needs above their own (Samter, 2003). Thus, adolescents are more loyal, supportive, and committed to their friends compared to younger children and talking becomes an important part of these relationships to strengthen the bonds. This need for sharing includes day-to-day experiences as well as important concerns. Anyone with a teenager knows how difficult it can be to separate him/her from the telephone.

Prosocial behaviors have also been linked to social competence (Wentzel, 1994). Well-accepted adolescents are found to be more prosocial than those who are rejected or socially isolated (Wentzel & Caldwell, 1997). Both peers and parents provide opportunities for the development of the behaviors of sharing and reciprocity of relationships. Cooperative and prosocial behaviors have been theorized to develop from peer interactions and those children who are well accepted will often show more positive and prosocial behaviors than those who are not (Wentzel & McNamara, 1999).

How friendships are viewed differs between the genders. Boys and young men tend to continue to define their friendships based on shared interests while girls and young women emphasize intimacy and support (McCoy et al., 1994). Similar to preadolescents, males tend to bond through activities and females from talking. These findings continue into young adulthood (Raffaelli & Duckett, 1989). To believe, however, that males do not value commitment and support would be incorrect. Recent studies have found that boys and young men place a high value on trust as well as empathy for the other person's feelings and problems (Burleson et al., 1996; Monsour, 1992). Moreover, both genders appear to have difficulty when a best friend is not present and report feelings of depression as well as loneliness (Samter, 2003).

Similar to findings at other age levels, adolescents and young adults who are sociable tend to have better adjustment in all areas of life. Adolescents, who communicate freely with others, even with strangers, tend to be happier and better adjusted than those who are lonely. Moreover, those who are shy and usually describe themselves as lonely often have difficulty approaching people, and are passive and nontalkative even when approached by others (Bell, 1985). Thus, those adolescents and young adults who do not have basic social skills often continue to be socially isolated partly due to their own behaviors and partly due to the perceptions of others that they are not approachable or sociable.

The ability to share confidences with a close friend appears to be an important task of adolescence. Samter (2003) suggests that ability to self-disclose is important for forming and maintaining friendships. This self-disclosure appears to be received better when the person already has established a relationship with the person. The ability to share intimate information is prized as well as the ability to elicit such information from another person (Miller et al., 1983). Such sharing appears to help the friendship to continue and to deepen. This sharing serves not only to help the adolescent to feel his/her way through conflicting feelings and concerns, but also to provide much needed emotional and social support.

Having a friend understand a feeling and then provide the necessary support is increasingly important in adolescence and young adulthood. The finding that one is "not so different" from the friend by itself can be supportive of feelings. When an adolescent is troubled and the friend merely indicates understanding, the friendship deepens and both participants are provided with an opportunity for intimacy.

There may be some ethnic differences in how emotional support is provided. For example, a study of the differences between Caucasian and African-American friendships found that the Caucasian friends placed more emphasis on talking about feelings compared to the African-American sample (Samter et al., 1997). In contrast, problem-centered talking was emphasized by the African-American sample above sharing of feelings. How problems are solved also differs between ethnicities. Ting-Toomey (1986) found that loud talking is viewed by African-American adolescents as supportive particularly when it emphasizes a solution to a problem. Moreover, while the discussion may be animated and intense, the discussion of negative emotions is not encouraged (Hecht et al., 1993). Similar to the African-American adolescents, Asian-American adolescents place little emphasis on talking about feelings or conflict and greater emphasis on problem-solving (Samter, 2003). Asian Americans have been found to show little distress in front of friends, to have fewer intimate conversations, and are relatively passive in their interactions with friends (Goodwin & Lee, 1994).

Loneliness. Loneliness appears to be an important issue for adolescents—even more important than for younger children (Roscoe & Skomski, 1989). Feelings of loneliness appear to be exacerbated when the adolescent has been rejected or feels not in control of a situation. Boys have been found to experience more difficulty with loneliness than girls particularly when the do not have an interest or activity to share with a friend. These feelings of loneliness are related to lack or loss of friends and not to how close the adolescent feels to their parent (Hoza et al., 2000). Adolescents will actively seek to not be alone and describe themselves as less happy when they are alone. If they find themselves alone, adolescents will often feel there is something wrong with them and that they should always have someone with them (Burger, 1995). Research has indicated that adolescents feel lonelier than any other group with the loneliest group being low-income, single adolescent mothers (Medora & Woodward, 1986).

One way that adolescents attempt to counter their feelings of loneliness is through activities in and out of school (Bergin, 1989; Dubois & Hirsch, 1993). The most popular students are those who join many activities as well as are active in sports. Landsheer et al. (1998) found that students who excelled in mathematics and science were consistently rated more poorly than those who participate in sports. Moreover, athlete-scholars have been found to be the most popular of students and admired by their peers.

Dating. Dating is an activity frequently associated with mid to late adolescence and beyond. It has been found to serve many purposes foremost of which is an ability to further define oneself and to understand how to relate to the other sex and as a primer for marriage. The ability to attain intimacy with someone other than a same sex friend can be very rewarding and confers ability for openness and sharing. Intimacy in dating has been found to be linked to higher social status and for learning how to support one's partner (Eaton et al., 1991).

Adolescents who have a girlfriend or boyfriend have been found to be either very popular or very unpopular (Bukowski et al., 1999). This dichotomy is interesting as it points to needs that may be met in only one manner for the adolescent who is unpopular. Moreover, of the children without a same-sex friend, boys were found to have a higher level of self-esteem while girls were found to have a lower level. Thus, it appears that dating may be helpful for boys who do not have a same gender friend but may be detrimental for girls—this conclusion may be related to the pressures placed on the girl to meet the boys needs but not her own as well as possibly not feeling included with other girls in typical sharing of feelings and thoughts that appear more important for girls than boys.

Parental Influences

During adolescence family interactions change to meet the developmental needs of the adolescent for independence and individuation. These issues can make family life difficult at best and conflictual at worst. Moreover, interactions that are positive between parents and the adolescent have been linked to social competence (Aronen & Kurkel, 1998).

Chu and Powers (1995) suggest that when the family and adolescent are in synchrony, the attachment bond continues to be secure and provides for improve social competence and adjustment. Synchrony is defined as the ability to change based on needs of both the adolescent and the parent and runs from infancy through adulthood. When the family is able to accommodate these changes, social competence is enhanced and a stage-environmental fit is present (Eccles et al., 1993). The quality of the interactions between the adolescent and parent and how responsive the parent is to these changes likely influences later growth as well as the resulting relationship. Chu and Powers (1995) suggest that if the relationship is asynchronous, then difficulties arise and developmental issues are not resolve optimally. They suggest the following dimensions to improve adolescent-adult synchrony.

- Allow for turn-taking, problem solving, and cooperative decision making.
- Active listening needs to be present on both the parent and adolescent's part—respect for varying opinions and the need for assertion should be valued.
- Frequent and direct interaction time is very important to further the relationships—activities need to be mutually agreed upon, shared, and enjoyed.
- Adjustment and adaptation is important for both parties—the interaction is dynamic and fluid and changes based on environment as well as activity.

Attachment

Similar to the concept of synchrony, attachment continues to play an important role in the adolescent's development. Theorists continue the construct of attachment to parent–adolescent relationships where it provides a base for the adolescent to experience new situations that are challenging (Papini et al., 1989). The adolescent's feelings of self-worth have been related to attachment particularly for high school students (Rice, 1990). Moreover, self-esteem has been linked strongly to parental attachment throughout all developmental ages even more so than peer attachment (Armsden & Greenberg, 1987; Weinfield et al., 1997). Peer attachment was linked more strongly to social competence (Lempers & Clark-Lempers, 1992). Noom et al. (1999) found that attachment was related to overall functioning and self-esteem but not to social competence with peers. Attachment to peers was related to social competence particularly when the adolescent showed high levels of autonomy. Thus, the confidence an adolescent has about the parental attachment appears to be a crucial variable relating to psychological adjustment and to reliance on the parent for support while peers provide an important support for the development of social competence (Bretherton, 1985; Ryan & Lynch, 1989).

Patterson et al. (1995) found that positive affect of an adolescent toward his/her parents was associated with higher self-esteem and coping. Both mother and father were found to play a significant role in the development of psychological adjustment, and support from both parents was found to be crucial to the adolescent's ability to develop feelings of higher self-worth. Attachment was not found to vary between the genders with both males and females relying on parents equally.

Family cohesion appears to be a protective factor for the development of depression or low self-esteem (Wentzel & McNamara, 1999). Poor family cohesion has been linked to emotional distress and lower competence at school (Wentzel & Feldman, 1996). Family structures that allow for sharing and resolution of conflict as well as an authoritative type of parenting style may well contribute to feelings of higher self-esteem as well as improved social competence. Social competence has been linked for both genders to families that are supportive, provide reasonable limits, and who are encouraging of personal growth (Margalit & Eysenck, 1990).

In a large study of the ethnic differences in attachment style, no differences were found between Black and White adolescents. Three attachment types were identified for this study: secure, anxious, and avoidant. Gender differences were found with girls showing higher levels of anxiety across all attachment styles with the highest level of anxiety associated with the anxiously attached adolescents (Cooper et al., 1998). Securely attached adolescents were found to show higher levels of coping, self-efficacy, and in general functioning. Those with insecure attachments showed significant difficulties in all areas and showed a pattern of maladjustment with the anxiously attached adolescents the most poorly adjusted. Avoidant adolescents were less hostile and depressed than the anxiously attached adolescents and were performing better in school.

Emotional Regulation

As stated earlier, emotional regulation is a cornerstone for the development of social competence (Rothbart & Bates, 1998). Eisenberg et al. (2000)

suggests that adolescents who experience difficulty regulating their emotions, particularly negative ones, have difficulty with over-arousal during emotionally charged social situations and show inappropriate behaviors. Reacting to a situation can vary depending on the individual and those who react quickly, intensely, and for an extended period of time appear to be at risk for social difficulties (Murphy et al., 2004).

Emotional regulation has been subdivided into two types—regulation of the emotion and regulation of the behavior. Regulation of the emotion refers to the ability to modulate the feeling present. Attentional control is an important part of the regulation of the emotion as moving attention from one situation to the next can assist in managing an intense emotion. Behavioral regulation is the ability to change one's behavior to manage the emotion (Murphy et al., 2004).

Emotional regulation has been found to continue throughout childhood and into adolescence. The compounding of difficulties over time on social functioning that arise when a child continues to show intense emotion of long duration reduce the social experiences the child will have and the acceptance of others for his/her behavior. These continuing problems extend into adolescence and generally result in problems with externalizing behaviors as well as poorer social relationships (Caspi, 2000). When these behaviors continue into adolescence, social difficulties continue particularly in the formation of intimate relationships in late adolescence (Masten et al., 1995).

Gender effects of regulation in adolescence have been found in a study evaluating emotionality and regulation (Murphy et al., 2004). Boys were reported to be rated lower than girls by parents and teachers on measures of regulation and higher on measures of problem behaviors. Social competence was related to low negative emotionality and high regulation for both genders for both parents and teachers. Consistency of ability to regulate behavior and emotion and social competence was found in this study over a 5-year period. Thus, adolescents who were low in emotionality and high in regulation showed stronger ability in social situations that continued throughout adolescence.

Conversely, those who were high in emotionality and low in regulation experienced difficulties with friendships and peer relationships throughout adolescence. A study of college students confirms this hypothesis. Reactivity and emotional regulation were found to be related to self-esteem, adaptability, and social competence in a group of college students (Klein, 1992). Thus, the continuity of the temperamental characteristic of emotional regulation appears to be an important variable for the development of social competence in later adolescence and likely into adulthood.

Maladaptive Behaviors and Social Competence

Both internalizing and externalizing behavioral difficulties have been associated with problems in social competence. Problems with sadness, anxiety, aggression, and conduct in childhood and continuing into adolescence have been found to be predictive of difficulties with social competence in adolescence (McGee & Williams, 1991). A history of early mental health problems has been linked to problems with social competence with the most vulnerable adolescents being those coming from socially disadvantaged homes particularly for boys (Feehan et al., 1995).

Rule breaking has been found to be continuous throughout development for some children and is linked to problems with social competence as well as problems academically and vocationally (Masten et al., 1995). Females who show difficulties with anger expression (express anger and have a higher level of intensity of their anger) also tend to have difficulties with social skills. Lower self-esteem and higher levels of impulsive behaviors were also seen with these girls. Interestingly, no difference was found between males who showed higher levels of anger and those who did not on measures of social competence (Sarris et al., 2000). Social withdrawal has also been linked to problems with social competence. Rubin et al. (1995) found in a longitudinal study that children who were high on measures of social withdrawal had difficulties with loneliness and low self-esteem while those high on measures of aggression showed poorer social competence. Thus, aggression, anger management, and social withdrawal have been associated with poorer outcome in adolescents.

Aggression

Aggression has been strongly linked to problems with social competence (Coie & Dodge, 1998; Coie et al., 1990). Hawley (2003) suggests that different types of aggression may be associated with varying levels of social competence. She rightly makes the point that many CEOs and successful people are also aggressive. However, their aggression may be channeled in a more constructive manner than that of adolescents who are traditionally viewed as having difficulty with aggression and social relationships.

Children who are socially competent have been found to score similarly to those with social difficulties on measures of aggression and may vary from prosocial and nonaggressive to rough and aggressive (Newcomb et al., 1993; Rodkin et al., 2000). Hawley (2003) suggests that aggressive behavior should be evaluated as to its utility for obtaining a goal—a process she terms as "Machiavellian." She studied adolescents based on their ability to manage strategies to obtain what they wanted. Children were typed based on their responses and may be seen as prosocial, coercive controller, typical, or a bi-strategic player (also called Machiavellian; using more than one strategy to obtain what was wanted). She hypothesized that modest aggression and manipulation that balanced coercive behavior and prosocial behavior would be linked to a positive self-image and peer regard.

Findings indicated that adolescents who showed high levels of prosocial behaviors were more accepted than those who used high levels of coercive behaviors. However, aggressive adolescents were viewed by peers, parents, and teachers as socially appropriate if their aggression was tempered by prosocial behaviors. She labeled these children "coercive controllers." They were viewed by their peers as likeable, effective, and important to the group. These controllers were also candid about their strategies and acknowledged their negative behaviors.

They were also skilled at understanding the motivation, feelings, and needs of their peers and were adept at providing these needs when it benefited their agenda.

This study is important for two main reasons. First it provides an alternative model that suggests aggression needs to be viewed for its utility rather than being solely seen as a negative characteristic. Secondly, aggression is not a homogenous characteristic and needs to be studied more fully to understand its implication for development, intervention, and relationship to social competence.

In contrast to the above study, aggressive behavior is generally linked to problems with social functioning as well as to cognitive processing. The social-information-processing model suggests that the aggressive adolescent has difficulty because they are unable to solve social problems through the use of strategies and/or language abilities (Crick & Dodge, 1994). When processing of information is faulty, the adolescent is unable to solve the problems and adjust his/her behaviors to fit the situation. Aggressive adolescents have been found to base their analysis of a situation more on their past experiences than on the situation itself. Moreover, they attribute more hostile and negative intent to the other person in the situation and infer intended harm (Bickett et al., 1996). In addition, aggressive boys have been found to a need to dominate a situation and will feel less need to provide support to others than those who are not as aggressive (Lochman et al., 1993). Thus, aggressive adolescents are found to have fewer strategies for solving problems outside of those that involve aggression than adolescents who are more prosocial in nature (Pakaslahti & Keltikangas-Jarvinen, 1996).

Along with fewer problem-solving strategies, aggressive adolescents view aggressive behavior very favorably and have been found to believe that their victims deserve what happens to them (Pakaslahti & Keltikangas-Jarvinen, 1996; Slaby & Guerra, 1988). They also appear to believe that their aggressive behavior will be rewarded and anticipate fewer consequences for this behavior (Lochman & Dodge, 1994; Slaby & Guerra, 1988). It is also possible that they do not look far in the future as to these consequences and may have a need for fast self-gratification of their needs.

Emotional regulation becomes an important aspect in aggressive behavior. Aggressive adolescents tend to make assumptions about a social situation based on their internal state—if they are very angry they will likely interpret the situation from an angry stance (Dodge & Tomlin, 1987). Forgas (1995) further suggests that these emotions will focus the adolescent's attention to the more negative aspects of the situation, and thus validate his/her feelings and actions. The emotion of anger has been found to restrict cognitive capacity and limit the search for alternative strategies (Bodenhausen et al., 1994).

Aggression appears to be fostered depending on the home environment and parenting techniques. Parental physical abuse appears to be related to a child's propensity to pay attention to negative and hostile cues and to ignore positive interactions (Dodge, et al., 1995). Parents of aggressive adolescents have been found to express more hostility when dealing with day-to-day situations compared to parents of nonaggressive adolescents (Pakaslahti et al., 1998). Parental indifference is also more likely to be present for adolescents with aggressive behavior as well as providing less guidance for the adolescent's behavior (Dix & Lochman, 1990; Pakaslahti et al., 1996, 1998).

Peer relationships also further aggressive behaviors with aggressive adolescents actively seeking out more aggressive peers (Dishion et al., 1994; Huesmann & Guerra, 1997). These adolescents differ from those who are rejected by the group. Those who find a peer group that is accepting of them generally enjoy higher status than those who are rejected (Cairns et al., 1988). For those adolescents rejected by most peers, social competence becomes an increasingly difficult aspect of development as the more rejection the less opportunity to practice skills. Boys, in particular, seek to belong in a larger peer group and will seek out such support while girls will gravitate to a few close friends (Baumeister & Sommer, 1997).

There are gender differences in aggression with girls using less direct means of aggression (relational aggression) and boys using more overt methods. Girls tend to attempt to harm social relationships and to isolate the victim. Moreover, they also believe that the victim of the aggression deserves to be victimized more than boys do (Pakaslahti & Keltikangas-Jarvinen, 1996). These gender differences may relate to girls stress on inter-dependency and boys on independence as well as how girls relate (talking, sharing) and boys (doing).

Thus, interventions will differ for aggressive adolescents in a smaller peer group compared to those who have fewer to no friends. Pakaslahti (2000) suggests that group interventions may be more effective for both of these types of adolescents than individual treatment. Providing appropriate models as well as supporting a different worldview may be the most helpful vehicle for change. She further suggests that many of these behaviors are learned within a family context and real change needs to assist the family in developing a different manner of interacting with others.

Summary

Social competence is an important aspect of development and changes depending on the age of the child/adolescent and the requirements of the environment. Temperamental characteristics are important in the development of social competence particularly in the areas of sociability, emotional regulation, and attachment. These characteristics have been found to be present at all ages and are continuous throughout development and into adulthood. The ability to attach to someone is learned early in life and the trust that these important caretakers will be there is not only important in infancy but equally important in adolescence. It is likely that attachment plays a role in the eventual ability to marry and have one's own family. Emotional regulation is also important. How we see the world, how the world reacts to us, and how we use that information is important in regulating our behavior and our emotions. Intensity, duration, and frequency of emotional outbursts are an important variable for relating to others.

Wanting to be with other people is another important variable and sociability not only relates to what we want but how other people see us. We have all seen babies who are very approachable and who just beg to be picked up and hugged. We have also seen children who are resistant to touch and who are not approachable. The social world of both of these individuals will differ greatly.

Infancy, childhood, adolescence, and young adulthood are important parts of development for all aspects but particularly for social competence. The ability to relate to others becomes more and more important as one leaves the home and plays into the development of self-esteem as well as competence in other areas of life. When difficulties are present in social relatedness whether due to aggressive behavior, social withdrawal, or problems in social understanding, the child and adolescent will experience problems with adjustment that often play into difficulty with academic and vocational attainment.

The following chapter briefly reviews assessment techniques to understand the child's level of social understanding. This chapter is, by no means, exhaustive and there are many measures to be evaluated. The goal of the chapter is to provide an overview for the interested clinician to adapt to his/her needs.

3

Assessment of Social Competence in Children

While the understanding for the components of social competence is continuing to be empirically validated, assessment for social competence is not as well studied and continues to develop in procedures. Many models assume that children who have appropriate social skills will respond more effectively across situations compared to those who are unable to access or utilize these abilities (Cavell, 1990). Thus, it is assumed that a child will show similar behaviors at school, at home, and in the neighborhood. This assumption may not be accurate as research has found different patterns depending on the environment in which the child is interacting socially (Bierman & Welsh, 2000). In addition to possessing appropriate social skills and using them effectively, social judgment can also be affected by a myriad of factors including gender, ethnicity, additional talents and skills, and attractiveness (Cavell et al., 2003). Each of these variables can also be affected by the setting in which the child is in or the environment, culture, and/or gender of the person completing the rating scale. For this reason, it is clinically prudent to gather information in a multimodal manner including observation, interviews, and rating scales.

While environment, culture, and gender can affect the child's performance, it is a mistake to believe that because a child has the skills, he/she can necessarily use them effectively. Comorbid diagnoses can also affect how the child responds to his/her environment and the adaptability of this response. When a child has an experience and his/her skills work well in that situation, they are often empowered to repeat these behaviors and reinforced for adequate performance. However, a child with the same set of skills may perform them less adequately and be accorded little to no reward for their behavior and thus feel inadequate and become less likely to attempt to interact in novel situations. It is also likely that the child will bring memories of these situations to the next occurrence that arises and the child's self-efficacy will be lower. Such lowered self-expectations make it difficult for the child to try the skills again and thus a vicious cycle continues.

A prime example of these difficulties is present in children with ADHD. Research has indicated that children with ADHD show the same levels of interacting with others and may even approach people for attention more often than children without ADHD. In addition, the intensity the children with ADHD show in their interactions is higher than those without ADHD and leads to fewer rewarding experiences as this very intensity results in the other child retreating from interaction. As the child matures it may become more and more difficult for him/her to approach others and expect a welcoming response. Such an interaction between social context and emotional expectation are irretrievably entwined, and thus become enmeshed and intervention becomes more and more difficult. For example, many children with ADHD may have the skills and frequently can even tell you *what* they should do, but they are unable to put the skills to appropriate use. In this case there isn't a skills deficit but rather a performance deficit that hinges upon problems with inhibition and inattention.

One of the areas lacking in understanding of social competence is the evaluation of social abilities. It is possible that the child can have difficulty in his/her understanding of the social interaction, the child's perception of facial expressions, voice intonation, and gestures, his/her ability to remember, organize, and retrieve information about social interactions, and/or the social skills themselves. In addition, the child's responses can be colored by the emotions that are attached to his/her past problem with relating to others. For these reasons, an assessment needs to measure all of these areas in order to be efficacious and ecologically valid.

Assessment of social ability needs to include an interview with the child, parent, and teachers if possible, observations of the child in structured and unstructured situations, assessment measures that may include rating scales completed by the child, parent, and teacher, and possible use of therapeutic techniques such as role plays and situational coaching. Having multiple informants also helps the evaluator in understanding how the child functions in various environments as well as the caretakers that are involved in his/her care. As will be seen in later chapters, the social skills that the caretaker possesses can transfer to the child and affect the child's functioning. Each of these techniques will be discussed in the following section.

Interviews

Interviews can be very helpful obtaining information not only from the child but also from the caretakers (parent and teachers). Such information may vary not only with the informant but also with the situation. For some children, assertive behavior may be prized in one situation (i.e., home) and not in another (i.e., structured classroom). Knowing when to use certain behaviors and to be able to be flexible in using these behaviors can suggest appropriate intervention targets for the child.

An interview with a child and/or adolescent must be geared to his/her developmental level. Many young children will tell the interviewer that "I have lots of friends" because the child already realizes that this is the socially appropriate answer. Or they may not understand what friendship entails beyond playing beside another child. However, when the child is pushed a bit during the interview to name these friends or to tell about experiences with these friends, it often becomes clear to the interviewer that close relationships are not present and that the child's understanding of friendship is generally superficial and revolving around close proximity. For adolescents it becomes even more difficult to admit to having few friends and the interviewer needs to move with even more caution. Talking about situations hypothetically can be very helpful in drawing out a withdrawn adolescent.

Questions during an interview need to draw out the child's strengths as well as difficulties. Some children may be very adept in a structured classroom or on academic subjects but when faced with art or gym classes or the lunchroom they may show different behaviors. It is important to help the child discuss activities that he/she is very good at and those that are harder for him/her. In addition, a discussion about what the child would like to do better and what the child thinks he/she already does well is also helpful to get a feel for how the child views the world. Finally, it is very helpful to have the child/adolescent describe how they think others see them and then to have them describe how they would like to *be* seen by others. I also find it helpful to have the child tell me how their parents see them with friends as well as how they see their parents interact with friends. Many times the children I have worked with who are not socially adept have parents who are also not socially adept. It is important during these interviews to gather informal observations concerning the skills present in the family for nurturing social competence and emotional efficacy.

Interviewing Young Children

Interviewing young children is generally less structured and often requires the use of materials such as crayons and paper as well as puppets or dolls. The use of short and concrete questions is very important. For example, I used to ask the child "What are your friends were like?" until I repeatedly was told the other child likes to play trucks or something like that. Better to ask closed ended questions than abstract questions—"who are your friends or what do you like to do with your friends" rather than "what do you like in a friend?"

Play can also be quite helpful particularly when using dollhouses or villages to spark talking. Action figures are also very helpful particularly with boys to demonstrate playing and making friends. Bierman and Welsh (1997) suggest having the doll or action figure express and emotion and then ask the child what the figure is feeling and then what the figure will do about it. Ablow and Measelle (1993) developed a puppet interview to evaluate young children's understanding of social relationships. This interview was particularly developed for younger children for whom other methods (i.e., behavioral rating scales) have not been developed. The Berkeley Puppet Interview (BPI; Ablow & Measelle, 1993) uses puppets to interview children about their understanding of their own social abilities, their acceptance by peers as well as evaluating indications of mood disorders, aggressive behaviors, and academic competence. This technique allows the child to respond either verbally or nonverbally to interview questions using the puppets.

On this interview, the social competence scale has 7 items that evaluate how well the child makes friends and plays with others. Nine items evaluate the child's acceptance by his/her peers. The mood scale has 16 items that measure the child's self-report of sadness, loneliness, anxiety, etc. Each item has two opposing answers that reflect the positive and negative answers. Of the items 32 focus on positive behaviors (I am good at . . .) and 28 on negative (I cause trouble/I don't cause trouble). There are two hand puppets which are puppies named "Iggy" and "Ziggy." The puppet states the question such as "I have lots of friends" while the other says "I don't have many friends." The child is then asked by one of the puppets "What about you?" The child can respond in any way and may use non-verbal means such as pointing or shaking their head.

This method was empirically evaluated with 97 families whose first child was entering kindergarten from preschool (Measelle et al., 1998). Gender was not found to be related to achievement competence or to the social scales. The study did find that girls scored higher on the measures of depression/anxiety while boys scored higher on the aggression-hostility scale. The study also found that the BPI was reliable and consistent over the age range. The BPI was also found to be significantly related to reports by mothers and teachers of the child's social competence. Father's ratings were not significantly related to the child's report. The BPI was also found to be consistent with teacher ratings.

Another method that has been successful in my practice has been to provide cartoons where the faces are missing or the mouth is missing and then have them fill them in and tell the story. Still another method is to use picture books and talk about the relationships within the story. There are many good children's books, some of which just have pictures and others that have stories, which can provide a good jump off for understanding how the child sees relationships and how they may interact.

Interviewing Older Children and Adolescents

Children above the age of 8 can generally talk about their feelings and relationships fairly well. Discussing with them the concerns they have as well as how they have solved the problem in the past can be quite helpful. In addition, it may be helpful to provide children in this age range with hypothetical situations and ask them to solve them. In this manner, one can get an understanding of the level of the child's social cognition as well as their understanding of consequences of behavior. Dodge (1993) suggests that children with peer difficulties will often generate aggressive strategies as well as to attribute negative intentions to the other child particularly when the examples are ambiguous.

For adolescents who are unwilling to discuss the particularly painful situation of having few to no friends, the use of video games or videos may be quite helpful. There are several teenage videos available that can provide a springboard to discussion in a particularly recalcitrant adolescent. In addition, the use of sentences such as "many teenagers have difficulty with this problem—I have seen several who have had trouble making new friends . . . etc." can help to assess the adolescent's understanding of their social relationships.

Observations

It is very helpful to observe the child in additional settings other than the office. Many times I can obtain interesting information about the child's social abilities but observing him/her in the waiting room of my office or, if in a school, observing him/her in informal situations broadens my understanding of his/her skills. The lunchroom is an area that is particularly interesting. Is the child eating alone? Or has he/she seated himself/herself near others but isn't interacting? Or does the child go out of his/her way to avoid lunchtime. One child I worked with was very ingenious in avoiding the lunchroom. Upon observation I found that his eating habits were atrocious and children were actively avoiding him. Although improving his table manners did not make him friends, it at least stopped the teasing.

Observing a child when classes are changing or when they are in unstructured situations is also quite helpful to understand his/her social ability. The playground is particularly helpful for younger children. For adolescents, observing them during class changes as well as during lunchtime can help one understand how they relate to others when adults are not present.

Observations can be formally conducted and the use of coding systems is readily available. However, for social competence it is very helpful to evaluate the context that is present as well as the behaviors. Observing situations that vary depending on activities can provide one with a multidimensional understanding of the child.

Self-Report Measures

Self-report measures are frequently utilized to evaluate the child's view of himself/herself as well as possible feelings of sadness and worry. Self-esteem is an important issue and has been linked to social adjustment (Edens et al., 1999; Hughes et al., 1997). Both overestimating and underestimating one's worth has been linked to poor social functioning. There are several measures for evaluating self-esteem and self-worth and they are listed in Table 3.1. Many of these measures provide a global rating as well as scores in other domains of functioning (i.e., academic, athletic, etc.).

There are also measures of social skills and these measures evaluate how the child sees himself/herself functioning in a number of areas that are both positive and negative. In some instances these self-report

Table 3.1. Rating scales commonly used

Measure	Informants	Ages
Social Skills		
MESSY (Matson et al., 1983)	Child	6–12
Social Skills Rating Scale (Gresham & Elliott, 1990)	Child, Parent, and Teacher	6–18
Loneliness and Social Dissatisfaction Questionnaire (Cassidy & Asher, 1992)	Adolescent	12–18
Friendship Quality Questionnaire (Parker & Asher, 1993)		8–16

(Continued)

Table 3.1. Rating scales commonly used *(Continued)*

Measure	Informants	Ages
Measure of Adolescent Social Performance (Cavell & Kelley, 1992; King, 1993)	Child, Parent, and Teacher	12–18
Global Functioning		
BASC II (Reynolds & Kamphaus, 2004)	Child/Adolescent, Parent, Teacher	2.5–21
CBCL (Achenbach & Edelbrock, 1991)	Child/Adolescent, Parent, Teacher	3–18
Conner's Parent and Teacher Rating Scales (Conners, 1997)	Parent and Teacher	3–18
Social Competence and Behavior Evaluation (parent and teacher versions; LaFreniere & Dumas, 1996; Kotler & McMahon, 2002).	Parent and teacher	3 years 0 months–4 years 11 months
Interpersonal competence scale (teacher, self; Cairns et al., 1995).	Teacher and Self	6–12
Joseph Pre-school and Primary Self-Concept Screening Test (Joseph, 1979)	Child	4–7
Pictorial Scale of Perceived Competence and Social Acceptance (Harter & Pike, 1984)	Child	4–7
Specific Measures		
Pier-Harris Self-Concept Scale (Piers, 1984)	Child and Adolescent	6–17
Self-Perception Profile for Children and Adolescents (Harter, 1985, 1986)	Child, Parent, Teacher	6–17
RCMAS (Reynolds & Richmond, 1978)	Child and Adolescent	6–18
Children's Depression Inventory (Kovacs, 1979)	Child and Adolescent	6–18
Reynolds Adolescent Depression Scale (Reynolds, 1996)	Adolescent	12–18
Direct Measures of Social Understanding		
DANVA 2 (Nowicki, 2002)	Child/Adolescent and Adult	6-adult
Children and Adolescent Social Perception (Magill-Evans et al., 1996)	Child and Adolescent	6–18
Social-Cognitive Assessment Profile (Hughes et al., 1993)	Structured Interview	
Revised Class Play (Masten et al., 1985)	Children	8–12

measures also have a parent and/or teacher form that allows one to compare the child's ratings with how a caretaker/teacher also sees him/her. It is interesting to compare the child's insight into any problems that may exist. A large study that is being conducted by this author obtained ratings from children with ADHD, Asperger's Disorder, and nonverbal learning disabilities (NVLD). The children with Asperger's Disorder rated themselves poorly and as having few friends while the children with NVLD or ADHD indicated that they had several friends. Parent reports for all of these groups found no differences with all groups having difficulties making friends (Guli et al., in process). Table 3.1 lists self-report measures for social skills.

In addition to directly measuring social skills, several measures provide insight into the child's emotional and behavioral adjustment. These measures may be omnibus in nature and evaluate several domains of functioning while others may select depression or anxiety as the main focus. Table 3.1 lists many of the most commonly used measures. Similar to the self-report, several of these measures also include a parent and teacher form and can be quite useful in comparing the scores across informants. It is common to have disagreement between sources and it is likely that different observers are providing information that can be quite helpful. Children with little insight into his/her own behavior will require a different set of interventions than one with good insight into his/her difficulties. These difficulties may be observed by the parent and/or teacher. A child may not show significant difficulties at home because he/she is in a situation where there may not be many children available to him/her and so opportunities are not present for problems to arise. It may also be that the child interacts with other children in a structured setting and so few problems are noted. Another possibility is that the child interacts with siblings or relatives with whom he/she is familiar, and so again the problems are not as noticeable.

There are far fewer measures of self-report of social competence for preschool children. The Pictorial Scale of Perceived Competence (Harter & Pike, 1984) and the Joseph Pre-School and Primary Self-Concept Screening Test (Joseph, 1979) are two that have been found to have adequate reliability and validity. The Social Competence and Behavior Evaluation-30 measure (cited in Kotler & McMahon, 2002) has been evaluated to evaluate social competence in children aged 3 years 0 months to 4 years 11 months. There were 218 in the original sample. From this sample 20 anxious/withdrawn children, 20 angry/aggressive, and 20 socially competent children were selected. Evaluation of these children found that the instrument reliably indicated children with mood disorders, behavioral disturbances, or who were functioning appropriately socially. A teacher version of the instrument has also been developed and found to have adequate psychometric properties (LaFreniere & Dumas, 1996).

The Interpersonal Competence Scale-Teacher (ISC-T; Cairns et al., 1995) is an 18-item questionnaire which uses a seven-point Likert scale and is completed by the child's teacher. It provides the following scale scores: popularity, Olympian (how the child does at sports), affiliative (how the child's affect appears), academic, aggression, and internalizing. Reliability coefficients are within the moderate level with test-retest reliability being between .80 and .92. It has been found to be related to direct observation and peer nomination measures and has also been shown to have adequate predictive validity over an 8-year period (Cairns & Cairns, 1994; Cairns et al., 1998). The Interpersonal Competence Scale-Self (ICS-S: Cairns et al., 1995) includes the same questions as the ISC-T with 3 detractor items. It has the same scales and the same factor structure. The reliability and validity has been found to be similar to the ISC-T (Farmer et al., 1999).

Another method for evaluating the child's social competence is through the use of direct measures of social interaction. These can include testing the child using standardized measures as well as providing tasks that the child completes in a laboratory setting under the observation of a trained clinician. Each of these will be discussed in the following section.

Direct Measures of Social Interaction

The Diagnostic Analysis of Nonverbal Accuracy (DANVA 2; Nowicki, 2002) provides an evaluation of the child or adolescent's ability to understand visual and auditory social stimuli. The child is asked to identify faces that show common emotions including anger, sadness, happiness, surprise, and disgust. These faces are presented on a computer screen and the child indicates what emotion goes with the face. The child also sees adult faces with the emotions and matches them with the correct emotion. The child then listens to sentences and matches the sentence with the correct emotion. The sentences are spoken by a child and then an adult.

The DANVA 2 provides scores that indicate whether the child was correct or not in the identification. It also provides intensity measures that allow the clinician to determine whether the child identified correctly less intense emotions (happy, sad) as well as more intense emotions (angry, surprised). In addition, the measure provides a comparison between being able to decipher emotions based on intensity.

The Children's and Adolescent Social Perception (CASP; Magill-Evans et al., 1996) task is a series of 12 vignettes. The vignettes are mostly adolescents acting out a situation that is emotionally arousing. The voices are masked so one can only hear the intonation and not the actual words. The child is asked to tell about each vignette after it ends and then to answer questions such as "why do you think he was feeling that way?" and so on. Scores are provided for nonverbal cues and emotions identified.

Performance task measures require the child to be observed in different settings using different methods. The methods may include observing the child in a laboratory setting using a play group, a friendship dyad, or a cooperative activity. The play group can be helpful to evaluate the child's interaction abilities as well as patterns of social responsivity while in a controlled environment. Generally 4–8 children are placed in a small group and observed while they play together. Different groups can be formed with some familiar and unfamiliar playmates to gauge how the child handles such variations in social comfort level. For the friendship dyads the child is asked to play with another child. During this time there may be free play or a task may be presented to the pair to solve. In this manner the child's ability to negotiate, deal with conflict, and to problem-solve can be observed.

The final type of observational method involves providing a performance task to the group. An example of one type of task may be entering an unknown group while another may be solving a social problem cooperatively with one or more peers. Each of these methods has been validated for use with the play group being most appropriate for the preschool child and the friendship dyad and performance tasks useful for children in elementary school and high school (Bierman & Welsh, 2000). One type of performance task that has been utilized to evaluate the child's conversational skills is to use a scripted interview where the interviewer asks the child to imagine talking to someone and then asks questions about that situation (Bierman & Furman, 1984). Some have found this technique helpful for children who have difficulty with impulsivity and behavior in evaluating the child's social skills (Hansen et al., 1988). The generalization of these results is questioned in the literature and further research is needed to evaluate how well they predict functioning in naturalistic settings (Bellack et al., 1979; Bierman & Welsh, 2000).

These performance tasks have been used not only for screening and evaluation purposes but also to evaluate the outcome of an intervention. Findings have indicated that when the intervention is targeted toward the child's deficits (i.e., social conversation) greater generalization to naturalistic situations occurs (Bierman & Furman, 1984; Ladd, 1981). Bierman and Welsh (2000) suggest that performance tasks may assist the examiner in understanding where the difficulties lie and then tailor the intervention to these problem areas. In addition, such interventions may show more generalization to other areas of the child's life than the usual social skills training approaches. Further research is needed to more fully understand the use of these techniques as well as their use for developing interventions.

Peer Nominations

Peer nominations have been used to determine the acceptance of a child within his/her peer group (Cillessen & Bukowski, 2000). There are several forms to this type of measure ranging from asking the children to rate the person they feel is most attractive to asking the child to rate all of the peers on a scale. The simplicity of this method is also its problem as it may be one-dimensional, and thus not provide sufficient information about the child's social skills. Maassen and Vershueren (2005) suggest that a person may not be nominated as being the most desirable peer and still be well-liked. When a two-dimensional classification is utilized, the child is asked to select attractive peers as well as unattractive peers. This typology allows for a continuous variable as well as better-demarcated groupings. The use of this technique has resulted in groups who are divided into two dimensions: social preference (popular, average, and rejected categories) and social impact (neglected, average, and controversial). Children who are controversial are those who are selected by equal numbers as liked and disliked.

An ethical issue has arisen concerning the use of negative nominations. Parents and teachers as well as selected researchers have suggested that eliciting negative rankings from a child sets up a possibility of labeling the target child unfairly. Asher and Dodge (1986) suggested that the child be asked for positive nominations and then having them rate the favorability of playing with the other members of the group. This technique allows for both negative and positive nominations in that the children infrequently chosen as playmates are placed in the more negative categories.

A more complex method was developed that is based on a probability method and labeled SSrat (Maassen et al., 1996). The sociometric scale is divided into positive and negative halves with an algorithm developed that converts the ratings into positive and negative halves using a single rating scale. Both of these methods have been found to be helpful in determining the social status of the child.

The stability of the SSrat and Asher and Dodge methods has been found to be good (Maassen & Vershueren, 2005). Validity was found to be good for the SSrat and the Asher and Dodge methods. When the pure nomination form was utilized (select the most attractive and least attractive peer) stability, reliability, and validity fell to unacceptable levels (Maassen & Vershueren, 2005).

An unusual type of performance task is included in the Revised Class Play which is a modification of the Class Play (Garmezy & Tellegen, 1984). Masten et al. (1985) revised this technique to include 30 roles, 15 positive and 15 negative. The entire classroom participates in this program and each child selects his/her peers for roles in the play. Only one classmate can have each role and the child cannot select himself or herself for a role. The role is read aloud to the class twice and the each child marks his/her choice independently. This type of nomination technique has been validated and found to be stable at intervals of 6 and 17 months (Masten et al., 1985). Children who had a profile of low positive, were chosen for more aggressive roles, and were more isolated showed the poorest levels of social competence.

Summary and Conclusions

The field of assessment of social competence is in its infancy compared to that of academic and cognitive evaluation. Although many techniques are now available, the psychometric properties of these measures are similar to that of measures of personality and emotional competence but not at the level expected for good psychometric properties. Most of the reported reliability and validity coefficients range from .50 to .80 rather than the generally expected level of .80 and above. It is important to recognize that these measures may not be as accurate as those of more tangible skills. However, these measures can assist the clinician in evaluating the child's skills. It is important to utilize multiple informants as the child's behaviors likely vary depending on the environment and the people associated with that environment. Parents may have a limited view of their child's social skills while teachers have a larger comparison group for the child's development. Mothers have been found to be more realistic about their child's social abilities than fathers. Thus, to have only one data point will restrict the understanding of the child's abilities and likely provide an inaccurate measure of the child's skills.

The age of the child also affects what measures may be possible. Behavior self-rating scales are not generally helpful for preschool children. Challenges to the validity of even the most common measures such as the Pictorial Scale of Perceived Competence or the Social Acceptance for Young Children are present particularly with the child's grasp of the rules of administration (Fantuzzo et al., 1996). For the preschool child the use of observation is likely the best method for evaluation. The Berkeley Puppet Interview is a novel method that is promising for use with preschool children.

For the grade school child coupling self-reports with teacher and parent rating scales is helpful. Observation of the child on the playground or in a friendship dyad is also helpful. Interviews with adolescents as well as observations can be useful tools.

Using performance techniques generally requires a laboratory and is likely unrealistic in a school or clinic setting. The techniques, however, may be useful in assisting the clinician in developing an intervention that targets the child's difficulties and there is research to support this type of use. What is clear from the above review of the literature is that more work is needed for our understanding of the child's social competence with better instruments developed.

The next section of this book provides a discussion of the challenges for children with learning, attention, and social relatedness in developing social competence. ADHD, Asperger's Syndrome, Autism, learning disabilities, externalizing and internalizing disorders can create significant problems for the child functioning in the school but more importantly relating to peers. These difficulties will be discussed in the following chapters.

4

Social Competence in Children with Attention Deficit Hyperactivity Disorder

John had difficulty in preschool with attention and impulse control. By kindergarten year he had experienced a great deal of difficulty in school and was frequently on the time out chair for blurting out answers and bothering other children. His teacher recommended that he be retained in kindergarten due to his immaturity. His parents decided to promote him to first grade despite the teacher's recommendation. His academic progress was described as average but John continued to have problems with attention and impulse control. Children in first grade began excluding him from their play at recess and he began hitting and fighting with many of the boys. He resisted teacher and parent attempts at behavioral correction and appeared to be angry a great deal of the time.

In second grade his grades began to fall and his teachers became concerned about a learning disability. His parents felt that he was learning adequately but that the teachers weren't teaching him correctly. They hired a tutor for him and John made progress in the one-to-one situation with his tutor. His grades improved but his behavior did not. His attention and impulse control were better with his tutor but she also reported the need to frequently redirect his efforts.

By third grade the school requested testing to determine whether John required special education support. His parents agreed and the testing indicated high average ability, low average achievement, and significant problems with attention, impulse control, and activity level. John was continuing to experience social rejection and had few friends that would play with him. It was confusing to his parents because John readily made friends—he just could not keep them! The evaluation pointed to a possible Attention Deficit Hyperactivity Disorder and John was referred to his pediatrician for an evaluation. The school was also concerned about his social interaction as well as his oppositional behavior and anger. John was subsequently evaluated by a child psychiatrist and was prescribed Adderall. Improvements were almost immediately seen in his attention and impulse control but problems remained in the area of social interactions.

ADHD

Attention Deficit Hyperactivity Disorder (ADHD) is a disorder defined by difficulties in attention, inhibition, impulsive control, and activity level. There is a diverse body of research into all aspects of ADHD including social competence. As discussed in Chapter 2, important functions such as working memory and executive functioning become more and more important in later development. These basic skills allow the child and adolescent to be able to monitor his/her behavior and to change it accordingly. When difficulties are present in inhibition, attention, and impulse control, the child or adolescent has difficulties applying previously learned rules to current situations and often problems arise in all areas of life—academic, social, and behavioral.

Previous research had viewed ADHD as a unitary diagnosis similar to the DSM IIIR (APA, 1987) conceptualization. DSM IV-TR (APA, 1997) defined ADHD as having three subtypes—ADHD: combined (ADHD:C), ADHD: predominately inattentive (ADHD:PI), and ADHD: hyperactive impulsive (ADHD:HI). The subtype of ADHD:HI is infrequently diagnosed after the age of 7 and will not be addressed here. Children with ADHD:C have been found to show higher levels of aggression, impulsivity, and poorer compliance than ADHD:PI (Gaub & Carlson, 1997). In contrast children with ADHD: PI show more withdrawal and more attentional difficulties than those with ADHD:C as well as higher levels of learning problems, anxiety and depression (Wolraich et al., 1996).

Comorbidity and ADHD

Attention Deficit Hyperactivity Disorder has been found to co-occur with other disorders including learning disabilities, anxiety, depression, conduct disorder, bipolar disorder, and oppositional defiant disorder (Biederman et al., 1991; Semrud-Clikeman, et al., 1992). Additional diagnoses likely contribute to a more severe form of ADHD and also impact the child's social functioning. Children with ADHD and aggression have been found to show the poorest level of social functioning and to experience more difficulties making and keeping friends (Landau, Milich, & Diener, 1998). These additional diagnoses further complicate the picture, as interventions require a multi-faceted approach and one that generally requires intense family and school interventions. Medications are more problematic for children with multiple diagnoses as side effects become more pronounced and medications move from simple stimulants to more potent drugs (Connor & Swanson, 1999).

Children with ADHD and externalizing disorders experience social problems as well as those with internalizing disorders. The behaviors that are targeted may differ. Where those children with comorbid aggressive or acting out behaviors require additional behavioral control, children with co-occurring anxiety and depression (or mood disorders) may require assistance with withdrawal behaviors and isolation. Social concerns are present for comorbid externalizing and internalizing disorders for children with ADHD. Specific discussion of these disorders without ADHD is present in succeeding chapters.

Social Competence in ADHD

Research has shown that children and adolescents with ADHD tend to be rejected by their peers fairly soon after their initial meeting and have fewer friends than those without ADHD (Bagwell et al., 2001). Some have suggested that the social difficulties found in children with ADHD are important enough to be included in the diagnostic criteria and may be a defining characteristic of the disorder (Landau et al., 1998). It has also been found that children with ADHD are more disliked than those children who are aggressive (Milich & Landau, 1989). These difficulties have been found even when unknown peers view videotape without sound and rate the social behaviors (Bickett & Milich, 1990).

Many children with ADHD have playmates that also have ADHD for friends and thus cooperative play becomes problematic (Hubbard & Newcomb, 1991). For those children with ADHD and aggression, social problems are more extreme and predictive of later social difficulty. These peer difficulties have been found in childhood and to extend into adolescence (Bagwell et al., 2001). Of greatest concern is the tendency for these problems to continue into adolescence and adulthood and to be resistant to change (Coie & Dodge, 1983). Bagwell et al. (2001) found social rejection to continue for adolescents previously diagnosed with ADHD whether or not the symptoms continued into adolescence. This finding indicates the problems learned in childhood translate into behavioral difficulties in later life and changing these behaviors has not been found to be successful even when the ADHD symptoms have subsided.

Previously it was believed that problems with substance abuse, delinquency, and acting out were regularly associated with ADHD (Barkley et al., 1990). Emerging evidence is present that ADHD may not be as strong a risk factor for such difficulties as is conduct disorder (Forehand et al., 1991) or when ADHD co-occurs with conduct or oppositional defiant disorder. Substance abuse appears to be related to involvement with a delinquent peer group rather than to solely a diagnosis of ADHD (Bates & Labouvie, 1995).

Greene et al. (1997) studied boys with ADHD over a 4-year period for social functioning and substance abuse. Findings indicated that social disability significantly predicted increased substance abuse for these participants. Of additional concern is a study by Greene and Biederman (1999) of siblings of these boys who did not have ADHD. These siblings were also evaluated for social competence. Findings indicated that those with social disability (even without a diagnosis of ADHD) were at higher risk for the development of substance abuse compared to those with at least average social functioning. Thus, the relationships between ADHD and substance abuse may not be due to the diagnosis of ADHD but rather to poor social functioning. This finding requires additional study but is important for our discussion because it links social competence disability to higher risk for substance abuse and poorer outcome.

A sole diagnosis of ADHD has also not been found to be a major risk factor for delinquency. However, when ADHD and conduct disorder co-occur, the severity of behavioral problems increases dramatically and the disorder does not respond readily to intervention (Teeter, 1998). When children with aggressive tendencies also have a diagnosis of ADHD, they have a higher risk factor for engaging in behaviors that eventually result in adjudication.

Thus, while children and adolescents with ADHD continue to have difficulties with social problems, those with comorbid conduct or oppositional defiant disorder face the poorest outcomes. Since the closest friends to children with a sole diagnosis of ADHD are those with the disorder also, it is likely that play and social relationships are problematic particularly in regard to difficulties with disinhibition and poor impulse control. These weaknesses likely contribute to higher levels of aggression and disruption in play and poor learning from appropriate models. Since many of the children with ADHD are not accepted by their peers without ADHD, opportunities to learn corrective behavior are limited and may contribute to Bagwell et al.'s (2001) finding that problems persist even when symptoms of ADHD subside.

Biederman et al. (1993) evaluated adaptive behavior functioning in children with ADHD. Adaptive functioning is the ability to relate to different settings and different social expectations. In their sample of 150 children with ADHD and 120 controls, 38% of the children with ADHD reported significant difficulties with peer relationships while only 2% of the controls reported these problems. Moreover, 20% of the children with ADHD reported difficulties relating to their parents compared to 3% of the controls. Of the children with ADHD, 23% reported difficulties relating to others in the leisure activities compared to 4% of the controls. The children with ADHD who showed the most difficulty were those who had comorbid diagnoses with conduct disorder, depression, and anxiety disorder each placing the child at higher risk of difficulties with adaptability. Thus, the controls showed the fewest problems, the children with ADHD the next level of problems, and the children with ADHD and any other comorbid diagnosis the most problems socially.

Medication

Many children and adolescents with ADHD respond favorably to medication with improved academic and behavioral functioning. However, research does not provide evidence that medication improves social relationships (Landau & Moore, 1991). Some improvement from medication has been found in sports and structured recreational settings (Smith et al., 1998) but not in unstructured interactions. Meichenbaum et al. (2001) suggests that many adolescents with ADHD stop taking medication, and thus social relationships are negatively impacted. Bagwell et al. (2001) found that continuing treatment with medication in adolescence was related to improved peer relationships, increased activities that were socially accepted, and less substance abuse.

A comprehensive study of the effect of medication on several aspects of functioning (academic, emotion, psychosocial, and social) has evaluated the effect of long-term methylphenidate and multimodal psychosocial treatment in children with ADHD (Klein et al., 2004). One-hundred–and-three children with ADHD who did not have any comorbid disorders and who responded favorably to methylphenidate were placed into one of 3 groups: (1) methylphenidate alone; (2) methylphenidate and multimodal psychosocial treatment including parent training, academic support, psychotherapy, and social skills training; or (3) methylphenidate plus attention control treatment. For the first year all children were on methylphenidate and for the second year children were switched to a single-blind placebo.

Abikoff et al. (2004a) found that there was no improvement in participants who had the psychosocial treatments compared to those with sole administration of methylphenidate. All children showed a relapse when the placebo phase of the study began and all were reinstated on methylphenidate within 8.6 days for group 1, 17.1 days for group 2, and 11.7 days for group 3. The authors concluded that psychosocial treatments did not add to improvement for these children and were not helpful. Support of these findings was presented from the MTA study from 1999. In that study (MTA Cooperative Group, 1999) psychosocial treatment alone was very poor compared to medication effects and psychosocial treatment with methylphenidate was no better than methylphenidate alone.

These findings were also present in a study of the child's academic and emotional functioning using the same groups as Abikoff et al. (2004a). Hechtman et al. (2004) found that academic assistance and psychotherapy did not provide any improvement beyond that seen by medication alone. These authors concluded that providing academic assistance for children without learning problems accorded no advantage to these children compared to those with appropriate levels of medication. Abikoff et al. (2004b) studied the social functioning of these same children. Social skills' training was not found to improve functioning beyond that seen in children with methylphenidate alone. Medication was found to reduce negative social interactions both by the treated children and by their peers toward the child with ADHD. These findings are intriguing as they somewhat argue against additional treatment beyond that of medication. However, as will be seen later in this chapter, the social skills training and psychosocial interventions may need to not only be multimodal but also utilize treatment at home and at school.

In summary, children and adolescents with ADHD have been found to experience difficulties with peer relationships as well as adaptive behavior. The existence of a comorbid diagnosis also predisposes a child/adolescent with ADHD to more severe problems. Medication issues cannot be ignored and must be addressed in any study or treatment protocol. Developmental issues are important for ADHD as well as for other disorders. ADHD progresses along a developmental path similar to the other aspects of development of social behavior discussed in earlier chapters. The following section briefly reviews the developmental issues important for the child or adolescent with ADHD.

Development and ADHD

Developmental issues are important in understanding difficulties in social functioning in ADHD. Children with ADHD have been found to show at least a 2-year developmental lag in adaptive behavior and in prefrontal functioning (the ability to plan and organize information and solve problems based on previous learning) (Amin et al., 1993; Chelune et al., 1986; Dykens, et al., 1990). Consistent developmental lags in children with ADHD have been found on tasks that need to be mastered at various ages. The child with ADHD appears to learn these skills at a different stage, thus causing a mismatch between the child with ADHD and his/her peers in social understanding and in behavior.

Barkley (2000) places important emphasis on four aspects of development important for social functioning. First, the child needs to learn to represent an event mentally for later use. Frequently this representation is in the form of language encoding of what happened as well as what he/she should do in that situation. This shift allows the child to hold the "rules" of social engagement in place to be applied to later similar situations. Secondly, the child needs to be able to shift control of his/her behavior from others to himself. In other words, the child needs to apply the rules learned in stage 1. Thirdly, the child needs to learn how to delay gratification. The child needs to be able to wait for a reward and to anticipate the reward if the behavioral rules are appropriately applied. Finally, the child needs to be able to anticipate the future—not to live in the here and now. All of these steps are intertwined and important for the child to be able to socialize with others. As discussed in the following paragraphs, the child with ADHD accomplishes these shifts later than his/her peers and such a delay causes significant problems in all areas of his/her life but particularly in the social area.

Infancy and Preschool Age

For the infant and toddler with attentional and/or activity difficulties, important issues are similar to that of typically developing children—namely attachment and temperament. Environmental issues have been shown to play an important role in development in conjunction with genetics. The interplay of environment on genetic makeup likely sets the stage for the child's eventual personality (LeFrancois, 1995; Sameroff, 1975).

One of the main tasks for the toddler and preschooler with ADHD is that of developing self-regulation and self-control based on environmental rewards. A child with ADHD frequently experiences difficulty in this area and likely has many more negative corrective situations where parents need to respond to problematic behavior. Frustrating situations can arise where the parent corrects the child and expects that he/she will learn over time to utilize correct behavior and such learning does not seem to be taking place. This learning of self-control may also not be as predictable for the child with ADHD and frequent reminders and corrections are necessary. For a parent who is patient and able to manage his/her frustration, these corrections are manageable. However, when there is a misfit between the parent's temperament and the child's (a low frustration tolerance in both cases), parenting difficulties become, at times, overwhelming. Moreover, there is a high incidence of ADHD in parents of children with ADHD which sets up another difficulty in that the parent with ADHD may well have more impulsive behavior and less tolerance for difficult behavior in their child. Given the finding that infants learn how to modulate their behavior based on parent reaction (Kopp, 1982; Teeter, 1998), it is likely that the child with ADHD will experience more frustration and possibly come to view social exchanges as reflecting a failure on his/her part.

A large minority of parents of children with ADHD indicate problems in the first year of the child's life which include sleep difficulties, problems with language development, feeding problems, and crying with fewer incidences of smiling and cuddling (Weiss & Hechtman, 1993). These children are also reported to be difficult to soothe and poor mother–child bonding is frequently reported (Teeter, 1998). These difficulties continue into the preschool age and toddlers are reported to be difficult to toilet-train and reported to be oppositional to the point of straining the mother–child relationship (Barkley, 1997).

Parents frequently rate their child with ADHD as more aggressive, more demanding of parental time, and less socially skilled (DeWolfe et al., 2000). Moreover, these same parents rate themselves as less competent parents who are more often negative than positive and who are experiencing significant feelings of stress. Fathers are found to withdraw from parenting thus isolating the mother-child dyad further and restricting the child's experience of both parenting styles. The parents are also likely to experience criticism from friends and extended family as to their parenting ability and an increase in stress, self-efficacy, and family conflict is often seen.

Play difficulties are also seen at this age. Preschoolers with ADHD have been found to have fewer interactions, poorer motor skills and thus poorer ability to join in group games, and to have difficulty following through on group activities (Alessandri, 1992). Moreover, these children also experience difficulty with being negative and oppositional thus driving away possible playmates.

Elementary School Children

Children entering elementary school are required to sit quietly, listen to the teacher, and work cooperatively with their peers. Children with ADHD may be able to maintain appropriate social behaviors in free play where they are able to do what they enjoy with minimal interference. However, when placed in a structured setting these children began to have many challenges and their peers are aware of the difficulty a child with ADHD has in the classroom. Since these children do not profit from previous experience in changing their behaviors, it is likely that they become more and more frustrated with both the situation and themselves. Children with ADHD often have poor school adjustment (Barkley, 1989), have problems with friendships particularly if they come from a disorganized and/or chaotic home (Campbell, 1990), and are often referred for evaluation with increased incidence of depression and anxiety disorders (Biederman et al., 1991; Wenar, 1994).

Problems with parenting continue to present with the child resisting completing chores and fighting with siblings (Barkley, 1990). Parents of children with ADHD consistently rate themselves as feeling more stress and needing to use more coercive methods of discipline (Buhrmester et al., 1992). Gerdes et al. (2003) found that mothers and fathers of elementary-aged children with ADHD perceived their relationship with their child as more negative than did parents of control children. Moreover, the children with ADHD did not differ from control children in how they perceived their relationship with their parents. Thus, while the parents were experiencing significant amounts of stress, the children with ADHD viewed their parents more positively and felt more positive in their relationship to both their mother and their father.

At this point in life, the child with ADHD is frequently rejected by his/her peers and receives higher levels of negative attention from the teacher and, most importantly, lower levels of positive attention (Milich & Landau, 1989). When aggression is also present, difficulties in social functioning are more severe and continue past the elementary school age (Johnston & Pelham, 1986). There are gender differences present with girls with aggression and disruptive behavior shown to have more social problems than boys even with the same level of aggressive behaviors (Carlson et al., 1987).

Adolescence

Adolescence has its own challenges even for the child with relatively few problems. For the adolescent with ADHD they become more difficult as peer relations are more problematic. There is evidence that adolescents with ADHD tend to be more thrill-seeking and engage in behaviors that are very risky and problematic (Wender, 1987). As with the younger children, adolescents with ADHD may have a developmental lag socially, and thus the development of empathy and perspective-taking is delayed and puts them at odds with their more typically developing peers. These difficulties may translate into higher rates of conduct problems at this stage. Research has indicated that these problems ameliorate for the majority of adolescents by their 20s again indicating that they "catch up" to their peers in understanding the consequences of their behaviors, albeit at a later age (Mannuzza, et al., 1993).

Adolescents with ADHD who are studied through adolescence and into their 20s have been found to show improvements in all areas particularly in the areas of substance abuse and aggression (Mannuzza et al., 1989). Moreover, of the adolescents in this study 18% were found to own their own business compared to only 5% of the controls. It is likely that these adolescents who were sensation-seeking were able to channel this behavior in a socially accepted manner. For the adolescent as well as for the younger child, aspects of development including the constructs of self-perception, executive functions, and working memory are important for understanding social competence. Each of these concepts will be described in the following sections.

Self-Perception in ADHD

Self-perception has been defined as how competent one sees oneself in differing domains often including perceptions of academic competence, or social acceptance (Harter, 1985). These perceptions are collectively known as global self-worth. The domains and the self-worth are linked to how a child feels about himself/herself in meeting the challenges of everyday life and not how they actually perform within their environment.

There are two strands of findings as to the self-perceptions of children with ADHD. The first indicates that boys with ADHD have lower self-perceptions than boys without ADHD and these perceptions may be realistic self-evaluations (Treuting & Hinshaw, 2001). The other group of findings indicated that boys with ADHD show an inflated sense of self and report competence on tasks that do not differ from controls or may even exceed self-evaluations of controls (Hoza et al., 2001). Hoza et al. (2001) term this inflation "positive illusory thinking" and view it as a coping response that may be adaptive for the child to encourage him/her to continue to try to establish relationships despite evidence to the contrary that his/her feelings will be reciprocated. Hoza et al. (1993) studied boys with ADHD and those without ADHD. Findings were of no differences between the groups on measures of academic, social, athletic competence, or physical appearance. There were also no group differences on global self-worth measures. The boys with ADHD reported lower scores on measures of behavioral conduct. These boys showed difficulties in all of these areas and thus the conclusion from this study was that they were inflating their self-perception. In addition, boys with comorbid aggression, ADHD, and poor achievement overestimated their abilities the most in the areas that they had the most difficulty in (behavior and academic competence). Moreover, boys with ADHD without comorbid depression overestimated social and academic competence compared to controls while those with ADHD and depression did not differ from the controls. Thus, boys with co-occurring depressive symptoms show less positive illusory bias and appear to not have as much protection from feelings of failure and inability to continue to try as those without depressive symptomatology. Therefore, when depressive symptoms are controlled, children with ADHD show higher levels of self-perception compared to those without symptoms school.

Taylor and Brown (1988) suggested that these positive illusions might be protective from depression and allow the child/adolescent to continue to try even when experiencing failure and/or setbacks. Others suggest that these illusions are actually detrimental as they do not allow for an accurate appraisal of the child/adolescent's functioning and hence the ability to change behavior (Colvin et al., 1995).

Studies have begun to evaluate differences in social functioning for the subtypes in ADHD. Owens and Hoza (2003) sought to investigate these inflated perceptions in children with ADHD and their eventual adjustment. They hypothesized those children with ADHD: C would inflate their competence while those with ADHD: PI would report lower or average levels of competence. They also hypothesized that there would be no differences between males and females on these reports. Owens and Hoza (2003) recruited 97 children between 9 and 12 years of age. Eighty two were recruited from a school population and 15 from a clinic-based program. Control children were matched to these children from the same school. The self-perceptions of the ADHD: C children did not differ from those of the controls despite significant difficulties reported by teachers and parents. The self-perceptions of the ADHD: PI children were lower than those of the control children in the areas of academic ability, physical appearance, behavior, and global self-worth. However, neither group differed from the control group on measures of social self-perception. On measures of academic and behavioral competence, additional information was gathered from teachers and parents as to the accuracy of the child's self-perception. It is unfortunate that Owens and Hoza (2003) did not obtain information as to the friendships these children had to verify their self-perceptions. Given the frequent findings of difficulties with peers (Barkley, 1997), it is reasonable to speculate that these children also had more problems than they either reported or of which they had knowledge.

Hoza et al. (2002) evaluated the relationship of the estimation of self-perception to social functioning in boys with ADHD as related to teacher report of social competence. Boys with ADHD were found to overestimate their skills in all areas and to overestimate more in the domain in which they were most impaired. Thus, boys with ADHD and aggression rated themselves better on social and behavioral domains than teachers while those with academic problems rated themselves equal to controls. These findings were replicated by Hoza et al. (2004) particularly in the area of social functioning. Boys with ADHD were found to overestimate their social abilities compared to teacher, mother, and father ratings as well as compared to typically developing children. These children had previously completed an intensive behavioral treatment for ADHD and this overestimation continued even after the treatment ended.

Hoza et al. (2004) rightly point out that although such "positive illusory self-perceptions" may protect against depression, they also prevent improvement in the areas continuing to be problematic for these children. Further study is needed to determine whether these inflated self-perceptions are related to the more negative outcome frequently seen for adolescents and young adults with ADHD. For social skills, some researchers suggest that these inflated self-perceptions may be needed until the child begins to experience positive reward and then can gradually be correct (Diener & Milich, 1997; Ohan & Johnston, 2002). However, the method for conducting this transition is not clear nor is the developmental trajectory for its accomplishment.

Difficulties with insight may be related to problems with executive function deficits that may be related to problems with self-awareness (Ownsworth et al., 2002). These difficulties likely influence not only insight but also the ability to change behavior adapt to the environment. The following section discusses the relationship of executive function and working memory deficits to social competence in children with ADHD.

Executive Functions and Working Memory

Executive function is a construct to describe a group of behaviors that generally encompass the concepts of planning, cognitive flexibility, inhibition, organization, and working memory. Executive functions have been defined as "those capacities that enable a person to engage successfully in independent, purposive, self-serving behavior" (Lezak, 1995, p. 42). Barkley (2000) further defines executive functions as the "when or whether aspects of behavior, whereas nonexecutive functions involve the what or how" (p. 1065).

These skills have been found to be problematic for children with ADHD (Barkley, 1997). In addition, difficulties have been found on direct measures of working memory as well as on response inhibition that are related to parent ratings for difficulties in attention, activity level, and persistence (Muir-Broaddus et al., 2002). These functions also underlie goal-directed behavior and the ability to inhibit a response that can interfere with the desired goal. Medication has been found to improve executive functioning particularly on measures of planning, cognitive flexibility, and working memory (Kempton et al., 1999). Its link to improvement in social skills has not been carefully studied and an investigation into these underlying mechanisms is poorly understood.

While there is a substantial body of research that has found difficulties with executive functioning in children with ADHD, a consensus about the particular measures to evaluate executive functions is not present with various studies finding equivocal results depending on the measure utilized (Pennington & Ozonoff, 1996). For example, some studies have found difficulties with set-shifting as measured by the Wisconsin Card Sorting Test (Gorenstein et al., 1989) while others have not (Grodzinsky & Diamond, 1992). Others found difficulties on continuous performance tests (CPT) and processing speed (Corkum & Siegel, 1993) while others have not (Grodzinsky & Diamond, 1992; Korkman & Pesonen, 1994). Barkley et al. (2001) reviewed the literature on executive functioning and concluded that the aspects of executive functioning that have empirical support include response inhibition, working memory, cognitive flexibility, and self-regulation or persistence.

Subtypes of ADHD have been found to differ on measures of executive functioning. Both ADH: C and ADHD: PI have been found to show deficits in response speed, vigilance cognitive flexibility, or inhibition with the ADHD: C evidencing more problems with planning (Nigg et al., 2002). As expected the children with ADHD: C had more behavioral problems and the children with ADHD: PI had more academic difficulties. Klorman et al. (1999) found differences between subtypes on measures of planning and working memory with the children with ADHD: C scoring more poorly than the children with ADHD: PI. Both subtypes have been found to perform more poorly on measures of pair-associate learning (Barry et al., 2002; Bayliss & Roodenrys, 2000). Thus, the subtypes of ADHD may show differing aspects of problems with planning, cognitive flexibility, and working memory. These difficulties may translate into problems with social functioning but have been relatively poorly studied for differences between the subtypes. Both subtypes may experience social problems for differing reasons. The children with ADHD:C may be more impulsive and disinhibited while the children with ADHD:PI may show more difficulty with withdrawal and problem-solving. Evaluating the social functioning for the individual child with ADHD is particularly important when designing interventions that would best meet the child's needs.

This conceptualization of executive functioning is particularly apt for the study of social ability in children with ADHD. Effective social functioning often requires the person to formulate appropriate actions and to change this action plan if difficulties arise. It is likely that children and adolescents with ADHD are uniquely unable to modify their behavior to fit the situation at hand. In addition, executive functioning allows the person to allocate the limited attentional resources needed to process a situation. Such attentional resources require working memory—both of these constructs have a limited storage capacity and require fast processing. If an individual needs to allocate more capacity to these processes, there is less left to accurately encode the situation. If the person becomes distracted during this process, these difficulties can prove problematic for accurate processing of the situation at hand (Barkley et al., 2001). Children with ADHD have been found to process information quickly and frequently inaccurately. Their responses have also been found to be more intense than would be warranted and the difficulties may be related to the inability to switch responses and interpretation of a situation to meet changing demands. The ability to monitor behavior is particularly important in executive functioning, and Damasio (1994) suggests that this monitoring is related to affective and motivational states for change.

The ability to communicate socially is particularly important for children with ADHD. Clark et al. (2002) found that children with ADHD were more likely to show poorer communication abilities as well as executive functioning and that these adaptive skills were highly related to their social functioning. Difficulties with executive functioning appear to be present for many children with ADHD from early childhood through adolescence. Particular difficulties in inhibition have been found to play a major role in the development of poor executive functioning and later problems in school and with friends (Berlin et al., 2003). Executive functioning has also been related to problems with emotional regulation in children with ADHD and to be specific to ADHD compared with other disorders (Berlin et al., 2004; Geurts et al., 2004). This link of adaptability, disinhibition (or emotional regulation), and cognitive flexibility may foreshadow significant problems with social functioning as well as the ability to change behavior to fit the situation.

The particular features of executive function particularly important for social functioning include the ability to shift a strategy as needed and to allocate the necessary resources in attention and working memory to successfully solve social problems. Nixon (2001) suggests that the understanding of these underlying aspects of executive functions possibly provide more appropriate interventions to enhance outcomes in later life.

Barkley (2000) suggests a framework to understand social functioning from an executive function network. Although his article is not directly intended for this purpose, he provided a link between the most commonly agreed upon aspects of executive functioning and social ability. Table 4.1 provides these links. Social ability is impaired by difficulties in these regions and may occur during development as the child or adolescent fails to make the changes expected of his/her age. Particular problems would be present in the child's ability to form relationships, to take care of himself/herself socially, and to understand this his/her current behavior impacts future relationships and the resulting perceptions of others.

Barkley (2000) suggests that play in early childhood and throughout life allows the person to understand how people relate, how to obtain a goal, and how to gauge one's behavior based on the other person's response to that behavior. During this time the child internalizes the rules and executive functioning allows for the person to become able to control his/her behavior. These reactions become internalized in what he terms "private motivational states" and provide the motivation needed for future behaviors. Difficulties arise for children and adolescents with ADHD when these executive functions are not adequately developed and when the disorder interferes with these developmental tasks. The inability to use these executive functions to learn from others, to apply appropriate rules, and to self-direct behaviors is likely tied to the difficulties children with ADHD have in social competence.

Thus, interventions that target these aspects of executive functioning may help children and adolescents adapt to changing environments and to develop appropriate behaviors. The following section discusses various types of interventions that have been utilized with children and adolescents with ADHD.

Table 4.1 Links between executive functioning and social competence

Executive function	Social competence
Response inhibition	Self-regulation
	Ability to wait for reward
Working memory	Retrieving previously learned material Holding information in mind while solving a social problem
	Organizing behavioral response
Cognitive flexibility	Changing responses to meet current needs
Self-regulation	Modulating behavior and emotional response

Social Interventions in ADHD

Studies have indicated that children with ADHD experience difficulties with both knowledge of social skills and the ability to act appropriately (or performance deficits) (Landau et al., 1998). Difficulties with social skills indicate that child does not understand interactions or does not encode the situations correctly. Problems in performance show that the child cannot implement their skills appropriately. Interventions would target the appropriate areas in order to improve social functioning. For those children with social skills, knowledge deficits direct training in skills would appear to be appropriate while for those with performance deficits training would improve their ability to manage their behavior. Unfortunately research has not supported these conclusions for children with ADHD. Social skill deficits have not been consistently found for children with ADHD with studies finding children with ADHD able to identify appropriate and inappropriate social behavior (Whalen et al., 1990).

It has been suggested those children with ADHD: PI may show social skills knowledge deficits while those with ADHD: C have problems with performance (Wheeler & Carlson, 1994). Those children with ADHD: PI show more withdrawal and anxiety compared to children with ADHD: C and that more problems are present in skills rather than in performance. The children with ADHD: C were found to have more problems in regulating their behaviors and thus often elicit rejection from others further limiting their interactions with others.

Social skills training most often utilizes direct teaching of social behaviors. This training is often accomplished in the school setting and occasionally in a clinic, and behaviors are practiced within those settings. Difficulties in motivation, self-regulation, and self-monitoring may also play into problems with socialization as discussed earlier in this chapter. Training in these areas may be also helpful for the child particularly in generalization of skills to various settings. Guervemont and Dumas (1994) suggest that social skills training incorporates four objectives: (1) increased awareness of appropriate social behaviors; (2) direct teaching of social behaviors; (3) increasing the use of appropriate social behaviors across settings; and (4) improving the social status of the child.

Social skills training have traditionally met with limited success for improving social functioning with children and adolescents with ADHD. These techniques include modeling, rehearsal, feedback as well as directly teaching appropriate social behavior in a group setting. These models are generally built on cognitive-behavioral training. Some improvement is seen following social skills training but the improvement is often not present at follow-up or does not generalize to similar situations (Semrud-Clikeman et al., 1999). Self-regulation and cognitive-behavioral training have not been found to improve social functioning but have been helpful for parents and teachers for managing the child's behaviors (Pfiffner & Barkley, 1990). Abikoff (1987) found that cognitive-behavioral training did not improve social functioning for children with ADHD. Programs for social skills training that build on cognitive behavioral therapy have improved social skills somewhat but not to the level of social competence (Pelham & Bender, 1982).

Since one of the difficulties with social skills training has been the problem with generalization, Pfiffner et al. (2000) pairing social skills training with teaching parents and teachers techniques that were useful shows promise. Findings indicated that improvement was seen for these children and that an increase in generalization across settings was found. Similarly, Antshel and Remer (2003) found pairing social skills training and parent training led to better generalization and more improvement in the child's cooperation and appropriate assertiveness at home. In addition, improvement in the child's understanding of empathy was also seen for both children with ADHD: C and those with ADHD: PI.

Cousins and Weiss (1993) paired social skills training and parent training in appropriate behavioral techniques and found improvement for children with ADHD. Particular emphasis was placed on the parent learning how to encourage appropriate peer behaviors, to teach self-evaluation techniques to their child, and to share information with other caregivers in the child's life to facilitate consistency between situations. When these treatments were combined, the improvement in social competence was reported to be stronger and to generalize across situations.

These findings were further supported by a study pairing social skills training and parent training. Sheridan and Dee (1996) paired social skills training with a parent group that met at the same time as the child's group. The parents were trained in problem solving and goal-setting. Findings indicated that parent's skills improved as well as the child's social skills. More importantly, the child's skills were found to translate into improved functioning in the classroom. Moreover, parents reported that the children showed fewer indications of anxiety, psychosomatic complaints, and learning problems than prior to the intervention. These studies conducted with five boys and their parents need replication with a larger sample and with concomitant behavioral observations to provide support for the finding but the results are instructive and may indicate appropriate interventions for the future.

Most social skills training is completed in groups of children with generally 5–6 in a group. Hoza et al. (2003) placed children with ADHD in dyadic groups reasoning that learning how to learn strategies for friendship may be better accomplished with one particular child. In addition, parents were encouraged to participate and to assist in the developing of the friendship. Findings indicated that those children who showed less aggression and whose parents were more highly compliant developed higher-quality friendships with their paired peer. In addition, teacher ratings for these dyads were also higher and indicated some generalization of social competence to the classroom.

Landau et al. (1998) suggest that for social skills training to be effective for performance deficits the training needs to be incorporated into the curriculum of the classroom. Moreover, they suggest that social problems be viewed as chronic rather than acute for children with ADHD. The shift of emphasis from acute (meaning solved in an 8–12 week program) to chronic provides support for ongoing training throughout the child and adolescent's school and home experience. These authors further stress the need to build in generalizability through the transfer of learning from the intervention to the classroom by use of journaling and direct teaching of self-monitoring. In addition, the inclusion of "popular" or accepted children in the training groups is necessary not only to provide appropriate peer models but also to reduce the stigma of working with a trainer outside of the classroom. In addition, the stress is on providing parent support and academic tutoring as appropriate. Direct training of self-monitoring strategies is also suggested.

One particular self-monitoring strategy, the use of verbal rehearsal or "self-talk," may be useful in helping the child with ADHD to monitor his/her behavior. Lawrence et al. (2002) evaluated children with ADHD on a video game task and on a less formal task of finding their way through a zoo. The ADHD children were found to use more self-talk than the controls. This self-talk appeared to assist them in focusing their attention and regulating their behaviors. Moreover, when working memory was strained due to multiple simultaneous demands, the children with ADHD performed more poorly. Social interactions frequently require many aspects to be attended to at once, and poor attention to one or more of these aspects may lead to social difficulties.

Teaching self-control directly to assist with monitoring behavior and focusing attention may also be useful for improving social competence. Including the teacher and parent would appear to be the most important aspect of working with these abilities to improve social functioning. Directly rewarding appropriate behaviors has been found to improve social functioning particularly when the behaviors are directly taught and supported (Hupp & Reitman, 1999). Medication has been found to improve social functioning and the efficacy of social skills training (Teeter, 1998). Combining direct teaching of skills, cognitive-behavioral self-regulation, and medication may provide the best support for the child with ADHD and social learning.

Difficulties with response inhibition likely impair social functioning. These problems have been linked to increased reactivity and intensity of response as well as difficulties with self-regulation (Barkley, 1997). Response inhibition may also interfere with the child's ability to understand the affect behind a social response and to determine the appropriate response (Friedman et al., 2003). Misinterpreting these social cues may lead to inappropriate responses and poor social performance.

Children with ADHD have been found to have difficulty with affect recognition as well as understanding auditory cues as to the sender's emotional message (Corbett & Glidden, 2000; Rapport et al., 2002). Adults and adolescents with ADHD have been found to show problems with facial affect recognition (Rapport et al., 2002) and with voice intonation (Becker et al., 1993). Higher levels of emotional reactivity may interfere with the adolescent with ADHD's ability to understand the message and react appropriately. If the person with ADHD is encoding the message inaccurately and then reacting to that inaccuracy, appropriate social functioning may be difficult. Using social skills training to improve social functioning may not be addressing the most salient difficulty present for that child. Thus, it is important to evaluate the child/adolescent's ability to decipher expressed emotion in order to provide the most appropriate intervention.

Friedman et al. (2003) found that adults with ADHD were poorer at accurately identifying facial affect and had little self-awareness of their subsequent misinterpretations. ADHD has also been linked to difficulties with engaging others in conversation particularly in sharing time during the conversation. Of greater import for interventions, the awareness of the response of the listener to conversations is decreased for people with ADHD (Friedman et al., 2003). These findings are consistent with those of Hoza et al. (2003) that children with ADHD also have higher estimations of their abilities and lower awareness of problems.

Thus, social skills interventions may not be fully helpful for children with ADHD due to problems with underlying skills in interpretation. These problems coupled with difficulties in executive functions may require interventions that specifically target these areas of difficulty in addition to appropriate social behaviors. They may also explain why social skills and self-regulation training have not been found to generalize across situations and settings and appear to be limited to the clinic or group setting. Developing more appropriate interventions would appear to be crucial for success. Including parents and teachers in the intervention as well as providing support for them in reinforcing learning of socially appropriate behaviors has also been found to provide the best support for the child or adolescent with ADHD.

Family Contributions

As discussed earlier in this chapter, parent support is crucial for helping the child/adolescent with ADHD develop appropriate social relationships. It is also important to realize that many children with ADHD have one or both parents who also have ADHD (Biederman, et al., 1994). Fischer et al. (1993) found that families who showed higher levels of parental competence had adolescents who were better adjusted socially than those who had families with more difficulties. Moreover, these variables were more predictive of social adjustment than earlier ratings of hyperactivity, conduct problems, or elementary school adjustment.

For families with high levels of social instability, teacher ratings of social competence were lower for those adolescents. Conclusions were that family stability was particularly important for the development of appropriate behaviors in all areas but particularly in the social area for adolescents with ADHD. Improvement in parent–child interactions would appear to be important for later social adjustment.

Families of children with ADHD often report significant problems in all areas. Copeland and Love (1991) found the following areas of interaction to be problematic for these families:

- Activities and social gatherings found unpleasant and avoided.
- Parental arguing over discipline and a pervasive feeling that nothing works.
- Parents spend inordinate amounts of time with the child with ADHD over homework with less time spent with children and activities that do not revolve around homework.

- Meals are fraught with conflict and at times end with arguing and someone leaving the table.
- Disagreements over chores and responsibilities.
- Parents feeling isolated and afraid for the future.

Children with ADHD show more negative behaviors during interactions with others and are highly active, intense in their responses, and more oppositional than those without ADHD (Befera & Barkley, 1985). Moreover, parents of children with ADHD have been found to give more negative and fewer positive comments, establish more control on their child, and initiate fewer interactions (Buhrmester et al., 1992). Mothers of children with ADHD are more negative and demanding than fathers of children with ADHD with their children responding less to these maternal demands than to paternal requests (Johnston, 1996). These findings have been replicated with children without diagnoses who also have behavioral problems (Russell & Russell, 1987) and indicate that mothers may engage in more negative interactions with their children than fathers, possibly because they are responsible for the largest amount of caretaking (Gerdes et al., 2003).

Patterson et al. (1992) suggests that families of children with externalizing behavioral difficulties may engage more in "coercion training" than those without such problems do. This training means that negative interactions begat more negative interactions that build on each other. The end result is that the family interactions are fraught with problems and are caught in a vicious cycle that breeds more problems. Hence the parents "train" their children in solving problems through negative means. As problems increase, the negativity and coercion process for problem-solving escalates even though the system is not working for either the parent or the child. The end result is severely impaired family interactions and low family cohesion.

For adolescents, parent training that directly teaches positive discipline techniques has been suggested (Alexander-Roberts, 1995; Phelan, 1993). Among the highlighted aspects of these approaches are (1) selecting areas that can be ceded to the adolescent for responsibility; (2) negotiating the behaviors that are acceptable and the consequences for rule-breaking; (3) providing alternatives for the child/adolescent to chose from when faced with a problem; (4) using a behavioral contract that includes consequences that are previously agreed upon by parent–child and that are written down; and (5) decreasing parental lectures and increasing positive problem-solving. Although these techniques may be clinically useful, they have not been empirically validated and further research is needed (Teeter, 1998).

Erk (1997) suggests that parents of children with ADHD require parental and family counseling that needs to incorporate the following points:

- Providing information about the disorder and the chronic nature of the disorder.
- Improving communication patterns.
- Establishing realistic goals and expectations for the child with ADHD in the following areas—behavior, school, and social.

- Providing consistent parental supervision, setting appropriate boundaries and using pre-agreed upon and fair consequences for behaviors.
- Observing closely the effects of medication both at home and at school.
- Providing a great deal of positive reinforcement for the child.
- Improve social functioning by providing opportunities for the child to interact with others appropriately—not expecting a child with ADHD to entertain a friend for several hours without supervision, etc.
- Utilize family therapy appropriately with a therapist familiar with ADHD.

When direct teaching of behavioral and social skills was combined with behavioral training of parents of children with ADHD, improvements have been found in both areas for children with ADHD (Tutty et al., 2003). These treatments were combined for a year and two groups were utilized—the intervention group and a control group. The parents of the intervention group were found to use the behavioral strategies more often and more effectively than did the control parents. No difference was found in use of stimulant medication between the intervention and control groups. Unfortunately the treatment was not found to generalize to the school setting and teachers were not included in the training. Thus, as described by Landau et al. (1998), training in all settings would seem to be most appropriate.

It is also important to recognize that home–school communications are often negative in nature and serve to increase conflict between the child/adolescent and his/her parents. These communications serve in turn to disrupt family functioning as parents are too often enlisted to solve school problems at home. At other times, parents can become protective and defensive when communications from school are overly negative and critical and over-reactions from the family and the school can render discussions unfruitful (Emery et al., 1992). Given the finding that social skills improve most dramatically when treatment includes all facets of the child's environment, it would be important to include parent and teachers in the interventions and encourage improvement in communication between the two settings to benefit the child.

Summary and Conclusions

Children and adolescents with ADHD face many challenges in their development in all areas of functioning but most importantly in social competence. Research indicates that poor social functioning places all children at risk for the development of substance abuse and delinquency as well as for depression, anxiety, and conduct problems. ADHD has also been linked to comorbid problems in these areas and the expression of the disorder with these additional diagnoses is more severe, and hence more problematic for development. The child with ADHD progresses through many stages as he/she develops and at each point must master various developmental tasks. Many children with ADHD appear to be "immature" and behind their peers emotionally, and thus, stand out as problematic even at the early ages. Problems with self-regulation and difficult temperaments may contribute to these problems and likely add to the challenges faced by these children. As the behaviors become more difficult to manage, peers and parents may seek escape from interacting with these children and this isolation even more fully restricts the child's ability to learn corrective behaviors.

Skills involved in problem-solving (executive functions) are impacted for children with ADHD and may also translate into difficulties socially. It is important in a social interaction to key into what the other person is saying, pay attention long enough to "hear' what is being said, and engage in appropriate social reciprocity. When developmental lags are present in these areas, it is difficult to make up the ground lost to be equal with the peer group. As the child attempts to interact, he/she may show more intensity and intrusiveness thus ensuring more rejection.

Findings from studies with parents of children with ADHD also show a negative interaction, as do those with teachers. As the child becomes less accepted, self-esteem may also suffer. Parents and teachers are rightfully frustrated but so is the child, as nothing he/she does seems to work. Coercion training likely interferes with teaching the child the most appropriate manner for solving problems. Add to this mix the finding that many parents of children with ADHD also have a diagnosis of ADHD and the problems become more intimidating.

The literature on interventions is mixed as to the effect that social skills training alone is helpful. In addition, medication has been found to show the most promise for improving social skills, partly due to the fact that the child is more able to regulate his/her own behavior and pay attention to important cues. However, emerging evidence is present that combining social skills training and parent/teacher support may pay dividends. The research studying methylphenidate utilized only systems that involved the child and not the parent or teacher. Comparing the child's functioning when parent and teacher training is provided may show improvement in skills particularly when medication is utilized.

It is only recently that social competence and ADHD has been studied and further investigation of these findings is necessary. That social competence has been found to be so very important in preventing the development of substance abuse and delinquent behaviors is an important beginning. Now it is important to find appropriate interventions that can be utilized both at home and at school.

5

Social Competence in Children with Learning Disabilities

A Case Illustration

Abigail is a nine-year-old third grader who has had difficulty with learning since she was a preschooler. She attended Early Childhood classes due to problems with language and later with academic readiness skills. She was dismissed from services when she entered first grade. Abby was always happy to go to school until second grade when difficulties were present in learning to read and write. First grade had been a challenge but she had brought skills learned during her Early Childhood support classes to first grade and had achieved in the low average range with a great deal of parent and teacher support. She started having significant difficulties in second grade and began complaining of stomachaches and resisting coming to school.

Abby was retained in second grade and, although the second time through the grade was better than the first, she continued to learn slowly and her ability to recall words and to read fluently was very problematic. Her parents began to see difficulties with other children in that Abby was teased about "flunking" and about her slow reading skills. To make matters worse Abby was tall for her age and towered over the younger children. She had difficulties with attention and frequently required reminders to stay on task. Abby was subsequently referred for an evaluation for possible ADHD but found not to qualify for that diagnosis although her attentional skills were considered below problematic.

Abby had made friends in kindergarten and first grade but had difficulty sustaining the friendships as she appeared to be more immature than her friends. These problems became more and more pronounced as she proceeded into third grade. Abby tended to play with first graders on the playground during recess. She struggled to interact with girls her own age but shared few interests with them and was generally "tolerated" but not included.

Abby's parents pressured the school for a full evaluation for her learning problems and this evaluation was conducted in the fall of her third grade year. Findings indicated low average ability with significant problems with sounding out words and with reading fluency. Her writing skills were problematic as she frequently had difficulty spelling words and her handwriting was very difficult to read. Her mathematics calculation skills were stronger and she was in the low average range in this area. The evaluation also described feelings of sadness and low self-esteem. An observation of Abby during her reading class and on the playground found a child who was frequently off-task, required redirection to complete tasks, and was isolated by her peers. Abby was placed in a program for children with learning disabilities and provided reading and written language support for 3 hours per day. The rest of the time she was placed in her regular third grade classroom. Although her academic skills improved with support, Abby continued to experience difficulties socially. Her Individual Educational Plan provided for her academic problems but did not address her social difficulties. Her teacher requested counseling support for Abby and she was enrolled in a social skills group. Some improvement was noted in her friendships particularly with the other girls in the group but problems continued socially.

Definitions

Learning disabilities have been defined in many different ways. Some have used the term "dyslexia" to be synonymous with learning disabilities when in fact dyslexia refers to problems solely with reading. In contrast learning disabilities may refer to problems in any one of seven areas of learning including listening comprehension, expressive language, basic reading skills (word identification, phonological coding), reading comprehension, written language, mathematics calculation, or mathematics reasoning.

Estimates place the incidence of learning disabilities (LD) in general to be at 5% of public school students. Learning disabilities is a heterogeneous grouping that generally includes children with difficulty learning despite adequate ability and instruction in one of seven areas related to language, reading, and mathematics. The definition generally assumes a significant discrepancy between ability and achievement that is often not well defined. Differences in defining this discrepancy has led to various incidences of LD across the country with some states defining the discrepancy conservatively (children achieving below the 2% for their age) and others more liberally (a difference of 16 standard score points between ability and achievement).

Many children may experience difficulties in more than one area as well as having difficulties with attention, emotional adjustment, and/or behavioral problems (Lyon, 1996a). The majority of children identified with a learning disability have difficulties in reading with many of these also experiencing difficulties with written language (Kavale, 1984). Poor phonological processing has been found to be the most predictive of continuing reading difficulty (Stanovich & Siegel, 1994).

When a severe learning disability is present, remediation is much more difficult and achievement of average reading ability may be questionable (Lyon, 1996a). It is likely that these children show significant problems with emotional adjustment and with social competence and thus academic interventions are complicated by these concomitant difficulties. Comorbidity with other disorders is present with learning disabilities similar to that with ADHD.

Comorbid Disorders

When a reading disability is coupled with other learning problems, a more severe form of the disorder is present. Very few children show a sole learning disability in reading with most showing problems in reading and written language (Lyon, 1996b). Difficulties in written language frequently involve problems with spelling, organization of ideas, planning of the writing process, and ability to utilize appropriate punctuation and grammar.

Children with difficulties with reading also have been found to show problems with mathematics. Approximately 6% of children have been found with a learning disability in mathematics (Fleishner, 1994). Problems with mathematics calculation are more common compared to those with mathematics reasoning for children with concomitant reading disabilities. It is rare for a child to be diagnosed solely with a learning disability in mathematics. When found problems with mathematics reasoning often are associated with difficulty with reading comprehension. Significant difficulties with mathematics found in conjunction with visual-motor or visual spatial skills have been associated with nonverbal learning disabilities and will be discussed in a separate chapter.

Attention deficit hyperactivity disorder has been found to be comorbid with learning disabilities in various estimates ranging from 35% to 75% depending on definition (Semrud-Clikeman et al., 1992). Attentional difficulties likely exacerbate problems in learning as the child experiences problems staying focused during classroom instruction. When a child already has a difficulty learning to read, attentional problems may be present due to that problem and may lead to a formal diagnosis of ADHD. Children with reading disabilities have been found to show a higher rate of attentional difficulties, particularly that of ADHD: PI compared to the general population (Shaywitz et al., 1994). In addition those children with a diagnosis of ADHD have a higher risk of showing problems with phonological processing compared to those in the general population (Lyon, 1996a). When children with ADHD and with and without LD were compared on social functioning, those children with ADHD: PI and LD showed the poorest functioning on measures of social desirability, social anxiety, and social self-confidence (Kellner et al., 2003). Those with ADHD: C and LD had more difficulties with interpersonal difficulties and social self-concept. Children with co-occuring ADHD tend to be more resistant to interventions and require more intensive support (Wood et al., 1991).

Children with LD also are more susceptible to emotional difficulties (Martinez & Semrud-Clikeman, 2004). These children are more likely to show internalizing disorders such as anxiety and depression as well as withdrawal and low self-esteem. These problems may stem from frustration with the learning process as well as lower expectations for employment and financial success (Lyon, 1996b). Difficulties in emotional adjustment have been found to extend into adulthood and to require ongoing treatment through psychotherapy for low self-esteem and social difficulties (Johnson & Blalock, 1987).

Externalizing behavioral problems (oppositional defiant disorder and/or conduct disorder) have also been found to be present with children and adolescents with a learning disability (Palacios & Semrud-Clikeman, 2005). Difficulties with acting out are frequently seen coupled with academic failure particularly when reading problems are severe. Findings indicate that for children and adolescents with below-average ability and achievement difficulties with delinquency and conduct are present while for those with average ability these concerns are not present (Nieves, 1992). It may be that those children who experience continuing academic problems and have less ability to deal with such difficulties will resort to expressing their frustrations through acting out. For those with fewer resources for vocalizing their concerns (lower ability and possibly more problematic information-processing abilities), the one way to express this frustration is by acting destructively.

Communication Problems and Learning Disabilities

Many children with learning disabilities also have a language disability and are thought to be at highest risk for social problems due to difficulties in communication (Vallance et al., 1998). Social discourse is thought to underlie many social skills and is particularly impaired in children with learning disabilities and language disorders (LLD: Lapadat, 1991; Wiig & Secord, 1989). Difficulties in understanding and communicating one's thoughts, feelings, and needs may impair social exchanges and hamper a child's exposure and learning of appropriate social abilities of perspective-taking, understanding figurative language, and drawing inferences (Liles, 1993; Wiig & Secord, 1989). Cantwell and Baker (1991) suggest that difficulties in communication may contribute to problems with modulating behaviors and interacting with others. Difficulties in understanding directions, following commands, and with listening comprehension may limit the child with LLD's ability to interact appropriately with peers and with significant adults. These problems in understanding the social meaning underlying may lead to higher-than-expected incidence of social competence found in children with LLD (Vallance & Wintre, 1997).

Vallance et al. (1998) suggest that repeated negative experiences both in the classroom and with peers increases the risk for the development of problems with emotional and behavioral adjustment. They studied the social discourse and social skills of 50 children with LLD and 50 children without LLD to evaluate the relationship between difficulties in these areas and the development of adjustment difficulties. Findings indicated poorer social communication and social skills for the children with LLD compared to those without learning and language problems. In addition, the children with LLD also showed more problem behaviors. Statistical analysis further found that deficient social skills accounted for the development of problem behaviors more than difficulties with social discourse. Children with LLD showed fewer positive social behaviors (i.e., assertion, cooperation) and more negative behaviors such as a lack of self-control. An inability to interact effectively with other children was more predictive of problems with adjustment than having difficulties with social language.

Vallance and Wintre (1997) found that primary language processing deficits, particularly an inability to understand figurative language, was related to a child's social functioning. In addition, these difficulties negatively impacted the child's ability to communicate with his/her peers and contributed to less communications. Social discourse requires a mutual understanding of information as well as the ability to understand the intent behind the communication. Children with LLD were found to be most impaired in this understanding and to interpret information very literally. Understanding the underlying meaning in a social exchange allows the child to predict behavior and to choose a response that would most appropriately correspond to that prediction. Children with LLD were found to have difficulty using language in a socially effective manner. For adolescents the ability to use appropriate slang has been found to predict social acceptance (Schwartz & Merten, 1967). Problems with figurative language are likely most problematic for adolescents and may increase their social exclusion.

Robertson et al. (1998) evaluated children with learning disabilities and those with a sole diagnosis of language disability in a sample of Latino/Latina children. Included in this study were also children at risk for a learning problem but not currently identified as well as those not at risk for learning or language problems. Girls were found to have fewer risk factors and more resiliency compared to males for all groups. The children with learning disabilities were rated more poorly on social skills by their teachers than any of the other groups including the children with language impairment. Those with LD also rated themselves more positively on social skills although they also rated themselves more negatively on level of social support compared to any of the other groups.

Of additional concern was the rating of children with language impairment who showed lower scores on measures of cooperation and self-concept compared to children at risk for learning problems but not currently receiving support. Moreover, these children also showed more alienation and less connection to their school. Language problems were identified for these children as central to their social and adjustment problems. Concern was expressed by these authors that although these children were in fourth and fifth grade, some would be transitioning into middle school where many would be dismissed from services and support would be very limited.

The number of children with language disorders who later are expelled from school or drop-out has been found to be quite high particularly after services are withdrawn (Morrison & D'Incau, 1997). This study was one of the few studying minority children with learning or language difficulties, and further study is certainly required to more fully understand the relationship between learning and language difficulties experienced by English as second language learners.

Thus, problems in social competence may restrict the child's ability to practice skills including social discourse. Social discourse is an important variable and likely contributes to the problems with social competence particularly given the finding that children with LLD had compromised higher-order social processing skills such as problem-solving and social reasoning. These two variables certainly affect the child's ability to not only understand (or encode) the social situations but to also react appropriately. It is perhaps significant that while most evaluations of a child's language skills center on syntax and semantics, inclusion of measure of social understanding may also be important particularly for the child's ability to communicate effectively with peers and adults.

Social Competence in Learning Disabilities

Reviews of the literature indicate that approximately 75% of children with learning disabilities also experience problems with social skills (Kavale & Forness, 1996). These difficulties have been identified at the kindergarten level prior to identification and continue throughout life (Bryan & Bryan, 1991; Vaughn et al., 1990). Moreover, social skills difficulties may worsen academic performance and provide additional impetus for referral (LaGreca & Stone, 1990).

Some studies have found no differences in number of friends between children with and without LD (Vaughn et al., 1993). It should be noted that these children showed milder learning problems and were in full-inclusion settings. In contrast, others have found children with LD to be rejected and/or neglected (Stone & LaGreca, 1990; Wiener et al., 1990). Similarly, children with a learning disability have been found to be lonelier (Margalit & Levin-Alyagon, 1994) and to have fewer mutual friends than those without LD (Tur-Kaspa et al., 1999; Vaughn et al., 1996).

Kavale and Forness (1995) evaluated 152 studies of children with learning disabilities to investigate the expression of social competence problems in these children. The meta-analysis indicated that three out of four children with learning disabilities showed problems in social relations compared to children without learning problems. Further evaluation evaluated whether there were differences between teacher, peer, and self-assessment of social skill deficits. Findings were consistent from the overall meta-analysis with 75% of the participants found to be rated as having social skill problems by both teachers and peers. Children with LD rated themselves more negatively than did their peers or teachers.

Kavale and Forness (1995) further evaluated the nature of these social competence problems. Teachers indicated the most significant areas of problems were in the areas of academic competence and interacting less frequently socially compared to children without LD. Academic competence was seen to be the primary difficulty for these children, similar to Abby, and to exacerbate social functioning. Approximately 80% of the sample showed both of these two areas to be problematic. Additional areas teachers endorsed as problematic included overactivity, distractibility, and adjustment. Problems with attention and completing tasks were viewed as particularly problematic and as contributing to poor academic competence. These difficulties combined with social isolation likely contributed to problems with adjustment. No significant problems were found in the areas of aggression, conduct, or withdrawal. While 70% of the students were found to show higher levels of anxiety than children without LD, Kavale and Forness (1995) attributed these levels to higher-than-average ratings on the activity and distractibility dimensions that also contribute to increasing the ratings for anxiety. These authors concluded that aggression and not heightened anxiety and distractibility were interfering with peer relationships.

Peer assessments indicated higher levels of rejection for children with LD with approximately 80% reported to be rejected by peers without LD. Children with LD were reported less often chosen to be a friend and few were considered to be a friend by their peers. Thus, peers reported that they did not have friends who were learning disabled and the only children reporting friendship with a child with a learning disability were those who also had a learning problem.

Self-assessments indicated that 70% saw themselves as add (Kavale & Forness, 1995). having social skill problems. Similar to the teacher ratings, the primary area of concern was academic competence—leading one to speculate that significant academic problems will contribute to difficulty making and keeping friends. In addition, 80% of the children with LD indicated that they experienced problems with interpreting nonverbal communication in their ability to interpret social situations, messages, and feelings. In addition, 80% of the children reported problems with solving social problems. Problems with self-esteem were also frequent in this population as well as a poor self-concept. In addition, children with LD were found to more frequently attribute outcomes for their problems to outside forces rather than feeling they had any control over these difficulties. This type of attribution indicates that they likely feel powerless to effect change for these problems. Such attribution indicates that empowering these children to take action will be difficult as they already feel helpless. Approximately 70% of children with LD were found to view their successes to luck, and effort, ability, or perseverance were not viewed by them as providing success. The same number of children with LD also saw their poor performance as due to low ability—something that is not viewed as changeable or under their control. Thus children with LD view their success as "luck" and their failures due to problems internal to themselves (ability or effort). Not only can they not take credit for their success, they blame themselves for their failure.

Although these findings are intriguing, it is not appropriate (Kavale & Forness, 1995). to interpret them as indicating that academic problems cause social problems. Approximately 20–30% of the population with LD does not show such difficulties and it is not clear how these children differ. It may be that they are successful in other areas of school and social life such as sports or with a particular talent (i.e., music or art). It may also be that they have fewer problems with attention and/or distractibility. What is clear from these findings is that social competence difficulties and LD co-occur for the majority of children with LD and that these problems are chronic, significant, and at a tremendous emotional cost to these children.

Developmental Issues in LD

As discussed in Chapter 2, developmental issues are an important aspect for our understanding of social competence. The model developed by Crick and Dodge (1994) suggests that a child brings a database of learned abilities and memories from previous experiences to the event at hand. In order to understand an event, the child must process the information appropriately and attend to meaningful information. For children it is important to understand when they develop these skills. Children entering school at the kindergarten level are expected to play appropriately with others and to be able to converse with their peers. It is not expected that children at this age would be lonely or feel that the world is unpredictable (also called a sense of coherence) (Antonovsky, 1987). Children who have a sense of coherence are those that feel able to cope with situations and who view challenges as doable.

Children who were at risk for LD in kindergarten have been found to show loneliness and a low sense of coherence *prior* to being identified compared to those children without academic delays (Margalit, 1998a; Most, Al-Yagon et al., 2000). Children with LD have also been found to have fewer friends and to be poorly accepted by their peers. Teacher ratings indicate more adjustment difficulties in kindergarten, a finding that continues into middle and high school (Gresham & McMillan, 1997).

Margalit (1998b) extended her previous study down to preschool children. Sixty children at risk for developing learning disabilities were compared to 76 peers without LD from the same preschools. Findings indicated higher levels of loneliness and lower feelings of self-efficacy in the preschoolers with risk for LD. Moreover, these children were also less accepted by their peers and their teachers viewed them as having more adjustment problems. These findings are important because at the preschool age friendships are beginning and become more and more important to the child's adjustment and in his/her day-to-day experience (Guralnick, 1994). These experiences lay down the foundation for social competence at later years and are predictive of future social relationships (Guralnick & Groom, 1987). Children at this age need to interact and play with others as well as to communicate with them successfully.

A study of kindergarten children at risk for LD found that girls had poorer social-information processing abilities and more difficulty generating appropriate solutions to resolve social situations (Tur-Kaspa, 2004). Similar findings were not present for boys. Others have found difficulties for kindergarten boys in their ability to navigate the social requirements and in their ability to regulate their behavior (Tur-Kaspa, 2002; Tur-Kaspa et al., 1999). It may be that the expression of social difficulty takes a different pattern for the genders. These findings are important because difficulties in establishing appropriate interactions with peers at a young age has been found to be related to increased loneliness throughout development and is predictive of future adjustment problems (Asher et al., 1990).

Difficulties with loneliness and lack of self-efficacy are also present in elementary school children particularly in their ability to solve social problems (Tur-Kaspa & Bryan, 1994). These findings suggest continuing problems with social information processing and in the ability to retrieve information in order to solve a problem appropriately. Similar difficulties have been found for adolescents with continuing problems present in solution generation (Hartas & Donahue, 1997).

Important for intervention is the related finding that a child with LD has the basic social knowledge but does not apply it appropriately (Carlson, 1987; Stone & LaGreca, 1984). Thus, the child can demonstrate the appropriate knowledge, but when asked to apply it to a social situation, he/she often selects a less appropriate response. It has been suggested that problems with language processes may interfere with the child's ability to process information appropriately and thus apply it accurately.

For adolescents difficulties with understanding peer relationships and increasing feelings of loneliness often intersect with less support academically and socially. More problems are noted with difficulties forming close intimate relationships and with dating often present. An increase in problem behaviors has been seen for some adolescents while others show increased feelings of sadness and anxiety (Forness et al., 1998). These critical years are important for developing appropriate behaviors and for learning how to cope with feelings and situations. For adolescents with LD particular problems may lie with information processing but also with problem-solving as more independence is expected at this age. It is important to understand how difficulties with social perception and development coincide for a child or adolescent with LD.

Social Perception and LD

As reviewed in Chapter 1, social functioning includes five steps: encoding, interpretation and representation, goal selection, deciding on the response to take, completing the selected behavior (Crick & Dodge, 1984). When problems arise at the earliest stages of this process, then the resulting behavior is frequently inappropriate and unhelpful. Children with LD have been found to show problems with the interpretation of emotions and the correct labeling of these emotions from facial expressions (Sprouse, et al., 1998). In addition, children with LD have been found to require additional time to process these facial expressions—as we well know social exchanges do not generally stop to give the child sufficient time to process this information. In addition, children with LD have been found to view social vignettes as more negative and unfriendly than do those children with LD (Weiss, 1984). Bryan (1997) evaluated studies of children with LD utilizing the first two steps in Crick and Dodge's (1984) model. She found that children LD had more difficulty encoding social cues and were less able to understand and interpret social cues.

As stated earlier, not all children with LD show social skill deficits. Meadan and Halle (2004) hypothesized that the difference may be due to differences in social status for these children given the finding that within the LD group there are significant difference in status ranging from low to high (Kuhne & Wiener, 2000; Sale & Carey, 1995). They utilized a qualitative approach and interviewed the children as to how they perceived social situations. They divided their sample into high and low social status through the use of a rating scale to evaluate the peer acceptance of children with LD. Teachers also rated the children using a similar rating scale. Three children with LD with high social status were selected as were three children with LD with low social status. For the first interview, the child viewed a videotape of two children putting a puzzle together and then was interviewed as to the feelings and emotions that were displayed by the children on the videotape. For the second interview the child looked at five photographs taken from the videotape and asked to describe what was happening in the pictures. The teachers were also interviewed about the child's social functioning.

Findings were coded by the authors along three themes: encoding and interpreting social situations, the experience of the LD label and academic problems, and characteristics of friendships and of a best friend. No difference was found between the two groups in how they attended to facial expressions and their interpretations of these cues. Moreover, both groups reported liking the resource room support but also reported negative feelings about their disability. Finally each student reported that he/she had a best friend and/or friends and was able to articulate the reasons for having friends (playing, sharing, supporting).

Important differences identified between the groups indicated that those children with low social status were less attentive to details in the pictures, and thus may interpret them differently due to this processing difference. Those with high social status indicated that they were no different from other children while those with lower social status felt different. Those with higher status reported behaving appropriately and attempting to control their behavior while those with lower status reporting more aggressive behaviors and indicating that when mad they could not control their behavior. In addition, those with higher status indicated liking to work and play with others while those with lower status stated they preferred to play and work alone.

Social perception requires one to process information both verbally and visually. It requires appropriate interpretation of this information including the intonation and facial expressions that accompany the social exchange. As seen from Meadan and Halle (2004) the cognitive set that the child brings to the social exchange can affect how he/she interprets what happens. Their study evaluated how the child interpreted the social exchanges. Research has indicated that visual cues are more easily understood than those that are solely auditory in nature. Moreover, when auditory and visual cues are combined they are also better understood than auditory alone but were not better understood than visual alone (Gross & Ballif, 1991; Hess et al., 1988). For children with LD findings have indicated less accuracy for perception of emotions using visual stimuli compared to children without LD (Nabuzoka & Smith, 1993). When auditory and visual input is combined, the children with LD perform better (Reiff & Garber, 1990; Sisterhen & Gerber, 1989).

Most and Greenbank (2000) sought to evaluate how children with LD process nonverbal communications as well as the verbal portion of the message. They hypothesized that difficulties with interpretation of nonverbal communication underlie comprehension of social situations. They utilized three conditions to compare the efficiency of emotional identification in children and adolescents with and without LD; auditory, visual, and combined visual-auditory. In addition, they evaluated the relationship between the child's social skills and his/her ability to utilize combined visual-auditory input. They had 30 participants with a sole diagnosis of LD and with average ability levels. The children viewed six faces and selected the emotion they believed was expressed. They also listened to auditory recordings of a neutral sentence stated with various emotional tones. Finally, they watched and listened to a videotape of a social scenario. Each child and teacher completed the appropriate form of the Social Skills Rating Scale (SSRS; Gresham & Elliott, 1990).

In each case, the children without LD performed significantly better than the children with LD. Post hoc analyses found that the auditory-visual mode was superior to the other two modes for both groups with the auditory mode being the poorest. Both groups evaluated themselves similarly on the SSRS while teacher ratings indicated significant differences between the two groups with the children with LD performing more poorly than those without LD. It was also found that the higher the score on the auditory-visual condition, the higher their social functioning was reported to be by the teachers for the total sample. Moreover, those children with LD who were rated as more assertive by their teachers were also found to show better skills at social interpretation using the auditory-visual mode.

Thus, those children who are more adept at negotiating and interacting despite a learning disability are rated higher than those who are not. Recommendations from this study were for interventions for children with LD who have difficulty understanding facial expressions and nonverbal cues. Moreover, an intervention for social skills remediation was suggested by these authors to particularly target difficulties with linking emotions to actions to responding appropriately to social situations. Interestingly, this study had more girls than boys and although no difference was found between the genders, further research is needed to extend these findings to boys. Kavale and Forness (1995) have found limited effectiveness of social skills training with children with LD—further discussion of interventions will be provided later in this chapter.

To shed further light as to the quality of friendships in children with LD, Wiener and Schneider (2002) evaluated the friendship patterns of children with and without LD in grades 4 though 8. Boys with a learning disability had fewer friends. Moreover, children with LD had more friends with learning problems and these friends tended to be younger. More conflict was found between these friends. Wiener and Schneider

(2002) suggest that children with LD may have acquaintances but not friends and that to work with these children most appropriately may require focusing on dyads rather than on classrooms or small groups.

Relationship of Social Competence to Level of Academic Functioning

While children with learning problems have been found to show difficulty with social skills, it is not clear whether particular problems are present just for this population or whether children with low achievement will also show social skills problems. Some studies have found that children with LD show more difficulties socially than those who are low-achieving (LaGreca & Stone, 1990) with others finding no difference (Vaughn, et al., 1990).

Haager and Vaughn (1995) evaluated the relationship between social difficulties and low academic achievement assuming that low achievement in general was related to social problems rather than any specific problems with learning such as LD. The three groups included those with LD, children with low achievement (LA), and those with high achievement (AHA). Children with LA had reading achievement scores lower than the 30th percentile and no scores higher than the 40th percentile and none were in special education programs. Those children in the AHA group had reading achievement scores above the 60th percentile and no subtest score below the 50th percentile. The children were evaluated through teacher ratings, parent rating, and self-ratings on the SSRS as well as peer ratings of the child's likability. Findings indicated those children with LD and those with LA had difficulties in social competence that were similar and were lower than those children with AHA. Students with LD were less accepted by their peers as were those with LA than children who were high achieving. This finding is not surprising.

Interestingly children with LD were rated as more socially competent by their special education teachers and also rated themselves with higher self-ratings compared to children with LA. There was low to moderate correlations between the ratings among the settings with poor agreement between parental ratings and general education teacher ratings and better agreement between parental ratings and special education teacher ratings. Thus, the setting in which the child is observed and the comparison group may be important variables that have not been fully studied.

Some have suggested that special education placement may be protective for children with LD and provides social support that is important for buffering stress (Robertson et al., 1998). Others have suggested that such placements assist the child in understanding and accepting their academic problems and as such provide additional support (Kloomak & Cosden, 1994). Additional variables that were present in the Haager and Vaughn (1995) study and not directly evaluated were the variability within the LD and LA groups in regard to gender, minority status, and behavioral characteristics. Most of the children in the AHA group were Caucasian and of middle to high SES while more children in the LD and LA groups qualified for reduced or free lunches.

Vaughn and Hogan (1994) studied the social competence of a group of children over 6 years to evaluate the effect of development on social skills for children with LD, LA, AHA, and average achievement (AA). Findings indicated that peer acceptance for children in all groups were similar with increases in peer acceptance found until third grade and then declining at that point. Kindergarten children later identified with LD were found to show less social acceptance than the children in the AHA group but did not differ from the LA or AA groups. When teacher acceptance was controlled, no difference was found between the groups as far as social competence (Vaughn et al., 1993). Other studies not controlling teacher acceptance have found poorer ratings for children with lower achievement (Coie & Krehbiel, 1984).

Vaughn and Hogan (1994) evaluated the within-individual variation of children with LD over a 6-year period for ten children. All children had full-scale IQs above 85 and were receiving special education services for less than half of the school day. No further information was present about the sample. Social competence was not found to be consistent over time for the seven boys with the social skill scores changing over time ranging from good to poor. In addition, three patterns were identified for children with LD with some children showing consistent competence, others showing resolution of their social problems at an early age, and others showing consistent and chronic problems. It is not clear what differentiated these groups and possibilities include problems with additional diagnoses (ADHD) or more severe types of LD for the children with continuing problems. Unfortunately, the authors do not address these possibilities.

Thus, differences between studies may be related to variables such as teacher acceptance, type and severity of learning disability, and classroom environment (resource or inclusion). Since many of these variables interact (children with severe LD are more likely to be in a resource room), it is important to view these as interlocking parts of the puzzle and to view the resulting research as suggestive as best. The differences in social competence may not be present between children who are low achieving and those with a milder form of a learning disability. Severity of a learning problem was not addressed in the series of articles by Vaughn and colleagues (Vaughn & Hogan, 1994; Vaughn et al., 1992; Vaughn et al., 1990). In addition, it is not clear whether children with LD were participated in many of these studies and compared to children with LA had social skills training or other interventions provided in their IEPs (Bryan, 1994). Certainly this type of information may be helpful. Is it possible that placement in a resource room environment may supply needed social support to enable the children to continue to have a relatively intact self-concept?

Special Education Placement and Social Competence

Vaughn and Hogan (1994) studied children with LA, LD, and AHA on social skills and found the diagnosis of LD did not predict problems with social status. Bryan (1994) rightfully asks the question whether special education placement may not have had a positive effect on these children. This controversial area continues to be debated in the literature and some have found that the social ability of children with LD to be problematic regardless of placement (Gresham & MacMillan, 1996). Others have found that children with LD who participate in a resource room score higher than others on social self-concept possibly particularly true for children who are socially rejected.

Arguments for mainstreaming in the 1970s and 1980s were that it would support the child's social development. In the 1990s and 2000s inclusion has been suggested to support children with LD both socially and emotionally. It was also suggested that these children will be less stigmatized and make friends more readily (Stainback & Stainback, 1996). Children with LD were found to show better progress academically *and* socially when placed in special education classrooms (Carlberg & Kavale, 1980; Pavri & Monda-Amaya, 2000).

The introduction of in-class aides, resource rooms, and team-teaching within the regular education classroom has also been suggested for children with LD to assist with their emotional and social functioning. Findings have been mixed depending on the type of intervention studied. Some have found no difference between children with and without LD in an inclusion classroom on measures of social competence (for example, Bear et al., 1993) while others have found problems with rejection and low acceptance (Margalit & Levin-Alygon, 1994; Pavri & Monda-Amaya, 2000; Vaughn et al., 1996).

When inclusion classrooms and resource room placements were compared, some found improvement on measures of social functioning and achievement motivation (Schmidt, 2000) while others found no difference in social outcomes (Merrell & Merz, 1992) or on measures of self-esteem and sadness (Howard & Tryon, 2002). Elbaum (2002) in a meta-analysis found no difference between the self-concept of children and special education placement. Others have found that self-contained placements may result in feelings of isolation and higher levels of feelings of social neglect (but not rejection) than other types of placement (Wiener & Tardiff, 2004). This finding is not terribly surprising as these children are likely not only more severely affected but also have additional diagnoses beyond that of LD. Using child interviews some have found that children with LD indicated a preference for an inclusion classroom so that they can make friends more readily (Klingner et al., 1998). It is not clear whether that outcome, in fact, occurred for these children.

To further evaluate the relationship between placement and peer relationships, Coleman and Minnett (1992) studied children with LA and those with LD in a large school district in the Southwest. Their peers rejected children with LD more frequently than those without a disability. However, these same children scored higher on the self-concept scale and rated themselves higher than children who were rejected, who were not placed in a resource room, and who also had learning problems. Coleman and Minnett (1992) suggest that although the children with LD who were also rejected likely were less competent socially, they were supported by their resource room peers and thus had a reference group that was more like themselves for comparison. Those children who were not identified as having an LD and were rejected in the regular education classroom did not have such a support system and thus did not have a second social comparison group. Recommendations from this study were for interventions for children in the regular classrooms that are generally used for children in special education placements (i.e., social skills training and support).

Wiener and Tardiff (2004) conducted one of the few studies that evaluated differences in social and emotional functioning of children with LD in different educational settings. For this study the children were enrolled in four different programs: in-class support, resource room support, inclusion, and self-contained. The children in the in-class support programs received assistance from a special education teacher within the general education classroom up to 90 minutes per day. Those in the resource room had support in a separate classroom for up to 90 minutes per day. The inclusion classroom included two teachers in the same classroom and the self-contained program children spent at least 50% of the day in the classroom with some integration into the general education program. Those children in the in-class or resource room placements were classified with mild to moderate LD while those in the inclusion or self-contained placements had severe LD. Comparisons were done between placements for children with similar levels of disability (in-class vs. resource and inclusion vs. self-contained).

A previous study using this same sample had found that children with LD had fewer friends, poorer quality for the friendships they did have, lower social acceptance, poorer social skills, and reported more loneliness, sadness, and had more problem behaviors than those without LD (Wiener & Schneider, 2002; Wiener, 2002). When these same children were compared on measures of social acceptance, quality of friendship, loneliness, and sadness, few significant results were found between the four different placements. Stringent analysis of these results indicates few differences between the groups on these measures with significant findings present that the children in the inclusion group scored higher on feelings of companionship with peers and that the children with in-class support scoring higher on feelings of competence in mathematics.

Conclusions from this study were that given this data special education placement cannot be seen as the major variable in predicting the social functioning of the child. Rather the authors suggest that a range of services needs to be provided by the schools to meet the individual child's need. While these services are certainly to be desired, larger school districts are more likely to be able to provide this range of services while smaller school districts will not. Emerging evidence that children with LD in inclusive settings that do not provide adequate support have very poor outcomes both socially and academically should give one pause in prescribing inclusion for children with LD without intensive support being provided (Coleman et al., 1992; Elbaum, 2002).

In summary, it appears that type of placement may not be as important for fostering social and emotional development as much as the presence of appropriate interventions for both academic and social competence. Wiener and Tardiff (2004) rightfully point out that the interventions studied have utilized trained teacher for interventions in the inclusive classrooms and not educational aides—something that is more commonly done. Further study is certainly needed to tease out what types of placement as well as types of interventions that are most appropriate. The following section briefly discusses possible interventions that are helpful for developing the social skills of children with LD.

Interventions for Children with LD

Social Skills Training groups have been utilized with children with LD with conflicting results. A meta-analysis of the research evaluating this training found a small effect for the training (Kavale & Mostert, 2004). Parent, teacher, and self-ratings were consistent as to the efficacy of this training showing less progress following social skills groups than was expected. This meta-analysis replicated an earlier one by Forness and Kavale (1996). The previous study evaluated 53 studies over a 15-year period. Findings were of a small effect size and few differences among teachers, students, and peers as to any improvement. Interestingly, this study found that the child with an LD rated himself or herself higher on social skills after the training. Importantly, this review found that social interaction between the child with LD and a peer was the least improved of all social skills. This finding is important as it highlights the need for the child with LD to be provided additional experiences in order to practice any of the learned skills. When such practice is not provided, it is not surprising that skills are not improved outside of the clinical experience.

Elias (2004) suggests that for interventions that improve social competence to be effective, the treatment must be comprehensive and link academic and social-emotional learning together. He suggests that targeting specific skills that are problematic for the child and then providing direct teaching would be more effective than a manualized approach frequently utilized in social skills training programs. Elias (2004) hypothesized that the areas of social-emotional learning that are problematic for children with LD include the ability to recognize emotions in others and oneself, to regulate strong emotions—negative and positive—and to recognize one's own strengths and needs.

Wiener and Schneider (2002) suggest that intervention needs to begin at the level of the dyad. Pairing a child with LD with a more socially competent peer in the classroom may assist in prosocial learning. To test this hypothesis, Wiener and Harris (1997) developed an individualized classroom-based social skills program that combined coaching and directly teaching social problem-solving. Forty-five children with learning disabilities, aged 9–12, were selected who attended a self-contained classroom. Thirteen children received an intervention that combined coaching and problem-solving strategies for social situations. Seven children received a similar intervention in a different classroom and 25 were clinical controls. The seven children in the second intervention did not show gains, a finding the authors suggested was due to classroom dynamics. However, the 13 children receiving the combined intervention showed a modest improvement in problem behaviors as well as stable peer acceptance.

In contrast the clinical control children showed deterioration in their peer acceptance and no improvement in problem behaviors.

Providing support from the teacher in coaching of appropriate behaviors as well as in utilizing cooperative learning may also improve social functioning. Similarly Meadan and Halle (2004) suggest that a more positive classroom environment that has a climate of tolerance would assist in the learning of socially appropriate behaviors. When classroom environment has supported the child with LD, findings have been of more acceptance of the child by nondisabled peers (Zygmunt et al., 1994; Wenz-Gross & Siperstein, 1997).

Peers have also been utilized for teaching prosocial behaviors. Improvements have been found when peers without a disability are paired with a child with a disability and directly taught social behaviors (Sugai & Chanter, 1989). Prater et al. (1999) compared teacher-led social skills training to peer-mediated social skills training for children with LD. The children providing the instruction were taught by their teachers the same skills and also had a learning disability. Skills targeted for intervention included how to give positive feedback, how to accept negative feedback, and how to contribute to a discussion. The special education teachers of the children involved in the study selected these skills. Findings indicated that both interventions improved social skills. Those children trained by their peers acquired the skills faster but unfortunately did not maintain these skills as long as those taught by the teacher.

Accepting negative feedback was the skill that required the most teaching and was not maintained as well as the other two skills. An important finding from this study was that the peer teachers improved more in applying these skills and maintained these skills better than either the peer- taught or teacher-taught children. Thus, the peer teachers appeared to be better able to generalize their learning and to apply it more appropriately. Since the peer teachers performed the best of all the children, it may be that teaching these skills allowed them to learn how to do the appropriate behaviors in a more tangible manner. Certainly this finding requires additional exploration. It may be that these children felt more empowered to use the skills they had learned and the subsequent improvement in their abilities increased confidence in their skills.

Margalit (1995) evaluated children with LD and those with a behavioral disorder (BD) using a social skills computer intervention. This intervention follows a script learned on the computer and then reinforced through teacher guidance. Each child participated in the program twice a week for 45 minutes. The child completed the computer program that included scenarios requiring solutions and then participated in a teacher-led group discussion of difficulties experienced by each child. All children were found to benefit from the program. Particular improvement was found for children who were lonely and had problem behaviors. Of this group the children with LD showed the most improvement in behavioral management and in feelings of less social isolation. Differences between the LD and BD groups indicated that children with LD may need more teaching on acquiring appropriate social skills and on coping with loneliness while those with BD require direct teaching of self-control skills to cope with their feelings of loneliness and isolation. Unfortunately, this study also found that none of these children improved in peer acceptance: a finding that questions the generalizability to this training to situations outside the special education classroom.

Emphasis on the child with LD's ability to hold a social conversation has not been present in many of the studies. Hartas and Donahue (1997) evaluated the ability of adolescents with LD to provide advice and to listen to advice. Adolescents with and without LD were paired and audiotaped as they role played an advisor and a caller on a telephone hotline. Three dyad types were identified: both adolescents with LD, one with and one without LD, and both adolescents without LD. Results indicated that adolescents with and without LD were equally skilled in asking for advice. Adolescents with LD, however, were found to have difficulty generating solutions to interpersonal problems. Thus, adolescents with LD were found capable of asking questions but not solving social problems. This finding is consistent with earlier findings that children with LD have difficulty with problem-solving skills in all areas including the social arena.

Summary and Conclusion

It appears that the interventions developed for improving the social skills of children and adolescents with LD have not delivered on their promise of improved peer acceptance and involvement. This finding is similar to that discussed in the chapter on ADHD and indicates that the problems are likely to be multi-faceted and to require more than one solution. It is interesting that few studies of children with LD were identified that incorporated a multi-site, multi-method approach and which included parent training as well as teacher support. The findings from some studies suggest that classroom environment, teacher support and/or coaching, and peer assistance may improve the generalization of skills from the small group setting to the larger social environment. An intriguing finding indicating children with LD who train other children with social problems actually show improvement themselves on these skills was present in the literature. Further study is certainly warranted in this area. A person modeling appropriate social behavior with a child with LD to provide social support for his/her peers with LD, possibly younger children, would serve to not only provide instruction for the younger child but also enhance the older child's feelings of self-efficacy.

The structure of the interventions is important but there are also issues about the type of instruction provided. The use of computers to instruct a child on possible solutions to a scenario may provide skill training and the first step in practicing these skills but certainly doesn't substitute for practice with other children. Improving the classroom climate is important for acceptance of children with a learning disability but requires a teacher who supports this acceptance. Similarly involving parents in supporting their child and providing instruction as to how they can provide social interactions are another important aspect of teaching social competence to children with LD. Further study is warranted in this area. In addition, when children with LD have co-occurring difficulties, social problems are more pronounced and are likely more difficult to remediate. Paying attention to the heterogeneity of these children is important.

Finally, it is important to provide support from an early age through adolescence. As Chapter 2 discusses, certain developmental tasks are expected to be mastered at different ages. When a child with a learning disability has problems with conversational speech and language, it becomes more difficult to join in on discussions that are important for social discourse. Moreover, difficulties with figurative language or interpreting speech in a literal manner have also been found to isolate the adolescent and impair the child's ability to respond appropriately in a socially effective manner.

The ability to read facial expressions and to understand vocal intonation is an important task that needs to be mastered in order to develop appropriate social skills. Empirical evidence that problems are present in these areas certainly indicate that for children with LD direct intervention may be necessary for these basic skills prior to the child's ability to benefit from the typical social skills training packages. Further understanding of the child with LD's ability to accomplish these skills is certainly needed. It is also important to note the finding that the child with LD may be able to express the appropriate social response but does not apply it to the situation appropriately. An inability to utilize good problem-solving strategies is an area that truly needs further study particularly for the development of appropriate interventions.

The social requirements for adolescents increase and the inability to meet those requirements often results in problems with loneliness and social isolation for adolescents. These demands occur at a time when the school structure provides fewer supports for the adolescent and he/she is required to deal with several teachers and academic demands that are not present at the elementary school level. It is important for middle and high schools to be sensitive to the adolescent's need and provision of a teacher who can act as a social coach may be necessary for appropriate social and emotional adjustment. My experience with middle school and high school teachers is of less investment in the adolescent and more interest in subjects and work completion. The special education teacher and/or consultant would be very important for the adolescent in his/her managing the system. This suggestion is particularly apt given the finding of increasing numbers of drop-outs when services are withdrawn or reduced for adolescents with learning and/or language difficulties.

6

Social Competence in Children with Nonverbal Learning Disabilities

Aaron is a ten-year-old boy who has had difficulty in learning to ride a bike, write legibly, and with making friends. His reading skills are fairly good but some difficulty is present in reading comprehension, particularly for material that requires him to draw inferences. Aaron's mathematics skills have always been problematic and he has recently been evaluated for a possible learning disability. The WISC III indicated a significant difference between his verbal and perceptual reasoning indices of 35 points with his verbal significantly higher than his performance ability. Mild difficulties were present in working memory and in his ability to process information quickly. Aaron's mathematics calculation skills were found to be significantly below expectations for his ability and age and difficulties were also present in visual-motor ability. Aaron qualified for a diagnosis of a learning disability in mathematics and was referred for further evaluation of his attentional abilities. This further evaluation confirmed attentional problems and Aaron was diagnosed with ADHD: PI.

His parents and teachers reported significant difficulties with attention but few problems with activity level or impulse control. His parents also reported that Aaron has experienced significant difficulties making and keeping friends and state that he "just doesn't get it" when playing with his peers. They have also been concerned about his motor development and he received physical therapy in kindergarten and first grade for what was described as "clumsiness."

Although Aaron was diagnosed with learning disabilities and received appropriate support, his full diagnosis is more than a mathematics learning disability. The type of learning disability which is generally verbally based described in Chapter 5 is the most frequently encountered form of LD. Aaron shows symptoms of the type of learning disability becoming more commonly diagnosed as a nonverbal learning disability (NVLD).

Children with NVLD generally show a different pattern of strengths and weaknesses than those with LD. While children with LD show difficulties in phonological processing, those with NVLD frequently do fairly well in single word reading and in spelling. In contrast, children with NVLD have significant problems with mathematics calculation, frequently misalign the columns in the computations, and have problems learning basic mathematics facts. They have particular difficulty in recalling information that is complex or novel but do very well with rote memory or information that can be recalled by verbal means (Rourke and Fuerst, 1995). In addition, children with NVLD also show problems with fine and gross motor development. Parents frequently report problems with learning to skip, tie shoes, and to write legibly.

Children with NVLD also have difficulties understanding nonverbal input in social situations and will be socially isolated. They are not often openly rejected as strange or weird but are infrequently chosen in games and often socially isolated. Significant problems are described in the child's ability to correctly perceive social relationships and with social judgment. Relationships with adults are better developed and the child with NVLD may cling to teachers and parents as a way of adapting to a confusing social situation. In addition, children with NVLD also have a tendency to show attentional difficulties. Older children with NVLD have also been found to have an increased incidence of depression, social withdrawal, atypical behaviors, and anxiety.

Children with NVLD have particular difficulties understanding situations that are novel and complex (Rourke & Fuerst, 1995). Particular difficulty is present in understanding situations that involve cause-effect reasoning and with generating solutions to problems (Semrud-Clikeman, 2001). Language skills are generally well developed for basic skills but problems are also present with more complex language, understanding figurative language and idioms, and with incongruities frequently seen with the understanding of humor (Glass, 2003). These more advanced skills likely interfere with social functioning as the child with NVLD has significant problems with social conversation as well as the give and take generally seen in child conversations. Some have described their conversation as having a "cocktail party" effect where content is limited as well as understanding (Rourke & Fuerst, 1995).

Rourke and colleagues (2002) characterize the NVLD disorder as having several principal features including the following:

- bilateral tactile-perceptual deficits more pronounced on the left side of the body than the right;
- bilateral coordination problems—again more on the left than right;
- problems with visual, spatial, and organizational abilities;
- problems adapting to novel and complex situations—use of rote or literal interpretation of behaviors that frequently result in inappropriate behavior;
- problems with problem-solving—more evident with nonverbal than verbal materials and situations;
- problems with benefiting from positive and negative feedback;
- a distorted sense of time;
- well-developed rote verbal memory;
- highly verbose with much repetition of previously stated ideas;
- poor speech intonation (prosody);
- problems with mathematics calculation with relative strengths in reading and spelling;
- problems with social judgment, social perception, and social interaction skills.

NVLD, Asperger's Syndrome, and High Functioning Autism

Some have suggested that NVLD is milder part of a continuum with Asperger's Disorder and High Functioning Autism (HFA) due to the similarities in weaknesses and strengths (Klin et al., 1995; Wing, 2000). There are, however, differences between the disorders that leave this question unanswered at this time. Children with Asperger's Syndrome have impairments in social reciprocity, understanding, and preoccupation with an item or concept (Barnhill, 2001). They have average to superior ability with average to superior literal language ability (Klin et al., 1995). Further discussion of Asperger's Syndrome (AS) is presented in Chapter 7.

Although some differences between NVLD and AS are present on neuropsychological measures, there are several similarities between the two disorders. Rourke et al. (2002) suggests that NVLD overlaps considerably with AS but not with HFA. Similarities are present with children diagnosed with either AS or NVLD showing clumsiness, problems with visual-spatial tasks, and poor social competence. Differences are qualitative in nature with the child with AS tending to be more pedantic in communication and to have extensive knowledge of a circumscribed area or topic based on rote memorization of facts compared to the child with NVLD.

Children with HFA also appear to be similar to NVLD and AS in that they have problems with reciprocal social interaction. However, children with HFA also experience difficulties with communication and language development and also appear to ignore others and to even strongly desire to be apart from others. Children with NVLD or AS desire social interaction and are hurt by not having friends while those with HFA are less likely to feel badly about not having a circle of friends. In addition, there are strengths in visual-spatial skills for children with HFA but these decline when tasks become more abstract and complex (Dennis et al., 1999; Siegel, 1998). Children with HFA have more difficulty on tasks that do not have set rules, have changing requirements, and require independent problem-solving (Ciesielski & Harris, 1997). While children with NVLD or AS may have some difficulty with these types of tasks, they do not struggle as significantly as do those with HFA. Academically children with NVLD and HFA show good word reading and spelling but poor reading comprehension. Differences are present in the area of mathematics, however, with children with NVLD having significant problems while those with HFA do not (Minshew et al., 1994).

Although there are similarities, at this time it is not appropriate to group these diagnoses together and further study is certainly needed to tease apart the similarities and differences. Klin et al. (1995) evaluated the neuropsychological profiles of children with NVLD, AS, and HFA. Eighteen of 22 children with AS met the criteria for NVLD while only 1 in 19 with HFA did. Thus, HFA is likely separate from NVLD and AS while the overlap between NVLD and AS requires further study. NVLD has been suggested to be related to white matter dysfunction of the right hemisphere (see below) while HFA shows more left than left hemispheric dysfunction (Rumsey, 1992).

Developmental Issues

It is important to recognize that social difficulties experienced early on in development can affect how the child relates to others. Problems with early development may easily transfer into difficulties with attachment. Children with NVLD show difficulties with motor development including a tendency to gaze to one side and to prefer right-sided activities (Voeller, 1995). Delays are often reported in reaching motor milestones while language skills are developed at appropriate ages (Strang & Rourke, 1985). Attending to faces and voice intonation is an important part of social development in infancy and toddlerhood. Infants as young as 2 months of age prefer to gaze at faces than at objects (de Haan et al., 1998). This preference has been related to the child's ability to understand emotion, social exchanges, and motivation (Buitelaar & van der Wees, 1997). Children with NVLD have been found to show poor eye contact and prefer playing with objects to people with an apparent lack of attention to faces (Gross-Tsur et al., 1995).

Children with NVLD are reported to experience tactile perceptual problems—these difficulties lead to difficulty with sensitivity to touch and to smells. Parents report that children with NVLD will resist being cuddled and appear to be tactilely defensive. They will also report a sensitivity to smells and tastes with some children refusing to eat various items due to texture and appearance. Others report that their child has difficulty tolerating the texture of some of their clothing and require that the tags at the back of shirts and underwear be removed. In addition, for younger children, problems arise with learning how to skip, how to ride a bike, buttoning and zipping, and tying shoelaces. These difficulties may lead to later problems with writing and spacing of words on a page. In addition, children with NVLD are reported to have difficulty with new situations and may actually shy away from these types of experiences thus limiting their exposure (Semrud-Clikeman & Hynd, 1990).

Problems with tactile defensiveness, understanding of novel information and situations, as well as difficulties with perception and spatial understanding appear to translate into difficulties in the elementary school years in attention. Problems with focusing on aspects that are important in the environment may increase difficulty with understanding of others. These difficulties often result in a misunderstanding of other's actions and a feeling that the world may be unpredictable (Semrud-Clikeman & Hynd, 1990). This situation would likely result in fewer incidences of exploratory behavior and less movement away from the child's comfort zone. Such restriction of activity decreases the child's ability to relate to others. By kindergarten, children with NVLD may be considered "shy" or withdrawn and teachers often need to encourage them to play cooperatively. Entry into a large classroom may exacerbate problems with attention and with activity level through increasing anxiety about the situation at hand. Continuing difficulty in understanding facial expressions and voice intonation may make relating to others fairly problematic particularly with peers.

The child with NVLD's good language skills generally protects him/her from significant academic problems prior to the middle of elementary school. As the academic tasks become more complex in third or fourth grade, the child begins to struggle academically and may be referred for evaluation due to organizational problems. Difficulty with planning and organization of tasks may result in poor work completion which in turn may lead to behavioral difficulties and resistance (Pennington, 1991). These difficulties are particularly seen on tasks that require sustained attention and organization such as in writing a paper or completing a long-term project. On these types of activities, the child may become bogged down by details and may quit in frustration. Such problems translate into difficulties with managing behavior as well as in the social context which now begins to require perspective-taking and sharing.

Social interaction becomes more and more important in the elementary years and children with NVLD are frequently left to themselves and socially isolated. Aaron, the boy described earlier, generally spent his recesses walking the perimeter of the playground or talking with the adult supervisor. In addition, during this time children with NVLD are often brought to the attention of their teachers and parents due to difficulties with mathematics and at times with reading comprehension particularly requiring drawing inferences.

In elementary school, children with NVLD also become painfully aware that they don't have friends, and unlike children with autism, they long for these friendships. However, difficulties with understanding of social nuances and with social conversation impede their development of these friendships and they are often seen as socially inept and socially isolated (Weintraub & Mesulam, 1988).

Rourke (1988) suggests that due to the perceptual deficits identified at infancy and in the preschool period, children with NVLD frequently have difficulties acquiring the social skills needed in order to function adequately. An inability to correctly identify facial expressions and tone of voice interferes with their ability to play. Children with NVLD do not understand how to manipulate items or how to engage in playful teasing and responding. Because they do not have this experience at young ages, children with NVLD are unable to apply this learning to the development of peer relationships. Since the child is not actively engaged in his/her social environment, learning does not take place as to how to approach others and how to understand the nonverbal cues so very important in a social exchange (Semrud-Clikeman & Hynd, 1990).

Executive functions begin to be important in elementary school and continue into adolescence. As discussed in Chapter 2, executive functions are those that allow a person to view their behavior, assess its appropriateness, and make changes if required. They differ from cognitive functions in degree as cognitive functions look at what a person knows while executive functions evaluate the person's ability to carry through with a plan of action (Damasio, 1994). Thus, a child or adolescent can know the appropriate plan of action in a social situation but be unable to carry through with it. For children with NVLD, it is hypothesized that they are unable to develop this plan of action due to faulty social perception. Children at this stage frequently rely on language skills rather than play-based activities to gather information.

Rourke and Fuerst (1992) suggest that children with NVLD "prefer to hear about the world rather than to see or touch it" (p. 407). This preference certainly translates into problems in learning how to develop a plan of action and then to correct mistakes that are made. The child with NVLD not only has problems learning from his/her mistakes, he/she also has difficulty with generating solutions to problems. They have developed a model that is illustrated in Figure 6.1 and adapted from their work. The secondary deficits section of Figure 6.1 shows the main problems present at the elementary and beginning middle school years.

The tertiary section of Figure 6.1 indicates the compounding of these early difficulties in the late middle and throughout the high school years. Children with NVLD often have difficulty learning the necessary skills for

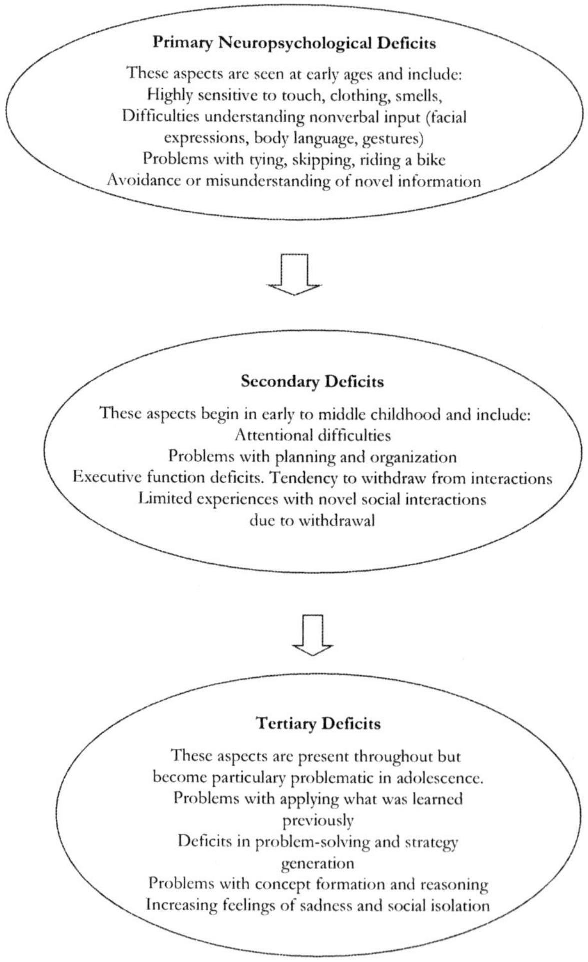

Primary Neuropsychological Deficits

These aspects are seen at early ages and include:
Highly sensitive to touch, clothing, smells,
Difficulties understanding nonverbal input (facial expressions, body language, gestures)
Problems with tying, skipping, riding a bike
Avoidance or misunderstanding of novel information

Secondary Deficits

These aspects begin in early to middle childhood and include:
Attentional difficulties
Problems with planning and organization
Executive function deficits. Tendency to withdraw from interactions
Limited experiences with novel social interactions due to withdrawal

Tertiary Deficits

These aspects are present throughout but become particulary problematic in adolescence.
Problems with applying what was learned previously
Deficits in problem-solving and strategy generation
Problems with concept formation and reasoning
Increasing feelings of sadness and social isolation

Figure 6.1 A developmental framework for NVLD
Used with permission from Dr. Guli and adapted from Rourke (1995)

social interaction as well as applying those skills appropriately. Difficulties with executive functioning are frequently present and these problems translate into difficulty in "formal operations" or the ability to step outside of oneself and evaluate the appropriateness and helpfulness of one's own behavior (Semrud-Clikeman, 2003).

Adolescence

Adolescents with NVLD have particular difficulty understanding another's point of view, as continued problems with executive functioning exist. Given that particular difficulty with fluid reasoning and concept formation continue into this period (Schnoebelen et al., 2003), adolescents with NVLD often seem out of step with their peers and may appear immature for their age. Continued dependence on teachers and parents for directions restricts their ability to develop the needed individuation expected of a child at this age. Continued difficulty in developing an action plan continues to be a problem and plays into difficulty with this individuation as well as with learning from mistakes. An inability to generate additional solutions to a problem further complicates the problems seen with adolescents with NVLD.

These difficulties continue to be present in the social arena but also now spread into the academic area as adolescents are asked to read and apply what they have learned to a novel situation. Difficulties become more evident in classes where the adolescent is asked to understand and apply information that he/she has learned. Additional difficulties become present when the adolescent is expected to write an essay or create something that is not rote in nature. Mathematics skills rarely develop past the sixth grade level and failure is generally present in the high school subjects of geometry, trigonometry, and physics which require abstract and visual-spatial reasoning (Pennington, 1991). Previous relative strengths in verbal ability become weaknesses at this point, as the adolescent with NVLD struggles to use more complex and figurative language.

The adolescent with NVLD has a higher incidence of sadness and social withdrawal than typically developing children. Rourke et al. (1989) suggest that adolescents with NVLD may have more serious emotional disturbance and suicidal behavior than those with other types of developmental disabilities. As the adolescent feels more isolated, the propensity for serious depression and withdrawal increases. Increases in psychopathology are present as well as lower self-esteem and problems with withdrawal. Some adolescents with NVLD can become oppositional while others are vulnerable to victimization or manipulation.

Adolescents with NVLD may also show an increased reliance on language to try and compensate for problems with nonverbal understanding. Some become highly dependent on adults and will seek out teachers and coaches as a means of allowing them to feel more accepted and as part of the social scene. Other adolescents may utilize antisocial means for getting attention. However, the main need for many of the adolescents with NVLD is structure and attention and they will seek out both of these needs in any manner that can help them attain their goals.

Brain Contributions to NVLD

The brain has two hemispheres—left and right. The left is believed to be important for language and sequential processing while the right hemisphere's functions include visual processing, wholistic understanding, and emotional processing. The motor and sensory systems are crossed—that is, the right hemisphere controls the left side of the body and the left hemisphere the right. The brain is divided into four lobes: frontal, parietal, temporal, and occipital. Goldberg and Costa (1981) found that the hemispheres are relatively equal in volume but that the right hemisphere has more white matter than the left. White matter is nerve fiber tracts that are myelinated. Myelin is the insulation around these fiber tracts that allows the messages to move more quickly from the front to the back of the brain and vice versa. In the left hemisphere the myelinated tracts are shorter and thus serve the ability to transfer information sequentially—a skill needed for language. For the right hemisphere the tracts are longer and lend themselves more readily to processing information in a more simultaneous manner (Semrud-Clikeman, 2001). White matter volume has been significantly correlated with the ability to process complex and novel information (Teeter & Semrud-Clikeman, 1997).

It has been hypothesized that the development of the right hemisphere in children with NVLD may be aberrant and result in problems with social understanding (Pennington, 1991; Semrud-Clikeman & Hynd, 1990). Using EEG to measure hemispheric functioning, Njiokoktjien et al. (2001) found that children with NVLD compared to those with verbal LD showed dysfunction with right hemisphere processing. Problems with understanding facial expressions, visual-spatial reasoning, and with social competence are consistent with the EEG findings and likely implicate the right hemisphere in NVLD. Further study is needed to understand the possible contribution of the right hemisphere to social understanding.

Developmentally the right hemisphere is more advanced than the left. In infancy the child is generally nonverbal and is beginning to understand his/her world through experience (Semrud-Clikeman & Hynd, 1990). As discussed earlier, for the infant with a propensity to NVLD, these tasks are problematic and retrospective reports find them to show less exploratory behavior and to be quite clumsy (Voeller, 1995).

Perceptual Processing in NVLD

Perceptual processing, particular visually, has been studied in NVLD. One of the first studies on visual processing in NVLD analyzed the responses of preschoolers with primary nonverbal learning disabilities using a picture vocabulary test and found difficulty recognizing commonly used objects when in picture form (Johnson, 1987). Myklebust (1975) analyzed perceptual accuracy of children with reported nonverbal deficits and found that difficulty was present in identifying a pictorial representation of a scene even though the children could accurately name the objects. Thus, initial deficits in identifying visual representations of objects translate into later problems with understanding complex pictures. Benton and Tranel (1993) suggest that the child needs to visually encode a complex picture, encode that understanding verbally, and report the integration. Problems with initial encoding make it difficult for the verbal portion of the response to be appropriately developed.

Myklebust (1975) suggested that since children with NVLD were able to identify the objects correctly, the difficulty was not in perception per se, but rather in the difficulty in integrating individual objects into a meaningful whole. Children with NVLD have been found to have difficulty in correctly identifying facial expressions and gestures compared to children with verbal LD or typically developing children (Petti et al., 2003).

Difficulties have also been identified with understanding emotional content of a social exchange (Worling et al., 1999) and with subsequent social isolation (Woods et al., 2000). The problems with understanding the emotional content appear to be related to interpreting complex relationships. Worling et al. (1999) compared children with verbal LD, NVLD, and controls on measures of language and inferential reasoning. There were no differences between the verbal LD and NVLD and both groups performed significantly more poorly than the control children on measures of language competency. However, when the learning disabled groups were compared, the children with NVLD showed specific difficulties on language tasks that involved the interpretation of spatial relationships. The children with NVLD did not have difficulty on tasks that required them to recognize individual items either for emotional content or spatial relationships. Difficulties were present when the child with NVLD was asked to integrate the findings and to make emotional inferences based on this integration.

Cornoldi (1999) evaluated visuospatial working memory and visual imagery in children with NVLD and those without. He also evaluated developmental trends in these tasks that differed between the groups. Visuospatial memory has been linked to the ability to generate and maintain mental imagery—a process likely important for social functioning (Logie, 1995). Children with NVLD were found to have difficulties on visual working memory tasks particularly in the areas of recalling visual and spatial information. Mental imagery difficulties were also found for both verbal and visual information. These findings indicate problems with higher-order mental reasoning that transcends the type of input. Thus, difficulty is present on tasks that require the child to learn new information by associating it with previously learned material. Cornoldi (1999) suggests that interventions need to be developed that do not overstress the working memory system. Strategies that improve working memory need to be directly taught. These strategies may include the use of writing lists, prioritizing work into smaller units, and giving more time for processing of material.

The problems recognized in children with NVLD in understanding complex pictures underscores the difficulties present in understanding dynamic social exchanges. These difficulties with integration make it problematic for the child with NVLD to understand facial expressions and pair them with gestures and language. When asked to interpret a scene where the verbal portion of the communication does not match the nonverbal portion, children with NVLD inevitably use the verbal portion to translate meaning. Thus, sarcasm or humor is not understood by children with NVLD and they often translate this type of communication literally (Semrud-Clikeman & Glass, submitted). Moreover, children with NVLD often make inferences based on language and interpretation of a situation using details without reference to the context (Worling et al., 1999). Thus, the child's interpretation may not be accurate for the context in which the information is given and his/her behavior is subsequently often inappropriate based on misperceptions. Borod et al. (1992) suggests that interpretation of emotion requires the ability to understand the relationship between emotions which in turn requires spatial organization—a right hemispheric integrative function. Working memory deficits present in NVLD also limit the child's ability to apply appropriate emotional inferencing to the situation at hand. Part of the difficulty is that system becomes overloaded attempting to process the details involved in any social exchange.

Visual Integration

The ability to integrate information presented visually has been suggested to be a primary difficulty for children with NVLD. Children with NVLD have been found to have more difficulty compared to children with ADHD or typically developing children on measures of visual-motor integration and visual-spatial skills (Wilkinson et al., 2002). When children with verbal LD were compared to those with NVLD on measures of visual-motor integration (Foss, 1991; Meyers & Meyers, 1995), both groups of children with learning disabilities performed more poorly than typically developing children. However, the children with NVLD performed the most poorly. Qualitative analysis of the findings indicated that children with verbal LD were able to copy the picture adequately but missed many details. The children with NVLD copied the picture in a piecemeal fashion with disconnected details.

Corlett (2002) evaluated the social perception of children with NVLD using projective measures. She compared children with NVLD and ADHD: PI with children with ADHD: PI and typically developing children. Children with NVLD frequently also a diagnosis of ADHD: PI. The children with NVLD were found to show significant difficulties with perception compared to the other groups whose difficulties were characterized by problems with integration. No differences were found between the ADHD: PI and control groups on perception, thus attentional deficits were not at the core of the problems with visual integration. Thus, it is likely that children with NVLD have difficulties integrating visual input accurately and may react inappropriately due to this inaccuracy. These social faux pas likely add up to increasing isolation and rejection from peers. This study also found that children with NVLD are interested in others but often react inflexibly to a social situation, possibly because of numerous negative experiences that serve to constrict the child's responses as a means of safeguarding him or herself from social rejection.

Children with NVLD have been found to show better skills on measures of sequential processing than those of simultaneous processing.
Simultaneous and sequential processing are based on Luria's (1980)
model of brain function that conceptualizes the brain function into three
networks that function independently as well as being integrated at
higher levels. The three networks are planning, arousal, and processing
(simultaneous as well as sequential). Sequential processing is the ability
to process information in a step-by-step manner and is primarily based
on left hemispheric processing. Simultaneous processing is a right hemispheric function and allows the individual to process information with
many facets and form an integrated whole. The individual uses either
style depending on the task at hand. Chow and Skuy (1999) evaluated
children with NVLD and those with verbal LD on measures of sequential and simultaneous processing. Children with verbal LD were found to
more commonly use the simultaneous processing style while children
with NVLD favored the successive processing mode.

The processing of social information likely involves the ability to interpret details as well as understanding the context of the social exchange.
If children with NVLD are processing social information in a piecemeal
manner, then it becomes more and more problematic for them to understand how the pieces fit together. When difficulty is present in integrating this visual information and if processing of the individual parts of an
interaction may be problematic, then it follows that significant difficulties will be present in interaction appropriately, responding to social
communication, and applying previously learned skills. The ability to
process social information is a complex skill that requires the child to
access previously learned information (recognition of facial expression
and labeling of emotions) and apply it to the situation at hand (Flavell
et al., 1985). Findings that children with NVLD prefer processing information in a step-by-step manner indicate that interventions that provide
support in this area may be most appropriate while also improving the
child's ability to process information simultaneously (Das, 1993).

Interventions

Interventions for children with NVLD are beginning to be empirically validated. The use of social skills curriculum developed for other children
have not been found to be a successful intervention without tailoring the
skills to the child with NVLD (Schafer & Semrud-Clikeman, submitted).
Most social skill programs begin at a level that is likely too advanced for
children with NVLD as it assumes appropriate interpretation of facial
expressions and body language. To be effective, interventions need to
begin with labeling of emotions and understanding of emotional labels.
Interventions need to be based on teaching social perception through the
use of practice, modeling, and role-playing. Breaking down social
perception into discrete steps and teaching rules to allow the child with
NVLD to process the information verbally plays on the strengths that
these children bring to the program. Pairing auditory and visual stimuli
together may also provide the type of support that is necessary for the

child to fully understand the complex nonverbal social communication that is problematic for his/her interpretation.

In order for these interventions to be helpful to children with NVLD, it is likely important that the program begin slowly and with a great deal of structure and then gradually move to the more complex activities that require the building of trust in order to attempt them. It is important for these interventions that practice is provided and that sufficient time is allotted for over-learning of these skills. To encourage generalization of the skills, parent involvement is necessary and particularly important for practicing newly learned skills in a naturalistic environment. Success with these interventions is more assured with the interventions continuing in the classroom and not solely in the small group or home settings.

There are different types of interventions that have been attempted with children with NVLD. Some of these interventions have not been studied as to treatment efficacy. One intervention developed at our laboratory has been studied for efficacy and will be discussed later on in this chapter. Generally the interventions fall into one of three types: parent interventions, social skills curriculum (including coaching and friendship groups), and a group-based intervention based on learning about emotions and social applications. Each of these types of interventions will be discussed separately in the following sections.

Parent Interventions

Parent interventions have been developed from programs such as Parent Effectiveness Training (PET: Gordon, 2006) and general program for parental involvement. These interventions are based on the assumption that parents are in the best place to assist their child and are the most committed to their child's improvement. Parents are encouraged to provide opportunities for the child to play with others and to participate in regular and structured activities such as Boy Scouts or Brownies/Girl Scouts. Providing experiences in clubs that are structured allows the child with NVLD to enter a program that reduces the ambiguity often present in unstructured social experiences—an area particularly problematic for him/her. At times family therapy may be most appropriate particularly when the parents have difficulties with their own social life. It is not uncommon for children with NVLD to also have parents that have difficulty with social skills and thus an intervention that expects them to teach the child such skills is problematic.

Interventions that provide parents of children with NVLD with experiences that can provide an outlet for the child socially can be quite helpful while expecting the parent to teach skills is likely to be an unrealistic goal. Parents are often unable to be objective about their child's abilities (rightfully so!). Moreover, parents have many roles to play with their child (disciplinarian, nurturer, manager, etc.) so that expecting them to teach these skills, particularly when they may not have the skills or patience themselves, may not be helpful. One parent who has a child with NVLD reported that it was very hard for her to be patient— "I tell him over and over what to do and then he doesn't do it! I get so impatient with him that it turns into a yelling match and then he storms off—my trying to help him make friends is hurting our relationship." Thus, it is important for the therapist or school personnel to be cognizant of the stresses that are often felt by these parents and not expect this type of support from most parents.

While parents may not be the best vehicle for teaching social skills, providing them with appropriate information and keeping them informed about interventions have been found to be helpful (Semrud-Clikeman & Schafer, 2000). Parents supplied with suggestions and support can provide additional experiences for their child that is more helpful. Many times the provision of a safety outlet for frustration and anxiety is the most effective type of support the parent can provide. Children with NVLD often experience rejection and isolation in school and in unstructured activities. A parent who can provide support through organized activities, a calm demeanor, and a place to decompress is likely giving the best support to the child. Setting up situations where the child is paired with one other child who may be more tolerant of the child's behaviors can also help. Trips to the museum, movies, or a structured activity are proactive for appropriate social exchanges. Situations that don't provide such structure are likely to be more anxiety producing and possibly less constructive as the child seeks to entertain his/her "friend."

Social Skills Programs

There are few empirical studies of social skill groups to validate their use for children with NVLD. Social skill groups, similar to those described in the chapters on ADHD and LD, generally include 4–6 children and meet for one hour or so weekly. There is often a discussion as to what children may profit from the technique. For children with NVLD it may be most appropriate to utilize groups with varying levels of skills rather than a group where all children have significant social problems. However, the developmental level of the children should be somewhat similar.

As discussed earlier, children with NVLD can profit from social skills programs as long as they have the underlying ability to understand emotions and emotional labeling. Most social skills programs begin assuming these skills, and similar to the findings for children with ADHD and/or LD, the programs are likely not as effective. These programs, however, can provide ideas for support for children with NVLD and allow practice of needed skills. Too often a child with NVLD will appear rude only because he/she does not have the appropriate behavior or misinterprets the situation at hand. Awareness of these difficulties or at least cognizance that the other person is unhappy with one's behavior is a beginning step in working on social exchanges.

Children with NVLD may benefit from classroom support with teachers matching a child with a more tolerant peer. It is important that the child's peer understands the difficulty that may be present. This type of "friend-making" is somewhat artificial and requires a very special child to support the child with NVLD. The advantages of peer-matching are that it occurs in a naturalistic setting and the child learns from a same-aged child. However, it is time consuming and requires a great deal of adult support for success both from the parent and teacher.

Suggestions in the field have been made for coaching interventions. These interventions occur in the child's environment and the adult observes the child. Following the observation, the child meets with his/her coach and discusses the behaviors seen and the situations. Corrective exercises are provided. It is likely that this method could be quite useful in assisting the child with learning appropriate behaviors in a naturalistic setting. I could find no empirically based studies that validated this type of treatment in the literature. At this point in time, it is a therapeutic technique that may be helpful. It requires a great deal of time from the adult as well as the opportunity to observe the child. The technique may also be problematic as it is difficult to observe a child without the other children wondering what is happening, and thus possibly isolate the child further.

Social Competence Intervention Program

We have developed a social competence intervention program (SCIP) designed to work with children with NVLD and Asperger's Disorder (Guli et al., 2007). SCIP is an intervention that is multi-sensory in nature and targets underlying difficulties in social perception as well as providing exercises to improve the generating of strategies for problem solving.

In SCIP, exercises were adapted from children's creative drama and theatre classes to practice the processes fundamental to social competence. These activities were originally designed to help actors develop accurate perception and response to cues and address various aspects of social perception. Spolin (1986) suggest that these activities fall in the following categories: sensory games, space/movement games, mirroring activities, communication with sounds, physical control, "part of a whole" and multiple-stimulus games. These skills are supportive of children with social difficulties due to faulty perception.

The exercises move from perception of emotions to interpretation and then to response. Within each of these areas, the exercises began with basic emotions and later involved subtler, less common emotions. Thus, the initial sessions involve direct evaluation, and if needed, intervention for understanding facial expression and nonverbal communication as well as decoding voice intonation as to intent of the speaker. As the child moves through the intervention, more complex emotions (disgust, frustration) are introduced and then integrated into role-playing situations. Since it is important for a child to be able to integrate these individually perceived stimuli into a correct interpretation, the introduction of more and more complex situations is required as the child masters the basic skills.

The exercises began with faces that are just pictures and with mastery the child is presented with faces that are in vignettes and skit to be closer to what is experienced in the world. As these skills are taught, the child is also introduced to understanding how his/her own body feels when angry, sad, happy, etc. and then how he/she imagines someone else would express these feelings. Children with NVLD frequently have difficulty managing new situations. The SCIP program provides new experiences that change with time but are built on situations that are familiar and thus not as anxiety producing as fully novel experiences would be. The work is constantly reviewed and supported throughout the time of the intervention thus providing for review and refreshing of skills.

Of course, it is important that the children trust each other during the groups and so the initial stages of the intervention are developed to assist with trust-building through several exercises. Exercises to reduce inhibition and to develop trust and group cohesion were included in each session. Relaxation exercises and exercises designed to increase physical self-control (Cresci, 1989) can potentially help those students with inhibited or restricted body movement (NVLD) and/or poor impulse control (ADHD).

Role-plays, for example, can be difficult to do in front of a group even for people without social perception difficulties. Through the use of activities that are manageable and less anxiety producing and with practice with different partners for several weeks, the child learns that the group is a safe atmosphere and anxiety and inhibition is reduced. The activities that are part of SCIP are reported by the children to be fun (Glass et al., 2000).

One common concern in working with children with NVLD is the tendency for problems in social competence to lead to isolation and fewer opportunities to develop or strengthen existing competencies. These children have few experiences of enjoying being with other children. The children also gain social experiences through the activities. Throughout the eight-week intervention period, activities and/or role-plays were frequently interrupted due to laughter and playing on the part of the group members. Indeed, it was difficult to believe one child's mother's assertion that he had "not a single friend."

Guli (2005) evaluated the efficacy of the SCIP program. She compared a treatment group and a clinical control group with deficits in social perception using several outcome measures before and after participation in the SCIP program. The outcome measures included a test of recognizing facial expressions and voice cues, parent ratings on behavioral checklists of withdrawal and social skills, and direct behavioral observations of peer interactions. Following the intervention, parents and children in the treatment group were interviewed about their experience.

Support of the SCIP was found from the quantitative and qualitative results. The children showed improvement in their ability to correctly recognize facial expressions as well as vocal cues following the intervention. Improvement was also found in the child's behavior within a social group based on observational data. Qualitative results showed that 75% of parents reported one or more positive changes in social perception or competence after participating in the intervention while 82% of the children reported one or more positive effects of the intervention. Thus, this study's results suggest that effects may generalize over settings (i.e., home and school). The results of this study lend support to efficacy of the SCIP program that targets specific difficulties in a very specialized population. Moreover, these findings strongly support research that stresses training in perception and integration of nonverbal cues for children with nonverbal learning disabilities (Barnhill et al., 2002; Bauminger, 2002; Carlyon, 1997).

Conclusion

Children with NVLD have specific difficulties interpreting information that is nonverbal in nature and which requires integration of varying pieces of information. Significant problems are found in the child's ability to understand social exchanges and to interact appropriately with peers. Neuropsychological deficits in visual-spatial processing as well as in executive functioning likely contribute to significant problems in functioning. Developmental shifts complicate these problems particularly for adolescents, and adolescents have a higher than average incidence of depression, anxiety, and suicidal attempts. Children with NVLD have many needs that are not often identified by the schools or provided with interventions unless significant emotional disturbance or a learning disability in mathematics exists.

Few studies have evaluated the efficacy of social skills interventions. There are promising developments in the area of interventions when particular skills are targeted and then are supported through creative methods for practice within a safe group and then practice outside of the groups. Further study is certainly needed to evaluate treatment efficacy and also generalization of these skills over time. The empirical base for interventions for children with NVLD is sparse and not well completed. Further study as to appropriate interventions is certainly needed.

One area that certainly requires additional evaluation is the role parents can play in the development of social skills. A sizable minority of children with NVLD have a parent with similar difficulties. Our ability to understand the family dynamics, family stress, and coping strategies necessary for success is just in its infancy. Further investigation is sorely needed in this area.

Teachers are an integral part of the process for intervention, and yet, few studies evaluate the child beyond behavioral rating scales from the teacher's point of view as to the efficacy of programs. These areas need to be more fully explored. Many teachers come to our program expressing frustration and concern because they do not fully understand these children and feel little to no support for working with these children through special education.

Both parents and teachers need support in working with children with NVLD and it is likely that a multi-modal intervention is probably the most efficacious model for these interventions. In order for the skills taught in small group interventions to generalize, it is important for the major parts of the child's life to work together on these skills. As you will see in the next chapter on Autistic Spectrum disorder, these difficulties are present for children with social competence difficulties and increase in importance as the disorder becomes more severe.

7

Social Competence in Children with Autism Spectrum Disorders

There have been many changes in our understanding of autism and related disorders. Under DSM IV TR (APA, 2000) autism, Rett's disorder, Asperger's Disorder (AS), and childhood disintegrative disorder have been characterized under the umbrella term Pervasive Developmental Disorder (PDD). PDD-NOS (not otherwise specified) is a diagnosis generally used when the child shows some but not all of the symptoms of either AS or autism. All of these disorders are defined by severe and consistent impairment in social interaction skills as well as significant problems with communication or stereotyped behaviors, interests, and activities. For these disorders problems are identified within the first 3 years of life.

Pervasive Developmental Disorder may also be seen with medical and chromosomal abnormalities and has been commonly associated with tuberous sclerosis. Common comorbid diagnoses with Autism Spectrum disorder (ASD) are seizures (Volkmar & Nelson, 1990), Tourette's syndrome (Baron-Cohen et al., 1999), ADHD (Ghaziuddin et al., 1992), anxiety (Kim et al., 2000), and mood disorders (Wozniak et al., 1997). Case histories suggest that some children with ASD were socially unresponsive from early infancy (Dahlgren & Gillberg, 1989); others report the onset of symptoms to occur sometime after the 2nd year of life (Volkmar et al., 1985, 2004).

Historically, definitional issues have been problematic for ASD but improvement in diagnosis and the standardization of this diagnosis have improved the reliability of the diagnosis. On the other hand, ASD has been expanded to include other disorders beyond autism and the conceptualization has become broader. Improvement in standardized instruments has also assisted with the diagnosis as well as interpretation of group studies of children with ASD.

Children are diagnosed with autism if they show significant impairment in social interaction including problems with eye contact and nonverbal understanding and difficulties with social reciprocity. Qualitative difficulties are found in communication with delays in spoken and receptive language, stereotyped and echolalic speech, and difficulties with play—both with peers and individually. Children diagnosed with autism also show a narrow pattern of behavior and interests, have repetitive behaviors, and become preoccupied with objects and items.

Delays are often seen in ability with many children with autism scoring the mentally handicapped range. However, with improved diagnostic capability, the IQ distribution has shifted upward and children with average to superior IQs have also been found to show autism and to be so diagnosed. Earlier studies indicated that a significant majority of children with autism were mentally handicapped with IQs less than 70 (Volkmar et al., 2004). More recent studies have found that less than half of children with autism now qualify for an additional diagnosis of mental retardation and have a brighter prognosis than was previously thought (Chakrabarti & Fombonne, 2001; Howlin, 2000; Tsatsanis, 2003).

Rett's Disorder/Childhood Disintegrative Disorder

Rett's disorder and childhood disintegrative disorder are also included under the PDD umbrella. Rett's disorder is not generally considered that similar to autism as it is a neurodegenerative disorder but was included in the ASD as a place marker (Volkmar et al., 2004). Rett's disorder is found only in girls and is generally not identified until the child is at least 5 months old and frequently at a later date but generally before the age of 3 (Swaiman & Dyken, 1999). Difficulty is initially seen with hand control and in loss of interest in others. Brain development slows and the head stops growing. Language and cognitive skills either regress or do not develop at all (Ozonoff & Rogers, 2003). As the child grows, repetitive wringing of the hands, clapping or rubbing of the hands is observed and the cognitive deficits increase. It is believed that Rett's disorder is transmitted by a mutation on the X chromosome and can be carried by boys who often show mental retardation but do not also show the Rett-like behaviors (Amir et al., 1999; Kerr, 2002).

Childhood disintegrative disorder (CDD) is a rare condition where the child shows a pattern of regression after normal development. This disorder appears to be genetically transmitted. CDD can be seen in girls or boys and is most common in males. The regression occurs abruptly and severely and can occur between the ages of 2 and 10. Normal development is seen up to this point and then the regression begins and is very severe. The child withdraws from social interactions, ceases talking, shows poor motor control, and has drops in ability and adaptive behavior. This regression lasts approximately 1–2 months and the child becomes very agitated and difficult to control. After this period the child appears to have severe autism and mental retardation. Unfortunately, there is little improvement with treatment and the condition is irreversible. It is not presently clear what the cause is but this disorder is different than the usual expression of autism (Ozonoff & Rogers, 2003). Neither of these two disorders will be discussed in any detail in this chapter.

Pervasive Developmental Disorders—Not Otherwise Specified (PDD-NOS)

Similar to AS, PDD-NOS is also very difficult to reliably diagnose and is frequently a fall-back diagnosis when the criteria for AS or autism is not met. These children show 2 of the 3 symptom clusters that identify children with ASD or AS (Ozonoff & Rogers, 2003). These clusters are the social responsiveness cluster, communication skill difficulty, and stereotyped or repetitive behaviors. For a diagnosis of PDD-NOS the child must show one area of concern with social reciprocity and one of the other two clusters. Mental retardation is not as common as found in autism and generally runs at a prevalence rate of 7.3% (Chakrabarti & Fombonne, 2001). Children with PDD-NOS have some autistic-like symptoms but either don't qualify for a diagnosis of autism as they do not have enough symptoms or do not qualify for a diagnosis of AS due to a language delay.

The PDD-NOS is probably one of the more unreliable diagnostic categories and the DSM IV field trials found that these children were often misdiagnosed (Volkmar et al., 1994). The field trials found that 33% of the children diagnosed with PDD-NOS met criteria for autism while another 33% did not qualify for any diagnosis in the autistic spectrum. These children generally showed language or learning problems with mildly delayed social skills or were hyperactive and very impulsive and distractible.

Incidence and Prevalence

The overall prevalence of the combined PDD diagnoses is approximately 26.1 per 10,000 (Fombonne et al., 2001). The most recent estimates of prevalence for ASD is 12.7 cases per 10,000 (Fombonne, 2003a). This estimate is somewhat larger than previous estimates of 4.4 per 10,000. Some of the increase is undoubtedly due to improved diagnostic measures while some is also due to the tendency for children with autism to be eligible for more services through the public schools than those with mental retardation. It is not uncommon for school psychologists and clinicians to be pressured to making a diagnosis of autism to receive these additional services. Children with autism are generally identified earlier compared to diagnoses of PDD or AS, approximately by the age of 30.0 months of age.

Epidemiological data reports an incidence of 8.4 per 10,000 children have a diagnosis of AS (Chakrabarti & Fombonne, 2001) while Rett's disorder and CDD have lower rates (<1 per 10,000 and 1 per 50,000 respectively). The prevalence of PDD-NOS is more problematic to study as the criteria is undefined and is generally provided when a child falls short of being diagnosed with autism. The prevalence of PDD-NOS was estimated from an epidemiological stay at 36.1 cases per 10,000 (Chakrabarti & Fombonne, 2001). Children with PDD-NOS were referred for evaluation later than those with autism and approximately at the age of 37.2 months.

Racial and ethnic differences have not been substantiated for the diagnosis of ASD or between social class and ASD (Dyches et al., 2001; Fombonne, 2003b; Ritvo et al., 1989; Wing, 1980). Gender differences do exist with a higher incidence of autism in boys found with ratios approaching 3.5 to 4.0 to 1 (Fombonne, 2003a; Lord et al., 1982). Further study has found that for boys with average cognitive functioning, the ratios are higher while those for boys and girls who are mentally handicapped the ratios approach each other (Lord et al., 1982). Volkmar et al. (2004) suggest that boys may be at higher risk for autism while girls require more neurological compromise for autism to be found.

Developmental Course of Autistic Spectrum Disorders

For most children with ASD the onset occurs prior to age 3. As discussed earlier a sizable majority does not show the disorder until after the age of 2. Most children who are later diagnosed with autism have irregularities and delays in development from infancy until diagnosis and these problems are characterized by difficulties with nonverbal communication, response to facial expressions, and lack of social responsiveness to the caretakers. Approximately 30% of children with autism show regression of skills generally between the ages of 1–2 years (Kurita, 1985: Tuchman & Rapin, 1997) and some have hypothesized that this regression is due to environmentally mediated occurrences (Hornig & Lipkin, 2001) or to genetic influences (Lainhart et al., 2002).

With early intervention, many children with ASD improve. Qualitative differences are present in the expression of some symptoms at different ages. Stereotyped and repetitive behaviors are most commonly seen in preschool and either improve or significantly decline in elementary school. For children receiving early intervention, it is estimated that 50% approach normal functioning by adolescence (McEachin et al., 1993). Although improvement is noted, most of these adolescents continue to have difficulty with social interaction and few are able to establish an independent life style in adulthood (Gillberg, 1991; Howlin & Goode, 1998). As with other disorders, the most predictive variable for a positive outcome is the level of intelligence present by the age of 5 (Rutter, 1984).

Neurodevelopmental and Genetic Contributions to Autism

Recent advances in genetic analysis have found that autism occurs in families approximately at the rate of 3–6% which is higher than the rate found in the general population (Bailey et al., 1998). Twin studies have found that monozygotic twins have a concordance rate for a diagnosis of autism of 60% while the rate was 5% for dizygotic pairs (Bailey et al., 1995). When all types of PDD were included the concordance rate increased to 90% for monozygotic pairs yielding a heritability estimate greater than .90 (LeCouteur et al., 1996). Ozonoff and Rogers (2003)] further point out that autism frequently co-occurs with other chromosomal abnormalities including tuberous sclerosis, fragile X syndrome, and in deletion syndromes including chromosomes 7, 15, and 18 (Semrud-Clikeman et al., 2000).

Fragile X syndrome is a commonly inherited cause of mental retardation that is transmitted by the mother's contribution to the sex chromosomes. Approximately 2–8% of boys with autism and Fragile X syndrome are also mentally retarded (Wassink et al., 2001). Tuberous Sclerosis (TS) is a genetic disorder where tubers or lesions are present throughout the body and particularly in the brain. Approximately 2–4% of children with autism have TS (Hansen & Hagerman, 2003). For further information about these particular disorders please see Chapter 12. Autistic symptoms have been reported in 43–61% of children with TS (Gillberg et al., 1994) with a higher-than-expected percentage showing brain lesions in the temporal lobe—an area of the brain particularly involved in language and emotion recognition (Bolton & Griffiths, 1997). Asano et al. (2001), using PET scans to visualize brain metabolism, found that patients with TS, both with and without autism, showed a higher metabolic rate in areas of the brain associated with impaired social interactions, language problems, and stereotyped behaviors.

Neuroimaging techniques have made it possible to view the develop-ing brain while the child completes various tasks. Thus, the ability to compare brain activity among groups as well as for different tasks allows us to understand some of the differences that are present that may account for problems in reasoning, social interaction, and with executive functioning. One of the more common techniques is functional magnetic resonance imaging (fMRI) and has been used to study children and adolescents with autistic spectrum disorders.

Because the behaviors associated with autism vary from social reciprocity/ understanding to language to stereotyped and repetitive behaviors, it is likely that many brain systems are involved and will vary depending on the severity of the autistic symptoms as well as the level of cognitive involvement. Children with autism have been found to have larger heads than the general population (Aylward, et al., 2002). It has been found that the brains of toddlers with autism are 10% larger than same-aged peers with the largeness of the head decreasing with age but continuing to be larger than matched aged peers throughout life (Courchesne et al., 2001; Herbert et al., 2003). Interestingly, there is no difference in head size at birth (Lainhart et al., 1997) and the brain growth that later occurs may be due to early overgrowth of neurons, glial cells, and a lack of synaptic pruning (Nelson et al., 2001). Findings have suggested that this increased brain size indicates that the extra tis-sue is not well utilized or organized—thus resulting in poorer skill devel-opment (Aylward et al., 2002). Specific findings indicate an increase in gray matter volume particularly in the temporal lobes (Herbert et al., 2002; Rojas et al., 2002). Autopsy studies have found that the cellular columns that make up the frontal and temporal gray matter areas were disrupted resulting possibly in an inability to inhibit neuronal activity in these areas and thus produce cognitive dysfunction and possibly behav-ioral overflow (Casanova et al., 2002).

Using structural MRI analyses, Courchesne et al. (2001) found smaller measures of white matter compared to gray matter in toddlers and adolescents. Other studies of adults with autism have found reduced measures of the corpus callosum (Hardan et al., 2000), a structure that connects the two hemispheres as well as difficulties with inter-regional integration (also a white matter function) using PET scans (Horwitz et al., 1998). Some have suggested that the larger brain, higher white matter volume, and disrupted gray matter cellular columns may contribute to the person with autism's difficulty in integrating information and generalizing this information to new situations (Schultz et al., 2000). These difficulties may interfere with the person's ability to put information together into an understandable whole—or interfere with establishing central coherence—a theory discussed in an earlier chapter.

The amygdala, anterior cingulate, and hippocampus have also been studied. These structures are part of the limbic system of the brain—or the emotional part of the brain. The amygdala is important in emotional arousal as well as processing social information. The hippocampus allows for the short-term and eventual long-term storage of information while the anterior cingulate works as a type of central executive directing attention where it is most required.

Abnormalities have been found in limbic system during autopsy with reduced size and fewer connections present (Kemper & Bauman, 1998). These abnormalities may contribute to the behavioral difficulties seen in people with autism in social reciprocity and social awareness. Further study is needed in these areas. Some have suggested that the amygdala may be important for mediating physiological arousal, and if it is not as active, the person may well not be as motivated for participating in social activities (Dawson et al., 1990; Klin et al., 2003).

More recent studies have begun evaluating discrete areas of the brain that may be disrupted in people with autism. An area of the temporal lobe that has been found to be important for recognizing faces has been studied in children with autism. This area has been found to be underactive in people with autism and the degree of underactivation is highly correlated with the degree of social impairment (Schultz et al., 2001). Of additional interest is that this area of the temporal lobe has also been implicated in successful solution of Theory of Mind tasks, skills that are also impaired in people with autism (Castelli et al., 2000; Martin & Weisberg, 2003).

Areas of the frontal lobes have also been studied in patients with autism. Both the frontal lobes and the superior area of the temporal lobes are important for understanding and perception of social interactions as well as the interpretation of facial expressions. The frontal lobes have been particularly implicated in the ability to take another's perspective—or in social cognition. These areas are intimately connected to the limbic system as well as the temporal lobe areas discussed earlier in this section. Studies of brain metabolism have found reduced activity in these regions of the brain in autistic patients particularly when asked to perform tasks that tap social cognition and perception (Castelli et al., 2002; Ernst et al., 1997; Haznedar et al., 2000).

Social Impairment in Autism

As discussed in earlier chapters, the theory of mind hypothesis is frequently used to describe the social problems found in children with ASD. Particular difficulty in understanding the mental state of another person interferes with the child's ability to construct a world that is social and in which the child is able to understand how people differ in beliefs, desires, and needs (Baron-Cohen et al., 2000). Others suggest that children with ASD process information in a piecemeal fashion and thus become over-focused on details and miss the full picture (Frith, 1989; Happe & Frith, 1996). This theory is called the "Weak Central Coherence Hypothesis."

Pennington and Ozonoff (1996) suggest that the main difficulty in social understanding for children with ASD is the "Executive Dysfunction Hypothesis." This hypothesis suggests that problems with perseveration and self-regulation make it difficult for the child to cope with changing social situations and result in ineffective problem-solving strategies as well as problems with responding to constructive feedback. Moreover, deficits in executive functions are strongly related to the rigid and repetitive behaviors seen in children with autism as well as the problems with language and social reciprocity (Joseph & Tager-Flusberg, 2004). In this view, social communication requires an ability to update information, evaluate the information, and select an appropriate response when presented with multiple sources of information that is multifaceted (verbal, auditory, kinesthetic, etc.) (Bennetto et al., 1996). The executive function hypothesis suggests that the deficits seen with theory of mind tasks are due to underlying executive function impairment. The theory of mind tasks as well as executive functioning has been found to be impaired in children with autism.

To study the relationship between executive functions and theory of mind, Joseph and Tager-Flusberg (2004) evaluated 31 school-aged children with autism who were rated as verbally facile using tasks that included assessment of executive functions as well as theory of mind. The children had a mean age of 9 years and ranged in age from 2 years 7 months to 14 years 2 months. As well as completing the false belief tasks, all children completed tasks tapping working memory, planning, and inhibitory control. These tasks were selected since working memory tasks have been found to be very poor in children with autism (Bennetto et al., 1996) while inhibitory and working memory skills together are also implicated in autism (Hughes, 1996).

The Tower of Hanoi and Tower of London are planning tasks that have also been found to be compromised (Ozonoff & Jensen, 1999). Tower tasks require the child to move disk on three pegs to match a model given a specific number of moves. Working memory and planning skills as well as some inhibitory abilities are implicated in these tasks (Roberts & Pennington, 1996). For this sample, symptom severity was also assessed as well as cognitive and language skills. These skills are important as they are highly correlated to theory of mind performance (Yirmiya et al., 1998) as well as executive function deficits (Russell et al., 1999). Moreover, the level of language skills and cognitive ability are also highly correlated with symptom severity—those children with more severe presentations of autism also generally show lower cognitive ability and language skills (Lord & Paul, 1997).

Of the sample, 27 showed autism while 4 showed a diagnosis of ASD. Each child was administered the Differential Abilities Scale (DAS; Elliott, 1990) as well as receptive and expressive language measures. Children generally showed below-average verbal skills and low average performance abilities. Each child also completed three theory of mind tasks to evaluate knowledge and false belief attribution. Five executive function tasks were utilized measuring working memory, working memory and inhibitory control, and planning. Findings indicated that nonverbal ability and language skills were significantly related to the theory of mind performance. A strong relationship independent of cognitive and language skills was found between a combined working memory and inhibitory control task and the theory of mind task measuring false belief attribution. The authors hypothesized that working memory combined with inhibition is necessary for the child to develop a mental representation that allows for the solving of the Theory of Mind task. If the mental representation is not present, the child has significant difficulties utilizing other environmental information to arrive at an appropriate social conclusion. One area that may become problematic due to problems with processing information and inhibiting or ignoring extraneous material may be present in the development of attachment for children with autism.

Attachment and Social Understanding

Children with autism have been found to show differences in their attachment to caretakers. Approximately 40% of preschool children diagnosed with autism have been found to be securely attached (Shapiro et al., 1987). These authors also found little relationship between secure attachment and the severity of autistic symptoms. Rogers et al. (1991) found that the degree of mental retardation in the autistic child was related to attachment security with those children with moderate to severe mental retardation showing the poorest attachment. Hence, cognitive ability may be more strongly related to difficulties with attachment than a diagnosis of autism.

Joint Attention

While some may interpret secure attachment as synonymous with normal attachment, for children with autism secure attachment may not be related to "normal" attachment. Capps et al. (1994) found that 40% of their children diagnosed with autism to be securely attached who also showed significant problems in the way the attachment was expressed. Difficulties were found in how they reflected back affect from the caregiver and in how they were linked affectively to their caregiver. The primary difficulties were present in what is labeled as a failure of joint attention (Mundy et al., 1993). These are skills that are important for the child/infant to mirror affect from another person in the form of eye contact, facial expressions, and gestures.

For children without developmental disorders, joint attention becomes established in the form of eye contact by 9 months of age and for gestures and facial expressions by the age of 18 months (Gutstein & Whitney, 2002). Typically developing children have been found to engage in communication with adults that involves both asking for help as well as talking for the sake of talking. Children with autism do not engage in spontaneous talking for social acknowledgement and their communication generally centers around asking for help (Wetherby & Prutting, 1984). These findings have been obtained with preschoolers as well as preadolescent children with autism. When children with autism have been compared to typically developing children as well as those that are developmentally delayed but not autistic, the findings of problems with joint attention remain particularly when more complex behaviors are required such as following an examiner's line of gaze and an examiner's pointing to an object that is hidden (Mundy et al., 1993).

Social Communication

An additional area of interest for social competence is the difficulty children with autism have with sharing their feelings with others. Children and adolescents with autism have been found to display fewer emotional responses than typically developing children or children who are developmentally delayed (Attwood et al., 1988). It has also been found that children with autism have difficulty producing positive affect and often show higher levels of negative affect when engaged in play than children without autism (Snow et al., 1987). Of additional concern is the finding that children with autism also show affect that is less recognizable by adults, more difficult to interpret, and thus limit appropriate reactions to the child. These findings were particularly noted when the child was "socializing" with others and was most apparent when engaged in attention-sharing activities. Similarly, Dawson et al. (1990) found no difference between controls and children with autism in looking at the mother's face and the number of times the child smiled. What was different was the finding that affect sharing (coordinating smiles between the mother and child) was significantly different for the children with autism. For these dyads the smiles were not coordinated, while for typically developing children when the mother smiled, the child reciprocated.

Emotional recognition in children with autism is another area that is particularly interesting and important for social competence. Children with autism have been found to perform similarly to those with developmental delays when cognitive ability is matched on facial recognition tasks. However, the interpretation of the expression is more problematic. Children with autism have been found to differ in their relationship to events and objects when required to pay attention to how others react to these situations (Sigman et al., 1992). For children with autism events and objects are a primary focus while people are secondary. Moreover, the child does not appear to respond to another's emotions.

Children with autism have been found to be adept at identifying basic emotions of happiness, sadness, anger, and fear but to have more difficulty with more complex emotions such as embarrassment and frustration. It is hypothesized that these emotions are more verbally mediated and thus require more complex and social reasoning thus providing more of a problem for the child with autism to understand the hidden or more subtle meaning. It has been suggested that these emotions are based on how people interact as well as how they judge and evaluate themselves and others (Tangney & Fischer, 1995). Pride, shame, jealousy, guilt, etc. are emotions that are likely established by social communication and which require a referent to another's perspective and needs—something that is quite difficult for children with autism. Tangney and Fischer (1995) suggest that the basic emotions of fear, anger, sadness, and happiness may be hard-wired since they appear to be cross-cultural while the more subtle and complex emotions are not shared universally.

The Theory of Mind hypothesis may be related to difficulties that children with autism have in developing joint attention skills and emotion-sharing—activities that have been found to be problematic. Tasks that measure the autistic child's ability to take another perspective have found problems in the child's ability to decenter even up through adolescents. For example, Baron-Cohen et al. (1985) had children with autism and those without watch a child moving a marble from a basket to a box after another child (named Sally) leaves. Questions are posed such as "where will Sally look for her marble?" The children without autism as well as the children with Down's Syndrome were able to understand that she will look in the basket while the children with autism almost always reply—in the box! When children with autism are asked to predict how someone else may feel about a situation, difficulty is present that appears independent of cognitive ability (Holyrod & Baron-Cohen, 1993). Of additional concern is the finding that for children with autism there appears to be a plateauing for this skills with little improvement seen after a period of time (Ozonoff & McEvoy, 1994). These findings have also been present on measures of executive functioning and appear not to be related to mental or chronological age.

Related to these difficulties with theory of mind and executive functions are difficulties with the ability to form a mental model of appropriate social behaviors. These types of behaviors require one to behave and think flexibly in order to understand another person's beliefs and thoughts. Since appropriate social interaction requires changing schemas and mental representations, children with autism are at a distinct disadvantage. It has been hypothesized that because they have an impairment in this area, they fall back on skills that are more elementary and are safer (i.e., their thoughts and feelings) rather than attempting to interpret ambiguous stimuli (Ozonoff et al., 1991).

These hypotheses have been somewhat substantiated from a study utilizing eye-tracking (Klin et al., 2002). A male with autism and above-average cognitive ability and an age- and gender-matched male were compared watching film clips. Differences were present between the two viewers in that the normal male viewed the eye gaze of the actors while the viewer with autism centered on the mouth of the actor even when the clip was silent in voice. This finding is consistent with previous research that indicated problems with reading eye expressions and more emphasis on mouths in children with ASD (Baron-Cohen et al., 1997).

These difficulties likely lead to problems in interpreting social situations. The child with autism has difficulty understanding and/or processing information particularly when a response to a complex situation is required. The ability to utilize working memory to form a mental representation of a social situation is important to understand social dynamics particularly when processing information that is either ambiguous or requires complex understanding. Children and adolescents with autism frequently interpret social situations literally or based on their own internal beliefs, and as such are often incorrect in their encoding of the social situations.

In addition to the difficulty with interpretation, social interactions often utilize movement and objects. Klin et al. (2002) suggest that people with autism may be drawn to the objects and ignore the facial and body gestures that are present. This situation may easily happen when there are more objects available. The findings of Klin et al. (2002) have indicated that people with autism are more sensitive to movement as well as objects and that they may well totally ignore changes in facial expressions when distracted by these extraneous items that most people ignore in order to focus on the more important aspect of the interaction—emotional expression.

The social difficulties found in children with ASD do not translate into more emotional and behavioral difficulties compared to other children with psychiatric disorders (Fombonne et al., 2001). In contrast, however, children with ASD, by definition, have more social difficulties than those with other psychiatric disorders. These social problems frequently translate into family stress and parental sadness (Konstantareas & Homatidis, 1991). How the family copes with this diagnosis is an important aspect for the adjustment of the child.

Family Issues in Autism

With all of the difficulties present in emotional understanding in autism, problems for the family in adapting to the challenges of autism have been documented. Given that the social difficulties are the most pronounced for this population, many parents may feel overwhelmed by the child's needs. This feeling may begin with the assessment for autism. The assessment often requires the parent to evaluate the child's functioning and the parent may feel that he/she is not a "good" parent. The assessment focuses on the tasks that the child cannot perform and thus can also be quite painful for the parent to experience. However, the feedback from the assessment is a therapeutic chance for the parent to find out what the child can do as well as what he/she cannot. Moreover, with the advent of recent treatments, early identification appears to lead to a much better outcome than had been previously believed possible.

It is important, then, for the parent and family to become an important member in the treatment of the child. Murphy et al. (2000) studied the personality styles of families of children with autism. Relatives of children with autism were found to show a higher tendency to be withdrawn or more anxious than those of children with Down's syndrome or of typically developing children. Related to this finding was the additional finding that the stress of coping with a child with autism's behavioral difficulties was not related to the level of withdrawal. The authors conclude that a genetic disposition toward autism may be present in these families and while a full expression of autism may not be present, the underlying tendency is expressed. Thus, families may have siblings or partners that have "autistic-like" tendencies that further complicate adjustment.

Autism is one of the two most common disorders in ASD. The other common disorder is Asperger's Syndrome (AS). Although there is some controversy whether AS belongs with autistic spectrum disorders, it has been placed there in DSM IV and is a relatively new diagnostic category. The following section seeks to discuss aspects of AS including diagnostic issues, neurobiological aspects, and the behavioral expression of this syndrome.

Asperger's Syndrome

Asperger's syndrome (AS) is a disorder that is not well characterized in the literature. AS has been defined as difficulty with social relationships that includes problems with nonverbal behaviors (eye contact, facial expression, and body gestures), difficulty sustaining peer relationship, and problems with social reciprocity. In addition, children with AS often show stereotyped behaviors and interests and may be inflexible in their adherence to routines. Often children with AS show problems with understanding another person's feelings and mood state, have poor eye contact, and are not aware of excursions into someone else's private space (Attwood, 1998).

Many children with autism are quite sensitive to sounds and tactile sensations (Rimland, 1990). This sensory sensitivity has also been found in children with AS with approximately 40% showing such sensitivity (Attwood, 1998). Sound can be particularly obnoxious for children with AS with sudden and unexpected noises being experienced very negatively. High-pitched continuous noises are also painful for some children with AS as are confusing and complex noises as experienced in a large crowd gathering or a closed-in large space (mall, gymnasium) (Attwood, 1998). One child I worked with was so very sensitive to loud noises that he had anxiety attacks when the routine fire alarm drills were set for his elementary school. The first time the drill occurred he screamed for hours as though he was in a great deal of pain. We needed only one more incident for us to understand what was happening and he was conveniently away from the school when fire drills were scheduled. These events were traumatic for him as well as his parents and peers until we found out what was occurring. This situation occurred prior to the existence of the diagnostic category of AS but I'm sure that would be the appropriate diagnosis now. He was classified with atypical autism at the time.

Tactile sensations can also be problematic for a child with AS. One child I worked with needed all tags taken out of his clothing and his clothing washed several times with large amounts of softener before he could tolerate wearing the clothes. When his clothes wore out or he outgrew them, the process of reacclimating him to the clothes was extremely difficult and his parents learned to have the next size up ready for him prior to his needing them.

Exclusionary criteria for AS include no general significant delay in language or cognitive development and not being previously diagnosed with autism or PDD. The prevalence of AS is estimated to be about 7.1 per 1,000 children. (Ehlers & Gilberg, 2003). Originally it was believed that AS was a disorder of males but continuing research has identified the disorders in both genders with a male to female ratio of 2.3:1.

Diagnostic Issues in AS

Definitions vary between studies and Volkmar et al. (2004) report seven different definitions of AS. Miller and Ozonoff (1997) reviewed studies and found that DSM IV (APA, 1994) and ICD-10 (World Health Organization, 1993) criteria are sufficiently vague that they do not result in a reliable diagnosis of Asperger's Disorder. Controversies as to whether AS is a milder form of autism or similar to high functioning autism (HFA) continues in the field. The exclusionary criteria of a history of language delay are being challenged currently as well as the presence or absence of mental retardation (Eisenmajer et al., 1996; Szatmari, et al., 2003). There is emerging evidence that differences between AS and HFA may lie in outcome (Szatmari et al., 2003), presence of other psychiatric disorders (Volkmar et al., 2004), neuropsychological functioning (Lincoln et al., 1998), and possibly genetics (Volkmar et al., 1998).

Volkmar et al. (2004) strongly suggests that these definitional problems need to be resolved before empirical findings can be translated to clinical use and that differentiation of AS from PDD-NOS and from autism are critical determinations for which a consensus has not been arrived. Volkmar et al. (2004) suggests that AS at times becomes a fall-back diagnosis when a child doesn't meet criteria for autism. When compared to PDD-NOS or autism, children with AS are diagnosed later and generally around the age of 47.5 months. Some children may not be identified until elementary school.

Differentiating AS from HFA can be challenging at best. Ehlers et al. (1997) suggest that HFA and AS are part of the autistic continuum due to the overlap of symptoms while others believe the two disorders are distinct and have different neurological underpinnings (Baron-Cohen et al., 1997, 1999). Williams (1995) suggests that differences in cognitive ability and language development as well as a higher level of social responsiveness may be the most clearly delineating features between the two disorders.

Neuropsychological differences have also been found between AS and HFA. Children with AS show higher scores on measures of adaptive functioning particularly in the areas of socialization, communication, and daily living skills compared to those with HFA (Szatmari et al., 1995).

Ozonoff et al. (1991) compared HFA and AS and found that children with HFA showed deficits on tasks involving perspective taking and verbal memory while children with AS did not. Children with AS often do show gross motor deficits—a finding not common in children with HFA (Klin & Volkmar, 1997).

There are also similarities between AS and NVLD. In both disorders, problems with social communication and reciprocity are present. Moreover, Klin et al. (1995) found similar neuropsychological impairments in AS and NVLD. For example, children with AS or NVLD show stronger verbal than performance skills (Gillberg, 1991; Klin et al., 1995) while those with HFA have stronger performance than verbal abilities (Klin et al., 1995). Klin et al. (1995) found children with AS showed age appropriate levels of verbal output, vocabulary, articulation, and verbal memory.

Gunter et al. (2002) compared the functioning of children with AS to determine whether strengths and weaknesses found were consistent with those previously found in children with NVLD. Eight participants with AS were identified as well as eight control subjects. Participants were matched on verbal IQ and age. No difference in verbal ability or age was present between the two groups. Mean age was 16.5 years and the mean verbal IQ was 117.4.

Participants with AS were found to show difficulties with nonverbal communication and pragmatic language particularly in humor appreciation. Moreover, significant deficits were found in visual-spatial skills which are consistent with previous findings of problems in this area in participants diagnosed with NVLD (Voeller, 1986). Difficulties were not found on measures of visual-motor integration, fine motor coordination, or for the ability to combine parts to make a whole figure.

These findings were not consistent with predictions based on the NVLD model—that is, participants with AS did not show the visual-spatial or bilateral motor deficits predicted by Rourke (1995) for a diagnosis of NVLD. Thus, the authors suggest that AS may not be one size fits all for diagnosis and that there may be subtypes of AS just as there are subtypes of LD and ADHD. Further study is certainly needed to understand this perplexing disorder. However, children with NVLD and AS share a common problem with social understanding and reciprocity that is very problematic for their adaptation to the world and success as adults.

Szatmari (1992) suggests that AS is not on the autistic continuum due to the higher level of social responsivity present in AS. Klin and Volkmar (1995) suggest that it is not possible with the level of our understanding of these disorders to make a judgment as to whether AS is or is not on the autistic spectrum. They suggest that more research is needed to validate the diagnosis of AS as well as to arrive at a consensus as to the diagnostic characteristics of AS. This suggestion could also be made for the diagnosis of NVLD. It is interesting that these two disorders share many similarities and may also share some similarities as to the underlying neurological substrates involved.

Neurobiological Underpinings in AS

Some researchers suggest that NVLD is a right hemisphere disorder (Semrud-Clikeman & Hynd, 1990; Voeller, 1995) and others make the same suggestion for AS (Gunter et al., 2002) while others suggest autism is a left hemispheric disorder (Green et al., 1995; Klin et al., 1995; Rumsey, 1992). It has been suggested that NVLD is due to problems with the white matter in the right hemisphere that in turn causes difficulty in the processing of complex and novel material. These same difficulties have been identified in AS.

McKelvey et al. (1995) studied patients with AS and found through imaging that all the patients had abnormal right hemispheric functioning. Described in a case study, Volkmar et al. (1996) found that the adolescent male had cerebral abnormalities in the right hemisphere that were more prominent than those in the left. Consistent with these findings, Berthier et al. (1993) studied seven children with AS and Tourette's Syndrome using quantitative measures of MRI scans. Findings were of right hemispheric abnormalities that were consistent with a neurological study of left-sided motoric and sensory impairments (Berthier et al., 1990).

Findings have also been reported of differences in the corpus callosum in participants with AS. The corpus callosum is a large band of myelinated (white matter) fibers that connect the two hemispheres and allow the hemispheres to talk to each other. Berthier (1994) found structural cortical white matter abnormalities in 53% of the patients with AS with thinning in the posterior region of the corpus callosum. Similarly, Lincoln et al. (1998) found a larger anterior corpus callosum. Thinning of the fibers in the posterior corpus callosum may be related to the difficulties patients with AS show in tying together novel information that is visual spatial in nature. To compensate for such difficulties it may be that the frontal lobes (or where the anterior corpus callosum connects) struggle to decipher this visual-spatial material through the over-reliance on verbal instruction. Further study is needed to determine the relationship between neurological differences and behavioral manifestations of AS.

Social Functioning in AS

Children with AS have been described as socially clumsy but socially assertive (Kerbeshian et al., 1990) and that they are excessively talkative and preoccupied with circumscribed topics (McLaughlin-Cheng, 1998). Language is generally well developed in children with AS but the rhythm and inflection is often poor or unusual. Moreover, language comprehension is generally good except when asked to complete tasks that are inferential in nature (Green, 1990).

Children with HFA do not approach other children as readily as do those with AS. Children with AS will become immersed in a play activity and resent being interrupted by other children who seek to be social. When thus interrupted the child with AS may become overly assertive and aggressive and thus push away these interactions. On the other hand if the peer is willing to acquiesce to all of the child with AS's requirements, then the peer is allowed to join the play (Attwood, 1998). Thus, the inflexibility often seen in their cognitive reasoning ability translates into rigid play patterns and serves to further isolate children with AS. Unfortunately, the child with AS has little insight into why this isolation occurs.

While the child with AS's symbolic play is stilted and unusual it does exist while for the child with HFA no symbolic play is present. As far as attachment, children with AS appear to show more responsivity to care-takers and peers than those with HFA. The frequency of these interactions is more evident although the quality is poor for both populations.

The child with AS also has difficulties with perspective taking that cause difficulty with his/her understanding of the rules of social conduct. Due to this lack of awareness, the child with AS will annoy and aggra-vate other children. When taught appropriate social manners and rules of conduct, the child with AS will apply those rules without regard to the situation or context and be very rigid in this application. Moreover, the child will often point out social "faux pas" on the part of his/her peers thus alienating other children even more. Peers and adults describe these children as rude and insensitive when, in fact, the chil-dren are unable to inhibit these responses and do not perceive the hurt or embarrassment their remarks cause the other person. They are truly "socially clumsy."

An important study by Church et al. (2000) studied children with AS retrospectively to determine what the social experience of these children was growing up. Forty children were identified consisting of 39 boys and 1 girl. These children were interviewed over time. The mean age of diag-nosis was 7.9 years of age. Each child had a comprehensive psychoedu-cational evaluation with an initial mean IQ of 107 and a mean IQ of 123 when retested 12–24 months later. The Vineland showed significant deficits in adaptive behavior relative to age and ability. Of the sample, 67% had auditory sensitivities, 62% tactile, and 73% had motor difficulty. Although the children with AS had social difficulties as preschoolers that were reported by their caregivers, these difficulties were not sufficiently significant for a referral for evaluation.

Most parents indicated their concerns for their child began about the age of 3.5 years. Identified problems were listed in social interactions, play skills, and problems with sensory integration. In contrast, the preschoolers were described as relating well to their parents and teach-ers. Problems were identified in separating from parents and four of the children had significant separation problems when beginning kinder-garten. The majority of the children with AS were described by their teachers as inappropriately silly, loud, aggressive, or withdrawn. The children were also reported to show a lack of spontaneity and a ten-dency to have a flat affect. Moreover, the preschoolers showed a need for routine and had specific things that they did over and over. When these rituals or routines were disrupted, the child reacted very poorly and had severe tantrums.

Transitions were particularly problematic and a great deal of prepara-tion was needed for these occurrences. Some stereotyped behaviors were noted including hand flapping and spinning—behaviors that served to set these children even further apart from their peers. Many of the children with AS had collections of items and enjoyed lining them up or placing them just so—they often did not play with these objects in any creative manner.

By the time these children entered elementary school, serious developmental problems were recognized. Over 90% of the children had been classified with other diagnoses prior to the diagnosis of AS. The most frequent diagnosis was ADHD, followed by autism and learning disabilities. Social skills became particularly problematic for children with AS and none of the children had close and intimate friendships. Few of the children were invited to other children's parties or in turn invited other children over to their house to play. Parents supported their children by teaching them "social" conversations and the children frequently used these scripts but not very effectively. Difficulties were noted in the child's ability to read facial expressions and gestures as well as problems with socially inappropriate behaviors. Two types were identified. The first was quiet, timid, and shy and the other was a child who was loud, active, and who violated personal boundaries. Patterns of negative interactions with peers increased during this time and the children were often ostracized or isolated.

The children continued to have a need for routines and support throughout their development. Stereotyped behaviors diminished during this period of time except when the child became quite anxious. Replacing these behaviors for many of the children was a tendency to obsess with certain objects or events leading to a preoccupation with certain themes or details. Playing games with other children was particularly problematic for the children with AS as they attempted to enforce all rules literally without any attention to the environmental context.

These children showed age-appropriate language abilities in preschool. By elementary school, difficulties were present in pragmatic language abilities and almost 96% of the children were reported to be receiving speech and language services. The children were described as having "cocktail" speech—speech that is voluminous but basically is about nothing. Long monologues about areas of their interest without regard to the listener were frequent at this age. The speech was often either too loud or soft and the children continued to have difficulty with modulating their sensory input.

Motor clumsiness became more noticeable and the children were seen as very clumsy and to have an unusual walk. Descriptions of parents and teachers indicated that many of the children had problems with boundaries—both physical and social. Participation in playground or after-school activities became more difficult and many of the children with AS preferred solitary activities such as watching TV, playing video games, or working with the computer.

Academically 56% of the children with AS were found to require some form of special education with a majority of children requiring occupational therapy and a third requiring physical therapy. Less than a fourth of the children were receiving any social skills support. Basic reading skills were found to be at or above grade level for the majority of children with significant difficulties present in reading comprehension. Handwriting was described as particularly problematic. Most children with AS had excellent computer and mathematics skills and these areas were seen as strengths for them.

Adolescence

By middle school the children with AS show more difficulties with behavior, particularly with oppositional behavior, and 46% were working with a therapist—either individual or family. Although the children had made one friend, the friendship was described as superficial and subject to change. Many of these "best friends" were 2–3 years younger than the child with AS and the friendships were formed surrounding a mutual interest. Play continued to be rigidly based on rules and the child with AS may abandon the friendship when the rules were not followed to his or her satisfaction.

Parents and teachers recognized difficulties with the child's ability to understand emotions—particularly ones that varied in intensity. These children often enjoyed silly comedy and slapstick but could not appreciate more subtle forms of humor or sarcasm. The children with AS continued to stand out from their peers through their unusual behaviors that included humming, drumming, awkward body posture and walking, poor eye contact, or "odd" behaviors. Routines and rituals continued to be important and often the child restricted his eating choices to a few foods. One child I worked closely with would only eat peanut butter and jelly for *all* meals. He could not tolerate any shift in food choices—trips to restaurants became quite difficult so that his mother brought his food in with them to prevent a meltdown in front of the other diners.

Academic skills varied depending on the child with some participating in gifted classes and others requiring support particularly for reading comprehension. Over three-fourths of the middle school children participated in social skills interventions. Unfortunately, most of these children had significant difficulty applying the knowledge to the fluid social scene in most middle schools. Most children at this age became unmotivated to complete homework that was not of interest to them or to continue to participate in social interactions or extracurricular activities.

By high school, the five adolescents with AS identified showed continued significant problems socially. Many were described as oppositional and defiant. On the positive side, all had made at least one friend of the same age and gender with the friendship based on common interests. All were interested in girls but were unable to approach the girls appropriately. Particular difficulties were found in these relationships as two boys became obsessed by a particular girl and almost stalked the girl. Others inappropriately touched or talked to the girls. The high school boys continued to prefer solitary activities and parents began to have more and more difficulty including these adolescents in family activities.

Rigidity, inflexibility, and strict adherence to routines continued into the high school years. Continued problems were noted in obsessive-compulsive behaviors. Four of the five boys were placed on medication to assist with these difficulties. Academically the boys had more problems with behavior than with learning. All of the boys used a computer for writing due to continued problems with handwriting. Continued problems were present in engaging in reciprocal conversations and the boys tended to be hyperverbal and given to monologues.

In summary, this study summarizes very well the challenges of a child with AS through preschool to high school. Consistent problems are present with pragmatic language, inferential thinking, social reciprocity, and obsessive-compulsive types of behavior. Peer relationship problems continued to dominate the child and adolescent's life, and although basic skills were learned, the fluidity and ability to think on one's feet never developed for these participants. Sensory issues continued to be problematic throughout the child's experience. Increased incidences of sadness and anxiety developed by middle school and continued through high school. At times the children became quite belligerent and oppositional and problems with motivation was certainly identified.

The authors concluded that the course of this disorder does not substantially change over development and that current methods of intervention are only slightly helpful. They also identified differences between children with AS and those with HFA as the children in this study were more motivated to form friendships, were brighter, and had much better verbal abilities than those with HFA. Moreover, their visual-spatial skills were identified to be much poorer than those children with HFA. An important aspect of this research is the finding that children and adolescents with AS appear *normal* and as such may not be tolerated as readily compared to those who have more obvious disabilities.

Given the findings for children with AS and autism, interventions may be particularly problematic. Similar to findings with ADHD, LD, and NVLD, typical social skills programs do not appear to assist with the development of social competence for children with ASD. The following section reviews programs that are available—most of which are experimental.

Social Competence Interventions

The development of social competence interventions for autistic disorders has been challenging. The most frequently studied treatment for autism is a behavioral treatment based on applied behavioral analysis (ABA) (Smith et al., 2000b). An empirical study to show the efficacy of this approach was conducted with two groups of 15 children. One group received ABA treatment 24 hours per week for a year and the other group received 3–9 months of parent training. Although the treatment group showed greater gains than the controls, the gains were not as significant as had been expected from the previous work of Lovaas (1987). Children with PDD-NOS and those with higher IQs made the most progress. Additional studies have shown improvement with individualized behavioral treatment (Eikeseth et al., 2002) or parent training (Drew et al., 2002).

Behavioral treatment has by far the most support, although improvement has not been as good as previously was predicted from initial studies (Mudford et al., 2001; Smith et al., 2000a). Improvements have been found in behaviors but findings indicate that the children require support to continue utilizing appropriate behaviors and that no gains in IQ have been found (Bibby et al., 2001). Although parent satisfaction is generally good with ABA and other behavioral treatments, gains are not significant when the children are followed 2–3 years later (Volkmar et al., 2004).

Additional approaches have utilized the use of social stories and written cues (Thiemann & Goldstein, 2001), incidental teaching, and the TEACCH program (Treatment and Education of Children and Adults with Communication Handicaps; McGee et al., 1999; Ozonoff & Cathcart, 1998). From the voluminous research being published in this area in the past decade, researchers and clinicians have strongly suggested that no one single approach is appropriate for each child with ASD and that the use of programs needs to be tailored to the individual child's needs (NRC, 2001). Volkmar et al. (2004) strongly suggests that approaches be combined that support the child's acquisition of basic skills as well as allowing for the child to develop more complex social skills and social reciprocity. Additional study indicates that the child needs to be motivated to participate in the programs and that the programs need to be tailored to family needs (Moes, 1998; Lord & McGee, 2001). Of importance is the child's ability to generalize basic skills to changing circumstances and empirical findings indicate that such generalization needs to be directly taught in order to occur (Hwang & Hughes, 2000; Strain & Hoyson, 2000). Teaching individual skills such as joint attention and social communication skills has led to improvements in social skills following a social skills program (Drew et al., 2002; Whalen & Schreibman, 2003).

In a review of ten studies of the efficacy of communication intervention, Delprato (2001) found that teaching social communication was most successful when it was directly related to everyday situations and possible communications. Similarly when language is tied to an intrinsic interest the child has, improvement has also been found in language and this improvement appears to be long-lasting (Siller & Sigman, 2002). An additional finding has been that the number of hours of treatment (more is better) and the skill of the therapist also appears to be crucial variables predictive of success (Volkmar et al., 2004).

Work with social skills appears to be most fundamental beginning in elementary school and continuing through adolescence and even for some into adulthood. Programs that utilized peer groups, classroom milieu, as well as social stories and directly teaching problem-solving strategies have been found to be helpful particularly when generalization is built into the programs (Strain & Schwartz, 2001; Weiss & Harris, 2001; Wolfberg & Schuler, 1999). It has been found important to continue to support skill development within the natural setting and to provide this support in all areas of the child's life (Strain & Hoyson, 2000).

Gutstein & Whitney (2002) suggest that interventions need to include specific occasions for the child to learn social skills that are apart from the traditionally scripted approaches most commonly seen with social skills programs. They suggest that to be effective intervention programs need to incorporate tasks that directly teach social referencing and interactions that are taught in a developmentally appropriate sequence guided by adults. Initially the interventions need to be ritualistic and predictable with inconsistency and novelty kept to a minimum. As the child learns these skills, more complexity and novelty is introduced and assist the child in generalization. The intervention needs to be in a quiet and distraction-free environment where the child feels safe. It is important to restrict the sensory input so that the child does not become overwhelmed. Actions, emotions, intonations, and gestures need to be overdone and amplified so that the child learns what is important. Emotions and environmental input that is subtle may be too difficult for the child to process and is most likely to be ignored. Finally the adult coaches need to move the child to a peer coach as readiness is perceived. The use of these techniques can assist the child in developing the abilities that are needed but more importantly to generalize the skills to the more dynamic nature seen in most social exchanges.

Due to the difficult nature of intervention studies, most empirical evidence comes from case studies or small groups. Further study is necessary to determine the parameters for the success for many of the interventions as well as to move much of the work into public schools. There are programs that are developing and that are promising for working with children with ASD. One approach, SCIP, was described earlier in the chapter on NVLD and won't be repeated here. It has been found to be successful with NVLD as well as with AS. It hasn't been tested on children with HFA or those diagnosed with PDD-NOS.

Carter et al. (2004) piloted a Friendship Club approach to AS to assist children in developing positive social interaction skills. The model was based on the Lifestyle Performance Model (Veld & Fidler, 2002) that combines commonly experienced activities of life to support learning adaptive behaviors. The club met for 5 consecutive weeks for 90 minutes. Activities were selected based on parent and child interviews that allowed for pinpointing of specific skills that each felt needed to be developed. Topics included how to learn about someone else, how to start a conversation, how to know if you have a friend, how to participate in parties, how to maintain a friendship, and how to develop trust. Findings from this very short intervention indicated improvement in participation during the meetings and increased social interaction. Unfortunately it was not clear from the study whether these gains were significant and whether they carried over into the regular classroom environment. While promising, the study was very short and did not provide statistical analysis of the findings or qualitative analysis. The reports were generally from exit interviews and were likely somewhat influenced by a "halo" effect.

Corbett (2003) has developed a video modeling intervention that appears to be very promising. Video modeling is based on Bandura's (1977), social learning theory that emphasizes the ability to learn new behaviors through observing a model engaging in a behavior the child would like to emulate. Four processes are involved in observational learning: attention, remembering what has been seen, producing the behavior, and responding to reinforcement. Video modeling involves the child watching a videotape of a desirable model producing a behavior. The behavior is then imitated and practiced with a therapist. The behaviors are additionally practiced and reinforced over time.

Corbett (2003) studied the efficacy of video modeling on social skill acquisition using a single case study design. The child was 8 years 3 months old and was diagnosed with autism. His IQ was measured at 60 with adaptive behavior being significantly lower at 37. The child watched the videotape showing expressions denoting happiness, sadness, anger, or fear. The videotape was shown for 10–15 minutes daily for two weeks. The child quickly mastered identification of the happy face with improvement seen in the other categories over the treatment duration. Certainly this study shows promise and replication and follow-up of the length of these gains is needed.

Social stories have also been used fairly successfully with children with ASD. In social stories the child is given a social situation that he or she describes and includes what the child should do and what the feelings are. The child is asked for his or her interpretation. Gray and Garand (1993) use four types of sentences for the social stories. The descriptive sentence describes where the situation is occurring and who the main character is. The perspective sentences describe the reactions of others and the feelings that the characters have. The directive sentences provide information about what the child is expected to do or say. Finally, the control sentence is generally written by the child to solve the situation. Most stories have 0–1 control and/or directive sentences for every 2–5 descriptive and perspective sentences. For those children who cannot read, the stories can be read to them and discussed as the therapist reads the story.

An example of a social story would be the following:

John rides the school bus to school every day (descriptive). He sits in the front seat next to the bus driver (descriptive). The ride takes about 20 minutes to get to John's school (descriptive). He knows that he can ask the bus driver for help if he needs it (perspective). John also knows that he can't always have the same seat on the bus if someone gets on before him (perspective). He can ask the other child if he can sit on the seat (descriptive). He is afraid to ask the child to move over (perspective). John asks the child and sits next to her (perspective). Buses have large seats (control). His mother will be proud that he solved his problem (perspective).

Social stories can help the child to solve a current problem or to resolve an issue that is troublesome to him/her. They can also be tailored to fit the child's particular interests to keep the story relevant to him/her. As with other interventions, this intervention appears promising but empirical support has not been developed at this time.

Summary and Conclusions

For children with autistic spectrum disorders, social competence is by definition a very difficult task to accomplish. Research has burgeoned in the past 10 years even as the identification of children with ASD has found an increased prevalence. As researchers and educators become clearer in the diagnosis of these disorders, it is hoped that improvements in the interventions will also be forthcoming. Currently there is a great deal of confusion as to the overlap between AS, HFA, and NVLD. It is likely that AS and NVLD are close cousins while HFA is more similar to autism and possibly less amenable to change in social understanding. Emerging evidence of a right hemispheric contribution to AS is intriguing. However, it is likely that it is not as simple as one hemisphere versus another. It is very possible that there is also frontal lobe involvement given the rigidity and difficulty with problem-solving that is seen with children and adolescents with ASD.

Of great concern is the toll that these disorders take on children as well as their families. These difficulties appear to be life-long with adults showing significant problems with unemployment or underemployment, social isolation, and problems with living independently (Venter et al., 1992). Interventions for families are an area that has not been well-researched and which needs further exploration. Studies have shown a tendency for subtle social and communication problems in relatives of people identified as autistic. These tendencies likely translate into problems with relationships but also increased stress in the home.

While there is support for interventions utilizing behavioral reinforcement, the generalization of these interventions to more complex and novel social situations is by no means documented. More and more interventions are showing promise but the one ingredient that appears to be consistent among these interventions is the necessity of intense intervention that begins when the child is quite young. Providing support for children in elementary, middle, and high school levels is also important. Some of the studies cited above indicate that many of the children did not have specific social interventions specified in their individual educational plans even though goals were stated. These interventions were not generally present until the child was in middle school—that is way too late and many children begin to feel sad, anxious, and unmotivated to change. While children with ASD may never be social butterflies, it is important that they be provided with sufficient interventions to develop appropriate understanding of the social world around them and to participate in it as they chose.

It is an exciting time in our understanding of ASD. With the advent of technology we begin to understand more readily these disorders. Hopefully our understanding will also allow us to develop appropriate interventions as well as to provide support both for the family and for school personnel.

8

Social Competence in Mentally Handicapped Children

Todd, a 12-year-old child with mild/moderate mental retardation, was referred for therapy to assist him with making friends. He had been in special education programs since the age of 2 and was currently mainstreamed into a 5th grade classroom. Although he was very friendly and smiled frequently, he had made few friends in his mainstream classroom and was older than most of the children in his special education program. His social skills were more similar to that of a 7-year-old child. This discrepancy between his chronological and social age was a hardship when attempting to make friends. Todd was still interested in the comic book figures of Bugs Bunny and Goofy and not as interested in the action figures and superheroes popular with his same-aged classmates. Although he was very friendly to his peers, Todd's behaviors are also younger than his age. When he attempted to play with the boys in his regular education class, Todd had difficulty because his gross motor skills are below average and he had problems playing soccer and four-square. His parents are very involved in helping Todd but at this point did not know what else to try. His one good friend who was in his special education classroom recently moved away and Todd's demeanor now is either sad or withdrawn.

Interventions with Todd were semi-successful. Willing peers were recruited from his classroom and volunteered to play with him first in a small group setting and then during recess. Basic gross motor skills were practiced with his father and brother including tossing and kicking a ball and taking turns. These skills were helpful in getting Todd into some of the playground games. In addition, working on conversational skills was a project the speech and language therapist agreed to begin working on. Family support was provided through the local Association of Retarded Citizens and Todd was linked with a play group from that organization of children his own age. The challenges faced by Todd are not dissimilar to those faced by many children with mental handicaps. As the child with a mental handicap ages, the problems may intensify as the discrepancy between the child's skills and his/her chronological age appear to be more substantial.

Diagnosis

Mentally handicapped children have been historically diagnosed through the use of individual measures of intelligence and adaptive behavior. The nosology has changed from mental retardation to mental handicap with some now utilizing the term "intellectual disability." The common issue for children with mental handicaps is that their abilities are in the significantly below average range with concurrent difficulties in adaptive skills in the following areas of communication: self-care, social, and community (AAMR, 2002). These difficulties must arise before the age of 18. General definitions require that the intelligence quotient be at least 2 standard deviations from average or a score of 70 and below. Some have agreed to use IQs as high as 75, a practice that has been criticized as including more people than should be diagnosed with mental handicaps (Sattler, 2003).

DSM IV-TR (APA, 2000) provides four levels of severity. Children with mild mental retardation are those with an IQ level of 50–55 to approximately 70. Those with moderate mental retardation have levels of 35–40 to 50–55; with severe 20–25 to 35–40 and finally with profound an IQ level below 20 or 25. Both the AAMR and DSM IV-TR have IQ levels as defined above as well as commensurate adaptive behavior levels for a diagnosis.

Demographics

Mental handicaps may occur as a primary diagnosis with no known cause, as part of a syndrome (i.e., chromosomal disorder, fetal alcohol syndrome, metabolic disorders), as part of another developmental disorder such as autism, or co-occurring with a neurological disorder such as epilepsy or cerebral palsy. Some children may be born with average developmental characteristics and fall ill with meningitis or other infections and toxins or have a traumatic brain injury and become mentally handicapped.

Many children with mental handicaps also have physical disabilities that can range from mild to significant. Fairly often children will require assistance from physical therapists and occupational therapists to improve gross and fine motor skills. Adaptive skills such as buttoning, tying shoes, and zipping are initial tasks that need to be mastered followed by eye–hand coordination needed for copying and writing. For gross motor skills the child often has difficulty with leg coordination and needs additional treatment to develop walking skills as well as those skills often associated with childhood such as skipping, riding a bicycle, and playing group games.

Most children with mental handicaps have concomitant difficulties with speech and language. For the most severely affected children, difficulties with articulation can significantly hamper social interaction while language comprehension can also be a difficult hurdle in attempting conversations. While for many children with mild handicaps language problems will not be as significantly impacted, understanding commonly accepted interests at specific ages will be an area of difficulty for relating to other children. In addition, these children may have interests that are much younger than their age. For example, one young girl of 12 years of age had an overwhelming interest in doll play which was incongruent with the interests of other 12-year-olds in boys and fashion. She was tolerated by her same-aged peers but not accepted. She preferred to play with 6-year-old girls who were nearer to her mental age and shared her interests.

The incidence of mental handicap is about 1% in the general population with 85% classified within the mild range of mental handicaps, 10% in the moderate range, 3–4% in the severe range, and 1–2% in the profound range (Sattler, 2003). There is not a significant gender difference in incidence. Cultural and ethnic differences are not found to be significant predictors of mental handicaps. However, a thorough assessment is needed to determine whether lack of experience or cultural differences account for mental delays rather than a true mental handicap.

Social Functioning in Children with Mental Handicaps

Each of the levels of mental handicap has corresponding developmental issues that reflect on social functioning. The following section will discuss the challenges faced by individuals in the various levels with an emphasis on mild retardation. The emphasis of this chapter is on the social development and possible intervention techniques. As such each area will be discussed with information also provided over the lifespan.

Mild Mental Handicap

In the early developmental ages the child begins to develop social skills such as eye gaze, smiling in response to a smile or interaction, and social communication abilities. At this age the child may show mild delays in language and motor skills but not appear significantly different from children his/her age. By the age of 6 years the child's academic progress and language skills will be significantly below average for his/her age. Social skills continue to develop very slowly although the child is very interested in other children and adults and will attempt to interact with various people. Difficulty may be present in the child's tendency to interact in a familiar manner with strangers and not appreciate the difference between known children and adults and strangers.

In middle school the child's attainment of academic skills slows significantly and most achieve a sixth-grade level overall. High school subjects are mostly beyond the reach of many of these children and special education is a necessary piece of their education. For many children with mild mental handicaps a transitional plan for beyond high school includes work-related experience to assist in determining appropriate vocational needs.

Moderate Mental Handicap

A child with a moderate mental handicap has difficulty with speech and language development as well as poor social awareness. In early development, children at this level need support for gross motor skills but generally master walking and running as well as fine motor tasks. These children require more supervision as they do not readily understand dangers or utilize common sense. In school they can generally learn functional academic skills to the fourth grade by late high school.

In late adolescence and early adulthood, they can manage self-help and independence as well as work at a semi-skilled occupation. When under stress their behaviors may regress and additional support is frequently necessary. Socially these individuals generally relate well to peers at younger ages or with similar handicaps.

Severe and Profound Mental Handicaps

For individuals with severe and profound mental handicaps motor development is generally very poor and they have minimal speech and language skills. In addition, self-help skills are very poorly if at all developed and in most cases nursing care is necessary. As the child with a severe handicap ages some speech and language abilities are developed as well as elementary self-care skills. Functional academic skills are not readily developed for either of these groups as for the children with profound handicaps total care is generally required. As the child with a severe handicap matures, he/she can be trained to participate vocationally with close supervision and can work in a controlled environment. The child with a profound mental handicap generally is incapable of self-maintenance and needs complete care and supervision. In both cases social skills are significantly impaired and relationships are generally with adults in a caretaker role.

Assessment of Social Functioning

Assessment of social functioning in children with mental retardation is a challenge as many of these children have delays in all areas of social functioning. Particular challenges are present in children with moderate to severe cognitive delays and often include problems with social deficits as well as excesses (hugging and talking with complete strangers in a very familiar manner) (Duncan et al., 1999). There is also a substantial overlap between autism and mental retardation with children with multiple handicaps showing the most impaired social competence as well as presenting the largest challenge for assessment and intervention (Bielecki & Swender, 2004). Studies have found that as the psychopathology increases in children with mental retardation, the social skills decrease significantly and negative social behaviors are more present (Matson, Smiroldo, & Bamburg, 1998; Njardvik et al., 1999). These social impairments are also correlated with aggression and self-injurious behaviors that further complicate the assessment picture (Duncan et al., 1999).

One of the challenges to assessment of social skills in children with mental retardation is the inability to provide a useful self-report. Most rating scales for social skill assessment utilize a parent, teacher, and child report. These rating scales are also not normed generally on children with mental delays. Thus, it is recommended that an assessment of social functioning is better conducted using observational methods as well as checklists and playing with the child (Zigler & Burack, 1989). The use of observations of the child in his/her general setting allows the opportunity to evaluate the child's performance and to provide information about how to assist the child with generalizing his/her skills to other situations.

Role-playing helps the child practice skills in a safe environment as well as providing the therapist with an idea of the speed of skill acquisition and the needs for additional scaffolding of skills. There are three techniques developed to assist with social skills development; the Behavioral Social Skills Assessment (Castles & Glass, 1986), the Social Problem-Solving Test (Castles & Glass, 1986), and the Means-End Problem Solving Procedure (Platt & Spivack, 1975). Each of these techniques presents an open-ended situation that the child must solve with assistance. These techniques allow the therapist to directly observe the child's skills as well as to use weaknesses to inform appropriate interventions. Bielecki and Swender (2004) rightfully point out that these techniques are verbally demanding and for children with moderate and below abilities may be inappropriate.

Behavioral checklists can also be utilized particularly those directly developed for children with cognitive delays such as the Vineland Adaptive Behavior Scales II (Sparrow, Galla, & Cecchitti, 2005), the AAMD Adaptive Behavior Scale-2 (Nihira et al., 1993), and the adapted Social Performance Survey Schedule (Matson et al., 1983). Each of these scales is an interview with the main caregiver and evaluate the child's ability to perform important skills that lead to social interactions. The Vineland and AAMD scales show very good reliability while the adapted Social Performance Survey Schedule has less information about its psychometric properties and has not been utilized with children with severe and profound mental retardation.

The MESSIER (Matson, 1994) was developed for children with mental retardation to evaluate the social functioning in children with severe and profound delays. Psychometric properties for this measure are acceptable and it relates well to the Vineland. It provides measures as to positive behaviors (sharing, approaching, eye contact) as well as negative behaviors (withdrawal, aggression).

In the past decade the above measures have been developed for children with mental retardation that are more ecologically valid and useful. These measures can also assist in developing appropriate interventions. Of particular importance is the beginning of our understanding of the social challenges and appropriate interventions for children with severe and profound mental retardation as well as for those with mild and moderate needs. The following section seeks to review the existing literature on the peer relations for children with mental handicaps.

Social Competence and Peer Relations

As discussed in earlier chapters, social competence is comprised of the ability to interact with peers and establish friendships. Children who have difficulty interacting with others often have fewer opportunities for developing the requisite skills needed to function successfully socially. Children with mental handicaps often experience difficulty establishing peer relationships and friendships due to problems with cognitive and language delays as well as frequent problems with motor skills.

Children with mental handicaps generally show problems in establishing a relationship with a peer by the age of 4 and 5 (Guralnick et al., 2003). Particular difficulties are present in their ability to initiate social activities as well as to play cooperatively. Additional problems are present in the ability to resolve a conflict and to problem solve a social dilemma (Guralnick et al., 1998). It has been found that these problems are present even when the child's mental age is taken into account and the child is compared to others at the same mental age (Gurlanick, 1999). Issues that impact these areas of social difficulty include problems with speech and language, working memory, and cognitive delays most of which have not been found to improve with training.

Children with mild cognitive delays have been found to have types of play activities that are more similar than different from typically developing children. For typically developing children three subtypes of nonsocial play have been identified. The reticient subtype is a child who watches others but does not join in the play or who may also remain unoccupied for extended periods of time. These children are often seen as anxious when faced with a social situation and appear to be shy as well as to experience more internalizing disorders (Coplan, 2000; Coplan et al., 2001). These children are also seen as less socially competent.

Those children who engage in solitary and passive play seem to prefer to be alone and often explore and constructively play with objects but are able to appropriately interact socially. These children do not appear to have difficulty with adaptability and psychological development. The final subtype involves children who have repetitive sensorimotor behaviors or engage in dramatic play alone even though there are available peers. Difficulties in impulse control and externalizing problems are often seen with these children as well as problems with social competence as these children are not engaged with others and eventually their peers neglect to include them in activities.

Guralnick et al. (2003) sought to evaluate whether these nonverbal subtypes are also present in children with cognitive delays. In addition, these authors sought to evaluate whether the social context can also influence the type of nonverbal play that is present. Twelve separate play groups of six children each with equal numbers of typically developing and developmentally delayed children were observed. Children with developmental delays were found to engage in more nonsocial play than the matched age typically developing peers. Solitary-passive play was the most common for type of play found for the children with developmental delays. In addition, more unoccupied time was also seen for this group. Solitary-passive play has been linked with difficulties in social competence particularly for boys (Coplan et al., 2001). Both this type of play and reticent behaviors seem to be related to problems with peer relationships with the reticent children possibly showing delays in the acquisition of social skills.

The above findings are important as additional work has found that children with developmental delays who have limited interaction with peers also show a higher risk for the development of psychological disorders (Bebko et al., 1998). When children have not established friend-ships, behavior adjustment and depression have been found to occur (Bebko et al., 1998; Laman & Reiss, 1987). Prevalence rates of psy-chopathology in this population have found rates ranging from 14% to 50% (Russell, 1985) with depression being diagnosed the most frequently (Menolascino, 1990). Researchers are currently viewing psychopathology in children/adolescents with mental retardation to be transactional between genetic/constitutional vulnerabilities and environmental stres-sors (Cicchetti & Beeghly, 1990; Dosen & Geilen, 1990; McGee & Menolascino, 1990). The most important environmental stressor appears to be the tendency to withdraw from social contact with peers and to become isolated. These findings are in agreement with that of Guralnick et al. (2003) finding of more solitary play for children with mental hand-icaps than for those without such difficulties.

Absence of peer relationships has been linked to a number of adjust-ment difficulties (Bebko et al., 1998). Bebko et al. (1998) have devel-oped a model for adequate social competence in children with mental retardation that includes biological/physical contributions, prior experi-ence and exposure to others, and the opportunity to improve and refine social skills. Interventions are important at every level of this model for children with mental handicaps in order to not only improve social rela-tionships but to also work as a preventative for internalizing disorders that arise when social interactions are not adequate for emotional devel-opment.

Play

Observations of children with mental delays found a tendency to utilize solitary and parallel play rather than interactive play as well as fewer incidences of social interactions that were bidirectional (Guralnick & Weinhouse, 1984). These children also had difficulty moving beyond simple requests to more elaborate and imaginative exchanges with peers. These difficulties are likely related to cognitive and language delays but were sufficiently present to inhibit the formation of more friendships and social exchanges. Language delays appear to be primary areas that negatively impact the child's ability to relate to others. When children with cognitive delays were compared to children at the same level of cognitive development, the ones with cognitive delays contin-ued to play alone or not at all and were not interacting with the other children—even those at the same cognitive level (Guralnick & Groom, 1987). Of additional concern these children showed an overall decline in their ability to interact with others generally because they removed themselves from such interactions. Moreover, when interventions have increased the child's approach to others and attempts to interact, the peers were not receptive to these overtures (Fischer Fritz, 1990).

Most research has found that children with cognitive delays are often isolated because behaviors and cognitive skills are different from typi-cally developing peers. For children with cognitive delays, it has been found that children who are in heterogeneous groups interact more often than when in a homogeneous group. Thus, when paired with children at their cognitive level, less interaction is seen than when in a more heterogeneous setting (Guralnick et al., 1996). Moreover, it has been found that children with cognitive delays prefer establishing relationships with nondisabled children rather than with other children with delays similar to their own (Guralnick & Groom, 1987). One of the reasons for this finding is that typically developing children are more socially outgoing and responsive to social bids from all children. Children with disabilities as a whole appear to be less responsive to social interactions and are thus less rewarding with which to interact than those children without disabilities.

Guralnick et al. (1996) brought together unacquainted groups of children to form play groups based on developmental status of the children and the social setting. The play groups either were homogeneous or heterogeneous in terms of developmental levels (all developmentally similar or a combination of normally developing children with those with communication disorders or developmental delays). Each group was observed by trained observers to evaluate social participation and the level of cognitive play that was present. Social participation included solitary play, parallel play, and associative play. Within each of these groupings, the child's play was coded by type: simple repetitive play, constructive play (learning and doing), dramatic play (role taking and pretend play), and games with rules. In addition the coders evaluate the child's observing but not joining in with play as well as engaging in conversation but not playing and moving from one activity to another.

Findings indicated that the children with developmental delays formed the fewest reciprocal friendships compared to those who were typically developing or those who have communication disorders. The children with communication disorders appeared to form more reciprocal friendships with similar children than when placed in more heterogeneous groups. Children with communication disorder and with developmental disorder distributed their friendships across types of development while those who were typically developing preferred friendships with other typically developing children.

Thus, these findings indicate that even within a small group setting that is led by trained professionals, typically developing children seek out other typically developing children. Children with developmental delays showed the fewest reciprocal friendships and also had the most difficulty establishing relationships with other children, even those with a differing handicapping condition. This study also found that preschool-aged children form friendships quickly and are selective with whom they chose to interact. In addition, reciprocal friendships were felt to rely on positive evaluation of the other child while unilateral friendships (which were more likely for the developmentally disabled group) relied more on toy possession and proximity. Moreover, the children with developmental disabilities preferred a typically developing child 85% of the time.

Another aspect of investigation in children with mental handicaps is the stability of the friendships over time. These relationships are crucial for the child's eventual acclimation to the community at large as well as contributing to his/her quality of life (Abery & Fahnestock, 1994).

One longitudinal study of the stability of friendships in adults with developmental disabilities in a group home setting over a 30-month time period found that only 2.6 adults interacted with another at least once in the year and only 1.2 socialized with another at least once in 20 months. These types of findings are of concern as they indicate that many people with developmental disabilities, particularly with the moderate to severe level, may not interact with others and also may not be encouraged in such interactions.

Newton et al. (1996) sought to evaluate the social skills in individuals with mental handicaps as well as the stability of these relationships. Their study evaluated 15 individuals who were in community-based apartments and were provided 24-hour support. Mental handicaps ranged from profoundly retarded to mild disabilities. Findings were of a strong relationship between the level of social skills and the number of interactions. Stability of relationships was not as strongly related to social ability while supported relationships was related to stability. Factors such as having a staff that supported the social relationships as well as support from fellow members seem to be more important than the sole possession of social skills (Newton et al., 1996).

These findings are consistent with those for children with severe mental handicaps. Evans et al. (1992) studied eight children with severe mental handicaps as well as typically developing children who were matched for gender. Social skills were not related to social acceptance or to the number of times they were approached socially. It appears that factors such as proximity, attractiveness, behavior, and supported relationships may be more important than just possessing the requisite skills.

It appears that it is not enough to just teach the appropriate social skills but one must also support the use of these skills as well providing proximity and opportunities for social interactions. The importance of the parent–child bond to later social competence has been found to be a crucial variable for the later development of social skills in children with mental handicaps as well as those who are developing normally.

Social Context and Social Competence

Similar to typically developing children, the first social experience of the child with mental handicaps is with his/her parent. Children with mental delays have been found to experience more difficulties with parent–child attachment partially due to problems with difficult temperament (problems with soothing, medical issues) as well as being less responsive to parental overtures and have more problems relating to the parent in the same manner as a nondisabled child (Bebko et al., 1998). In addition, differences have been found between noncognitively delayed children and children with cognitive delays in the parent–infant relationship that is likely partly due to the child's differences in reaction, soothability, and response to stimulation and the parent's response to these issues. In addition, these differences in early relationships likely have an effect on later interactional styles. Children who have mental retardation have been found to be at higher risk for an atypical relationship with the parent due to the prevalence of a more difficult temperament and the need for more interaction and direction by the parent (Bebko et al., 1998).

As the child develops, the parent begins to require more of the child and to restrict the child in his/her behavior. It is expected that the child will comply with directions and also form independence in leaving the mother and approaching others: adults and children. The mother must allow the child to explore while also making sure the child is safe: a task that has been titled as "maternal scaffolding" (Bruner, 1998). Offering a child choices as well as providing clear directions have also been associated with development of social competence (Crockenberg & Litman, 1990).

It is believed that this maternal scaffolding assists children with developmental disabilities in a very important way due to the language difficulties frequently present as well as difficulty in initiating social interactions in an age-appropriate manner (Beeghly et al., 1989; Kopp et al., 1992). It has been found that mothers of children with Down's syndrome utilize a more active role in helping the child develop social relationships than those with typically developing children (Kopp, 1990; Marfo, 1990). These directive methods have been found to be more productive for children with Down's syndrome, than more suggestive ones (Landry & Chapieski, 1989).

Landry et al. (1994) evaluated the use of maternal scaffolding with mothers of children with Down's syndrome. It was expected that these mothers would be more directive with mothers of typically developing children being more suggestive when a task requires more cognitive challenge. The Puzzle task requires the child and mother to assemble a puzzle while the tea task is pretend play of participating in a tea pary. For example, the puzzle task is a more cognitively challenging task and thus the number of directive requests was hypothesized to be higher. For the tea party task which is more social but which might involve more possibilities of actives, the mothers of Down's syndrome children were hypothesized to impose more restrictions. Praise of the child's efforts was also evaluated with the hypothesis being that both groups would utilize similar incidences of praise. It was also expected that both groups would use more praise during the puzzle task due to its cognitive requirements. In addition to the behavior of the mother, the children were also evaluated as to the level of compliance to maternal requests and unsuccessful attempts to carry out a directive.

Findings indicated that both groups showed more directives during the puzzle task with no difference between the groups in the number of directives. Interestingly it was found that expressive language ability interacted with the use of directives with children with more expressive language problems requiring more use of directives. This finding held true for both tasks. The mothers of typically developing children showed a higher use of suggestion than those of children with Down's syndrome for the puzzle but not the tea party task. It was also found that the typically developing children were more compliant with maternal requests during the tea party but not the puzzle task. A higher proportion of unsuccessful attempts to comply were present during the puzzle task for the typically developing children than for the children with Down's syndrome. In addition, it was found that the mothers of children with Down's syndrome needed to be more consistent in their use of directives across situations and that there was a perception that their children needed more structure in order to complete the tasks and to behave appropriately. The use of praise did not differ between the groups and the use of praise did assist on tasks that required more direction.

The ability of the child with Down's syndrome to comply with adult directions was poorer compared to the typically developing child when presented with a less structured activity (the tea party). This finding may indicate that novelty and a loosely structured activity are important variables in teaching the child how to manage a socially demanding setting. Part of the reason there was more difficulty in the tea party task for these children may have been the ambiguous nature of the tasks as well as difficulty in understanding exactly what was required of them. Children with Down's syndrome showed more compliance when the expectations were clear and structured, thus indicating that the child with a mental handicap may well respond better to tasks that are directive and show more compliance when the social context is more defined. It may well be that the social context defines how the child would respond and what types of support are necessary for social success.

Landry et al. (1994) also found that children with Down's syndrome showed fewer attempts to direct their mother's attention to social interactions and had fewer incidences of turn taking. This finding was independent of expressive language difficulties possibly indicating that more structure and direction is needed to assist in social participation. Thus, children who are typically developing may have internalized appropriate social behaviors that are not present in children with cognitive delays. The ability to generalize these abilities across social context is an area that the child with a cognitive delay will need additional support. The following section evaluates the effect of family variables in the development of social competence particularly in the effect of parent directiveness and social support.

Family Issues in Mental Handicaps

While the child's cognitive delays and expressive language deficits likely cause difficulty with social development, family factors may also play a role in the child's social and emotional development. Emerging research indicates that when parent–child relationships are characterized with sensitivity and reciprocity as well as the use of language to reinforce learning of key social competence practices, the child shows improved social competence with peers (Guralnick & Neville, 1997; Isley et al., 1999; Mize & Pettit, 1997).

The parent–child relationship is an important variable in understanding the development of social competence in children with mental retardation. Sameroff and Chandler (1975) have stressed a model of environment–child interactions which include a transactional effect. A transactional effect is one that emphasizes both the genetic and physiological elements of a person as well as the environment the person is in and these elements are bidirectional in nature. In other words, what the child brings to the relationship relates to how the child manages his/her environment and how the environment in turn changes the child.

The child with mental handicaps generally matures much more slowly than the typically developing child. The parent's relationship to the child and the child's to the parent are dynamic and change with the environment and the demands placed on both of them by each other. In this model, the child is an active participant—the parent doesn't just control what is happening—the child modifies what happens between him/her and the parent with influences added from the environment or context that is found. As was discussed earlier, the social context has an important influence in how the child reacts and relates to others. For children with mental handicaps it may be even more important in the influence it plays in their social development. Sameroff and Chandler (1975) summarize this well when they state, "The child and his caretaking environment tend to mutually alter each other. To the extent that the child elicited or was provided nurturance from the environment, positive outcomes were a consequence" (p. 236).

Mink and Nihira (1986) utilized three family types to evaluate possible different patterns of influence for children with mental retardation. It was expected that in some types the child would be the most influential while in others it would be the parent. It was also expected that the family pattern would be related to social competence in the disabled child. The first pattern was of a learning oriented (LO) family where school grades and formal education was valued. Learning and good behavior were strongly rewarded in these families and the child was involved in family decision-making. The second pattern involved achievement oriented (AO) families where competition was emphasized in the different activities. These families were generally top down in organization with rigid rules that were frequently enforced. The final pattern was a family that was considered to be outer directed (OD). Achievement orientation was low in these families and competitiveness was not emphasized. Family rules were either not defined or not followed through on. The expression of feelings was discouraged in these families.

In this study, 218 students and their families were followed for 4 years with questionnaires completed during this time as well home visits completed. For the LO families the child was found to influence the family and these children also showed the strongest social competence. For these families when the child's behavior was maladaptive, the family was less involved in outside activities in the community. For the AO families the family had the most influence on the child's personal and social adaptation. For these children they were encouraged to relate to their community and to participate appropriately. Findings for the OD families found few areas that were significantly impacted. In the case of the OD families in some cases the parent affected the child while with others the child affected the parent. Direction of effect was not consistent and was directly tied to specific environmental variables. These families showed the most psychological stress and rejection of the handicapped child.

Thus, when a child is in a situation where parental openness and awareness of the child's ability is present as well as the provision of a safe environment, the child's social competence is most highly developed. A family that is strongly connected to their community and values participation also had children who were more socially aware and competent. In addition, families that value the child's contribution and who are not experiencing significant amounts of psychopathology or discord also promote children's social responsibility and social independence.

To further evaluate the relationship of the child–parent bond in children with mental handicaps and its interaction with the environment, Keogh et al. (2000) studied 80 children with developmental delays identified before the age of 3. These children and their families were studied at the ages of 3, 7, and 11. One important finding was that a child who experienced more difficulties triggered more intense family accommodations. Significant difficulties present at age 3 significantly predicted more intense family accommodations by the age of 7 and again triggered more intense family interventions for social competence by the age of 11. In addition, a child with significant communication difficulties at age 3 predicted more intense accommodations by the age of 7. Children who showed more significant problems with behavior at age 3 were more likely to have more accommodations made for their behaviors within the home by age 11. In addition, when there was accommodation efforts required the child's behavior was generally poorer. In this study the transactional model was not strongly supportive; rather the paths were found to be predictive rather than interactive.

In summary, a child with significant mental handicaps does react to his/her environment and the environment in turn reacts to him/her. The best setting for learning social competence appears to merge direct teaching, support, additional experiences in the community, and openness to expression of feelings. For children with cognitive delays, it appears that problematic behaviors and significant delays in communication trigger additional parental direction and intervention that increase in intensity with the child's age. While the transactional model was not fully supported, by the research cited above the findings do indicate that for children who have parents are involved and interactive, their social competence is optimal, while for parents who are more rigid or less supportive, social competence is not as well developed.

Beyond the parent–child relationship are also direct influences parents can have on their child. An example of such an influence is when a parent teaches a child how to enter a peer group and then provides hands on instruction as to how to do this and supervises the outcome. However, if the main caretaker is very controlling and directive, the child's resulting social competence has been found to be poor and the child frequently experiences more behavioral difficulties (Russell & Finnie, 1990; Rubin & Mills, 1990). Thus, it appears that there is a good middle ground for parent support to develop peer relationships. A parent that encourages and provides scaffolding for learning these behaviors while not highly controlling generally has a child that is more competent than a parent who is highly controlling and demanding (Ladd & Hart, 1992).

This type of support can be challenging for many parents given competing demands on their time. Ladd and Golter (1988) found that over 50% of middle-class families do not arrange for additional social contacts for their children outside of the school experience. Factors that are associated with active parent involvement in promoting social competence include parents who believe that they can improve the child's social functioning with those that believe the child's cognitive delays preclude social development developing fewer contacts for the child with peers (Mize et al., 1995).

The amount of social support that is present for the family also appears to relate to the child's resulting social competence. When the family is stressed by factors such as economic disadvantage or family discord and there is little social support for the parents, the child's social competence suffers. Social support present for parents of children with mental handicaps often serves as a protective influence for relieving or ameliorating parent stress (Krauss, 1993).

Guralnick et al. (2003) developed a model that includes seven constructs involving the child's competence, parent constructs of arranging, control, attitude, stress, social support, and child risk. As the parent becomes more controlling and believes that the child requires more assistance, the child's peer competence appears to decrease (Guralnick et al., 2003). In this model a parent who arranges play dates and has an attitude that this will help their child without being overly controlling generally has a child with higher social competence. In contrast when a parent is very controlling and believes the child needs such control, the child does not develop the requisite skills needed to be socially competent. In addition, when a parent directly teaches the child social skills, the child's resulting competence does not appear to be related to such teaching (Booth, 1999), perhaps because one cannot teach all of the possible variations on a theme for social competence.

When a parent has a child with compromised cognitive and language abilities, increased stress is reported to be present and resulting poor social competence has been found (Booth, 1999; Guralnick & Groom, 1987). Guralnick et al. (2003) sought to test the model by utilizing 74 families with children between the ages of 48 and 78 months who had an IQ between 52 and 90 and who were reported to be experiencing difficulties with social competence. Findings were that parental stress and parent action in setting up socialization strategies were related directly to child peer competence. Greater parental stress was found to be related to lower peer competence and the authors suggested that difficulties in attachment, feelings of incompetence in parenting, tendencies toward depression and isolation may have impacted the child–parent interactions and affected the child's social competence (Guralnick & Neville, 1997).

In addition, it was found, as was expected, that the more controlling mothers had children with poorer social competence. In addition, lower levels of social support for the mother were related to more controlling strategies. Surprisingly, the number of play dates and social outings arranged by the mother was not related to child peer competence. This finding differs from that for typically developing children where more social exposure is related to better competence. For children with cognitive delays it may well be that the type of play setting and the experiences are more important than the number of exposures.

Parent attitude has not been found to be significant predictor of social competence. Guralnick et al. (2003) suggest that the parents may have been attributing their child's difficulty to internal causes which are not changeable rather than to external causes which could be changed. Further investigation of the attributions of the parent to the child's difficulty is needed to determine whether this finding is indeed true. If it is the case that these parents do not believe that the child can change, intervention it is important to work on these attitudes and to change the parent's focus to what can be done with interventions. It would be very important to provide support for social support systems as well as actions to be taken to assist the child in his/her development. A comprehensive approach that not only selects behaviors and interventions for the child is recommended but also involving the family, particularly those families of limited means and education, in the intervention for the child. This suggestion is bolstered by additional study by Guralnick et al. (2002) that found that mothers of children with developmental disabilities did attribute problems in social competence to internal causes and monitored the child's play more carefully but in fewer instances than did mothers of children without developmental delays.

Thus, when the parent believes that the child's problems are not caused by external events, interventions are more controlling and directed and thus reduce the child's ability to learn independent skills even more than would be necessary given his/her delays. These types of behaviors are very important to study as they provide a window into appropriate family interventions. Mothers of children with developmental disabilities, while supportive of mainstreaming of their children, have been found to believe there were significant drawbacks to such a practice in that their child was not provided sufficient support (Guralnick, 1994). In this case, the parent's view that the child needs additional support in a mainstreamed class is consistent with the findings that the parent feels the need to provide more control for the child: control that is not necessarily proactive in helping the child learn skills on his/her own. In this type of controlling behavior the parent does things for the child rather than believing the child can learn these skills himself/herself.

Siblings

The siblings of children with developmental disabilities can also have an effect on the child with disabilities as well as on the sibling's social competence. There is some evidence that children with siblings with developmental disabilities may be at risk for developing behavioral difficulties (Dyson, 1993). Similar to the child with disability, the family's ability to cope with the child with disability also appears to affect how the sibling copes with the additional stress (Crnic et al., 1983). Additional studies have found that when social support is provided, siblings of children with disabilities show a higher self concept and more positive family relationships particularly when there is a low level of parental stress (Dyson et al., 1989).

Dyson (1993) studied the effect of a sibling with a developmental disability on the development of the nondisabled sibling. Two groups were compared with the first group having a disabled sibling who was younger and the second group having a younger nondisabled sibling. These families were followed over 4–5 years. Findings indicated that the participants with disabled siblings did not differ significantly from those without disabled siblings in terms of behavior and self-esteem. In fact, both groups showed more behavioral difficulties and lower self-esteem at the time of retesting. Moreover, the psychosocial functioning of these children was found to be stable over time with behavior and social competence being most stable and self-concept being least. In addition, family psychological factors also interacted with the findings. Positive family relationships and emphasis on personal responsibility were linked to better social competence. Conversely, negative family experiences were related to poor self-concept which decreased over time.

Interventions

Interventions that have generally been utilized include social skill training, modeling, direct instruction, role play and social reinforcement. The use of social reinforcement appears to be very helpful in developing opportunities for social play, sharing, and reciprocal support. One of the difficulties with these types of interventions is that the skills are not maintained without additional support and they did not generalize beyond the treatment setting (Bebko et al., 1998). It has been found that placing children in a mainstream class without additional intervention does not improve social interactions (Asch, 1989). In fact the child engages in more and more solitary play than if in a special education classroom when no efforts are made to improve socialization (Jenkins et al., 1989). Others have found that any intervention needs to be intensive and continual. For example, Fischer Fritz (1990) utilized a one-time intervention to increase elementary school children's sensitivity to children with mental handicaps. The children with cognitive delays were found to approach others and attempt to interact but that these overtures were rarely returned by the nondisabled peer and interactions by the nondisabled peer were rarely initiated.

Given the above findings of difficulty with interactive play, researchers evaluated how the child responds to being mainstreamed into a regular classroom. Many have found that just placing the child in a mainstream class without additional support does not promote social competence and may actually serve to reinforce solitary and parallel play (Asch, 1989; Jenkins et al., 1989). When a play program was introduced that included interactive experiences, the children showed good improvement not only in social abilities but also in language skills.

Studies have found that when additional support is provided the child will develop reciprocal friendships that are rewarding to both children. This finding has held for children with mental handicaps as well as those with handicaps and typically developing children (Hamre-Nietupski, 1993; Strully & Strully, 1993). Thus, continuing support and direction is required in order for the child to interact with his/her peers and to develop the prerequisite skills needed to forge a successful peer relationship.

Most of the interventions that have been used include direct instruction, modeling, role plays, and reinforcement of learned behaviors. The use of social reinforcement has been found to be very helpful in the shaping of prerequisite social behaviors necessary for social success by children with cognitive delays (Strain et al., 1984). The difficulty that is present for children with cognitive delays is similar to that of children with other disabilities; that is, the child can perform the necessary behaviors in isolation or in the clinical setting but cannot generalize these behaviors to settings that are somewhat different.

Bebko et al. (1998) suggests that research has not currently been published that provides a good idea of how to assist children with mental retardation in generalizing these skills to the larger environment. Findings from studies indicate that it is likely that children with mental retardation have a different developmental trajectory for learning social skills from that of typically developing children or children with other disabilities. The lack of information about these key variables makes an informed intervention difficult and may be why intervention strategies do not carry over into the "real" world. As discussed above, support both in the school and home setting is crucial for the child to learn appropriate social skills and to develop reciprocal friendships. These friendships, whether with typically developing children or children with similar disabilities, are important for the child to continue to develop socially and to adjust to the ever-changing landscape of the social world. This support needs to continue past the elementary school age and into adulthood. Given that people with mental handicaps are vulnerable to depression and social isolation, the support provided to young children needs to be applied as the child develops and to change with the varying expectations for different life stages.

Conclusion

Children with mental handicaps are social beings and flourish best when provided with interactions first with their parents and then with peers. Research as to the effect of differing care-giving strategies and challenges for parents of children with mental handicaps is incomplete at best and needs to be expanded. There is strong evidence that these parents face differing challenges and that a child with mental handicaps is often more difficult to parent and requires additional parenting skills compared to a typically developing child. These differences are important particularly for the development of appropriate intervention skills. Beginning to assist parents in helping children acquire appropriate adaptive behavior skills at an early age is a good first step in the child's ability to learn appropriate social ability.

Cognitive and language handicaps have been found to have an impact on the child's ability to share experiences and converse with peers. These difficulties are compounded for a child with mental retardation particularly as the child develops and language becomes more and more abstract. Some have suggested that difficulty in understanding and use of emotional language may be tied to social competence problems in children with mental retardation (Cicchetti, 1991). These problems indicate that intervention that specifically targets such understanding may be helpful.

One of the difficulties with research in mental handicaps/retardation is the heterogeneity of the population. Children with mental retardation due to organic or genetic causes may have different challenges socially than those who have mental handicaps that are not attributable to internal causes. Family functioning may well differ between these subtypes as well as the resources needed for a child who is medically fragile. Further understanding of the relationship between the type of mental retardation and the resulting social challenges is necessary and we do not currently possess sufficient research to elucidate these issues.

Finally, the research indicates the support the family has from others and from organizations assists in how well the family can provide early interventions that have a better chance of improving the child's performance. Family issues that include marital discord, financial stress, economic hardship, and social isolation certainly may contribute to difficulties the child later faces in developing appropriate social skills. These issues also are rarely addressed within the school setting where many of the interventions for children with mental retardation are provided. Family support and therapy appear to be issues that can be more readily addressed and which research supports as beneficial to the child's overall functioning but also for his/her social and emotional development.

9

Social Competence in Children Who Are Gifted and Talented

Stefan was in second grade and a gregarious seven-year-old child when the author first met him. He had always been interested in materials and information since before the age of two. He began reading at age 2 and was doing double-digit mathematical problems by the age of 3. His language skills began at the age of 7 months and he was speaking in full sentences by the age of 18 months. He had no difficulties in development in any area and enjoyed people, ideas, and sports. Stefan was well accepted by his peers and had a number of friends. He was described as sensitive and caring and a "good friend" by his peers. Stefan was frequently picked first in games and excelled at soccer and T-Ball. By second grade he had mastered most of the middle school curriculum and his parents and teachers were very concerned about what types of instruction could be provided to him in as normal a setting as possible. Although his parents were well educated, they described themselves as above average in intelligence but certainly not as smart as Stefan. They were invested in his developing to his highest potential but they also prized his social and emotional development and wanted him to remain in as normal a setting as possible for as long as possible.

A psychological assessment found his ability to measure approximately 170—he scored above the ceilings on most subtests of the WISC. Achievement tests found him at college level in most subjects and he was beginning to study calculus and higher-order geometry on his own. Stefan had already built a computer from scratch with some help from his father.

He continued to have friends in his second grade classroom and was friendly with all children. Educational programming for him was a very difficult area and the plan eventually included classes at the local community college in the mornings and then classes in his second grade classroom in gym, music, art, and health in the afternoons. This arrangement was very helpful throughout elementary school but additional challenges were present for middle school when he had already fulfilled requirements for a Bachelor's Degree. Special arrangements were made with a local university for Stefan to take advanced graduate level classes while attempting to stay connected with his peers. It was a tribute to Stefan that he was able to cope with these challenges with equanimity. Eventually he attended an Ivy League school at the age of 14 and obtained a doctorate in computer science by the age of 19. His social and emotional maturity continued to be above his age level and commensurate with his ability levels.

What Is Giftedness?

The definition of "giftedness" has been an area of controversy for several years. The definition adopted for the reauthorization of the Jacob K. Javits Gifted and Talented Students Education Act of 1988 indicated that this term is reserved for children who show high potential for performance in the following areas: intellectual, artistic, creative, leadership, or in a specific academic field. Conceptual models have been proposed including that of Renzulli (2000). This model suggests three factors necessary for giftedness: higher levels of intelligence, and creativity, and task commitment. For a child to be considered gifted in this model all three conditions need to be present. Renzulli's model includes children with IQs as low as 115 and looks at giftedness in terms of a talent pool. This talent pool is an ability to excel in at least one area of endeavor. Other models require at least an IQ of 130 to be considered gifted.

Sternberg and Zhang (1995) defined giftedness using a pentagonal implicit theory. In this theory the person must meet these five criteria: excellence, rarity, productivity, demonstrability, and value. Excellence means that the child is superior in some way to his/her peers. Rarity means that this excellence is unusually high and not frequently seen in other children. Productivity means that the child accomplishes a task at a high level. Demonstrability indicates that the child performs in the superior range on one or more assessment measures. Finally, value indicates that this performance is valued by the society in which the child lives.

In the past, giftedness was often viewed as unidimensional—in other words, you were either gifted or not. Currently, giftedness is frequently viewed as domain-specific (Gagne, 2003; Gardner, 1999). That is, a person may be gifted in one or more areas. An interesting theory of giftedness is tied to Goleman's (1995) theory of emotional intelligence. In this theory emotional intelligence is an important factor whether children and youth with high intelligence succeed in life or not. Emotional intelligence is defined as self-awareness, impulse control, persistence in the face of adversity, empathy, and social competence. He attributes success for children and youth who are gifted to high ability as well as high social intelligence. By definition, children who are gifted and talented tend to have questioning minds and may not always accept a teacher's explanation. They may also challenge the status quo and overwhelm a parent or teacher who is unsure of their own abilities.

Initially theorists believed that giftedness was present at birth and continued throughout life. The Fullerton Longitudinal Study in California (Gottfried et al., 1994) followed children identified as merely "healthy" for 18 years starting at the age of 1. Parents were found to be accurate as to the potential of their child and at times more accurate than early instruments utilized to predict later giftedness. For children scoring above 130 on an IQ test it was found that scores fluctuated over time with some children showing precociousness and then their development smoothing out while others were found to be "late bloomers." Thus, this study concluded that children with high potential should be evaluated at various points in development rather than at one time. It is also possible to speculate from this study that giftedness is not necessarily immutable and that some may be precocious early but not retain that label and others may not show giftedness until they are older.

Prevalence and Etiology of Giftedness

Given the problems with definition, the prevalence of giftedness depends on the definition utilized. If ability is the main measure of giftedness, then the prevalence may range from 2 to 3% and if a multidimensional definition is used the incidence may be around 15% (Kaufmann et al., 1986). Generally giftedness is defined as an IQ above 125–130. When this definition is used, then the incidence is around 3%. However, when additional measures of talent and skill are added then the incidence comes closer to 15% particularly when the IQ threshold is lowered to 115 (Renzulli, 2000). While neither method has become the gold standard, logic would indicate that a combination of both methods not only provides for adequate identification but will also identify unusual learners or those who come from less advantaged homes.

It is also important to use measurements that allow for determination of giftedness that are not solely cultural or experiential specific. A child who is gifted nonverbally is likely to score better on a measure of performance while one who is linguistically gifted will do better on a measure of verbal ability. Using multiple instruments can assist in identifying children most accurately. Of course, no matter what instruments are used, some children will be missed and others will be identified incorrectly.

Etiology of giftedness is generally assumed to be a combination of genetic and environmental factors. Previously it was believed to be mostly genetic but with additional studies environmental influences have also been implicated (Kauffmann et al., 1986). Generally children who are gifted have parents that are also intelligent. Studies have also found a correlation between higher socioeconomic status and ability; that is, children with more advantages score higher on measures of cognitive ability (Richert, 1985, 1987). This finding is likely due to both genetic and environmental advantage.

Social Issues for Children Who Are Gifted

Previously children who were gifted were thought to have social difficulties—to have difficulty fitting in due to their high ability. Robinson (2002) rightly indicates that the range of skills, temperament, and personality traits of children and youth who are gifted is more similar to the general population than different. Lewis Terman (1925–1929) began a study of 59 children in California with an IQ above 135. Contrary to frequently held beliefs that gifted children are social misfits, these children tended to show the same tendencies toward social and emotional adjustment as the general population. Terman's work is and was incredibly important for the field as it allowed some demystifying of giftedness and talent and indicated that mental, physical, and creative abilities tended to go hand in hand.

One of the difficulties with Terman's study was that it generally studied children of university faculty who were Caucasian and were not representative of the population as a whole. By definition the families of these children were committed to education and to enriching experiences. Terman found that these children were above average in many areas and including height and leadership. It is sobering, however, to note that when these children reached senior citizen ages, they were not more successful financially than others from the same socioeconomic groups. Thus, giftedness does not ensure financial success. It is not clear from the studies as to the quality of life for these adults or their feelings of satisfaction with their lives. These findings have been replicated in several studies including those of Subotnik et al. (1993) and Schaie (2005).

Similar to Stefan, children who are gifted face challenges in development and educational progress that may not be present for typically developing children. Davis and Rimm (1998) found that gifted students tend to have more difficulty with anxiety, sensitivity, feelings of isolation, and may have a tendency to become easily over-excited. Others have found children who are gifted to be very motivated but often motivated in only a specific area of interest and may seem unable to make a transition to other topics when necessary (Leal et al., 1995). While there is no empirical evidence that children who are gifted have more difficulties emotionally and socially than typically developing children, the above tendencies and differing maturity levels from their peers may put them at risk for problems if their needs are unmet by the educational system (Robinson, 2002).

Stefan was able to bridge his two worlds (academic and social) when he was young but this area became more and more difficult as he aged. Generally gifted children are more mature socially and valued by their peers more than typically developing children. They also tend to have social networks that extend beyond the school. In addition, they have a more mature understanding of what a friend is than their peers and may feel they don't have "close" friends—just people that they can do things with. Robinson (2002) suggests that at times the gifted child may attempt to fit in by hiding or even denying their special gifts. Some children who are extremely verbally facile may experience more social difficulties as they attempt to share experiences, thoughts, and ideas that are beyond the level of the children with whom they are relating. Robinson (2002) hypothesizes that these differences may cause significant social difficulties and the gifted child may become less socially adept and more socially isolated particularly when the child is exceptionally gifted.

To investigate emotional and social adjustment in gifted children, Sayler and Brookshire (2004) studied children who were gifted and were accelerated in school, children who were gifted but not accelerated, and typically developing children. Surprisingly there was a gender distribution differences with more females in the accelerated group than the nonaccelerated group and more males in the entire sample (56%). Both groups of children who were gifted tended to come from the highest socioeconomic categories while the typical group was spread evenly across all categories. The students in the accelerated group showed the highest level of internal control followed by the gifted and then the typically developing group. The self-concepts of both gifted groups were higher than the typically developing group. The accelerated group showed the best academic achievement compared to the other two groups. The gifted group reported that they had higher level of social acceptance than did the members of the other two groups. These findings indicate that there are trade-offs in trying to match the interests that differ between gifted and nongifted children. When gifted children were accelerated, they showed good self-concepts as well as a strong internal locus of control. Gifted children who were not accelerated also showed good achievement but not as high as that of the accelerated children. They, however, showed greater peer acceptance than the accelerated group and were self-reported to be more popular and athletic. These findings indicate that there are pluses and minuses to both choices—acceleration or not.

There may also be gender differences in how "being smart" is viewed as a positive or a negative characteristic. Rimm et al. (1999) found that women who were gifted felt that they were different whether or not they had been singled out. Of additional concern is a finding by Luftig and Nichols (1990) that when adolescents were rated for popularity, gifted boys ranked as most popular followed by nongifted boys; nongifted girls with gifted girls being the least popular.

Additional studies have looked at the degree of giftedness with those with very extremely high IQs showing more difficulty with social acceptance than those with moderately high abilities (Feldman, 1986). Of those children with IQs higher than 160, the vast majority (80%) reported extreme social isolation and ongoing emotional stress (Gross, 1993). Others have found that extremely bright adolescents will seek to avoid or withdraw from honors classes and other activities that mark them as different (chess club, computer club, debate club, etc.) with the percentage higher for females than males who withdraw (Davis & Rimm, 1998).

These difficulties carry through from Caucasian to African-American females. Ford (1994, 1995) found that in a group of gifted African-American girls at least 50% had been teased unmercifully by their peers for high achievement while a sizable minority (33%) were called "acting White." Reported feelings of isolation, rejection, and withdrawal as well as underachievement were present.

Studies have found that while gifted children are more intelligent than others, their overall achievements may not be any more impressive than those of lesser abilities (Freeman, 2006). Findings have linked self-esteem and motivation as well as opportunity to later success (Freeman, 2005; Shavinina & Ferrari, 2004). Positive self-esteem has been found to be the most reliable predictor of later success with intelligence accounting for only 30% of this success (Trost, 2000). Optimism has also been found to be an important predictor for later success for children who are gifted both achievement-wise as well as socially

(Peterson, 2000). Personality studies (Shavinina & Ferrari, 2004) have found that the majority of gifted students as well as Nobel Prize winners score high on the intuition scale of the Myers Briggs Indicator (Mills, 1993). Such intuition likely relates to their ability to think of aspects of a problem that are not readily evident to most other people; that is, to bring a fresh perspective to the solution.

Cornell (2004) contrasted popular and unpopular gifted children with typically developing children. Rating scales were utilized that were completed by the child as well as by the parents. Differences were found on measures of social status, social self-concept, and academic self-esteem. No differences were found on measures of achievement or any internalizing disorders. In terms of social status, the fathers of the unpopular students were in the lowest range for the study followed by the typically developing group and the popular group scoring the highest. Although social self-concept was found to be poor for the unpopular students (an expected finding), other areas were not found to be an area of low self-esteem including their attractiveness, athletic ability, or academic skills. Teacher ratings indicated that the unpopular gifted students were less independent in their work, had difficulty making decisions, and did not readily undertake new challenges and/or tasks. The teachers also reported that these children were more difficult in class and did not have favorable self-talk about their own abilities. An interesting study would be to contrast unpopular gifted with unpopular typically developing children to determine whether these issues are specific to this population or similar across ability groups. It may well be that these differences are more highlighted because the child who is gifted is assumed to succeed more readily than those who are not.

Social context has also been suggested to be important in understanding the eventual development of children with giftedness. Vygotsky (1978) has suggested that the environment shapes the child's perceptions and thoughts and can be optimized by various settings. A study of children who were prodigies found that none lived up to their abilities in adulthood (Feldman, 1986). Similarly, a study of 115 very high ability Chinese children found extremely accelerated achievement skills (reading and writing) with very poor social skills (Zha, 1995, cited in Gross, 2002). Others have found that parents who are invested in their child's giftedness tend to be achievement oriented and actually encourage less emotional expression and have children with more adjustment problems than would be expected (Cornell & Grossberg, 1989; Freeman, 2001). These findings suggest that very special treatment may not be beneficial as it does not provide the breadth of experiences or the environmental context so necessary to develop appropriate life skills.

In contrast, there are some demonstrations that an enrichment program that is within the general education setting may be of benefit to gifted children socially. Peer relations of fourth, fifth, and sixth grade children in a pull out gifted program were compared to those not in the program. The gifted children were found to be rated with good social acceptability and competence and were valued members of the peer group. However, these children did not have more friends than their peers—they were more valued as a friend or social contact (Cohen et al., 1994).

Another study evaluated adolescents and their self-image. Findings indicated that there was excellent socioemotional functioning in those adolescents scoring the highest on measures of creativity and they also showed more self-assurance (Smith & Tegano, 1992).

While the majority of children who are gifted show social and emotional development similar to typically developing children, there is a sizable minority that show emotional difficulties. Freeman (2006) found that children who are labeled as gifted were significantly more likely to show emotional problems than those who were equally as gifted but who were not labeled. There were also more family problems (divorce, etc.) in the labeled group than the other group. By the age of 40 these participants showed fewer emotional difficulties but continued to evidence sadness. In addition, findings have indicated that children who engaged with supportive adults as well as having outside supports (extended family, schools, etc.) showed fewer emotional difficulties despite family challenges. In addition, children from advantaged backgrounds generally show higher self-esteem and academic achievement than those from disadvantaged background (VanTassel-Baska et al., 1994). Thus, similar to other children the social context, family factors, and intangibles (motivation, optimism) may be more important predictors of the child's social functioning than his/her giftedness.

Degree of Giftedness

McCallister et al. (1996) suggest that children who are gifted are fairly heterogeneous and that research indicating good social and emotional development may not be accurate for the total population of children who are gifted. Gifted children who are moderately gifted (IQ 130–160) may differ from those who are exceptionally gifted (IQ 160–179) or profoundly gifted (IQ 180 +). There is not a great deal of study with these children as by definition they are rare. However, McCallister et al. (1996) indicate that the literature finds no emotional/social difficulties for children who are gifted and yet clinically there are many reports of children with these very difficulties.

Gross (2002) reviewed the literature and found evidence that the children who were the highest in IQ had the most significant social difficulties and adjustment. These findings were also present in Terman's study where a child with an IQ higher than 170 was found to have social difficulties and to be socially isolated (Burks et al., 1930). Other theorists (Hollingworth, 1942) suggested that IQs ranging from 125 to 155 were optimum for social adjustment among the gifted while IQs 160 and above were related to difficulties with peer relationships, social isolation, and withdrawal. These hypotheses have been somewhat borne out in the research. Gross (1998) and Dauber and Benbow (1990) found that children who were profoundly gifted in mathematics or verbal skills showed significant social difficulties and had the lowest social standing compared to moderately gifted children with the children with profound verbal intelligence scoring the most poorly of the four groups.

Peer Relations

Studies have found that gifted children generally relate better to other gifted children or to older children (Gross, 2001, 2002). Interviews have found that exceptionally gifted children report having older friends, too few friends, and the feeling that their intellectual ability made it more difficult to make friends. Their parents generally report the child has only one close friend or none (Janos et al., 1985).

An interesting finding is that mental age is a better predictor of a child's progress through social development than chronological age (Gross, 1998). For example, an exceptionally gifted child has a different conception of what friendship entails at a younger age than his/her peers. For younger gifted children expectations are for intimacy and confiding while their same-aged typically developing peer may be solely looking for someone with which to play. This misfit of expectations likely leads to difficulties forming close ties with a similar aged child but explains why older children are preferred as friends. These differences appear to be most apparent during the elementary school years and are reported to be most acute before the age of 10 (Gross, 2002). When adolescence occurs, there is a shift in experience and a widening of choices that makes it easier for the gifted adolescent to find some peers with which to relate appropriately.

Asynchronous Development

In addition to difficulties finding same-aged peers with similar interests and abilities, children who are gifted may have a mismatch between their intellectual maturity and their affective maturity. While they may appear more emotionally mature than their same aged peers, their ability to regulate their feelings, understand their emotions, and translate this understanding into words is likely below the level of their cognitive skills. Parents, teachers, and other adults may expect behaviors and emotional discharges that are consistent with their ability while ignoring the fact that all skills are not going to mature at the same level simultaneously with affect regulation likely to lag behind other areas (Robinson, 2002). It is interesting that gifted children at the elementary level tend to be well liked but that by early adolescence this tendency appears to disappear (Rimm, 2002; Udvari & Rubin, 1996). Rimm reports that when 3,500 Minnesota high school students were asked whether they would rather be best looking, most athletic, or smartest in their class, most did selected being most intelligent followed by most athletic and then best looking. However, the essays indicated an awareness that there may well be a stigma to being "too smart."

Differences in areas of development has been termed "dyssynchrony" and is indicative of uneven development in gifted children in the areas of intellectual, affective, and motor development (Terrassier, 1985). Terrassier (1985) divided dyssynchrony into two types. Internal dyssynchrony is different rates of development in the gross and fine motor, cognitive, and emotional areas while social dyssynchrony occurs when a child feels out of place in his/her social context. Silverman (2002) suggests that the use of the term "asynchrony" is more appropriate for the gifted child as the prefix "dys" may indicate a dysfunction rather than just a feeling of being out of step with one's own age. She goes on to point out that to have the cognitive ability of an adult in a child's body and with a child's emotional control must be very difficult particularly for children who are exceptionally gifted.

Twice Exceptional Children

Emerging research indicates that children who are "twice exceptional" experience more difficulty with adjustment. These are children that have a learning disability and are gifted or those with ADHD who are gifted. In both cases these children experience a misfit between some abilities and others.

Learning Disabilities (LD)

Children who are gifted and learning disabled generally have exceptional ability in one or more areas but also have significant problems in learning likely due to the processing deficits frequently seen in learning disabled individuals (Semrud-Clikeman, 2006). While many of the children with a dual diagnosis may compensate for these difficulties and achieve at an average level, their achievement is significantly below expectations for their ability, and their learning disability may, in fact, be hidden by exceptionally high intelligence (LaFrance, 1995). An additional difficulty for children who are gifted and learning disabled is that teachers may have more problems seeing the areas of high ability than they do for other gifted children.

As difficulties in reading, writing, and/or arithmetic are present in gifted children with learning disabilities, their ability to express their ideas or to find materials that are in line with their interests are disparate and likely cause significant problems with adjustment (Silverman, 2002). Moreover, they may be able to solve complex problems but not complete easier skills such as basic word reading, spelling, and mathematics calculation.

Social-emotional characteristics that have been found in gifted/LD children include lower self-concepts, poor feelings of self-sufficiency, mood swings, anxiety, and low frustration tolerance (Dole, 2000). A study by Waldron et al. (1987) compared children who were gifted and achieving at an average level with those who had average ability achieving at an average range. Findings were that the gifted LD child had increased anxiety and lower self-esteem than the average achieving peer.

Minner (1990) surveyed classroom teachers and found that they (including teachers of gifted children) held preconceived ideas that children with learning disabilities are not considered for gifted programming despite high scores on standardized tests. Instead the teachers generally focused on the areas of disability (reading, spelling, writing) rather than on the creative and talented potential of these children. In addition, the teachers were reported to refer children who were gifted LD from higher socioeconomic status families for a gifted program than children from middle to lower socioeconomic status families.

In contrast to the preconceived ideas of the teachers described above, Olenchak and Reis (2002) surveyed the literature and reported that children with LD and giftedness were more likely to show persistence and to develop individual interests. However, these children were also more likely to show poor academic self-efficacy. Gardynik and McDonald (2005) suggest that many children who are provided appropriate support at home and school who have a dual diagnosis will show resilience and good adjustment. Without such support, she also suggests that these children have an increased vulnerability to academic failure as well as depression and anxiety. Successful children/adults with LD and giftedness have been found to be proactive, have realistic educational plans, and adapt to changing life circumstances (Gardynik & McDonald, 2005).

The discontinuity between high ability and learning problems has been related to affective difficulties for these children. Recent studies have found that gifted college students with a learning disability recall painful experiences in elementary and high school particularly in regard to retention in a grade, repeating work that was done poorly, difficulties with work completion in a timely fashion, and placement in special education classes with less adept students (Reis et al., 1997). Most also recalled being told that they needed to work harder, to get with it, and to not be so lazy.

Studies have found affective characteristics that tend to be associated with giftedness and a learning disability. These include a strong need for excelling on tasks, more perfectionism than is expected, very intense emotions, intense frustration on tasks that are problematic, disruptive and/or withdrawn behavior, and low self-esteem (Baum & Owen, 1988; Baum et al., 1991; Olenchak, 1994; Reis et al., 1995; Whitmore & Maker, 1985). In one study more than one-third of postsecondary LD/gifted adolescents had entered therapy for social and emotional problems (Reis et al., 1995).

Olenchak and Renzulli (2004) used case studies to evaluate the effects of a curriculum that stressed gifted skills to study the effects these curriculums had on children who are gifted and LD. Findings were that increased negative effects were found in this type of curriculum and the child who was gifted LD felt even more isolated from his/her peers than when in regular classes. However, when adjustments were made to the curriculum to assist the children who were gifted and LD, substantial improvements in social status and emotional development were found. Helpful strategies included assisting these children with developing study strategies, support provided through computers and other technology, counseling, an individualized academic program, and a focus on executive functions and cognitive strategies (Olenchak & Reis, 2002).

ADHD

Some researchers have hypothesized that a minority of children diagnosed as ADHD may in fact be gifted and not ADHD (Baum et al., 1998). These children may be active, intense, interrupt, and show attentional difficulties when faced with boring, repetitive tasks due to giftedness rather than ADHD. For this reason, careful diagnosis of ADHD is important particularly when the child is very bright. However, it may also be difficult to identify children with ADHD as gifted for similar reasons as discussed above for children with a learning disability. Castellanos (2000) found that a gifted child with ADHD will not be identified with ADHD until much later than a child with a sole diagnosis of ADHD with a negative relationship between level of IQ and identification of ADHD.

Children with ADHD and giftedness are often told to try harder, work harder, or experience frustration (both their own and their parent's, teacher's) but continue to have problems with organization, day-dreaming, and social immaturity (Leroux & Levitt-Perlman, 2000). In addition, the child may not be identified as gifted as children with ADHD have been found to score lower on IQ tests than those who are not ADHD. The pattern that has been found generally shows excellent verbal scores but performance subtests showing scores in the average to below average range (Castellanos, 2000). In addition, children with ADHD have been found to become over-focused when working on projects of great interest to them. For a child who is gifted and ADHD and who has this tendency, Moon (2002) suggests a significant danger that the child's attentional problems will be attributed to motivation rather than an attentional disability and more pressure applied for the child to apply him/her to the task at hand. This behavioral profile may also lead the teacher not to nominate the child for a gifted program due to lack of motivation.

For those children with ADHD who are also gifted, problems with impulse control and attention may impact their ability to produce work at the level for which they are capable. Kaufmann and Castellanos (2000) suggest that children who are gifted and ADHD may show less advancement in social, emotional, and motivational development compared to other children who are gifted. A misfit in their cognitive skills with executive functioning and response inhibition likely sets them up for additional areas of stress and problems particularly in the social and emotional areas (Moon et al., 2001). Zentall et al. (2001) found that children with ADHD with and without giftedness experience significant adjustment problems with the ones with ADHD and giftedness experiencing the most.

It has also been found that gifted children with ADHD experience problems with affect regulation (Moon et al., 2001). The difference between this child's emotional maturity and their cognitive complexity leads to the asynchrony spoken of earlier in this chapter. Moon (2002) suggests that younger children with a combination of ADHD and giftedness need express instruction in understanding, labeling, controlling, and expressing their emotions in an appropriate manner.

Social rejection is more likely for children with ADHD and giftedness as their behaviors are likely to be obnoxious, intrusive, and intense. Moon (2002) suggests that this social rejection may be exacerbated through placement in pull-out programs for gifted children. By definition, children with giftedness are generally more mature while children with ADHD are less mature. The behaviors seen in a program for gifted children are likely to be more adult-like than the child with a dual diagnosis of giftedness and ADHD is ready to manage. For many of these children peer rejection occurs in this setting and is particularly hurtful for these twice exceptional children.

Consistent with these findings is a study by Moon et al. (2001) which used a case study of three groups of boys: one with giftedness and ADHD, one who was gifted without ADHD, and one with ADHD but who were not gifted. Those with combined ADHD and giftedness were found to be the least mature and have the poorest emotional adjustment. In contrast the other two groups showed fairly good maturity and emotional functioning. Socially the combined group showed more difficulty with immature behavior and social rejection particularly within a self-contained class for gifted students. The other two groups showed adequate social skills and had friends. Many of the boys in the ADHD group participated and excelled at sports which may have helped their acceptance by their peers.

Emotional Development

Children who are gifted have been found to be sensitive and to express emotions and thoughts in a more intense manner than others. The research as to the emotional development of children who are gifted is equivocal. Some research links this sensitivity and intensity to an increased incidence of internalizing disorders (i.e., anxiety, depression, etc.) as well as social difficulties (Keiley, 2002). Some have suggested that the stress society places on children who are gifted can lead of obsessive perfectionism as well as a fear of failure (Weisse, 1990). Still others have linked these stresses to problems with eating, underachievement, substance abuse, and suicide (Nugent, 2000). Keiley (2002) suggests that children who are gifted experience difficulty managing failure as most things come easily to them. When failure is experimentally induced, gifted children have been found to show significant feelings of physiological stress and more negative affect compared to those children who are not gifted. Other researchers have found that gifted children show no differences in the incidence of internalizing difficulties compared to nongifted children (Garland & Zigler, 1999; Galluci et al., 1999). Again, these differences in findings may relate to the level of giftedness as well as other mitigating circumstances (family stress, low income, etc.).

Externalizing problems in gifted children have not been studied as prominently. As mentioned earlier in this section, children with ADHD who are also gifted have been found to show difficulties with social adjustment that is more similar than different from those problems experienced by children with a sole diagnosis of ADHD. Most studies have found the same incidence of externalizing diagnoses in groups of children who are gifted compared to those who are not (Keiley, 2002).

Some studies have looked at delinquents and the incidence of giftedness in this population. Samenow (1998) found that although some delinquents scored poorly on traditional ability tests, they showed excellent ability to "assess other people for their own purposes and carry out elaborate schemes (p. 67)." Neihart (2002) defines these abilities as "untaught" intelligence that is developed through experience. Seeley (1984) found that a sizable minority of adolescents in an adjudicated sample were gifted, but gifted in fluid reasoning (the ability to think on one's feet and learn from previous experiences) with relatively lower skills in verbal and academic knowledge. For the most part, however, most gifted children do not show delinquent types of behavior and tend to reach advanced levels of moral reasoning at earlier ages (Janos et al., 1989). Niehart (2002) suggest that this advanced moral reasoning is likely related to lower levels of delinquency in this population and that it serves as a mediating factor against the development of such difficulties.

In addition to the research looking at specific types of diagnostic categories in groups of children with giftedness, findings as to the resilience of children who are gifted have indicated that many of the children have high self-efficacy, sensitivity, and have developed effective coping strategies for stress (Mendaglio, 1995; Merrell et al., 1996; Tomchin et al., 1996). It is likely that the gifted child's high cognitive ability has assisted him/her with developing strategies that are successful in combating problems in adjustment and although normal stressors occur they are managed with more success than same-aged peers are able to accomplish.

Parenting Issues in Social Competence with Gifted Children

Research has begun evaluating the role that parents play in developing social competence and independence in their children. Windecker-Nelson et al. (1997) found that the mother's attitude toward independence and their willingness to tolerate this independence were related to the preschooler's resulting social competence. A moderate level of strictness (not permissiveness) was related to higher social competence. In a large study of parents of advanced Head Start children, the families appeared to have more resources and to use those resources constructively as well as fewer stresses in their family life (Robinson et al., 2002). In addition, these parents took a positive approach to parenting and directly encouraged their child's school performance. These children were followed through grade 3 and found to maintain high achievement and ability throughout these years.

The study of factors involved in parenting of gifted children is a fairly new area of investigation. Bronfenbrenner (1986) first suggested that the social context in which the parent participates influences the child's development. Some have found that the perceptions the parent has of the child's abilities are more utilized by the child to estimate his/her ability than objective feedback such as grades (Phillips, 1984).

There are many challenges to parenting a child who is gifted that differ from the developmental obstacles faced by parents of any child. One of the areas of difficulty lies around the establishment of family roles. Since gifted children are more mature and exert more control over what they are interested in, the role of the gifted child in the family can be problematic (Windecker-Nelson et al., 1997). Difficulty in establishing an appropriate role for a child who is gifted may be an area of great concern particularly as the child ages. Due to the challenging nature of a child who is gifted, the parents' own self-perceptions of their abilities may be an area of difficulty as well as their perceived competence in managing the child's attitudes and behaviors (Colangelo & Dettman, 1983).

Many of us experience these challenges with adolescents while for the primary school aged child who is gifted, these challenges may occur at a much earlier age. Additional challenges have been found in preventing and/or reducing sibling rivalry. Some parents have reported that they feel inadequately prepared to cope with a gifted child, that it changed their marriage, and that difficulties in communicating with their partner as to expectations were present (Dettman & Colangelo, 2004). It is important to note that these parents were also concerned about the adjustment of their child and held the previous views that giftedness translates into social and emotional difficulties.

Parents may also become concerned about the child's ability to "fit in" with neighborhood children and games. Since at times the interests may differ the child may feel more of an affinity for older children and/or adults either of which is not at the child's age and may be inappropriate as sole social outlets (Hackney, 1981). Keirouz (1990) suggests that parents of gifted children may not feel comfortable confiding in neighborhood parents because their children are so very different. Creel and Karnes (1988) found that support networks of parents with gifted children are the most prized networks for parents of gifted children.

Parenting a gifted child with a disability (LD or ADHD) appears to be significantly more difficult than with either condition alone. When the child has ADHD and giftedness, the parent has the difficulties described for gifted children as well as the challenges of a child with ADHD. Moon et al. (2001) found that parents of children with combined diagnoses had somewhat unstructured and disorganized processes. Difficulties were also present in establishing consistent routines, more conflict within the family, and had more isolation from each other. While this was a very small study, the findings are of interest and instructive for additional research. Parenting a gifted child with a learning disability also has challenges but they tend to be more in the academic area than in behavioral control (Vespi & Yewchuk, 1992). Further study is needed to elucidate the effects of "twice-exceptional" children and parenting and family issues.

Conclusion

Early myths that children who are gifted have significant social and emotional difficulties appear to be fading with more and more empirical evidence that they show good if not excellent social competence. However, it has also been found that children who are exceptionally or profoundly gifted experience more difficulty with peers than those who are moderately gifted. As the child's ability moves farther from the norm, more social problems as well as difficulty in emotional adjustment appear. While this is a minority of children in the general population, it is important to recognize that the diagnosis of giftedness is not homogeneous but is rather heterogeneous in nature of degree. For the vast majority of gifted children, social skills are present and the challenge is to match social development with intellectual development particularly given the propensity toward asynchronous development.

In addition, there is very little research conducted on children with a dual diagnosis—those who are now termed "twice-exceptional." It appears from the few studies that exist that these children have significantly more social difficulties as well as behavioral problems and adjustment. The misfit between ability and behavioral or learning skills is a painful mix for these children and their parents. Parenting is a challenge for most parents of gifted children but appears to be even more so for parents of children who are gifted and who have externalizing behavioral problems.

Tied into these issues are the problems with assessment of giftedness. Most theorists and clinicians now envision giftedness as including high ability as well as creativity. Measures for high ability are difficult as they are generally ceiling out well below the potential for an exceptionally or profoundly gifted child. Moreover, measures of creativity are also problematic and there is no good consensus as to what makes up creativity. The most common definition is to assume that talents can be unidimensional (athletic, music, drama, etc.) or multidimensional. Matching these talents to appropriate academic programming can be very tricky. The assessment of giftedness in minorities as well as in children with unusual learning patterns (high performance skills and low verbal ability) is an important step in understanding the heterogeneity of giftedness and eventually providing the support to families and children.

10

Social Competence in Children with Externalizing Disorders

David was in kindergarten when he was first referred for behavioral difficulties. He had shot a rubber band toward another child's eye and had shown no remorse about this action. In fact, David had expressed disappointment that he had not hit his classmate. Therapy was recommended as well as parental support and he continued in his current placement. Behavioral difficulties continued but for the most part he responded to the management plan that had been established for him. His parents had divorced when David was three and he was living with his mother who was an accountant with a degree in psychology as well as in business. He had little contact with his father following the divorce and after 2 years did not see or hear from his father at all. His mother began therapy to assist in managing David's behavior which she described as having "always" been challenging. After a few sessions she ended her therapy and felt that David's problems had been "exaggerated."

In first grade David's teacher re-referred him for an assessment. He was reported to tease other children and to require them to give him their lunches as "payment" for not getting hurt. His learning skills were described as somewhat below average but his teacher felt these difficulties were due to motivational problems rather than to a true learning disability. His assessment found above average ability as well as academic achievement. Personality and behavioral assessment found anger at his mother and father as well as at his teacher. He felt he had many friends and reported that other children liked him.

David's teacher reported that he frequently challenged her directions and was often noncompliant. When she confronted him, he frequently denied the misbehavior even when his teacher had directly witnessed the problem. David scored high on the aggression and externalizing scales on a behavior rating scale as well as in the at-risk range on the scale measuring social skills. David's mother did not report any clinically significant problems on a behavior rating scale or during the interview. She also reported that his behavior at home, while challenging, was manageable. David's mother had been promoted to a position with a great deal of responsibility and she was not home as often as she had been in the past. Family therapy was again recommended but David's mother refused. Placement in a program for children with emotional disturbance was not found to be appropriate as David showed few emotional difficulties, and thus did not qualify. He continued to be a low average student and to be in frequent altercations with his peers and his teacher.

David was again referred in third grade and the referral question at this time involved his harm to another child in his class. He had hit the child repeatedly when he refused to give David a toy that he wanted. David showed little remorse about this incident and reported that it was the peer's fault. His reasoning was that if he had given David the toy there would have been no problem. David was referred for counseling within the school as his mother again refused private treatment. He was also placed on a behavioral management program that controlled his behavior within structured settings. Recess, lunch, art, gym, and music classes continued to be problematic for him as he continually challenged the limits.

A psychiatrist was employed by the district for a diagnostic interview and David was diagnosed with conduct disorder. It was also revealed during this interview that David had been reported to police for killing squirrels and skinning them when they were alive. He also had a reputation in his neighborhood for cruelty to other children. David could be very charming and made friends easily but generally had friends that were either socially isolated or rejected by others. David, again, did not qualify for special education services but was provided with behavioral support throughout his elementary school years. By middle school David was arrested for shoplifting and for animal cruelty. He was placed in a juvenile facility for fire-setting at the age of 14 and continued in this facility until age 16. David graduated from high school and dropped out of sight until he was 25 when he was arrested for a scam that took money from elderly people.

David's difficulties began at an early age and of particular concern was his use of people to meet his needs without regard to their needs and his lack of remorse. These problems escalated as he aged and David learned how to hide many of the troublesome behaviors from adults. His peers either feared and avoided him or looked up to him. He did not seem to require close, intimate relationships and appeared to view people solely as a means to an end. David's diagnosis of a conduct disorder included the three symptoms that are most predictive of later antisocial behaviors in adults: stealing/lying, fire-setting, and cruelty to animals and smaller children. He did not meet criteria for a program for emotional disturbance because his difficulties were mostly behavioral in nature and there were few to no indications of significant emotional problems.

Externalizing Diagnoses

Externalizing behaviors are defined as those actions that are overt, often include aggression and high activity levels, and are disruptive to the child's ability to form relationships with adults and with peers. DSM IV-TR (APA, 2000) includes conduct disorder, oppositional defiant disorder, and ADHD under the category of disruptive behavior disorders. Since an earlier chapter has discussed ADHD, this chapter will concentrate on conduct disorder (CD) and oppositional defiant disorder (ODD).

Conduct disorder is defined as behaviors that are disruptive to relationships, involve contact with the law, and which are significantly behaviorally challenging. Behavioral difficulties are frequently referred for psychological and psychiatric treatment and have been found to comprise one-third to one-half of all clinical referrals (Webster-Stratton, 1993). These children have been found to be at risk for peer rejection as well as parental and sibling abuse (Coie, 1990; Herbert, 1991; Reid et al., 1981). Many children with CD also have a diagnosis of ADHD (approximately 75%) which further complicates the picture for treatment. Waschbusch (2002) suggests that the combination of ADHD and CD are additive and that these children show a more severe manifestation of the disorder.

Conduct disorder is not generally diagnosed prior to the age of 7 and most preschool children are diagnosed with ODD. A diagnosis of CD requires the existence of problems that have lasted at least 6 months during which time at least three of the following symptoms must be present: physical cruelty to people and/or animals, stealing/breaking and entering, lying and cheating in games, aggression toward others often with a weapon, destruction of property, fire-setting, truancy, and running away from home at least twice during this period of time (APA, 2000).

The incidence of CD has been found to be between 1.8% and 8.7% (Esser et al., 1990; Kashani et al., 1987) with many of the behaviors seen in most children to one degree or another (Moffitt, 1993). For ODD the difficulties are less severe and may be seen as related to problems with adjustment. ODD has not been found to translate into antisocial personality disorder in childhood unless the difficulties are severe and early in onset.

For ODD the difficulties are less severe and may be seen as related to problems with adjustment. ODD has not been found to translate into antisocial personality disorder in childhood unless the difficulties are severe and early in onset. ODD is often seen as transitional and related to difficulties in environmental demands that resolve with treatment and with age.

As with many diagnoses, it is the severity of the symptoms as well as the frequency that trigger a diagnosis of CD. Aggressive behavior and noncompliance is seen in both CD and ODD. These difficulties have been linked to problems in social functioning including rejection by peers and poor social problem-solving skills (Dodge et al., 1990). Although these difficulties are found in both CD and ODD, children with CD tend to overestimate their social functioning (Hymel et al., 1993) while those with ADHD or ODD often show lowered self-esteem and more accurate views of their social functioning (Grizenko et al., 1993). When depression is found to co-occur with CD, the psychopathology that is present is more pronounced and more disabling (Ferro et al., 1994). In one epidemiological study, more than half of the adolescents with an affective disorder also qualified for a diagnosis of CD or ODD and had a poorer prognosis (Bird et al., 1988; Harrington et al., 1991).

It has been hypothesized that the development of CD may differ depending on age of onset. The early onset "pathway" has been described as the presence of ODD in early childhood with lying, stealing, and fire-setting appearing in early elementary school and progressing to significant difficulties with aggression, interpersonal violence, and property destruction in late elementary school and early adolescence (Lahey et al., 1992). When CD begins in adolescence, it is believed the prognosis is more positive and may be due to developmental issues (Webster-Stratton, 1993). For the early expression of CD it appears that these children and adolescents may be more chronically antisocial with behaviors that extend throughout the lifespan (White et al., 1990). Thus, not all children with ODD go on to develop CD and not all with CD go on to develop an antisocial personality disorder. There are a number of influences that increase the likelihood of more difficulty in adolescence and on into adulthood.

Influences Related to CD

In a review of the literature in externalizing disorders, Webster-Stratton (1993) identified the following factors as influencing the continuation of CD into adulthood. These factors are early age of onset, having problems in many environments, having several different symptoms, and family and parent characteristics (Kazdin, 1987). Some have postulated that the child's temperament also contributes to the severity of CD, and thus the propensity for this type of problem may be partially genetically programmed. The characteristics of high activity, low adaptability, and negative mood have been related to difficulties with aggression at older ages (Bates et al., 1991). It has also been recognized that negative family factors such as conflict and poor behavioral management techniques support later development of antisocial behaviors particularly when paired with a more difficult temperament. On the positive side a difficult temperament coupled with a favorable family environment is not related to externalizing behaviors (Maziade et al., 1989). Thus, it appears that a difficult temperament in and of itself does not lead to significant externalizing behaviors unless coupled with environmental difficulties.

Related to these findings are those that indicate children with externalizing behaviors often misinterpret social cues and ascribe more hostile and negative intent to fairly neutral situations (Milich & Dodge, 1984). Moreover, Dodge and Newman (1981) found that children who are aggressive often focus on aggressive cues from their peers more than children without aggression (Goutz, 1987). Therefore, children who are aggressive are more sensitive to aggression from others and respond with higher levels of aggression when threatened. For a child with ODD or CD, peer rejection is frequently experienced. This experience also colors the child's perception and attribution of other's intents to a more negative focus and thus engenders a more aggressive response. This aggressive stance likely further alienates peers and limits the child's ability to develop prosocial behaviors.

On top of the tendency to respond aggressively, these children also appear to have difficulty with social problem-solving usually using a more aggressive answer when a prosocial solution is likely a better response to the problem at hand (Asarnow & Callan, 1985). Due to the fact that children with CD/ODD tend to have difficulties with prosocial behaviors, they are also rejected and distrusted by their peers. Such distrust often confirms the child with CD's reading of aggressive intent in their relationships with friends and further precipitates reciprocal aggressive reactions (Dodge & Somberg, 1987). These difficulties increase over time and thus effectively limit the child's interactions with others.

Parenting a Child with CD/ODD

Parenting skills have also been linked to CD/ODD. Webster-Stratton (1993) found that parents of children with CD/ODD tend to show fewer positive behaviors, to use aggression toward their child and to be less positive in verbal interactions with their child, to be less consistent in their management of the child's behavior moving from permissive to restrictive without warning, and to ignore or even punish prosocial behaviors. Patterson (1986) has suggested that children with CD/ODD get their needs met through escalating negative behaviors which results in the parent becoming more negative and coercive also. Such patterns lead to higher rates of maladaptive behavior and noncompliance and more conflict in the family.

Children with CD have also been found to show fewer positive verbal and nonverbal behaviors and to use more negative and coercive body language, voice prosody, and gestures when interacting with their parents compared to children without externalizing behavior disorders (Webster-Stratton & Spitzer, 1991). Webster-Stratton (1993) suggests that due to the child's response to the parent as well as fewer positive affects noted, the child is less reinforcing to the parent to interact with, and thus a negative vicious cycle is established that further degrades the parent–child attachment and bond.

Parents of children with CD/ODD also tend to have difficulties with their own psychopathology. Maternal depression, paternal alcoholism, and antisocial behavior in either or both parents have been linked to increased risk for the development of CD in the child (Webster-Stratton, 1993). Maternal depression has been linked to CD because the mother does not respond as readily to the child's needs and demands and may be more negative and critical than would be otherwise warranted. The mother with depression has also been found to make more demands on the child with the result being that the child with a propensity for CD subsequently becomes more and more noncompliant (McMahon & Forehand, 1984; Webster-Stratton & Hammond, 1990). Both fathers and grandparents of children with CD show a higher-than-expected incidence of CD and criminal behaviors. These findings have been linked to genetic theories for criminal behaviors but can also be explained by a negative environment or an interaction of the two variables (Frick et al., 1991).

In addition to the individual parent's psychopathology contributing to the child's development of CD/ODD, family factors also relate to the child's difficulty with maladaptive behaviors. Parental discord and divorce have been found to be associated with CD but not necessarily causative (Kazdin, 1987). O'Leary and Emery (1982) were able to further elucidate the relationship between parental conflict and the development of CD and found that the level of discord between parents was more diagnostic for later development of conduct problems than divorce per se. Marriages that are characterized with aggression, inconsistent parenting, negative exchanges between parent and child that quickly escalate, and parents who are stressed and/or depressed tend to have a higher incidence of children with CD (Forgatch et al., 1988; Webster-Stratton, 1990). It is also important to note that families that have children with CD tend to struggle more with poverty, illness, and unemployment than those families who do not. These difficulties are not directly related to the development of CD but likely increase the risk for a child with a propensity for these difficulties.

For our purposes of understanding social competence in this population, the finding that mothers who have negative and poor social relationships with extended family, outside agencies, and friends tend to have children more likely to develop antisocial personalities (Wahler & Dumas, 1984). Webster-Stratton (1993) suggests that such "social insularity" contributes to the child's perception of social exchanges as aversive and unproductive rather than supportive or helpful. She has found that this combination of variables is related to a relapse of the family in treatment or the child's resistance to treatment.

Developmental Course

Early onset of CD is of particular concern as it is stable over time and the prognosis is very poor when severe behavior disturbance is present at this early age (Loeber, 1991). In 30–40% of cases early onset CD has been found to continue into adulthood as an antisocial personality disorder (Zoccolillo et al., 1992). Early onset CD has been associated with criminality, substance abuse, and impaired social and occupational adjustment (Kazdin 1987).

Webster-Stratton and Lindsay (1999) sought to examine the social competence of young children with conduct problems. They compared a clinic-referred group of preschool children with ODD or conduct problems to a matched group of typically developing children on measures of social information processing, conflict management skills, and social play interactions with peers and with parents. It was found that children with conduct problems tend to overestimate their social skills and to attribute negative intentions to others. In addition, this group was found to have fewer prosocial behaviors and knowledge of coping strategies than the typically developing children and was also more immature in their play skills.

Others have found that young children with conduct problems tend to have difficulties in understanding how to approach their peers to play with them and how to be positive rather than negative in their interactions (Putallaz & Wasserman, 1990; Toupin et al., 1997). This lack of prosocial behaviors contributes to peer rejection at later ages as well as to the distrust that their peers have of their intent. It has also been found that young children with conduct problems frequently experience difficulty entering a play situation appropriately and in matching their behaviors and intensity of emotions to others in the play group (Webster-Stratton & Lindsay, 1999).

Children with CD/ODD have been found to show verbal and physical aggression as well as being threatening when attempting to join their peers. Instead of asking to join a game, it is not uncommon for children with CD/ODD to push their way into the game and to bully the others or conversely to whine and cry when not included as they had demanded (Brotman et al., 2005). Once they have gained entry into the play group they often will become easily frustrated and then disrupt the game particularly when it does not go their way (Putallaz & Wasserman, 1990).

Campbell (1994) studied boys with behavioral difficulties in preschool over a 2-year period. Those children with poorer social competence had consistent difficulties with behavior over the time span while those with higher social abilities showed fewer behavioral difficulties. Their families also appeared to have more difficulties with conflict and discord with the families with more difficulties having children who experienced problems at a younger age. In addition, boys with lower intelligence and whose mothers were depressed showed the most behavioral difficulties which were also more persistent.

Investigators studying teenagers with CD have found that the immature understanding of another's intent and emotional response to provocation continues with age (Panella & Henggeler, 1986). Moreover, adolescents with CD have been found to use inappropriate perspective taking in their interactions with others and in their use of appropriate prosocial behaviors (Gottman 1983). Adolescents with CD have been found to experience difficulties with executive functioning particularly in regard to developing appropriate friendships (Clark et al., 2002). As with the younger children, difficulty in developing appropriate strategies for coping is present in adolescents with CD. These difficulties make it difficult for the child to develop appropriate alternatives to their general way of solving problems and to improve the effectiveness of these solutions. Such difficulties likely contribute to the problems that these adolescents have in adapting to ever-changing environmental demands and to assessing the appropriateness of their responses.

Comorbidity

Social functioning in children with more than a sole diagnosis of CD has not been clearly researched. Some have found that when an affective disorder is present as well as CD social functioning is significantly compromised throughout development (Asarnow, 1988; Harrington et al., 1991). Children who have been rejected by their peers have also been found to show more conduct problems as well as higher levels of depressive symptoms (Cole & Carpentieri, 1990).

In an attempt to further understand the relationship between affective disorders and conduct disorders, Renouf et al. (1997) studied children with depression, conduct disorder, and other psychiatric diagnoses between the ages of 8 and 13 years. The social functioning of all children was evaluated at two points in time with most children assessed approximately every 7.7 months. Findings indicated a significant association between conduct disorder, depression, and socioeconomic status (SES) over time.

Lower SES was found to be associated with poorer levels of social competence. Measures of social competence were found to be consistent over time and were not associated with race or gender. Children with depression were found to show lower self-esteem while this finding was not present for children with CD. It was also found that children with depression and CD had poorer self competence than those with a sole diagnosis of depression or CD.

Thus, having more than one diagnosis is related to poorer social competence. In addition, having fewer family resources also contributes to lower social functioning and adjustment. It was also found that when CD occurred early on in life in conjunction with depression, the outcome was significantly poorer than a later diagnosis.

Renouf et al. (1997) concluded that since a sole diagnosis of depression or CD appeared to influence later social competence less than a combined diagnosis, the comorbidity of these disorders appears to be more permanent and a possible psychological trait. Conversely, a sole diagnosis of CD or depression appeared to be more transitional and a function of the environment and the child's adjustment at a certain point in time. Conduct disorder also appeared to be more chronic than depression and to be related to more detrimental effects on social competence. Children with CD have been found to be more aversive and hostile in their peer relationships and these behaviors may negatively influence their ability to develop prosocial skills. In contrast, children with depression are approached by their peers and after recovery seem to be able to reintegrate into their social environment (Altmann & Gotlib, 1988). They also appear readily able to develop appropriate social relationships; a skill not frequently present in children with CD.

Gresham et al. (2005) found that children with ADHD + CD have unrealistically high views of their own social abilities and social competence compared to others with attentional problems or no difficulties. In addition, these children also were viewed by their teachers as less academically and socially competent than children with attentional difficulties or with no disorder. In contrast, children with difficulties with attention were rated by their teachers as average in social competence and in social skills. It may be that solely having difficulties with attention, in and of itself, does not relate to problems with social functioning. When these difficulties are combined with problems with behavioral control, then social competence becomes more difficult and more problematic.

Conclusion

Thus children with CD/ODD show difficulties in establishing appropriate social interactions at very young ages with those experiencing these problems early being at the highest risk for the development of antisocial behaviors in adolescence and into adulthood. Problems including difficulty with social information processing, attributing hostile intent to others where none is present, and having a low frustration tolerance all appear to place the child at significant risk for conduct disorder. In addition, the families of these children often have their own psychopathology with criminal behavior and alcoholism being present for many of them. In addition, maternal depression, although not causative, certainly contributes to problems for a child with a difficult temperament and one who experiences difficulty with developing appropriate social behaviors.

As with other children, when appropriate parental models for socialization are not present, children at risk for CD/ODD experience difficulty learning necessary prosocial behaviors as well as valuing other's needs and desires as much as their own. Such early teaching may be invaluable for these children and may set the stage for assisting the child in valuing others as well as in the development of empathy. Interventions are beginning to target these areas with particular attention to the child's ability to encode information accurately and respond appropriately to this interpretation. In addition, the ability to generate alternatives and select the most appropriate one is another aspect that requires intervention. Given the finding by Webster-Stratton and Lindsay (1999) that parents with depression and those with ongoing aggressive marital discord tend to experience a higher rate of relapse and resistance to treatment, it may well be important to assess these possible difficulties prior to beginning any treatment. The following section briefly reviews some of the more recent intervention attempts with children with conduct problems.

Interventions

Since young children with conduct problems are at highest risk for the development of life-long difficulties, many interventions have centered on children in preschool and in elementary school. Studies have sought to examine the child's risk for serious externalizing behavior through using many points of evaluation throughout the child's early years. Such practices are felt to strengthen our understanding of a child's risk for difficulty and to establish the stability of the child's difficulties (Lahey et al., 2002). Teacher and parent screening reports have been found to be the best predictor of later difficulties particularly when the child has been studied in fourth and fifth grade (Hill et al., 2006).

Most studies have found that the most effective intervention utilizes many components that address the child's difficulty as well as parental support and guidance (Tremblay et al., 1995; Walker et al., 1998). The Coping Power program (Lochman & Wells, 2004) provides social-cognitive interventions coupled with behavioral parent training and has been found to lower the rate of delinquent behaviors, substance abuse, and teacher-reported difficulties at a 1-year follow-up.

The Fast Track program has been found to produce some improvement in the child's behavior particularly when begun in early elementary school. It is designed to be utilized in many sites and using many components to study children who are at highest risk for externalizing behaviors continuing throughout their lifespan (CPPRG, 1992). It has been demonstrated to work well in early elementary school and improve behaviors for this aged child. It is meant to target behaviors in a preventative manner to assist with difficulties with poor parenting skills, difficulties with social problem-solving, and with improving coping skills. It also provides support for the development of appropriate academic skills, improvement of home–school interactions, and to improve socialization abilities (Bierman et al., 1996). Focus is also placed on the parents' ability to cope with the child's behaviors, family risk factors such as divorce, conflict, and poverty, and home–school difficulties (McMahon et al., 1996).

Early results have found improvement in the home–school collaboration for the child, improved rates of aggressive and oppositional behaviors observed in the school and improvement in behavior at home (CPPRG, 1999a). In addition, the children were less likely to be placed in special education, had better social interactions and peer acceptance, and showed better coping skills following participation in this program when measured at the end of first grade (CPPRG, 1999a,b). Changes in parents were also found with parents showing better communication with their children and to utilize consistent and more positive discipline methods (CPPRG, 2002). An important finding was that 37% of the intervention group was found to be functioning within average expectations by the end of third grade compared to 27% of the control group. The parent's skills as well as the child's social competence continue to improve from first grade through third.

The Conduct Problems Prevention Research Group (2004) sought to study the effects of this program when administered in fourth and fifth grades. Three cohorts were selected of children with the most significant externalizing behaviors. The schools that participated in this study were divided into those that participated in the interventions and those that did not. There were 445 children in 191 first-grade classrooms for the intervention group and 446 children in 210 classrooms for the control groups. All children and their parents in the study were followed from first grade through fifth grade. For the children in the Fast Track Program, improvements were found in social competence and in their ability to solve social problems compared to the control group. While these improvements were noted, it was also reported that the children at highest risk for continuing problems continued to have significant difficulties in the school setting despite the interventions provided.

Other researchers have focused on the family and parenting skills testing the hypothesis that significant conduct problems are the result of poor parenting. Work by Patterson and colleagues have studied the response of parents to a parent training program with fairly good results. The program rests on five family management practices including teaching on how to pinpoint problem behaviors, direct teaching of reinforcement techniques moving from tangible to social reinforcers, teaching of discipline techniques (time out, taking away privileges, etc.), and finally improved monitoring of the child and improved problem-solving and negotiation strategies. In addition, Patterson and Chamberlain (1988) report that 30% of the time in these groups involves working with the parent's own psychopathology.

Webster-Stratton (1984) also developed a parent-training program for parents of young children with CD. This program, entitled BASIC, utilizes helping the parent play appropriately with their child as well as teaching differential-attention techniques and use of compliance training. The novel piece of this intervention is the direct teaching of parents in interacting with their child. Videotapes are used that show correct modeling of behaviors in natural situations and assisting the parents in developing these skills. This program requires 13 sessions at 2 hours each in a group situation facilitated by a therapist. The children do not attend these sessions but the parents videotape their interactions with their children at home and complete homework assignments under the guidance of a therapist.

Webster-Stratton (1993) reviewed the various types of interventions and basically found improvement in all of these that was superior to family therapy alone. However, there were children that continued to experience difficulty despite participation in these programs. She suggests that when treatment begins too late, the child does not respond due to established behavioral patterns as well as entrenched parenting skills. In addition, a negative reputation with teachers and peers has likely been established. Webster-Stratton (1983) also suggests that parents whose psychopathology remains untreated have children who respond less favorably to intervention. Families who did show significant improvement were also found to have improved marital functioning and satisfaction. She also suggests that for programs that solely focus on parent training and parent guidance, the child's part in the difficulty is not present and may be a crucial area for intervention. In this case, programs such as Fast Track seek to utilize a multiple component intervention that stretches across environments as well as including the child as well as the parents.

Fewer projects have utilized teacher training within their focus. Teachers play an important part in the child's life and their ability to control peer interactions, at least within the classroom. Thus, this oversight may be crucial for some of the children. Teachers may experience significant difficulty with some of these children and have little support. For a child like David profiled earlier, special education was ruled out and the teacher was left to deal with David's misbehaviors as well as his resistance to learning. For other children, delays in academics can contribute to increased behavioral difficulties. Some have focused on supporting the learning (Fast Track; Coie & Krehbiel, 1984) and have found improvement in disruptive behavior. These areas need to be further studied and collaboration between home and school is an important step in assisting these children.

Greenberg and Kusche (2006) developed the Promoting Alternative Thinking Strategies (PATHS) curriculum. This curriculum is designed for use by classroom teachers and stresses the teaching of children for understanding social cognition and social competence as well as improving behavioral compliance. Findings over the past 20 years are improved ability of the children to manage their behaviors as well as their emotions as well as a more harmonious classroom setting. This curriculum has been found to be helpful for preschool and elementary aged students in both regular and special education classrooms. It has also been found that the principal of the school and other administrative specialists need to be supportive of the program as well as having effective teaching of the teachers for implementation. This program is one of the few teacher-focused programs for children with conduct problems that is available.

In summary, programs that include multiple components and which continue for several years appear to have the most promise for working with children at highest risk for conduct disorder. These programs are not only intensive for time and personnel required, they are also quite expensive and generally beyond the reach of most families and/or school systems. Funding is generally provided through research dollars, and increased exposure to these programs is important for these children in particular. In addition, teacher support appears to be an area that has not been addressed adequately by most programs and which requires further research. Teacher training programs may not provide the necessary training in working with these extremely challenging children and their families and may also need to have further information about possible new directions. Given the finding that these interventions need to begin at an early age, it appears crucial that further implementation occur at the local educational levels. Social competence for these children has been the one variable that has been found to consistently improve with intervention. Given the importance of this variable to later adjustment, this finding is very important and provides justification for introducing these skills in preschool and beyond. For children without significant behavioral difficulties, these interventions are also helpful and can assist with their adjustment particularly in light of social functioning.

While Fast Track, BASIC, and other programs show promise for these children, the children at the highest rate of deviance do not respond as readily to these interventions. The families of these children also appear to have the highest risk for deviance and psychopathology. Introducing programs at the preschool level has been found to be helpful in reducing later behavioral difficulties particularly with regard to social competence and improvement in parenting (Brotman et al., 2005). Continued work is certainly needed in this area to promote our understanding not only of the process seen with these children but also to determine which factors place them at higher risk for difficulty and which of these factors can be improved with intervention.

11

Social Competence in Children with Internalizing Disorders

Kevin was in third grade when he entered the school psychologist's office and asked to talk to her about his feelings. He indicated that other children didn't like to play with him and that he felt very lonely. When asked about his mood, Kevin said he was fine and smiled throughout the interview. Kevin reported that the other children did not choose him to play on teams and that he had no one to play with during recess. When asked what he did during recess, Kevin reported that he just walked around or talked to the teacher on recess duty. He also told the therapist that he began having these problems in second grade and that he had had friends before that time.

Kevin came to the office several times to talk about his concerns but was very guarded when asked about what was happening at home. When asked to draw pictures of his family, the pictures were generally of smiling stick figures holding hands and walking together. After a few sessions, he was again asked to draw a picture of his family doing something together. This time he drew a picture of his father lying on a couch watching TV with beer bottles next to the couch and his mother and he in the kitchen eating dinner. The faces on all the figures were smiling but Kevin's picture showed smiling with tears on his cheeks. When asked to explain the picture, Kevin said, "That's just what we do at night." He continued to smile throughout the interviews and subsequent meetings.

After a month of sessions, Kevin's mother came for a meeting. When she was shown the pictures, she broke into tears and began talking about her husband's withdrawal from the family, his drinking, and her feelings of social isolation. She shared that she had thought Kevin was doing well as he told her all was fine except his lack of friends. She reported that approximately 18 months earlier her husband had been fired from his position as a mid-level manager. After that time he had taken a series of positions that were below his previous level of education. Kevin's father had begun drinking heavily every night and withdrawing more and more from his family.

We talked about depression and dysthymia and how Kevin was likely trying to protect her and take care of her. It was also likely that he was feeling a sense of loss of his father's love and attention. The sadness was also noted by his teacher and was beginning to impact his learning. He appeared to be tired a great deal of the time and did not seem to be interested in activities in which other children participated. Kevin was showing indications of depression that were beginning to influence not only his social relationships but also his academic progress.

A first look at Kevin would make one think he was a happy child with few difficulties. Only after talking to him did it become readily apparent that he was sad and feeling very isolated not just from his friends but also from his father. It required several more meetings with Kevin and more family meetings for his father to agree to family counseling in order to assist with these difficulties.

Internalizing Disorders

Internalizing disorders are those where the child experiences a mood disorder that impacts his/her functioning. These have been defined by DSM IV TR (APA, 1997) as including major depression, dysthymia, bipolar disorder, and anxiety disorders. Each of these is a disorder of affect and for children depression and anxiety can appear remarkably similar in nature (Semrud-Clikeman et al., 2003). In many cases the term "mood disorder" may more accurately capture the difficulties the child is experiencing.

In the case of bipolar disorder, obsessive compulsive disorder (OCD), and social anxiety, characteristics differ and it is important to evaluate the difficulties the child is experiencing. While Kevin's difficulties were mostly depression related, he did experience anxiety when asked to attempt new tasks and meet new people. This chapter will discuss depression, bipolar disorder, anxiety, and OCD separately for diagnostic purposes followed by a discussion of social impairment found with each of these diagnoses. In some cases, social competence studies in depression and anxiety overlap and may be discussed together as appropriate.

Depression

Conceptions about depression in children have changed over the years initially in the 1970s it was believed that children could not experience depression. The current view of depression in children is that it is a syndrome that can be present at an early age and which is able to be diagnosed (Bell-Dolan et al., 1993). Interpersonal theories of depression stress the role of impaired relationships with others as well as a tendency to provoke negative interactions with peers and caretakers (Joiner & Coyne, 1999). Social behaviors that, in particular, define depression include poor eye contact, lack of social reciprocity, lack of social conversation, and a sense of disconnectedness in conversation (Segrin & Abramson, 1994). These behaviors serve to isolate the child even more and to increase the tendency to withdraw from interpersonal contact as such contact becomes more and more unreinforcing (Gable & Shean, 2000).

There has been conflicting evidence as to whether children and adults who are depressed have deficits in social skills as well as in social interaction (Gable & Shean, 2000). Self-report studies have found that people who are depressed view themselves more negatively (Dykman et al., 1991). While it is not clear that deficiencies in social skills are present, a meta-analysis found that negative self-perceptions were common in depression but social skills deficits were not (Segrin, 1990).

Most studies have used observers to rate the child or adolescent's social skills. Gable and Shean (2000) utilized ratings of people who interacted with depressed subjects. The following aspects of the conversation were evaluated with these participants: a show of interest in the other person, ability to relate to the person, expressiveness, and conversation etiquette (taking turns, listening, not interrupting). Subjects were college students classified as depressed by the Beck Depression Inventory. It was predicted that the participants would rate the depressed partners as less expressive and less interested in the nondepressed partner on a rating scale of social conversational skills. The study found that negative self-perceptions were found to lead to lower social responsiveness scores on the self-report scale. In addition, the depressed subjects rated their partners more negatively than did nondepressed dyads. The authors interpret these findings to indicate that depression flavors the interactions due to negative self-perceptions rather than to any social skill deficits.

Most of the studies looking at self-perception have involved college age and adult populations. It would be interesting to examine whether this is a developmental process and whether children show the same aspects in their conversations and interactions with peers. These types of studies were not available after a literature search, and research in this area is sorely needed.

Depression in children and adolescents has been linked to low academic and social competence (Cole et al., 1998). Rudolph and Clark hypothesized that the behaviors of children with depression may lead their peers to share the belief that the depressed child is not open to friendly gestures due to social withdrawal. Moreover, because of neglect or rejection, the depressed child may come to view his/her peers as untrustworthy and negative toward him/her.

Findings have indicated that when children enter social interactions with a negative feeling or impression, they generally key into the negative interactions that can occur and attend solely to those aspects of any social gathering (Rudolph et al., 1997; Shirk et al., 1998). It is likely that the confluence of these negative experiences reinforces the feelings of depression as well as limiting the child's social contacts. These difficulties then, in turn, relate back to feelings of unworthiness and social isolation characteristic of children and adolescents with depression. This idea has support from the empirical work finding that depressed children appear to elicit negative reactions from their peers, show hostility and withdrawal, and have poorer-quality relationships (Altman & Gotlib, 1988; Baker et al., 1996; Goodyer et al., 1990; Rudolph et al., 1994).

Self-Perception

The longitudinal effect of depression on the self-evaluations of children with depression is unknown at this time. Previous studies have been equivocal with two finding a relationship between underestimation of social competence and depression (Cole et al., 1998; Kendall et al., 1990) and one finding that self-estimates of social competence were accurate. Rudolph and Clark (2001) sought to evaluate the relationship between skill deficits and self-perception of social competence in children with depression, aggression, those with depression and aggression, and those with neither depression nor aggression. They utilized teacher reports of the child's social experiences and peer social status and self-report as to the child's conception of their relationships to their peers. Findings indicated that the children in the depressed and depressed-aggressive groups had poorer self-evaluations than controls or children in the aggression group. These groups also viewed their peer groups more negatively. Teachers reported the control children had the highest levels of prosocial behavior while the aggressive-depressed group had the lowest. Interestingly, the aggressive-depressed group did not differ from the aggressive group in level of prosocial behaviors. The depressed group showed the most difficulty with withdrawal behaviors among the four groups. Aggressive children showed more aggressive behavior compared to the other groups with aggressive-depressed children showing similar levels to the control and depressed groups.

Teacher ratings indicated that the control children were the most popular with the aggressive-depressed group being the least popular. Children in the aggressive-depressed group were also rated as the most neglected or rejected among the 4 groups. When the children were regrouped according to popular–unpopular, the depressed children showed a more negative self-evaluation within the same social status category even when they were seen as desirable friends by their peers. Thus, a child who was depressed but accepted ranked himself/herself less favorably than one who was not depressed but accepted. This finding did not hold for the aggressive group with aggressive children showing few negative conceptions of themselves and even ranked themselves more positively than matched control children.

Thus, children with depression have been found to consistently rate themselves more negatively and less socially competent than those without depression or those with aggression. Children with aggression do not appear to differ from typically developing children on these aspects. The clinical groups showed social impairment with the children with depression showing more prosocial behaviors than those with aggression or aggression and depression. These findings may support the developmental idea that with continued negative exposure children who are depressed persist in their negative self-conceptions and thus become more socially withdrawn and isolated. It also indicates that children who are depressed do have appropriate prosocial behaviors that are not often utilized due to their withdrawal. This isolation, in turn, relates back to fewer and fewer positive social interactions and thus less social competence. This hypothesis needs to be tested using a longitudinal rather than a cross-sectional study and at this time remains tentative.

Support for this hypothesis comes from a study by Shah and Morgan (1996) who compared children who scored low and high on a depression inventory. Teachers rated each child on how the child would respond in various social situations. Findings indicated that the teachers consistently rated children with high rates of depressive symptoms to have difficulties in social competence particularly in the areas of entering a play group, responding to provocation, and responding to success. It was also found that the teacher ratings corresponded to the child's self-rating of depressive symptoms 85% of the time for high levels of depression and 77% for low levels.

Similarly, Bell-Dolan et al. (1993) studied children in an elementary school who were nominated by their peers for evidencing depressive symptomatology as well as teacher reports of depressive symptoms to evaluate the relationship between depression and social status. Each child completed the Child Depression Inventory (CDI; Kovacs & Beck, 1977) as well as a rating scale evaluating social functioning. Findings indicated that children scoring high on the CDI were rated by their peers and teachers as more socially withdrawn as well as evidencing more negative social behavior. In addition, the depressed child's self-rating showed inaccurate ratings on social competence: a finding not shared by his/her peers. Approximately 50% of the children underestimated their social competence while 50% overestimated their skills. These findings point to the sensitivity of peers to depressive-like symptoms as well as to inaccuracy of self-awareness as to the child's own behaviors on their social interactions. Such inaccuracy likely reflects in unsatisfactory social relationships which in turn may exacerbate their feelings of social withdrawal and isolation.

Prosocial and Aggressive Behaviors

The relationship between fewer prosocial behaviors seen in children with depression and aggression is an intriguing one as there has been some evidence that early aggressive behaviors are linked to depression in childhood and adolescence as well as to lower levels of social competence and peer acceptance (Patterson & Capaldi, 1990). Some have found that depression and aggression frequently co-occur, and when they do, the child experiences significant difficulties with social interactions and is frequently rejected from peer groups more than children with depression alone (Kiesner, 2002). In addition, when depression and aggression co-occur in adolescence, adult adjustment appears to be very poor compared to adolescents with a sole diagnosis of depression (Capaldi & Stoolmiller, 1999). For children who are aggressive, it has been hypothesized that this behavior leads to poor relationships across settings which in turn leads to depression due to failure (Boivin et al., 1994; Cole & Carpenteri, 1990; Patterson & Capaldi, 1990). It may well be that these children tend to be rejected more than neglected and that they may not key into the reasons why such rejection occurs.

Kiesner (2002) sought to test the model of aggression of depression leading to poorer social relationships. He studied relationships in Italian children who had shared the same teacher and peer group for at least 3 years. Children were evaluated at two time periods at least 1 year apart. Problem behaviors and peer status were significant predictors of depression at the second time period. Those children with more behavioral difficulties had lower peer status and higher rates of depression. Kiesner et al. (2002) found that when children were rejected inside the school but had sufficient social engagement in other areas of their life, they showed fewer depressive symptoms. Thus, problem behaviors and peer status may be separate variables while other aspects of the child's life may mediate whether these two issues lead to depression. It is also very possible that there are common risk factors that interact with both problem behaviors and peer status in a causative manner (Fergusson et al., 1996). One aspect that needs further discussion is the relationship between the child's social difficulties and his/her ability to regulate emotions.

Emotional Regulation

Tied into social competence is the finding that emotional regulation is a cornerstone for good social interactions. The ability to regulate one's emotions when under stress has been linked to developmental psychopathology and to poor adjustment across the lifespan (Sandstrom & Cramer, 2003). There is an important distinction between emotional regulation that is purposeful and those processes that are more automatic and involuntary and possibly linked to temperamental characteristics (Compas et al., 2001; Cramer, 2000). While emotional regulation that is purposeful has lent itself to training programs that have been helpful, investigations into more automatic responses have not been as clearly studied in children. Most studies have utilized adolescent and adult populations.

For children who are over-reactive or under-reactive to stress, there may be a link to later feelings of depression and emotional avoidance (Laor et al., 2001; Wolmer et al., 2001). Sandstrom and Cramer (2003) evaluated the relationship between how the child manages stress and his/her social competence. When the child showed an immature manner of handling stress (denying its presence, avoiding), social maladjustment was higher. However, conversely the child also did not perceive, or at least report, themselves to have difficulty. Such misperceptions likely make intervention far more difficult and also increase the likelihood that the child cannot correct inappropriate or unhelpful social behaviors. These children scored higher on measures of depression and social anxiety than those children admitting to difficulty under stress.

These findings are consistent with other research that indicates psychopathology is strongly related to problems with emotional regulation particularly in the social competence area and with internalizing and externalizing adjustment problems (Lengua, 2003). Temperamental issues have been tied to social development as it has been hypothesized to be the nucleus around which personality develops in relationship to environmental events (Caspi, 2000; Rothbart et al., 2000). For a child who is over-reactive, difficulties may be present in social relationships in terms of intensity of response as well as for irritability and lability. For a child who is under-reactive, there may be few opportunities to interact, and thus, problems develop in social development.

Tied into these aspects are the ideas of two emotionality systems: positive and negative. Negative emotionality includes arousal tendencies that operate when one is faced with fear-provoking events or frustration. Positive emotionality is linked to smiling, laughing, and seeking pleasurable activities (Rothbart, 1989). A child who is fearful in many situations has a higher incidence of depression as well as social withdrawal (Biederman et al., 1990; Rothbart et al., 1994). In contrast, positive emotionality has been linked to social competence and prosocial behavior with fewer behavioral difficulties (Eisenberg et al., 1996; Lengua et al., 1998). Children who show a tendency toward negative emotionality paired with poor emotional regulation tend to have higher levels of internalizing disorders. Thus a child who experiences the world with fearfulness and avoidance of social interactions will often also have a higher incidence of negative emotions and thus a higher risk for depression and other internalizing disorders.

In order to test the relationship between negative emotionality and poor self-regulation, Lengua (2002) studied third through fifth grade children and their mothers. Measures included a 2.5 hour interview as well as tasks that the child completed that were designed to provoke stress. Irritability was found to be related to higher levels of both externalizing and internalizing problems as well as lower levels of social competence over a 2-year time span. This finding was far more robust than the relationship between fearfulness or self-regulation in predicting social relationships. In contrast, positive emotionality was more highly related to better social competence compared to self-regulation, attention, or impulse control. Negative emotionality is also likely to be related to peer rejection of the child.

Peer Rejection

An aspect of social competence particularly important for understanding the link between depression and social deficits is peer rejection. Peer rejection has been found to be extremely important for understanding how a child manages such a stressful event in childhood (Nolan et al., 2003). Peer rejection has been linked to loneliness, depression, and social anxiety (Boivin et al., 1994). Since the majority of children experience peer rejection at one time or another, how the child manages such rejection is strongly related to later difficulties with emotional functioning and adjustment (Reijntjes et al., 2006). Early and frequent peer rejection has been linked to aggressive behavior as well as to depression and social anxiety (Dodge et al., 2003; Joiner, 1999). Studying the co-occurrence of peer rejection and depression, Vernberg (1990) found that each is a strong predictor of the other in adolescents. Findings have indicated that non-aggressive rejected children show an increased need to monitor their environment and to become very sensitive to negative cues and to possibly seek them out to confirm their negative view of social relationships (Zakriski et al., 1997). These behaviors in turn lead to feelings of social isolation and increased withdrawal from social interactions which in turn lead to depression.

It has also been found that children who are depressed react differently to rejection. Those who were depressed tended to show more negative and passive reactions to cope with their hurt feelings with girls showing the most passivity (Dodge & Feldman, 1990). Bowker et al. (2000) studied peer-rejected children who were withdrawn and those who were aggressive. The withdrawn children tended to focus on their feelings and to ruminate on the difficulties they were experiencing. The aggressive children tended to respond with a behavioral coping strategy that was inappropriate while the popular aggressive girls used a problem-focused strategy. Thus, withdrawing from contact is likely to reinforce the feeling that one is not competent socially to encourage the development of feelings of helplessness and sadness. To be more active (or aggressive) seems to be related to a higher chance of developing strategies to overcome such difficulties. The passivity that is generated by peer rejection of withdrawn children serves to maintain these social difficulties over time and to make intervention even more problematic.

Reijntjes et al. (2006) had children view peer-rejection vignettes. It was predicted that better social competence would be associated with more problem-based coping strategies to solve the problems illustrated by the vignettes and that depressed children would show more distress, withdrawal, and more negative emotional reactions to the vignettes. The findings indicated that girls showed more sadness in reaction to the vignettes than boys did. In addition, those children with depressive symptoms felt more emotional distress when discussing the scenarios. Previous studies have found that children who are depressed have experienced more peer rejection than those who are not (Nolan et al., 2003). Thus, hearing the vignettes and having higher levels of depressive symptoms likely triggered memories of previous times when the child had been rejected and thus revisited those negative mood states.

With increased peer rejection, children with depression are likely to withdraw even farther from social contact. As they withdraw they increasingly have fewer chances for appropriate interactions with others, and thus may experience even more isolation. In addition, their cognitions are likely to be more negative about peer relationships making it more likely that they would anticipate peer rejection where there may have been none. In addition, the study by Reijntjes et al. (2006) found that children who showed more social efficacy were more likely to utilize problem-solving techniques and behavioral confrontation while those with lower social efficacy were more likely to withdraw and utilize denial as a means of passive but ineffective coping. These findings support the hypothesis that children with lower social competence (or efficacy) and with depression will likely have fewer chances to practice appropriate social skills and to become even more isolated.

These findings are also consistent with theories suggesting that high levels of depression, feelings of hopelessness, and dissatisfaction with life are related to difficulty in expressing emotions appropriately. Ciarrochi et al. (2003) suggest that the cognitive effort required to inhibit responding emotionally to provoking stimuli as is often seen with depression is an additional stressor and actually works against the person's ability to develop appropriate coping strategies. Moreover, these children, by definition, have less social support systems and are not adept at utilizing the support systems they do have. It may well be that the child has attributed his/her difficulty to internal states that are stable and will not change and are his/her "fault."

Attribution Style

In line with the work in peer rejection are findings that the attributions youths make about their social skills are related to depressive symptoms (Gladstone & Kaslow, 1995; Joiner & Wagner, 1995). Children and adolescents who believe their difficulties are due to their own personality (internal attributions) believe these problems won't change (stable), and that it is a large part of their world (global) that shows higher levels of depressive symptoms. These attributional styles may also color both positive and negative experiences so both types are interpreted in a negative fashion. When this type of style occurs the level of depressive symptoms appears to increase (Schwartz et al., 2000). In addition, it has been found that attributional style is stable over time and that negative attributions may be more stable than positive ones (Nolen-Hoeksema et al., 1986). It was also found that the depressive symptoms and attributional style of girls appear to be more stable over time than for boys. Girls retained a high level of depression in their attributions while boys' depressive attributional style decreased over time in adolescence (Nolen-Hoeksema & Girgus, 1995).

Gotlib et al. (1993) found that even when the depressive state has remitted, a more negative attributional style remains, thus setting up the person to be at higher risk for a reoccurrence of depression. This negative attributional style is more pronounced than the style found in people who have never been depressed. Schwartz et al. (2000) studied adolescents with and without depression to evaluate the relationship between psychological, self-esteem/coping skills, and social competence variables and attributional style. Findings indicated that a negative attributional style was related to more psychological distress as well as problems with social competence, self-esteem, and coping in adolescents. This negative style was stable and strongly correlated with depression. It takes time and experience for an attributional style to develop and family and early experiences likely contribute to this development. Thus, it is important to recognize the contributions that family life and maternal/paternal psychopathology brings to the development of depression and poorer social competence in children and adolescents.

Family Issues in Social Competence and Depression

An area that is increasing in interest is that of family support in children with depression. There are two main aspects of this research. The first evaluates differences in father and mother perceptions of the child's psychological functioning and social competence. The second aspect evaluates the effect of parental depression on the developing child's social competence and adjustment. Each of these will be discussed in the following paragraphs.

Mothers and fathers tend to relate to their children in a different manner and this difference extends to how they help their child cope with social difficulties and develop social competence. Previous research has found that parents who are very controlling in their interactional styles generally have children who experience significant problems socially. In addition, parents who are perceived by their children as critical tended to have children who as adults were more depressed (Randolph & Dykman, 1990). Family conflict has also been linked to feelings of loneliness in older adolescents with warmth being associated with less loneliness (Jones, 1992; Stocker, 1994).

A warm, parental interactional style has been linked to more positive social outcomes (Pettit & Harrist, 1993; Putallaz, 1987). Additional studies have found that mothers who encourage the child to join a group in a positive manner tended to have more socially competent preschoolers (Finnie & Russell, 1988; Mize et al., 1993). Direct advice giving was also found to be more successful in helping the child develop appropriate levels of social competence in preschoolers (Laird et al., 1994). The ability of parents to allow emotional expressiveness has also been linked to social competence and the ability to maintain adaptive peer relationships (Cassidy & Parke, 1989).

Paternal advice-giving for social relationships has not been well studied and emerging work indicates that both parents may play a unique role in the development of the child's social skills (McDowell et al., 2003). Some have found that how the father responds to the child's emotionality to be a stronger predictor of social competence than the mother's style (Gottman et al., 1997; McDowell & Parke, 2000). The fathers who allowed more emotional displays from their children were found to have children who were more socially competent (Gottman et al., 1997).

McDowell et al. (2003) studied differences in parental advice for socialization at two different time periods: the first was in third grade and the second, one year later. The child and the parent were videotaped in discussing problematic social scenarios. In addition, sociometric interviews were conducted to assess each child's social relationships. Teachers also provided assessments of the child's social and behavioral characteristics. Similar to previous studies, McDowell et al. (2003) found a maternal or paternal controlling style to be related to children being rating more negatively by their peers. In addition, it was found that parents who gave a lot of advice and who attempted to solve the social problems for their child had children who were more negatively rated by peers and teachers. This finding is consistent with that of Laird et al. (1994) which found that mothers of children with social difficulties tend to encourage peer interaction more than those of children who do not have such problems. It may be concluded that these mothers are invested in their child developing appropriate skills and may be trying to overcome the child's difficulty through pressure and encouragement. They may also be quite anxious about the child's social competence: a feeling that is often communicated nonverbally to the child who perceives the increased emphasis on the child's social abilities as meaning—"you can't make friends."

The strong link between a controlling parent and poor social competence may be related to the unspoken message that the child is not good socially and so needs help from the parent. Moreover, that negative message may also convey the impression that the child is not competent in many aspects of his/her life and needs the parent to assist him/her. This inhibition of a positive self-schema has been linked to depression (Cole et al., 1996).

In contrast, the amount of advice provided by the father was related to the child's social competence both initially and 1 year later. Fathers who were directive and warm tended to have children who were more socially adept. It may be that the advice of fathers is perceived by the child as helpful and nonintrusive while maternal advice may be viewed as more negative and anxious. Further study is needed in this area.

Hamilton et al. (1996) studied psychiatrically hospitalized children and their families. As expected the children with depression showed difficulties in forging and maintaining social relationships. In addition the parents of these children tended to have negative affect particularly when the family attempted to solve a problem together. In this punitive environment, the child frequently withdrew from the interactions. It is likely that the combination of social competence difficulties interacts with the negative parent–child relationship and has an effect on increasing the child's depression as well as the child withdrawing from emotionally provoking situations.

Epkins (1998) sought to evaluate the differences between father and mother ratings of social competence and depression. Findings with a large sample of elementary school children indicated that depressive symptoms as rated by the mother, father, and child were inversely related to social competence; the more symptoms the lower the social competence. When the mother scored high on the depression scales, she and her child also tended to show increased depressive symptoms and problems with academic competence. Similarly, Luoma et al. (2004) studied both parents and their child as to perceptions of depression. The concordance of the reports was generally high with fathers reporting fewer social problems than mothers particularly for boys. When the mother was also depressed, more difficulty in social competence for the child was reported by both the father and the mother. The relationship between maternal depression and the child's social difficulties is an important variable to study, and increasingly, researchers are evaluating the effects of parental depression on the resulting social competence of the child. This link between possible parental psychopathology and the child's social competence is an area that is beginning to be investigated.

Prinstein and LaGreca (1999) studied the relation between mother's and children's social competence. They studied the mother's social skills, the mother's recollection of their own childhood peer experiences, and the number of social contacts the mother now has. In addition, their children were rated as to their social competence by teachers and peers. Participants in the study were mothers and children in kindergarten. It was found, as expected, that mothers with good social competence had children who were well accepted by their peers. Of the three types of social competence evaluated in the mothers, the mother's own social skills were the most strongly related to the child's social competence. In particular, the mother's ability to initiate social contacts was the strongest predictor of the child's social acceptability and was related to the number of playmates and acceptance by his/her peers. Moreover, mothers who had experienced peer rejection as a child tended to have children who also have social difficulties. Mothers with the most social contacts tended to have children with more social opportunities and with more social contacts. It was felt that these mothers had more opportunities to provide experiences for their child and to model appropriate behaviors. They may also communicate nonverbally that it is expected that the child will be accepted by his/her peers and that the world is a pleasant place. For children of mothers with a history of peer rejection, the converse is likely true; that is, that the world isn't a safe place and that rejection can occur.

Gender may also influence the effect of maternal social experience on the child's resulting social skills (Prinstein & LaGreca, 1999). Mother's social competence was linked to both girl's and boy's acceptance by peers while it was more strongly linked to the girl's ability to develop appropriate social skills. Similar to other research, mothers' depressive and interpersonal problems were related to the child's social competence. The authors suggest that interventions need to target the mother's distress as well as the child's in order to be effective in assisting with the development of appropriate social skills.

Maternal Depression and Social Competence

There have been several findings of a link between maternal depression and the child's poor psychosocial adjustment (Beardslee et al., 1998; Goodman & Gotlib, 2002; Weissman et al., 1999). It has been suggested that this impairment may contribute to intergenerational transmission of depression (Cicchetti & Toth, 1998; Lewinsohn et al., 2005). Maternal depression has been linked to the following problems in adolescence: delinquency, substance abuse, academic problems, and social difficulty (Davies & Windle, 1997; Hammen & Brennan, 2001). Paternal depression has also been linked to problems in adolescence including problems in learning, and parent–child conflict (Kane & Garber, 2004).

Lewisohn et al. (2005) studied adolescents with depressed parents to determine the effect of parental depression on psychosocial functioning. Findings indicated that paternal depression contributed to problems with psychosocial functioning particularly for younger adolescents. Maternal depression appeared to interact with psychosocial functioning most prominently for older adolescents and young adults. No differences were found for gender indicating that both boys and girls are susceptible to problems with social competence when either parent was depressed. Psychosocial impairment was found to be the most important and stable variable in children with depressed parents, and thus, the authors suggest, may be the most important target for intervention.

To further study the intergenerational transmission of depression and its link to problems with social competence, Hammen et al. (2004) studied 800 depressed and never-depressed women and their 15-year-old children. It was found that maternal depression as well as depression in the maternal grandmother was linked to chronic problems in social adjustment for the adolescents. This link was found to be associated with poorer outcome for the adolescent as well as linked to increased interpersonal stress in the family.

Childs et al. (2001) studied the adjustment of adolescents of depressed mothers. Maternal depression was highly predictive of child adjustment with significant ramifications for the child's social competence. In addition, those adolescents with higher social competence, even with maternal depression, showed more resilience than those with poor social competence and a mother with depression. In families where the mother is depressed but the father is psychologically healthy, it has been found that children are rated as less popular by their teachers (Goodman et al., 1993). In addition, when a divorce occurred, the child showed more difficulties with social and emotional competence with older children being more vulnerable than younger children.

Similarly, in a large population study, Luoma et al. (2001) found that maternal depression at any point in the child's life from prenatal to postnatal significantly impacted the child's well-being and his/her social adjustment. In addition, it was found that boys were more vulnerable than girls for problems in adjustment. It was hypothesized that, prenatally, stress hormones in depressed mothers have direct and indirect effects on the unborn child.

Mouse models have indicated that maternal stress during pregnancy had long-term effects on the fetal brain, a finding that is important when working with pregnant women as to the resulting effect on the child (Nelson & Bosquet, 2000). In support of this hypothesis dysregulation, difficulties have been found in newborns of mothers with depression during gestation (Field, 1997). These difficulties were also found to disrupt the mother–child bond whether the mother continued to be depressed or not. Thus, dysregulation related to maternal depression during pregnancy may well disrupt the attachment of the child to the mother and vice versa. Such problems with attachment have been well documented to be related to problems with later adjustment and social competence.

Bipolar Disorder and Social Competence

Bipolar disorder is also in the DSM category of mood disorders. It is considered to be highly debilitating with high rates of disability, substance abuse, and suicide risk (Dalton et al., 2003; Goetzel et al., 2003; Judd & Akiskal, 2003). This disorder has also been found to be genetically linked, and thus children of parents with bipolar disorder are at higher risk to show psychopathology at an early age. Some studies put the risk for children of parents with bipolar disorder to be between 1–to 3% (Wals et al., 2001) while others place it at 27% (Klein et al., 1985). During the depression stage of bipolar disorder, problems occur with social interactions as well as daily living. Mania introduces another aspect to the disorder as daily activities and social interactions are significantly impaired and hospitalization may be required to prevent harm to self or others (Schapiro, 2005). Irritability may be present during a manic phase and can be characterized as intense, severe, and persistent thus significantly impairing social encounters with peers (Weckerly, 2002). Age appears to also be an important variable as some have found that children at risk for the development of bipolar disorder may show few signs at an early age but develop behavioral and social difficulties in later childhood, a time that is particularly important to develop social contacts and practice social skills (Radke-Yarrow et al., 1992).

Adolescents and adults with bipolar disorder have show many social difficulties as well as problems with behavior and learning. The social difficulties appear to be related to negative affect, lability, and poor self-esteem (Bentall, 2005; Hirshfield-Becker et al., 2006; Knowles et al., 2003). Jones and colleagues (2006) suggest that poor coping strategies and lability of affect are related to problems with social functioning. Further, the authors suggest a diathesis-stress approach where genetics, personality, and biological risk factors interact with the environment to produce an earlier onset of illness or to increased lability and poorer adaptive functioning. Jones et al. (2006) found that children of bipolar parents showed a tendency to ruminate about their difficulties and to engage in more risk-taking than those of parents without bipolar disorder.

To study psychopathology in children of parents with bipolar disorder, Henin et al. (2005) evaluated 117 unreferred children of parents with diagnosed bipolar disorder and 171 matched children of parents without bipolar disorder. Findings indicated that children of parents with bipolar disorder were at higher risk for academic and social difficulties as well as having a higher risk for anxiety. In addition, problems with anxiety, social phobia, ADHD, and depression were found to be present at younger ages while older children showed higher rates of bipolar disorder, OCD, and substance abuse. Bipolar disorder was most frequently diagnosed after the age of 12 with 20% of the sample showing this diagnosis during adolescence.

There has not been a great deal of study in this area apart from adult work. Social competence in children with bipolar disorder is likely an important developmental issue that requires further study. When families have bipolar disorder in their pedigree, it is very important to be cognizant of the high risk factor as well as the disruption in family life, and thus, in child development, that occurs when a parent has bipolar disorder. If the child is at risk it is likely that his/her temperament is more brittle, that he/she is more irritable and more emotionally labile, and that social contacts are either restricted or more negative in nature.

Summary

In summary, for children with depression, social competence is a major issue and encompasses concerns in psychological functioning as well as in adjustment and attributional style. These symptoms appear to be stable over time and change only when a drastic improvement in depressive symptoms is present. In addition, children who are depressed tend to be either ignored or rejected by their peers. Such rejection further isolates these children and research suggests they become less adept at coping and tend to focus on their emotional distress. As the child becomes more withdrawn and socially isolated, opportunities for positive social exchanges likely decrease, and thus the practice needed to become social adept is lacking. Empirical work has also found that these children often perceive negative intent where none is present. Such a tendency likely increases their reluctance to engage socially further limiting their social contacts.

This type of withdrawal is particularly important for our understanding as it appears to begin at an early age and to color the child's perceptions of his/her world. If the child begins to see the world in a negative light and himself/herself as socially inept, the ability to change such attributions is quite resistant to change and appears to be particularly pervasive in terms of psychological and cognitive functioning. For girls in adolescence these difficulties are even more stable and may forestall attempts at therapeutic intervention. Findings have indicated that generally social skills are intact; what is problematic are the perceptions of self and others as well as a tendency to become very distressed over commonly experienced situations and to lack adequate coping skills. Thus, interventions appear to be best placed in the realm of individual therapy and to developing appropriate perceptions as well as coping skills possibly through the use of cognitive-behavioral therapy.

Family issues are also important in understanding social competence in children with depression. When mothers and/or fathers are depressed, the social competence of the child is significantly compromised. Maternal depression is most influential with adolescents while paternal depression appears to be more operative at younger ages. In addition, boys appear to be more vulnerable than girls when either parent is affected. Depression in the mother during gestation has also been linked to higher risks for the child in cognitive and social/emotional adjustment. Interventions that are proactive in nature may be very important for pregnant women who are experiencing depression.

The social competence of children with bipolar disorder has not studied as often as that of children with depression. Findings indicate that, similar to depression, family style, genetics, and family environment may all contribute to the development of social difficulties in early childhood which are exacerbated in later life. Given the relatively strong inheritance of bipolar disorder, social problems may occur at younger ages given the disinhibition, lability, and irritability frequently seen early in the illness. This area needs further study to elucidate the difficulties present in these children during development particularly when seeking to develop appropriate assessment as well as intervention programs.

Anxiety Disorders

Anxiety disorders are another type of mood disorder and include obsessive-compulsive disorder (OCD), social phobia, general anxiety disorder, and post-traumatic stress disorder. This section of the chapter will discuss generalized anxiety disorder and obsessive-compulsive disorder (OCD) as well as social phobia. Post-traumatic stress disorder is not discussed in any depth due to lack of research in this area in social competence.

Anxiety often serves a positive purpose of perceiving a threat and allowing protection from that threat. However, children who are highly anxious may seek to avoid many social encounters and thus fail to develop appropriate social prowess. As discussed in an earlier chapter, inhibition may well serve as a protective device until it is carried to an extreme. Kagan et al. (1984) coined the term "behavioral inhibition toward the unfamiliar" which is a tendency to withdraw in new situations. This inhibition applies to social as well as nonsocial activities but for our purposes we are most concerned with the social applications. Inhibited children tend to show strong negative emotional reactions when faced with a new social encounter and show physiological changes that are consistent with significant feelings of stress (i.e., increased heart rate, and reactivity; Snidman et al., 1995). In addition, this type of inhibition has been found to be quite stable over time particularly during childhood (Bengtsgard & Bohlin, 2001). This type of inhibition when more pronounced has been linked to higher levels of anxiety and risk for social difficulties (Lonigan & Phillips, 2001; Thorell et al., 2004).

Rubin (1993) suggests that anxious children feel an approach-avoidance to social situations. On the one hand they wish to engage in social interaction while on the other hand they want to avoid new social situations. Thus, these children may engage in parallel play, be an observer to group activities, or withdraw from social encounters. Any of these behaviors would limit their experience and their opportunity to practice their social skills. Bohlin et al. (2000) found that this lack of practice translates into poorer social competence as well as fewer prosocial behaviors (helping, empathy, etc.). Derryberry and Rothbart (1997) suggest that such reluctance to engage in social behaviors is the result of overregulation or excessive activity in the fear regulatory system leading to less ability to cope (Newman & Wallace, 1993). Such overregulation serves to protect the child while at the same time limiting his/her experiences and taxing the cognitive system which is on overload against a perceived threat.

Rubin and Burgess (2001) studied children with high inhibition and found that they were at increased risk for not developing appropriate social skills. As the children developed, it was found that negative self-perceptions and internalizing behavioral problems increased and that these children generally engaged in passive play or solitary play. By adolescence these children showed anxiety and depression and were disliked by their peers.

Thorell et al. (2004) sought to study the relationship between inhibition to the unfamiliar and social problems in children. Those with high levels of inhibition to the unfamiliar were contrasted with children with low levels of inhibition. It was found that social competence was related to higher levels of inhibition to the unfamiliar, particularly in the child's ability to enter into social exchanges. Of particular importance, this study found that those children high on inhibition to the unfamiliar were more fearful of negative evaluation of themselves by their peers. Such fear preceded entry into social interactions and likely prevents the child from approaching unfamiliar peers and making new friends. These findings are consistent with that of other researchers that implicate such fears as detrimental to the development of appropriate social skills and social experiences (Rubin & Burgess, 2001). Thorell et al. (2004) suggest that inhibition to the unfamiliar is likely to lead to peer rejection due to the child's unusual fearful behaviors and withdrawal. Such rejection further reinforces the child's fear of negative evaluations by his/her peers.

Consistent with the above findings, children with anxiety may experience problems developing appropriate peer relationships integral to healthy emotional development. Research has been equivocal about the social development of anxious children. Some have found that anxious children are less popular and may be actually disliked while others find them to be withdrawn and neglected (Kendall et al., 1997). Still others have found no problems with peers or social anxiety (Crick & Ladd, 1993). Self-report studies have indicated that anxious children perceive themselves as shy and socially inept as well as lonely and with few self-reported friendships (Puig-Antich et al., 1985; Strauss et al., 1989). It may be that the anxious children who are experiencing peer rejection or neglect are higher on the scale of anxiety than those who have fewer problems. The severity of the anxiety is particularly important to evaluate when assessing these studies and when the child shows high anxiety and over-inhibition it may be that social problems are more pronounced than with milder difficulties. Families who provide support and nurturance for these anxious children may also ameliorate the difficulties compared to families where anxiety is high and parents also have difficulties in this area.

Expectations that children who are anxious have about social interactions may be negatively skewed where they expect threats and danger in their social environment. A study of social competence in children with and without anxiety found lower self-perceived social competence and higher levels of social anxiety compared to controls. These children also expected that they would experience peer rejection and isolation, and thus were reinforced for such beliefs when this rejection actually occurred. These perceptions were verified by lower ratings of social competence by teachers and parents (Chansky & Kendall, 1997). This study found that social anxiety was the best predictor for social difficulties as well as the self-perceptions of children with anxiety as to their social competence.

In a study contrasting depression and anxiety, children were compared on several measures evaluating competence in social situations, academics, behavior, and physical appearance (Smari et al., 2001). Social anxiety was found to be strongly related solely to the perception of poor social competence while depression was related to many aspects of perceived competence including social competence, physical appearance, and academic competence. There was also a gender difference. Girls reported lower physical and overall competence than boys and viewed social interactions with a more threat-based approach than boys. It was also found that adolescents who were anxious tended to show more threat-sensitivity and thus avoidance of fear-provoking situations than those who were depressed. Such avoidance serves to reduce anxiety but also reduces opportunities for mastery of anxiety and social skill development. In addition, a child who is fearful of social encounters might attempt to gather as much information about the situation as possible in order to contain his/her anxiety. This process will actually increase anxiety as the child becomes more hypervigilant and notes small differences between their behavior and that of the peers (Derryberry & Rothbart, 1997).

Thorell et al. (2004) suggest that children who are depressed have a pervasive negative view of their competence while those who are anxious appear to have increased perceptions of possible negative social events. This distinction is important particularly for developing interventions. For the child who is anxious, desensitization and therapy stressing relaxation techniques may assist in approaching social situations, while for a child who is depressed, work on the negative perceptions is more highly indicated.

Panella and Henggeler (1986) studied peer interactions of conduct-disordered, anxious-withdrawn, and well-adjusted Black adolescents. Each adolescent was asked to bring his best friend to the sessions. Each session required the adolescents to complete a form indicating personal preferences on two lists. They also participated in a 30-minute interaction session where they interacted with their friend and then with a well-adjusted stranger. During this period of time they needed to reach agreement on the lists (ranking athletes, football teams, and famous, attractive women). These interactions were videotaped and later coded for interactions. Findings indicated that both clinical groups showed poorer social competence and less positive affect than the controls. In addition the anxious adolescents showed more reluctance to talk in the dyads compared to the other two groups. The anxious adolescents were more outgoing with friends than with strangers. Moreover, the anxious group appeared less happy and more anxious in all settings but most particularly when interacting with strangers. Given the more negative affect and the tendency to be quieter and more subdued with strangers for the anxious group, these findings are consistent with studies discussed earlier that indicate the tendency of anxious children and adolescents to withdraw from social interaction and to engage less readily in approaching novel situations and unfamiliar people.

The study of anxious children and peer relationships needs to be conducted with peers and with families. A child who is anxious requires parenting that is calm and reassuring as well as encouraging him/her to attempt social interactions. The following section briefly reviews the issues that parents of anxious children face and what types of interventions have been helpful.

Parenting Issues

Parents of anxious children have been described as more involved in their child's day-to-day life and to be intrusive and limiting of the child's autonomy (Parker, 1983). Studies of parents of anxious children have found that they tend to be less accepting of the child's need to individuate and to expect the child to be more easily upset and to cope less readily to frustrating and fearful situations even when such expectations were not observed (Kortlander et al., 1997; Siqueland et al., 1996). Such expectations are likely communicated to the child and reinforce his/her feelings of incompetence and fear. As the parent attempts to protect and shield their child, these attempts further reinforce the self-perception of the child as inept socially.

Howard and Kendall (1996a, 1996b) developed a cognitive-behavioral family treatment procedure to assist with helping parents develop strategy to support their child's learning of coping strategies. Following treatment, children who were anxious showed significant clinical gains particularly in coping skills. These gains were found to be maintained over a 4-month period after treatment ended. Assisting parents in allowing their child to individuate as well as directly teaching coping methods for anxiety appears to be a promising treatment for anxiety. It is also important to recognize that treating the child in isolation will not change family patterns that may assist in maintaining anxious behaviors.

Biederman et al. (2006) studied a large sample of parents and children with various anxiety disorders. Findings indicated that children with social phobia and separation anxiety had parents with these same disorders. Parents with panic disorder had a higher risk of having children with diagnoses of OCD or agoraphobia. These findings indicate that social phobia runs in families and may have a different trajectory than other anxiety disorders. Behaviorally if a parent has a social phobia it is unlikely that they will be social with their peers. Thus, children not only have a genetic risk to develop anxiety disorders but the environmental risk is increased as well as the risk for problems with socialization. The Biederman et al. (2006) study suggests that a different path may be present for panic disorder and anxiety and OCD. OCD will be discussed in the following section.

Obsessive Compulsive Disorder

The incidence of OCD is approximately 2% in children and adolescents. OCD can have significant ramifications for the development of social relationships as well as disruption of family. As found by Biederman et al. (2006), OCD also appears within families compounding the difficulties not only in family functioning but also for the development of social competence in the child. Children with OCD show obsessions or compulsions that are severe, time-consuming and interfere with everyday functioning. Obsessions are intrusive thoughts and ideas while compulsions are behaviors that are repetitive and intentional and generally performed in response to an obsession (McGough et al., 1993). Both obsessions and compulsions require an enormous amount of time and effort which in turn impacts very negatively on the child/adolescent's academic and social relationships. Valderhaug and Ivarsson (2005) found, in their sample, that most of the children and adolescents showed severe symptoms at home with significant social difficulties also present at school. These social difficulties translated into the child spending more time at home, and thus increasing the conflict found in the home. Given that OCD tends to run in families, family disruption may be increased particularly when the parents share the diagnosis—this demographic was not reported in the study.

Piacentini et al. (2003) studied adaptation and emotional development in children with OCD. Parental report indicated that at least one-third of the sample had social difficulties. Particular concerns were voiced by the children as to being with strangers and entering public places. Boys were found to be more impacted than girls in their social relationships while girls had more difficulty with their relationship with their siblings.

Attention deficit hyperactivity disorder has been found to co-occur with OCD with rates varying from 10 to 50% (Sukhodolsky et al., 2005). This comorbidity has been found to be related to a more severe presentation for both of these disorders. Sukhodolsky et al. (2005) studied the emotional and family functioning in children with OCD with and without ADHD. The clinical groups all scored more poorly on a measure of socialization with the OCD/ADHD group scoring the most poorly. The OCD/ADHD group also showed the most difficulty with internalizing behaviors with the OCD and ADHD groups also showing impairment socially and with internalizing disorders. The families of children with OCD and ADHD showed higher levels of dysfunction compared to controls. Both the OCD and ADHD groups showed higher levels of family dysfunction than controls with higher scores on conflict and lower scores on measures of family cohesion. A diagnosis of OCD alone was not related to negative social functioning while a diagnosis of ADHD did have significant ramifications for social functioning and depression as well as family dysfunction.

Family Contributions to OCD

Family has also been found to affect the nature and severity of the child's difficulties. Younger children are more reliant on their families and have less control over most aspects of their lives. In a family where the parent also has OCD or has other mental health issues, difficulties are likely compounded and problems with social development are particularly magnified (Freeman et al., 2003). This difficulty is bi-directional as the child also affects the family system and the family's mental health (Lenane, 1989). For younger children the rituals may be actually maintained by the parent in an attempt to contain the child's anxiety. In addition the parent's interpretation of anxiety-provoking stimuli may increase the child's vulnerability to withdrawal and fear and thus increase the child's isolation from normalized situations (Steketee, 1997).

Freeman et al. (2003) strongly suggest that treatment must include the family and that the child cannot be effectively treated outside of this system. This belief is particularly pronounced for younger children. Przeworski et al. (1999) evaluated family conflict and problem-solving using mother–child dyads viewing OCD- and non-OCD-provoking situations. The mother and child were asked to discuss the videotaped situation and generate solutions. The style used by the mother was similar whether the situation was OCD provoking or not and showed fewer agreements between mother and child, fewer questions posed to solve the problem, and more anger present between mother and child. Thus, the parent was not instrumental in assisting the child to learn appropriate behaviors and may have, inadvertently, made things worse with teaching of coping skills. Interventions that focus on assisting appropriate parent–child dialogues would be most helpful.

Barrett et al. (2002) studied families with children with OCD, anxiety disorder, separation anxiety disorder, and social phobia and compared their interactions with families with a child with oppositional defiant disorder or ADHD. The families with a child with OCD were found to interact in a much different manner than the other families. These parents tended to show less confidence in the child's ability to solve the problem and did not allow the child the necessary independence to solve the difficulty compared to the families without OCD. As a result, the children were less confident, were less open to warmth, and were less likely to solve problems constructively. Thus, the family system differed for these children and was affected and was in turn affected by the child's difficulty.

Conclusion

For children with anxiety disorder socialization is a challenge. Similar to children with depression, children with anxiety tend to withdraw from situations and to have difficulty developing appropriate skills. For children with depression problems are present in significant feelings of social isolation. They also tend to have negative perceptions of their own social ability. In contrast, children with anxiety disorder tend to become very hypervigilant of their surroundings and to read negative intent from their peers. In addition, children with anxiety tend to also have a parent with anxiety who may withdraw from social encounters and fail to develop a social network. Children with OCD also have social challenges and tend to withdraw from new activities. In addition, they frequently feel "different" from their peers and attempt to hide their symptoms. Research indicates that parent–child interactions are characterized by poorer problem-solving and more conflict than children with externalizing disorders or with other types of anxiety disorder.

Importantly, for both diagnoses, family treatment is strongly recommended particularly for younger children. In addition, when the diagnosis is shared between parent and child, interactions are fraught with more conflict and more difficulty. There is little research about families with dual diagnoses; that is, the father has one type of internalizing disorder and the mother another. This type of situation would be most intriguing but also significantly problematic. It would appear that family therapy by a knowledgeable clinician would be most appropriate particularly in assisting parents and children with social difficulties to expand their social network and support system. Given the lasting imprint of social competence difficulties for these children's lives, it is particularly important to intervene at an early age. For Kevin family treatment as well as individual support was particularly important and was most successful in assisting him not only in feeling better but also in developing appropriate social exchanges.

12

Social Competence in Children with Acquired and Chronic Disorders

Joel was in third grade when his social difficulties became more noticeable. Prior to that time he had some problems with his peers but was generally tolerated and included when participating in teacher-led activities. In nonstructured activities, Joel was often observed playing next to same-aged peers but not often cooperatively. Joel had a diagnosis of Tuberous Sclerosis, a genetic disorder where tumors generally grow in the central nervous system. In his case, they were located in his brain and spinal cord. It was found that his mother was a carrier when the family was genetically evaluated. Joel began school at age 3 due to delays in language, speech, and general development. He was retained in kindergarten and was a year older than his classmates. Joel was mainstreamed into a general education third grade class with special education programming in a class for children with learning disabilities. He also received speech and language therapy, occupational therapy, and adaptive physical education.

At the age of 9 Joel began to experience intractable seizures. He had been diagnosed with a seizure disorder at the age of 4 with seizures that progressed from partial-complex (involving a portion of his brain) to generalized (involving his entire brain). He experienced several seizures in his classrooms; both regular and special education. Initially his peers were confused and frightened by his behavior. His teacher and the school psychologist met with his class to explain his seizure disorder in an attempt to allay the child's fears. While this intervention helped for a while, his peers soon moved on to other activities.

Joel experienced another seizure on the playground, which was witnessed by most of the school. The seizure was particularly intense and the paramedics were called. He was taken to the hospital and hospitalized for several days to titrate his medications. When he returned to school his peers felt that he was "strange" and he was ignored and avoided despite the best efforts of his teacher. When on the playground he was teased as "Frankenstein" or "Freddy Krueger" and rarely asked to join a play group. When the principal intervened, the teasing ended but Joel was generally isolated and neglected.

As Joel entered fourth grade he began to show signs of sadness and anxiety. He began to withdraw from social interaction and developed stomachaches and physical complaints generally around recess time. His schoolwork began slipping and he was not keeping up with his homework in either of his school settings. Joel's parents noticed that he was not participating in family activities at the same level and became concerned about his emotional and social development. In an effort to help him feel less "strange" they enrolled him in a summer camp for children with seizure disorders. In the camp he attended group therapy meetings and was encouraged to try activities that were scary for him with his seizure disorder (biking, climbing, and swimming). The support given him from his camp counselors and the fellow campers helped to increase his self-esteem and assisted in bringing him out of his shell in that environment.

When Joel returned to school in fifth grade, his parents decided to transfer him to a different school where he would not have a history to overcome. The school staff and his parents were proactive in designing his curriculum and social contacts as well as explaining to his peers and the school Joel's difficulties. Although he continued to struggle in school academically (something very common in children with Tuberous Sclerosis and seizure disorders), he made a friend in his special education class who had Hirschprung's Disease (a disorder of the colon leading frequently to bowel movement accidents). The support these two children gave each other helped them to manage the difficulties associated with late elementary school into middle school.

Introduction

This chapter will discuss the social competence challenges faced by children with acquired and chronic disorders. Although there are several disorders and this chapter cannot address all of them, difficulties in social functioning are fairly common across the disorders. This chapter will briefly discuss the following disorders. In chronic diseases diabetes, asthma, cystic fibrosis, and seizure disorders will be discussed. In acquired disorders childhood cancer, traumatic brain injury, and brain tumors will be reviewed. In addition, common genetic disorders such as Tuberous Sclerosis, Fragile X, Turners syndrome, Phenylketonuria, Neurofibromatosis, Tourette's Syndrome, and Williams Syndrome will be examined. While this is not a comprehensive list, these disorders are instructive and can be used as exemplars for other disorders within their categories.

Chronic Diseases and Social Competence

In the general pediatric population there is an incidence rate of approximately 10–15% with chronic physical illnesses (Perrin et al., 1987). These disorders create physical and medication issues. Most importantly for our purposes difficulties are often present in the child's response to his/her illness as well as that of his family and peers. The empirical evidence indicates that most of the children have adjusted fairly well to their disorders. It is not clear from the data what aspects of support help many of these children to adapt. This section of the chapter will discuss the social adjustment of children with select chronic disease as well as issues that may arise in working with these children and possible appropriate interventions.

Diabetes

Insulin-dependent diabetes mellitus (IDDM) is a one of the more prevalent diseases in childhood and has serious consequences for the child and his/her family in management. The primary goal is good control of blood glucose through diet, exercise, and medication. As the child matures, more and more of the monitoring and control is turned over to him/her. In addition, choices become present in eating decisions and exercise particularly when with the peer group. Heinbaugh (2006) found that when diabetes is discovered at an early age, the child makes a better adjustment to the diabetic regimen than when the child was older at first diagnosis. Age differences in onset as well as family support are likely aspects of the child's life that have a significant impact on their adjustment to their disorder.

There have been several studies evaluating the psychological adjustment of children with IDDM. Some have found difficulties with adjustment (Jacobson et al., 1990) while others have not (Hanson et al., 1989). Empirical evidence indicates that temperamental and environmental demands may be related to the child's adjustment. Individual differences in activity level, lability, ability to cope changing requirements and general attitude may influence the child's adjustment. Different expectations in classroom settings as well as family context may interact with temperament and also contribute to the child's emotional and social adjustment (Weissberg-Benchell & Glasgow, 1997).

Thomas and Chess (1977) suggest that how a child adjusts to his/her illness is partially determined by the environment as well as the match between the child's environment and his/her temperament. Thus, a child with IDDM who has a flexible environment and a difficult temperament will fare better socially and emotionally compared to a child who has a rigid environment and who has difficult temperament. Rovet and Ehrlich (1988) evaluated temperament in children with IDDM in elementary school. It was found that children who were active and inattentive, had a negative mood, had a set routine, and did not respond strongly to stress had better diabetes control. In contrast, Garrison et al. (1990) found that children with strong attention spans as well as negative mood had better diabetes control. Neither study evaluated the context social competence of the child.

Weissberg-Benchell and Glasgow (1997) sought to evaluate temperament, environment, and social competence in children with IDDM. It was hypothesized that children who were persistent, task oriented, and flexible would have higher social competence and better diabetes control than those who had a different temperament. Children aged 5–18 were included in this study with approximately even numbers of males and females included. The population was generally from middle to upper-middle socioeconomic status family and was basically in good diabetes control. Social competence was found to be related to higher levels of persistence and lower levels of distractibility. Thus, the child who is able to persevere in managing their disorder generally has better social competence.

Research has indicated that high stress can increase hormones which raise blood glucose levels. Stress can also decrease the child's ability to manage their diet and adherence to glucose monitoring. Hanson et al. (1987) investigated the relationship among social competence and parental support in managing stress in children with IDDM. They hypothesize that if social competence and parental support assist a child with IDDM in a direct manner then they provide a sense of self-worth and stability independent of the stress level experienced by the child. If there is an indirect effect, social competence and parental support may buffer the child against negative environmental events.

To help determine the inter-relationships among stress, social competence, and parental support, Hanson et al. (1987) studied adolescents with IDDM and their families. Adherence to diabetic regimens was positively and significantly related to social competence whereas high stress and poor adherence to diet were related to higher levels of stress in adolescents with poorer social competence. Parental support was not associated with stress levels, adherence, or glucose control.

Collectively, these findings are important for our understanding of social competence in children with IDDM. Children who have good diabetic control have been found to show fewer psychiatric disorders than those who are hospitalized for diabetic ketoacidosis (Blanz et al., 1993). These children also show lower self-esteem and poorer social competence (Daviss et al., 1995). In addition, many of the children with poorer control come from more disordered families. Liss et al. (1998) studied children hospitalized with diabetic ketoacidosis (a condition which occurs when there is poor blood glucose control). Social competence was found to be poor in this population of children and more psychiatric difficulties were noted. Importantly the families showed more difficulty on tasks requiring problem-solving strategies and showed less warmth in the family–child relationship.

The tie between social competence, parental support, and blood glucose control is just beginning to be understood. The child's ability to manage his/her relationships appears important for overall adjustment as well as managing this illness. While the empirical support for this hypothesis appears strong, it is not clear from the research what appropriate interventions should be utilized. Certainly based on the work of Liss et al. (1998) a lack of parental support appears to negatively influence the child's adjustment to both his/her disease and to developing appropriate social relationships. Given the importance of the child–parent bond for compliance with the demands of this disorder, it appears important to include the family in any type of intervention. Moreover, the relationship between the child's temperament and adherence is another important aspect for treatment.

While a child's temperament may be very difficult to either change or manage, it appears important to assist in matching the child's temperament to the demands that are placed upon him/her. A child with a more difficult temperament who is not flexible and who has attentional difficulties may be far more difficult to parent. In addition, he/she may have more difficulty establishing reciprocal peer relationships and developing the social competence that is also related to good management. Family therapy and education about the disease would appear to be crucial in helping the child develop appropriate peer relationships. Further study is certainly needed to examine these inter-relationships and their impact on treatment.

It is important to note that there are very few articles directly evaluating the social competence of children and adolescents with IDDM. Developmental shifts may occur. As the child grows, more independence is expected in management of the disease. For a child with social difficulties such shifts may be particularly problematic as the child may not be ready for such responsibility. If immaturity is present and the parent–child bond is not strong, the child/ adolescent will have more difficulty developing such independence. Moreover, children who are immature have also been found to be less socially competent. They may not comply with their glucose monitoring requirements or diet in the face of trying to fit in with their peers. Going to McDonald's or the Dairy Queen may be more important to this adolescent than managing his/her blood sugar. For a more independent and socially secure adolescent it may be possible to turn down treats or to follow moderate consumption. Such a strategy is likely impossible for a less mature child and by definition a more socially incompetent individually. Studies need to compare children and adolescents with IDDM along the continuum of social competence to determine the most important variables for intervention to assist children/adolescents at all levels.

Asthma

Asthma is another very common disorder in childhood and affects a sizable minority of children and is life-threatening in a more direct manner than IDDM (National Heart, Lung, and Blood Institute, 1995). Anxiety disorders have been found in children with asthma particularly in children with severe asthma (Bussin & Burket, 1993). This finding is understandable as the child has experienced times when he/she couldn't breathe and feels like he/she is being suffocated. Such episodes are not expected and thus the child feels, and rightfully so, that they could occur at any time.

In order to understand the psychiatric difficulties associated with asthma, Vila et al. (1999) compared children with asthma with those with IDDM using a semi-structured clinical interview to determine prevalence of psychiatric disorders in this sample. Findings indicated that there were far fewer disorders in the children with IDDM. The children with asthma showed more internalizing and externalizing disorders compared to the children with IDDM. This finding is consistent with that of Biederman et al.

(1994). In addition, there were no differences on the variables of age, gender, or socioeconomic status in frequency of externalizing and internalizing disorders. Both boys and girls showed similar rates of these disorders unlike the general population where boys show more externalizing disorders and girls more internalizing (Butz & Alexander, 1993; Vila et al., 1999). In addition, children with asthma who had psychiatric disorders also tended to have more difficulties with social competence. Vila et al. (1999) recommended that, given the high rate of psychiatric difficulties in children with asthma, they should be screened routinely for these difficulties. Although this study did not directly address the social competence of these children, it is likely that difficulties may be present particularly given the relationship between internalizing and externalizing disorders and poorer social competence.

Vila et al. (2000) studied children with asthma for anxiety disorders in a different sample of children aged 8–15. Their asthma ranged from mild to severe. The sample was divided into four groups of severity: intermittent, mild-persistent, moderate-persistent, and severe-persistent. These children were compared to healthy children with no history of asthma. In general, children with asthma were not found to have lower self-esteem compared to the controls; however, 35% of the children with asthma had at least one type of anxiety disorder with 17% showing two anxiety disorders and 3% showing three anxiety disorders. When the children with asthma had an anxiety disorder, they were found to have lower self-esteem and poorer social competence. They also participated in fewer social activities and were more withdrawn. These children showed these difficulties compared to the healthy children as well as other children with asthma that did not show anxiety disorders.

Thus, taken together Vila and others' work indicates that children with anxiety and asthma, particularly those with severe asthma, may show more difficulties with social competence and self-esteem. Such difficulties likely translate into more social withdrawal and possibly more social difficulties. As the literature on anxiety disorders without asthma indicates (see Chapter 11), social competence difficulties are often present due to fear of failure. For a child with asthma and anxiety, it would appear that social isolation may be a real risk. It is important to note that the literature on social competence in children with asthma is extremely limited and a literature search turned up very few studies. Given the gravity of this disorder and the prevalence, it would appear extremely important to study this issue more fully in this population. In any event, a child with asthma and anxiety should be screened for social difficulties, and interventions similar to those for children with a sole diagnosis of anxiety should be instituted.

Cystic Fibrosis

Cystic Fibrosis (CF) is a common genetic disorder that affects 1 per 2000 live births in Caucasians (Lloyd-Still, 1983). It is a disease which causes abnormal secretions of thick mucus that settles in the pancreas and lungs. Thus, children with CF suffer from malabsorption as well as from chronic pulmonary disease (Simmons et al., 1987). With improved treatment the death rate from CF has decreased in the past 20 years.

Early studies documented emotional difficulties in the children and their families partly due to the stress of the deadly diagnosis (Tavorima et al., 1976). More current findings are equivocal as to improvement in psychosocial functioning. Some have found improvement in coping skills while others finding the more severely affected children showing continuing problems (Drotar et al., 1981). Simmons et al. (1987) sought to further evaluate the behavioral adjustment of children aged 6–11 years with a diagnosis of CF. To study effects of age as well as gender, a sample of 108 children was used. The group was divided into two groups depending on response to treatment. Combining both groups it was found that females showed higher levels of social competence than males. Males tended to show more behavioral difficulties compared to females. It was suggested by Simmons et al. (1987) that the way that children with CF tend to deal with their potentially fatal disease is generally through feelings of sadness and anxiety while still remaining socially appropriate.

Pumariega et al. (1990) compared children with CF to age-matched peers with neurological problems. The children with CF were found to show fewer externalizing behaviors and better social competence than those with neurological problems. These studies taken together indicate that children with CF seem to show better adaptation particularly with behavior and social competence adjustment.

DiGirolamo et al. (1997) studied adolescents with CF and their parents. Each was interviewed as to their concerns about their disorder. The children with CF showed moderate levels of depression with girls showing the highest number of depressive symptoms compared to boys. Socially it was found that social functioning was generally in the average range. Males were found to rate themselves as more competent on measures of athletic competence, physical appearance, and global self-worth as well as on the measure of social acceptance compared to the girls. Participants who rated their problems more severe during the interviews also showed higher ratings of depression and lower social competence. It was also found that the parent–teen relationship was problematic in this sample.

Taken together, these studies indicate that most children with CF show fairly good social competence but that the disease is related to problems with sadness and worry. Those adolescents who view more problems in their illness also showed more difficulty with adjustment both behaviorally and socially. It may be that interventions which target assisting these children with their adjustment may assist the child in developing strategies that are helpful. It is also important to note that moderate levels of depressive symptoms, particularly in girls, are seen in this population. Attention by medical personnel as well as others is an important aspect in treatment. Given the additional findings of parent–teen discord these difficulties need further assessment and possible appropriate family treatment. It may well be that as the child strives for individuation they may show more difficulty in coping with the necessary treatment and required restrictions to their activity levels and their participation in typical adolescent past-times.

Seizure Disorders

Children with seizure disorders have been found to be susceptible to difficulties in social competence. These difficulties have been found to be more pronounced in children with asthma or orthopedic disabilities (Austin et al., 1994; Perrin et al., 1987). A relationship between social competence and pediatric seizure disorders was found most prominently in children with poorer seizure control, a disorder that was discovered at an early age, and treatment with valporic acid, a common antiepileptic medication (Herrmann et al., 1988). Several researchers have found a relationship between social competence and poor seizure control (McCusker et al., 2002; Williams et al., 1996).

Poor seizure control also is related to lower neuropsychological functioning (Herrmann et al., 1988; Semrud-Clikeman & Wical, 1999). Such lower neuropsychological functioning has also been linked to difficulties in social competence in children with seizure disorders (Caplan et al., 2005a). Caplan et al. (2002) found that children with seizure disorders frequently have social communication difficulties which are linked to their seizures. Such social communication problems have not been studied in light of social competence behaviors.

Caplan et al. (2005b) sought to study the relationship between neuropsychological functioning, seizure disorder, and social competence in children aged 5–16 years. Children with complex partial seizure disorder (CPS) and absence seizures (CAE) were compared on measures of social competence to healthy children. For the most part the children with either type of seizure disorder were found to have average social competence. However, 33% of the CPS group and 30% of the CAE group had clinically significant difficulties in social competence compared to 6% of the healthy group. When age, gender, spoken language quotient (SLQ), and IQ were covaried, the CPS group showed the poorest social competence of the three groups but the difference was not statistically significant. It was also found that the presence of psychopathology as well as low FSIQ significantly predicted difficulties in social competence. Those children with behavioral disturbances showed the poorest social competence while those with lower IQs also showed significant social problems. This finding was true independent of group membership. IQ and psychopathology were found to account for 40% of the variance.

The importance of this study underscores the need to evaluate the child's level of ability to predict social competence. When IQ is controlled, the link of seizure disorders and social competence difficulties declines. When difficulties in learning or behavior are present in conjunction with the seizure disorder, social competence difficulties are frequently present. This finding is consistent with the case study presented early in this chapter. Joel had learning difficulties, an IQ around 80, and a seizure disorder. These difficulties combine for the child to experience significant problems in socialization. Similar to Chapter 10, these behaviors were also linked to social isolation and rejection in children with seizure disorders.

Difficulties with brain functioning is likely linked to problems with social competence as deficits in cognition may affect not only the child's ability to understand his/her environment but to also adapt to this environment (Nassau & Drotar, 1997). These findings have been replicated in other brain disorders where neuropsychological functioning is impaired (Hoy, 1992; Mulhern et al., 1993; Noll et al., 1999). Further study is needed of children with seizure disorder with social difficulties to determine the most important variables. The extant research indicates that when additional disorders co-occur with seizure disorders the risk for social competence increases. Interventions certainly need to fully understand the child's neuropsychological functioning and its relationship to the child's social functioning, particularly with children with seizure disorders.

Summary

It appears that children with chronic diseases face obstacles that are not present for healthy children in developing socially competent behaviors. Issues such as frequent doctor and hospital visits and medications may interfere with the child's participation in many peer-related activities, particularly sports (Perrin et al., 1991). Peer rejection and problems with social competence is present for children with chronic disease particularly when additional problems are present with additional psychopathology, lower cognitive functioning, and possible neuropsychological deficits (Sandstrom & Schanberg, 2004). Research is just beginning to pinpoint important areas of research in these disorders. Evaluations of the child's temperament, environmental aspects, and behaviors/ psychopathology are needed to more fully understand not only the social challenges faced by these children, but also how to tailor interventions to meet the child's needs.

Reviews of the literature indicate that this type of research is just beginning and is in its infancy. Many children with chronic diseases show little difficulties outside of their disease. Since these disorders are relatively frequent in children, it is important to study those children who fall outside of the normal range of social development to determine what areas are deficient and what interventions may be of most use. At the very least the data indicates the necessity of a complete assessment of the child's functioning as well as the parental support and family issues that may interact with the child's adjustment.

Chronic diseases generally are lifelong and require constant monitoring. The next section of this chapter will review the social competence literature in disorders that can be life-threatening (cancer, leukemia, and brain tumors). Similar to the literature on chronic disease, the social competence research in these areas is also fairly limited.

Childhood Cancer

The incidence of childhood cancers of all types is approximately 8,000 children each year (American Cancer Society, 1997). The chance of survival from childhood cancer has improved drastically in the past 20 years with 60% surviving their disease (Varni et al., 1994). Childhood cancer includes leukemia, brain tumors, and tumors outside the CNS (i.e., kidney). These diseases are, by definition, life threatening and pose challenges in all areas of the child's life as well as in family functioning. Initially the emphasis is on securing appropriate treatment and undergoing procedures which are pleasant and frequently painful. These treatments can extend for years in the child's life and are fraught with anxiety and stress. For example, for acute lymphoblastic leukemia (ALL) treatment can last for 3–4 years prior to remission. During this time there are numerous doctor visits, hospitalizations, and procedures.

After the child enters remission, attention turns to other aspects of the child's life such as his/her academic and social functioning. The literature is equivocal as to the effects of cancer on the child's psychosocial functioning (Bessell, 2001). Some have found difficulties in self-esteem and social skills (Greenberg et al., 1989; Varni et al., 1994) while others have not found difficulties in psychosocial development (Kazak, 1994; Noll et al., 1993). It has been suggested that the differing findings may be due to the heterogeneity of the samples in terms of age, diagnosis, and severity of the disease and treatment (Varni et al., 1998).

Bessell (2001) suggests that school and social adjustment are affected by increased absenteeism due to doctor and treatment requirements, difficulties maintaining peer relationships as the child's friends move on with their relationships while the child is absent, and for some children, resulting school phobia from the change in their physical status and their lack of participation in school life. Coupled with these difficulties is the emerging evidence that the treatment may produce cognitive neuropsychological effects that may not be available immediately following treatment but may emerge months or even years later (Brown et al., 1996).

Madan-Swain et al. (1998) found that nearly one-third of the childhood cancer survivors were enrolled in special education with 7% in full-time special education programs. Most of the children qualified for special education under the other-health impaired category. In addition, a sizable majority of these children were retained in a grade due to absenteeism from the disease and treatments (Mulhern et al., 1989). In both of these cases, the child is not in the mainstream when reintegrated into school or is with a different peer group. These changes in his/her life are likely to have significant effects on the child's social life and depending on the age, possibly on his/her social competence.

Bessell (2001) sought to study the psychosocial functioning of children with cancer. Children were included in the sample if they were between the ages of 8–17 years, had a diagnosis of cancer except for brain tumors, and had cancer treatment that ended 6 months prior to the study. Fifty-one children and their families were enrolled in this study. It was found that children were more anxious than adolescents. In addition 42% were found to show poor peer acceptance and lowered self-perception compared to standardized norms. It was also found that the children who were retained viewed this retention as the worst that had happened to them.

Whole brain radiation treatment has been linked to possible late-effects including difficulty with learning and attention (Stehbens et al., 1991). The link to behavioral difficulties is less well established with some finding no link (Mulhern et al., 1989) and others finding behavioral difficulty

(Anderson et al., 1994; Deasy-Spinetta et al., 1988). Noll et al. (1997) sought to study children with ALL who had whole brain radiation treatment and those who did not on measures of behavior as well as social functioning. Findings indicate good resilience for these children in general. For our purposes the important finding was of fewer social difficulties than would be expected. The majority of children were not found to experience social difficulties unless there were concomitant family problems, or major changes in parenting such as overprotection or lack of monitoring.

The findings from this study as to the effect of the family on the child's resulting social adjustment are important. Horwitz and Kazak (1990) were interested in a complementary aspect of adjustment, namely how the family reacts when a member experiences cancer. How the sibling's cancer affects the adjustment of the brother or sister is an important emphasis for this study. It was predicted that the siblings of children with cancer would show poorer behavioral adjustment and poorer self-perceptions but stronger social competence and prosocial behaviors compared to those without cancer in the family. It was also expected that the sibling's adjustment would be related to how well the family adapted to the stress of the child's cancer and the cohesion that was present in the family. The siblings were found to be quite well adjusted socially and behaviorally, contrary to the hypothesized findings. Siblings who make good adjustment socially to the situation also appear to have fewer behavioral problems (Evans et al., 1993).

Over half of the families in the oncology were described as either rigid or chaotic while less than a fifth of the comparison group showed such profiles (Horwitz & Kazak, 1990). There were also findings of stronger cohesion than expected in the families of cancer patients for those families with siblings without behavioral difficulties. Horwitz and Kazak (1990) suggest that the rigidity or chaotic aspects of these families may be actually a positive coping strategy in light of the illness. The chaotic families may be more flexible in dealing with a very stressful, uncontrollable event while the rigid families are attempting to put control on this same type of event. Increased cohesion in these families has been linked in the past with better adjustment of the siblings and family of chronically ill children (Daniels et al., 1986).

Summary

These findings are important for thinking about appropriate interventions. School interventions that forestall the need for retention should be strongly considered particularly in view of the child's resulting anxiety and poorer peer acceptance. Providing support, psychologically, academically, and socially, is an important aspect in assisting these children with the transition back into the school environment. Too often the bridging of the child's medical and school/social needs are neglected and need to be thought of in a planful manner as the child progresses through treatment and beyond. Transitioning the child back into the school requires that the teacher be educated as to the child's difficulty as well as providing a case manager knowledgeable concerning chronic illness.

Support for these families is also an important aspect of their treatment. For the most part, the families are found to be coping relatively well with a very stressful situation. For those families that become more chaotic or rigid, it may well be that this is a coping mechanism for the heightened anxiety associated with a life-threatening illness. Particular attention needs to be paid to those families who do not cope well and who either over-protect or under-protect their ill child (Semrud-Clikeman, 2000). Providing support for these overwhelmed families is particularly important for the psychosocial adjustment of the patient as well as the siblings involved. It is promising that the siblings generally show good adjustment when the family is cohesive and supportive.

For children with childhood cancers treatment is generally time-limited and recovery is related to success of these treatments. In traumatic brain injury (TBI) the symptoms, particularly in the case of severe head injury, may last for the life of the child. The continuing challenge of severe traumatic brain injury is not only stressful but also psychosocially challenging. The following section briefly discusses the psychosocial affects of TBI.

Traumatic Brain Injury (TBI)

The incidence of TBI is approximately 180 per 100,000 for children and adolescents aged 1–15 years (Kraus, 1995). Problems are often found in executive functions, cognitive flexibility, memory, language, irritability, lability, and impulsivity (Semrud-Clikeman, 2001). Children with TBI have been found to show more difficulties with social competence compared to children with other types of injuries not brain related (Dennis et al., 2001; Papero et al., 1993).

Psychosocial and behavioral difficulties may be particularly problematic for children with TBI as they interact with academic and cognitive progress and may affect later social competence (Rosenthal & Bond, 1990). For example, cognitive deficits have been found to affect the acquisition of social skills in children who experienced TBI prior to age 7 (Ewing-Cobbs et al., 2000). Children who are infants or in preschool generally experienced head injury due to child abuse (Semrud-Clikeman, 2001). These children have been found to show poorer adaptive behavior following recovery (Prasad et al., 2000). Thus, for children with TBI due to child abuse it appears that the caretaker–child relationship is even more predictive of poor outcome than the injury itself.

Children with TBI have been shown to evidence hyperarousal and become easily frustrated with many children showing more headaches and stomachaches than those with non-TBI injuries (Vriezen, 2000). Depression is more commonly seen in this population with the depression not responding as easily to treatment particularly for those children with severe TBI and possibly to a lesser extent in children with moderate TBI (Janusz et al., 2002). Most importantly the difficulties with arousal and low frustration tolerance persist more than a year following the injury and may have a significant effect on the child's re-entry to school and re-entry into their peer group. If the child is irritable and labile, his/her peers will likely back away from close relationships, thus isolating the child and increasing his/her feelings of being different. Such feelings of social isolation may translate into difficulties with friends and with social competence at all ages.

The suggestion that children with TBI will show social difficulties is consistent with the above findings for the persistence of depressive and anxiety symptoms as well as the likelihood that younger children will experience difficulty in developing social competence. Some researchers have suggested that children with TBI may show a deterioration in social skills over time due to an awareness of previously obtained but now lost skills (Begali, 1992; Fordyce et al., 1983). Warschausky et al. (1997) studied the child with TBI's ability to generate solutions to social difficulties and found significant difficulties in this ability. Moreover, the children with TBI most often generated solutions that were less positive and less assertive than those generated by children without a head injury. It is not known what the premorbid level of problem-solving was present but all of the children were reported to be functioning adequately socially prior to the head injury.

Self-awareness deficits have been found as well as difficulties with the development of insight in children with TBI (Semrud-Clikeman, 2000). The younger child may not be accepted by previously made friends and may resort to social withdrawal or aggressive behaviors in order to regain social standing. These strategies frequently backfire with the child feeling more and more isolated. In addition, research indicates that children with TBI show difficulty in social communication skills which further affect their friendships and peer interactions (Ylvisaker, 1993).

Janusz et al. (2002) sought to evaluate how children with TBI solve social difficulties and the relationship of this ability to the social outcomes experienced by the child. It was found that children with severe TBI showed more difficulty solving social problems at the level expected for their chronological age. This discrepancy of age to problem-solving level was found to significantly predict difficulties in social and adaptive functioning. These findings indicate that a child with TBI is likely to have difficulty coping with social events that occur and will respond in a less developmentally advanced manner. Such responding may well be inappropriate for their age and result in peers preferring not to associate with the child. Such isolation may well contribute to continuing difficulties with social competence and social development. It is important to note that this study found deficits in social reasoning that may be subtle unless a more comprehensive interview is conducted. On basic rating scales, the child may show no difficulties as he/she is aware of the appropriate answer being sought. It was only after a further examination of the child's social reasoning was conducted that Janusz et al. (2002) found the areas of difficulty that were translating into poor social functioning.

Thus, interventions may need to target the child's ability to reason when confronted with a socially provocative situation. Traditional social skills intervention generally assumes that the child's difficulty is due to poor knowledge of social conduct. For most children and adolescents with TBI, the knowledge of social conduct is generally intact; problems are present with disinhibition and regulation. Meta-analysis of social skills training has not found long-term or generalized changes in the social competence of children with high incidence difficulties (Gresham et al., 2001). For children with TBI, interventions that focus on inhibition, social communication, and coaching may provide the most promise for intervening effectively in helping the child to develop social competence (Ylvilsaker et al., 2005).

In summary, children with severe TBI tend to have social difficulties. After a period of convalescence the child re-enters the school environment and has been found to have difficulties with attention, disinhibition, executive functioning, and lability. These problems have been found to interfere with the child's social functioning. In addition, many children with TBI have had normal social functioning up to the time of their injury. They re-enter school with changed cognitive, neuropsychological, and behavioral functioning. Emerging research indicates that these children are at risk for social difficulties, social isolation, and poorer social competence than children with nonbrain injuries and those who are healthy. Interventions that appear promising include coaching for executive function skill development and cognitive behavioral therapy. As with other disorders in this chapter, further research is needed for the child's social functioning and adjustment to a different world than the one he/she inhabited prior to the injury. The following section describes the challenges faced by children with genetic disorders. These disorders generally differ from TBI and chronic diseases as they are present from the birth of the child.

Genetic Disorders

There are a myriad of genetic disorders. A genetic disorder is present from birth and either inherited from one's parents or a result of a de novo combination of genes and chromosomes to form a disorder. A de novo combination occurs because the chromosomes unite in a different manner than usual. Such a disorder is 18q- where neither parent is a "carrier" of the gene—it is the result of the combination of the genes and chromosomes during meiosis. There are some terms that need defining. A genotype is the genes and chromosomes that are present from the parental contributions. The phenotype is the interaction between the genotype and the child's environment which produces the visible behavior and traits seen in the child.

There are several major groups of genetic disorders. In chromosomal disorders entire chromosomes or portions of the chromosomes are missing or added. Syndromes such as Down's Syndrome and Turner Syndrome are examples of this type of genetic disorder. Monogenic or Mendelian conditions are those where there is an alteration in DNA structure. These are autosomal dominant or recessive as well as X-linked. The autosomal dominant genes are those that only one parent needs to have for the child to have a 50% chance of inheriting the disorder. Neurofibromatosis is an example of an autosomal dominant disorder. A recessive disorder is where both parents must have the gene and the child has a 25% chance of inheriting the disorder. Disorders such as phenylketonuria are automosomal recessive. X-linked disorders are those that are linked to the X chromosome donated by the mother for males and by the father for females. Fragile X is a type of X-linked disorder.

Another type of genetic disorder is that of a multifactorial or polygenic type (Carey & McMahon, 1999). This type of genetic disorder is the result of a combination of genes or gene–environment interactions. These disorders often do not follow the usual rules of inheritance and include many of the diseases. Finally, there are new types of genetic disorders now termed "mitochrondrial disorders." These disorders have recently been identified and involved differences in the mitochrondria within the cell.

This chapter cannot describe all of the disorders present and so will provide a sample of the more common types. It is instructive that literature searches provide few articles in many of these disorders as to the child's social competence. Most articles discuss the physical and genetic characteristics of the disease followed by the cognitive and neuropsychological functioning present. There are only a handful of articles concerning social competence in children with various genetic disorders. This chapter will discuss Williams Syndrome, neurofibromatosis, tuberous sclerosis, phenylketonuria, Turner's Syndrome, Fragile X, and Tourette's Syndrome. This is by no means an exhaustive list but does give the reader an idea of the challenges experienced by these children.

Williams Syndrome

Williams Syndrome (WS) is characterized with dysmorphic facial features, cardiovascular disease, connective tissue abnormalities, delayed development, and a typical cognitive and personality profile (Dykens, 2003; Morris & Mervis, 1999). WS is caused by a submicroscopic deletion of chromosome 7 and must be identified through the specialized technique called FISH (fluorescent in situ hybridization). This technique uses a DNA probe containing the missing gene that is labeled with a fluorescent dye. When applied, normal chromosomes will show the fluorescent marker. For the WS chromosome the marker will not be present. The incidence of WS is approximately 1 in 20,000 live births (Morris & Mervis, 1999). It occurs throughout families and can be either passed from mother or father. The deletion is generally large enough to contain several genes with 13 mapped to the region that is missing at this time (Jurado et al., 1996; Wang et al., 1997).

There are many physical difficulties found in these children including hypotonia, hyperextensible joints, difficulties with feeding, problems with cardiovascular disease, and a voice that is generally hoarse and low-pitched. Cognitively these children have many areas of difficulty particularly in the areas of visual-spatial skills and in fine motor skills such as drawing. Strengths are found in language, particularly in conversation, and rote memory. Their overall cognitive skills are generally in the below average to mentally handicapped range.

Behaviorally children with WS have difficulties with attention as well as social difficulty. They often appear more immature than their age-mates and may act unusually in a social setting. Morris and Mervis (1999) suggest that this immaturity may be linked to the child's lower ability levels rather than to the syndrome itself. When children with WS were compared to those with other types of cognitive difficulties, it was found that they had more difficulty with attention, appeared more restless, and seemed more fearful of specific situations (Sarimski, 1997). Other studies have found that children with WS tend to be more fearful, had more difficulties with concentration, and were more solitary compared to other children with similar ages, genders, and Verbal IQ (Gosch & Pankau, 1994; Udwin & Yule, 1990). Einfeld et al. (1997) found that children with WS showed more difficulty with social behaviors including problems with being over-affectionate, overreacting to sounds, high activity levels, and constantly sought out attention, were described as inappropriately happy, and seemed to wander without a destination.

Morris and Mervis (1999) rightfully suggest that children with WS should be compared to other children with genetic disorders with compromised cognitive functioning to determine if there are social competence deficits that are due to their disorders rather than to lower ability. Rosner et al. (2004) compared children with Prader-Willi, Williams, and Down's syndromes on measures of social competence. Prader-Willi Syndrome is characterized by relatively higher levels of intelligence compared to the other two syndromes with strengths in visual processing and visual-motor tasks and weaknesses in behavior. Due to these behavioral difficulties, children with Prader-Willi often experience difficulty with socialization and frequently are more solitary and may show lower social competence. Children with Down's Syndrome (DS) have the lowest cognitive profile compared to Prader-Willi and WS but have relative strengths in visual memory and visual-motor skills. Weaknesses are present in expressive language and speech articulation (Dykens et al., 2001; Miller et al., 1995). Behaviorally children with DS have good social skills and are friendly and engaging. They can be noncompliant but research has indicated fewer emotional and behavioral difficulties than other syndromes (Dykens et al., 2002; Einfield et al., 1999).

Rosner et al. (2004) hypothesized that children with DS would show the best scores on measures of social competence with children with WS and Prader-Willi performing more poorly. In addition, the study sought to determine what variables were most related to social competence in these groups. As predicted the children with DS were found to score higher on measures of social competence with the children with Prader-Willi showing the poorest response. Children with WS or DS were rated as stronger on behavioral measure compared to the children with Prader-Willi. For children with WS or DS, age was directly related to higher social competence with older children showing better scores. This finding was not present for children with Prader-Willi. The social competence scores were found to be negatively correlated with measures of externalizing behaviors for all groups. For the Prader-Willi group internalizing behaviors were also negatively correlated with social competence.

The findings from this study underscore the need to study children with similar types of disorders rather than comparing children with these types of genetic disorders to typically developing children. When compared with children with relatively similar ability levels, children with WS or DS were found to score relatively well on measures of social competence. In contrast, children with Prader-Willi not only showed difficulties with social competence but also increased difficulty with externalizing and internalizing behaviors. Similar to typically developing children, children with WS or DS showed poorer social competence when accompanying externalizing behaviors were present.

Thus, the additional difficulties seen may be more due to comorbid diagnoses of ADHD, ODD, or conduct rather than solely to the diagnosis of WS or DS. It is also important to note that the children with Prader-Willi did not improve with age in social competence while the DS and WS groups did. This finding is disconcerting as the children with Prader-Willi may require targeting of these behaviors in order to facilitate appropriate functioning. Dykens and Cassidy (1996) suggest that long-term treatment is needed for these symptoms as well as case management throughout the lifespan.

Consistent with the above report, studies of adaptive behavior found that children with WS have found good socialization skills compared to their cognitive ability (Mervis et al., 2001). Difficulties were found on measures of daily living skills and for preschoolers in the motor domains. The socialization domain of the test utilized (Vineland Adaptive Behavior Scales) rewards children for interactions with others and for understanding others' emotional states. The children with WS did very well on these aspects of the Vineland but performed more poorly on aspects involving structuring their play and leisure time and coping with areas of difficulty.

Thus, for children with WS it appears that specific social skills are very intact. However, the difficulties with fearfulness, high intensity, inattention, and coping are areas of concern for these children and likely interfere with social functioning, particularly at older ages. It is recommended that children with WS utilize verbal self-talk to assist them with difficult tasks (Morris & Mervis, 1999). This technique may also be helpful with their social development. In addition, children with WS who have comorbid difficulties with externalizing behaviors fare more poorly in developing social competence than those without. These findings are similar to those with children with externalizing behaviors without WS and indicate that a comprehensive evaluation is important to determine what factors may be interfering with the child's ability to function socially. Moreover, awareness that cognitive delays may be related to the immature functioning seen in many of these children rather than to social delay per se is an important aspect for the clinician's attention.

Neurofibromatosis

Neurofibromatosis (NF) is an autosomal dominant genetic disorder that results in benign and malignant tumors in the central and peripheral nervous systems (Huson & Hughes, 1994). There are two forms of neurofibromatosis, NF1 and NF2, with more research present in children with NF1. NF1 involves abnormal peripheral nerve cell growth with frequently co-occurring brain tumors present. The incidence is approximately 1 in 4,000 live births and diagnosis is by clinical criteria (Nilsson & Bradford, 1999). The disease is progressive in nature with symptoms frequently present in childhood and increasing into adolescence and adulthood.

Diagnosis is generally by the age of 10 with pain present due to the neurofibromas that are growing in the peripheral nervous system. Tumors are present in the optic pathways and can compromise vision, create hydrocephalus, and may require surgery for removal (Listernick et al., 1995). NF2 is less prevalent than NF1 with an incidence of 1 in 40,000 live births (Nilsson & Bradford, 1999). Cataracts and hearing loss are often associated and the symptoms can be progressive and can result in death. NF1 has been linked to chromosome 17 with 50% of cases result of direct genetic transmission while the other half are due to new mutations (NIH Consensus Development Conference, 1988). NF2 has been linked to chromosome 22.

Children with NF show increased incidence of a learning disability as well as ADHD. Cognitive ability ranges from mentally retarded to gifted. Research has also suggested a higher prevalence of nonverbal learning disabilities in this population accompanied by difficulties with visual-spatial skills, perceptual-motor, and higher-order language difficulties. Problems are also frequently present with attention, sensory-motor difficulty, and psychosocial delays. While the incidence of learning disability and ADHD may be found in many children with NF, there are also several that do not show such a profile (Hyman et al., 2005; Philip & Turk, 2006). Therefore, this population is likely quite heterogeneous and there may well be subtypes within this disorder, thus NF should be studied with an eye to individual differences (Nilsson & Bradford, 1999). Moore et al. (1994) suggest that when NF is present with other Neurodevelopmental disorders (i.e., LD or ADHD), the presenting picture is more complex and likely more deleterious.

Emotionally children with NF frequently show difficulties with irritability, lability, impulsivity and mood disorders (i.e., depression, anxiety). In addition, parents who also have NF may show difficulty in adjusting to their child's disease based on their own experiences (Nilsson & Bradford, 1999). They may over-react to their child's difficulties or conversely under-react. Neither of these strategies is likely helpful for the child. Family support and therapy may be very important for these children. Findings of social functioning indicate that these children tend to be bullied more often, have fewer friends, and are openly rejected by their peers (Dilts et al., 1996; Johnson et al., 1999). Many of the studies have had heterogeneous populations of children with NF1 with many having ADHD and/or LD. As mentioned earlier and in other chapters of this book, these disorders can contribute in and of themselves to problems with social functioning, and the social difficulties found in children with NF1 may be more due to these comorbid disorders than to the disease itself.

Barton and North (2004) sought to evaluate the contributions of ADHD and LD to the social difficulties found in children with NF1. They selected children between the ages of 8 and 16 with diagnoses of NF1 and excluded children with CNS pathology. The total sample size was 79 children with NF1 and 46 unaffected siblings. Children with NF1 were found to show difficulty with total social skills by both parent and teacher ratings. In contrast the students rated themselves above average on measures of social competence. When the sample was divided by moderate/severe NF1 and mild/minimal NF1, as expected the more severe manifestations of the disorder showed more difficulties with social skills. Moreover, higher scores on measures of attention, aggression, internalizing and externalizing problems were significantly related to poorer social skills in both the affected groups and the siblings.

When children were compared using comorbid diagnoses, the following groups were formed: NF1/ADHD, NF1/LD/SLI, and NF1. The NF1/LD/SLI group showed the poorest scores on academic scales and IQ while the NF1/ADHD group had the poorest social skills and social competence ratings with scores indicating severe difficulties in this area (more than 2 standard deviations below the mean). The NF1/LD/SLI and NF1 did not differ on social skills and scored within the average range. These findings substantiate the idea that children with comorbid diagnoses may have significantly more difficulty socially than children with only one diagnosis with a comorbid diagnosis of ADHD being the most detrimental to the formation of social relationships.

While there are suggestions about social difficulties in children with NF, a comprehensive study of these difficulties is not present in the literature. The literature tends to focus on the neurological presentation as well as the academic difficulties found rather than on adjustment. Given the emotional difficulties documented in this disorder as well as the physical differences, children with NF face challenges that may not be present in other disorders and likely complicate their social adjustment. For example, Sobel (1998) studied patients with NF1 and found a wide range of disabilities ranging from significant disfigurement to no signs of any physical difference. When the disfigurement was fairly significant, the children were found to show poor social adjustment but to have appropriate social skills and competence. Findings indicated that social support was very helpful for these children and their families particularly for adolescents. Such studies underscore the need for a full assessment of the child's needs as well as the need for family and child/adolescent support.

Tuberous Sclerosis

Tuberous Sclerosis complex (TSC) is a multi-system disorder with a prevalence of 10 per 100,000 and has been linked to genes on chromosomes 9 and 16 (European Chromosome 16 Tuberous Sclerosis Consortium, 1993). It includes growths in multiple organs including the brain, skin, eyes, heart, lungs, and kidneys (Gomez, 1999). Approximately one-third of cases are a result of an autosomal dominant condition while another two-thirds are new mutations (Povey et al., 1994). Seizures are frequent with

TSC and are associated with poorer intellectual functioning (Joinson et al., 2003). Some have described behavioral symptoms of hyperactivity, destructiveness, and autistic-like behaviors (Gillberg et al., 1994; Hunt, 1993; Hunt & Dennis, 1987; Smalley, 1998). These autistic signs are more likely to be present in children with more neurological impairment. Frontal and posterior growths in the brain have been associated with autism in children with TSC particularly when a seizure disorder is also present. Temporal lobe growths appear to place the child at the highest risk level for developing autism (Bolton & Griffiths, 1997; Bolton et al., 2002; Zaroff & Isaacs, 2005). Steinhausen et al. (2002) found significant comorbidity with ADHD, oppositional defiant disorder, and separation anxiety disorder in a study of children with TSC.

There are very few studies evaluating the psychiatric difficulties seen in TSC with some finding higher rates of depression and anxiety (Lewis et al., 2004). Raznahan et al. (2006) express concern about the findings of mental illness in this population due to the high level of intellectual disability and the difficulty these clients have understanding questions posed in a standard psychiatric interview. These authors sought to evaluate the psychiatric functioning of 60 adults with TSC. Findings were of higher–than-expected affective disorders with major depression being the most common. It was also found that intellectual disability was negatively associated with mental illness. Such findings are consistent with other studies that have controlled for IQ when interviewing the child/adult and when the language in the interview is adjusted for mental age (Borthwick-Duffy & Eyman, 1990). It was felt that the vulnerability of this group to depression is likely related to having a chronic multi-system illness as well as possible neurobiological causes to such disorders.

It is important to note that there were very few to no studies on social competence and/or psychopathology found in the review for tuberous sclerosis. The Raznahan et al. (2006) study was one of the few looking at functioning in adults with TSC controlling for IQ. This research area really needs additional study but is hampered by difficulty in finding sufficient subjects to allow for the power needed to evaluate the child's functioning. Controlling variables such as epilepsy and degree of mental retardation as well as multi-organ involvement makes studying this population particularly difficult. Given the high risk for the development of autism in this population, it may well be that these children experience significant social difficulties similar to children with autism and that their social competence abilities are significantly compromised apart from their intellectual disability. Further study is certainly needed in this area.

Turner Syndrome

Turner Syndrome (TS) has a rich history of empirical study and is characterized by extremely short stature, is a female disorder with lack of secondary sexual characteristics, a broad chest, webbed neck, and many abnormalities (Powell & Schulte, 1999). It is linked to a loss or an abnormality in one of the two X chromosomes present in females and has been found to lead to many physical, neuropsychological, and emotional difficulties. TS occurs in 1 out of every 2,000–3,000 live births of females (Orten & Orten, 1992). It is thought the incidence for conception is much higher but that only 1% of pregnancies with the TS chromosomal abnormality actually result in a baby (Temple & Carney, 1993).

Neuropsychologically cognitive ability appears to be stronger on measures of verbal IQ with lower-than-expected performance abilities particularly on tasks that require visual-spatial processing (Rovet, 1995). Additional difficulties have been reported in visual memory, visual con-structional skills, math calculation, and in working memory (Berch, 1996; Buchanan et al., 1998; Rovet 1993; Temple & Carney, 1995). Diffuse right-hemisphere dysfunction has been found in women and girls with TX (Rovet, 1995; Shucard et al., 1992) consistent with the visual-spatial processing difficulties found in this population. In addition, Rovet (1990) found an increased signal in the left hemisphere when interpreting non-verbal information which she interpreted to mean that the girls with TS have compensated for a weaker right hemisphere. Such compensation was thought to be the result of the normal lateralization of function generally seen for nonverbal tasks to the right hemisphere and verbal tasks to the left hemisphere.

Psychosocially girls with TS seem to have fewer significant external-izing behaviors than other genetic disorders (Powell & Schulte, 1999). In contrast they experience more difficulties with peer relationships, lower emotional reactivity, high stress tolerance, unassertiveness, compliance with authority, and to be more emotionally immature (Downey et al., 1989; McCauley et al., 1995). Studies have particular difficulties in the areas of self-esteem, peer relationships, and social withdrawal (McCauley et al., 1995; Powell & Schulte, 1999).

One of the areas of difficulty for girls with TS is their short stature. Holmes et al. (1985) studied the relationship between short stature and social competency. They compared children with a growth hormone defi-ciency, a constitutional delay, and TS. It was found that all children in this study showed a decline in adjustment beginning in early adolescence. Parent ratings of social competence differed significantly for younger and older groups of children. During this time the child's school competence also fell as well as rates of social interaction. It was found that for the younger children all had more than one friend but at follow-up after the age of 14 one-third had no friends or only one with fewer contacts with the remaining friend. By late adolescence the child had reformed friendships and the incidence of peer contact approached that expected of a child that age. By the age of 17 these children's social competence abilities appears to approach normal functioning and the child "rebounds" from the years of adolescent angst. These findings were also present in a study by McCauley et al. (1995) which found a decline in social relationships and self esteem in girls with TS from the age of 7 to 14. In addition, these children were also seen as more immature than the control comparison group.

Thus, children who enter adolescence are at higher risk for social and school difficulties and additional support is very appropriate at that age. Their shorter stature and emotional maturity likely make them targets for other adolescents and likely increase their discomfort with their peer relationships. Rovet and Ireland (1994) found that height was correlated with social competence with shorter girls showing poorer social skills and peer relationships. These height differences likely become more evident as the peers grow during early adolescence.

It is important to note their resilience at the end of adolescence but the pain and turmoil experienced between the ages of 14 and 17 were substantial. Thus, school, medical, and clinical personnel should be aware of this vulnerability and thus provide support for these children at that time. Parents also should be provided with education and support for their children both before early adolescence and during. To have information that assists in understanding what the child is experiencing as well as the types of support that would be needed may be extremely helpful for these children and their parents.

While improvement in peer relationships is seen in late adolescence, this improvement should not be taken to mean that, as adults, these women do not experience social difficulty. Problems with self-esteem, lower levels of secondary sexual characteristics, and infertility have been found to be related to lower self-esteem in this population (Skuse, 1987; Pavlidis et al., 1995). It has also been reported that women with TS are more emotionally mature and continue to have a lower number of peer relationships than others their age (Powell & Schulte, 1999). Lower rates of marriage and a tendency to remain dependent on their parents have been found to be common in women with TS (Orten & Orten, 1992). On a positive note, women with TS have been found to have average to above-average academic and occupational success (Orten & Orten, 1992).

Faust et al. (1995) studied the reaction of mothers with girls with TS and the subsequent adjustment of the child. Mothers who utilized problem-solving coping strategies had children who adjusted relatively well while those who were emotional and used wishful thinking had children who had more social and academic difficulties. The administration of growth hormone was also found to significantly increase the mother's ability to cope with the child's difficulties with fewer mothers reporting depression in this sample. Stress has been reported in parents due to needs to assist school personnel in programming for the child, providing social outlets for their child, and dealing with medical personnel with growth hormone injections (Williams, 1995). In addition, for parents who had psychopathology, their children tended to have more difficulty and to have a poorer psychosocial outcome (Powell & Schulte, 1999).

Thus, social functioning in children with TS appears to be related to their age as well as parental psychopathology and the administration of growth hormone. These children appear particularly vulnerable between the ages of 12 and 17 and additional support is justified particularly in social environments. Support for parents has also been found to be helpful particularly during these age periods but also likely in early adulthood to assist the young adult in individuating from her parents. Interventions appear to be most important to assist parents with coping with the child's differences as well as supporting the child throughout development.

Fragile X

Persons with Fragile X syndrome (FXS) show problems in learning and emotional development as well as mental retardation. It is caused by a mutation in the gene entitled FMR1 on one of the X chromosomes (Hagerman & Lampe, 1999). Prior to this mutation, a carrier has an X chromosome which has fewer repeats of the DNA code for that gene. Individuals who carry the disorder may have a higher incidence of anxiety or depression but not generally intellectual difficulties (Franke et al., 1996; Hagerman 1996). The full mutation occurs when the FMR1 gene is passed onto the next generation through a woman who carries the permutation. With a father with the permutation he will pass on the permutation to all of his daughters but none of his sons. Daughters who receive the mutation from their father carry a high risk of having mentally retarded children (Hagerman & Lampe, 1999). A carrier mother can have affected females as well as males as the risk of passing on the mutation to the next generation is 50% with each pregnancy.

The prevalence of FXS is approximately 1 in 1,250 males and females respectively for those who are mentally retarded due to FXS (Hagerman & Lampe, 1999). Studies have also found that 1 in 259 females and 1 in 700 males are likely carriers of the permutation (Rousseau et al., 1996; Rousseau et al., 1995). Sherman (1996) suggests that FXS is the most common genetic cause of mental retardation and is involved in 30% of all X-linked forms of intellectual disability. Research has found that 2–3% of males with mental retardation of unknown cause had FXS while 6% of males with autism also had FXS (Brown et al., 1986; Slany et al., 1995). Hagerman (1996) has also found that most of the males with FXS will show autistic-like features.

Physical features may include large ears, a long face, finger joints that extend more than usual, double-jointed thumbs, flat feet, soft skin, and a high palate (Hagerman, 1996). Difficulties in children with FXS are frequently present in delays in language and motor skills as well as hypotonia and hyperactivity. These children are also very sensitive to sound, visual stimuli, and tactile stimulation. Due to this sensitivity to environment, these children are also prone to tantrums and aggression. Perseveration is common in children with FXS including repeating words and sentences (Abbeduto & Hagerman, 1997). Autistic features are seen with hand flapping, toe walking, poor eye contact, and social anxiety being more prominent in this population than in age-matched peers. These children are described as interested in social interaction but will often avoid such involvement due to their hypersensitivity to the environment (Cohen, 1995; Belser & Sudhalter, 1995).

There are gender differences in the expression of this disorder. Males are most often mentally retarded while females have less vulnerability as they have two X chromosomes. Females are able to inactivate one X chromosome—if they inactivate the fragile X chromosome they frequently show learning disabilities as well as attentional and organization problems in the face of an average IQ. Those females with the full mutation will show intellectual functioning in the borderline or mildly retarded range (deVries et al., 1996).

A review of the literature found very few articles that discussed social competence in this population. Given the high rates of ADHD and/or autism, it is likely that difficulties are present in social competence. Hall et al. (2006) studied the tendency of children with FXS to socially withdraw from social interaction. These authors were interested in the environmental contributions to the child's difficulties with social and behavioral control. In some syndromes it has been found that the antecedent and consequent demands placed on the child were directly related to inappropriate behaviors (Hall, Oliver & Murphy, 2001; Oliver et al., 1993).

Social escape has been found to be common in children with FXS. Cohen et al. (1988) studied 12 males with FXS in interactions with their mothers. These children showed high incidences of turning away from the adult, running away from the adult, or looking away compared to others with autism, DS, or who were typically developing. These behaviors were more pronounced in children with FXS both with their mother and a stranger with the stranger evoking more behaviors than even children with autism.

Hall et al. (2006) studied 114 children with FXS between the ages of 6 and 17 for social escape. These children were observed in their home where the child was videotaped in a set activity. The conditions were an interview, the child doing silent reading, then doing oral reading and then singing. Male participants showed high levels of face-hiding, fidgeting, refusals, and eye-rubbing while females showed face-hiding, fidgeting, and refusals. Females were more likely to establish eye contact with the interviewer with some males never establishing eye contact. Eye-rubbing and face-hiding were significantly correlated and may be a response class that is utilized by these children to avoid social contact. The singing task evoked most escape behaviors and appeared to be more problematic for these children than the interview condition. It is recommended that behavioral interventions be initiated with these children to reduce these difficulties and to increase eye contact.

Given the higher rate of prevalence of FXS with children with mental retardation and autism, it is likely that these children experience problems with socialization and with subsequent development of peer relations. It appears important to study this disorder more carefully with an eye to appropriate interventions for social adjustment. Comparing children with FXS and autism/mental retardation would be helpful to understand the challenges that are present in their development as well as in developing appropriate interventions.

Phenylketonuria

Phenylketonuria (PKU) is an autosomal recessive disorder and inherited from each parent. It affects males and females similarly. It produces a defect in the liver enzyme phenylalanine hydroxylase which block the conversion of phylalanine to tyrosine, a necessary amino acid. Without treatment, mental retardation frequently occurs. Treatment is diet based and must be started in the first few weeks of life. For the most part untreated subjects will suffer with mental retardation.

Phenylketonuria is a common genetic disorder with 1 out 50 people being carriers and an incidence of 1 in 11,000 in the U.S. It is rare in populations of African descent but more common in European countries. Every child born in the U.S. is screened for PKU. If untreated, mental retardation, eczema, seizures, ataxia, motor deficits, and behavioral problems frequently occur (Waisbren, 1999). Autism is fairly common in children with PKU. PKU is not generally seen until after 6 months of age and then is a progressive form of brain damage that probably begins right after birth (Waisbren, 1999).

The diet generally restricts phenylalanine and must be followed throughout life. A special formula is generally used that contains important amino acids in protein minus the phenylalanine. The diet allows for sugars, fats, limited amounts of vegetables and fruits, and special low-protein pasta products. No meat, fish, eggs, or dairy products are allowed.

With early treatment mental retardation is generally prevented. However, there is documentation of other neuropsychological deficits including visual-motor delays, slowed fine motor speed, poorer executive functioning as well as planning, reasoning, and sustained attention. Fast processing of information is problematic and presentation of lessons needs to be slowed down considerably to allow the child with PKU to appropriately process information (de Sonneville & Njiokiktjien, 1988; de Sonneville et al., 1990; Schmidt, Rupp, Burgard, & Pietz, 1992; Schmidt et al., 1994). It has been found that even in early treated children with PKU, frontal lobe functioning is compromised particularly on tasks requiring working memory and inhibition (Diamond et al., 1997; Stemerdink, 1996).

Socially children with PKU have not been found to show particular difficulties in social competence. They have been reported to interact well with peers and to show similar behaviors as adolescents and adults (Stemerdink et al., 1995). These findings are encouraging for children with PKU. For those whose treatment is less than optimal and who have significant intellectual difficulties, it may well be that their social skills are similar to children with mental retardation. There are few studies that test this hypothesis and this conclusion is speculative.

Tourette Syndrome

Tourette Syndrome (TS) is also known as Gilles de la Tourette syndrome. It is a genetic disorder that has motor and vocal tics that are present for a year prior to diagnosis (Brown & Ievers, 1999). A tic is a recurring movement or sound that is spontaneous. It occurs suddenly and is generally quick. Anxiety and emotional upset can increase the rate of tics and these may change over time and with development (Silva et al., 1995). The tics may be simple motor and vocal tics such as blinking or clearing the throat or may be more complex (i.e., shrugging and words).

The prevalence of TS is between 1 and 8 cases per 1,000 males and .1 and 4 cases per 1,000 females (Peterson et al., 1995). Children show higher incidence estimates than adolescents and it is thought the tic severity decreases at puberty (Apter et al., 1993; Peterson et al., 1995).

Onset of tics generally occurs around the age of 7 and the disorder develops gradually. Initially tics are generally in the facial region moving to the head and neck and then lower extremities (Brown & Ievers, 1999). Attentional deficits may be present and generally occur at the same time as the tics and often by the age of 4. Obsessive-compulsive behaviors are also often seen and show after the tics begin generally by adolescence (Leckman et al., 1994). The severity of TS is thought to be related to the child to adult course with mild presentations in childhood showing milder signs in adulthood (Bruun, 1988).

Tourette Syndrome is thought to be a familial syndrome that may have a genetic vulnerability. It is believed to be an autosomal dominant disorder with varying frequencies for the expression of this condition (Hyde & Weiberger, 1995). The frequencies of males showing the disorder is likely due a higher vulnerability for transmission. TS has been linked to other diagnoses and thus may share a genetic transmission with these other disorders. TS and OCD have been linked and OCD has been found to be over-represented in many families with TS. Females are more likely to show TS when also diagnosed with OCD (Peterson et al., 1995). Monozygotic twins have been found to be concordant for this disorder also with a 50–90% concordance rate with much lower rates for dizygotic twins (Hyde et al., 1992).

The severity of tics has been found to be related to the child's anxiety level and emotional adjustment (Shapiro & Shapiro, 1988). Zhu et al. (2006) evaluated children with TS on measures of school and social competence. They evaluated 69 children between the ages of 8 and 16 years using the CBCL. Findings indicated that the TS had poorer social competence compared to typically developing children. Attention, anxiety, depression, and unusual thoughts were characteristic of the children with TS. Severity of tics was significantly related to these difficulties. It was believed that these tic symptoms were related to problems with acceptance by their peers and resulting teasing and social isolation that occurred. Some children were found to withdraw from school through truancy and frequent absences while others became more aggressive and noncompliant.

Others have also found difficulties with peer teasing and stress over movements that cannot be controlled or managed (Bawden et al., 1998). These children have also been found to show more social withdrawal and isolation than children with ADHD or who are typically developing. Problems in family functioning have also been linked to problems with adaptability. The family systems of children with TS have been found to be more rigid and under more stress than those without TS (Matthews et al., 1985). Hubka et al. (1988) found that the daily activities of the family were significantly compromised by the child's TS. Others have found that when parents were more accepting and proactive, the child with TS shows less anxiety and stronger self-concepts than those with poorer parenting skills (Edell-Fisher, 1989; Edell & Motta, 1989).

Due to the high comorbidity of OCD and ADHD with TS, it is difficult to determine the contribution of each of these to the child with TS's difficulty socially. O'Donnell et al. (2000) sought to study children with TS with and without ADHD with matched numbers of children in each group showing additional difficulties (OCD, depression, anxiety, etc.). All children completed a comprehensive neuropsychological battery as well as an assessment of their social and emotional functioning. The children with TS + ADHD showed more difficulty on measures of social functioning compared to the TS and control groups. Difficulties were more pronounced on all measures of functioning for the combined group. The TS group differed from the control group only on measures of internalizing behaviors. This study underscores the need to view comorbid conditions when evaluating the child's functioning. For the children with a sole diagnosis of TS no difference was found in social functioning from those without TS. When children with TS also had ADHD significant problems were found in almost every area. Thus, it may not be TS solely that contribute to social difficulties but rather behaviors associated with TS and ADHD combining to negatively influence such problems.

This study also found a strong relationship between family functioning and social competence. Families that were higher in conflict and lower in cohesion generally had children with poorer social functioning. Thus, the support provided by families may be crucial in assisting a child with a diagnosis of TS and ADHD in adapting to environmental demands. This study did not provide information concerning the number of parents with OCD- or TS-like symptoms—such difficulties would like provide more stress to family functioning as well as concern about how the child would adapt and cope.

Thus, TS is related to several neuropsychological problems that may impact social functioning particularly when a comorbid diagnosis of ADHD is also present. The social difficulties that occur when ADHD is linked to TS appear to be more similar to those experienced by a child with ADHD than those of one with a sole diagnosis of TS. Thus, a careful diagnosis of the child's needs is crucial. In addition, family support and acceptance of these behavioral difficulties is important in the child's resulting social and emotional functioning. Further study is needed to tease apart the social and familial contributions to the child's difficulty in and out of school.

Conclusion

In many of these disorders the child's social functioning is linked to their adjustment to their disorder, parental support, lack of family discord, and additional support provided by the medical community. The adjustment also appears to be related to the severity of the disease or disorder. This adjustment is tempered by family acceptance of the problems as well as the mental health of the parents. For chronic diseases such as asthma and diabetes, diagnosis is often made at an early age. The adjustment to the disease happens gradually and the child is more prepared for dealing with these challenges as he/she ages. For older children diagnosed with the disorder adjustment may be more problematic as the child attempts to individuate from his/her parents and yet is dependent on them for treatment and disease management.

An important finding in the research is that depression symptoms are not uncommon. Although the child may not qualify for a diagnosis of depression, there are indications of stress and of sadness concerning these disorders. For most of us we do not need to face our mortality until much older. For children with chronic diseases such mortality is frequently present at a very young age and prior to the maturity needed to deal with such issues. The astute clinician will assist the child with his/her adjustment as well as understand the mismatch between the child's problems and his/her developmental level. For many children an assessment is important to determine the emotional and social functioning of these children.

While these adjustment problems are certainly important to note, it is also important to recognize that many of these children and adolescents make good adjustment to their difficulties. Families that are supportive and that are stable generally have children who are more able to cope constructively with their diseases. These findings indicate that when treatment may be required, it is important to involve the family in therapy and in support of the child.

References

AAMR (2002). *Mental retardation: Definition, classification, and systems of support*. Washington, DC: AAMR.

Abbeduto, L., & Hagerman, R.J. (1997). Language and communication in fragile X syndrome. *Mental Retardation and Developmental Disabilities Research Reviews, 3,* 313–322.

Abery, B.H., & Fahnestock, M. (1994). Enhancing the social inclusion of persons with developmental disabilities. In M.F. Hayden and B.H. Abery (Eds.), *Challenges for a service system in transition: Ensuring quality community experiences for persons with developmental disabilities* (pp. 83–119). Baltimore: Paul H. Brookes.

Abikoff, H. (1987). An evaluation of cognitive behavioral therapy for hyperactive children. In B. Lahey and A. Kazdin (Eds.), *Advances in clinical child psychology* (Vol. 10, 171–216). New York: Plenum Press.

Abikoff, H., Hechtman, L., Klein, R.G., Weiss, G., Fleiss, K., Etcovitch, J., Cousins, L., Greenfield, B., Martin, D., & Pollack, S. (2004a). Symptomatic improvement in children with ADHD treated with long-term methylphenidate and multimodal psychosocial treatment. *Journal of the American Academy of Child and Adolescent Psychiatry, 43,* 802–811.

Abikoff, H., Hechtman, L., Klein, R., Gallagher, R., Fleiss, K., Etcovitch, J., Cousins, L., Greenfield, B., Martin, D., & Pollack, S. (2004b). Social functioning in children with ADHD treatment with long-term methylphenidate and multimodal psychosocial treatment. *Journal of the American Academy of Child and Adolescent Psychiatry, 43,* 820–829.

Ablow, J.C., & Measelle, J.R. (1993). *Berkeley Puppet Interview: Administration and Scoring System Manuals*. Berkeley, CA: University of California.

Achenbach, T.M. (1991). *Manual for the Teacher's Report Form and 1991 profile*. Burlington, VT: University of Vermont.

Achenbach, T.M. and Edelbrock (1991). *Manual for the Child Behavior Checklist/4–18 and 1991 profile*. Burlington, VT: University of Vermont

Ainsworth, M. (1979). Infant-mother attachment. *American Psychologist, 34,* 932–937.

Alessandri, S.M. (1992). Attention, play, and social behavior in ADHD preschoolers. *Journal of Abnormal Child Psychology, 20,* 289–302.

Alexander-Roberts, C. (1995). *A parent's guide to making it through the touch years: ADHD and teens: Proven techniques for handling emotional, academic, and behavioral problems*. Dallas: Taylor.

Altmann, E.O., & Gotlib, I.H. (1988). The social behavior of depressed children: An observational study. *Journal of Abnormal Child Psychology, 16,* 29–44.

American Cancer Society (1997). *Cancer facts and figures*. Atlanta: Author.

American Psychiatric Association (1987). *Diagnostic and statistical manual of mental disorders (3rd ed., rev.).* Washington, DC: Author.

American Psychiatric Association (1994). *Diagnostic and statistical manual (III).* Washington, DC: author.

American Psychiatric Association (1997). *Diagnostic and statistical manual of mental disorders (IV.).* Washington, DC: Author.

American Psychiatric Association (2000). *Diagnostic and statistical manual of mental disorder (IV-TR).* Washington, DC: Author.

Amin, K., Douglas, V.I., Mendelson, M.J., & Dufresne, J. (1993). Separable/integral classification by hyperactive and normal children. *Developmental Psychopathology, 5,* 415–431.

Amir, R.E., Van Den Veyver, I.B., Wan, M. (1999). Rett syndrome is caused by mutations in X-linked MECP2, encoding methyl CpG binding protein 2. *Natural Genetics, 23,* 185–188.

Anderson, V., Smibert, E., Ekert, H., & Godber, T. (1994). Intellectual, educational, and behavioral sequelae after cranial irradiation and chemotherapy. *Archives of Diseases in Children, 70,* 476–483.

Antovsky, A. (1987). *Unraveling the mystery of health.* San Francisco: Jossey-Bass.

Antshel, K.M. & Remer, R. (2003). Social skills training in children with attention deficit hyperactivity disorder: A randomized-controlled clinical trial. *Journal of Clinical Child and Adolescent Psychology, 32,* 153–165.

Apter, A., Pauls, D.L., Bleich, A., Zohar, A.H., Kron, S., Ratzoni, G., Dycian, A., Kotler, M., Weizman, A., Gador, N., & Cohen, D.J. (1993). An epidemiological study of Gilles de la Tourette's syndrome in Israel. *Archives of General Psychiatry, 50,* 734–738.

Armsden, G.C., & Greenberg, M.T. (1987). The inventory of parent and peer attachment: Individual differences and their relationship to psychological well-being in adolescence. *Journal of Youth and Adolescence, 16,* 427–451.

Aronen, E.T., & Kurkel, S.A. (1998). The predictors of competence in an adolescent sample: A 15-year follow-up study. *Nordic Journal of Psychiatry, 52,* 203–212.

Asano, E., Chugani, D.C., & Muzik, O. (2001). Autism in tuberous sclerosis complex is related to both cortical and subcortical dysfunction. *Neurology, 57,* 1269–1277.

Asarnow, J. (1988). Peer status and social competence in child psychiatric inpatients: A comparison of children with depressive, externalizing, and concurrent depressive and externalizing disorders. *Journal of Abnormal Child Psychology, 16,* 151–162.

Asarnow, J., & Callan, J. (1985). Boys with peer adjustment problems: Social cognitive processes. *Journal of Consulting and Clinical Psychology, 55,* 80–87.

Asch, A. (1989). Has the law made a difference? In D. Kerkner & A. Gartner (Eds.), *Beyond separate education: Quality education for all* (pp. 181–206). Baltimore, MD: Brookes.

Asher, S.R., & Dodge, K.A. (1986). Identifying children who are rejected by their peers. *Developmental Psychology, 22,* 444–449.

Asher, S.R., & Williams, G.A. (1987). Helping children without friends in home and school contexts. In *Children's social development: Information for teachers and parents* (pp. 1026). Urbana, IL: ERIC Clearinghouse on Elementary and Early Childhood Education.

Asher, S.R., Parkhurst, J.T., Hymel, S., & Williams, G.A. (1990). Peer rejection and loneliness in childhood. In S.R. Asher and J.D. Coie (Eds.), *Peer rejection in childhood* (pp. 253–273). New York: Cambridge University Press.

Aspendorpf, J.B. (1993). Beyond temperament: A two-factorial coping model of the development of inhibition during childhood. In K.H. Rubin & J.B. Asendorpf (Eds.), *Social withdrawal, inhibition, and shyness in childhood.* Hillsdale, NJ: Lawrence Erlbaum Associates, Inc.

Attwood, A.J. (1998). *Asperger's Syndrome*. London: Jessica Kingsley Publishers.

Attwood, A.J., Frith, V., & Hermelin, B. (1988). The understanding and use of interpersonal gestures by autistic and Down's Syndrome children. *Journal of Autism and Developmental Disorders, 18*, 241–257.

Austin, J., Smith, M., Risinger, M., & McNelis, A. (1994). Childhood epilepsy and asthma: Comparison of quality of life. *Epilepsia, 35*, 608–615.

Aylward, E.H., Minshew, N.J., Field, K., Sparks, B.F., & Singh, N. (2002). Effects of age on brain volume and head circumference in autism. *Neurology, 59*, 175–183.

Bagwell, C.L., Molina, B.S.G., Pelham, W.E., & Hoza, B. (2001). Attention-deficit hyperactivity disorder and problems in peer relations: Predictions from childhood to adolescence. *Journal of the American Academy of Child and Adolescent Psychiatry, 40*, 1285–1294.

Baker, M., Milich, R., & Manolis, M.B. (1996). Peer interactions of dysphoric adolescents. *Journal of Abnormal Child Psychology, 24*, 241–255.

Bailey, A., Le Couteur, A., & Gottesman, I. (1995). Autism as a strongly genetic disorder: Evidence from a British twin study. *Psychological Medicine, 25*, 63–77.

Bailey, A., Palferman, S., & Heavey, L. (1998). Autism: The phenotype in relatives. *Journal of Autism and Developmental Disorders, 28*, 369–392.

Bandura, A. (1977). Social learning theory. Oxford, England: Prentice-Hall.

Barkley, R.A. (1989) Attention-deficit hyperactivity disorder. In E.J. Mash & R.A. Barkley, (Eds.), *Treatment of childhood disorders* (pp. 39–72). New York: Guilford Press.

Barkley, R.A. (1990). *Attention-deficit hyperactivity disorder: A handbook for diagnosis and treatment*. New York: Guilford Press.

Barkley, R.A. (1997). Behavioral inhibition, sustained attention, and executive functions: Constructing a unifying theory of ADHD. *Psychological Bulletin, 121*, 65–94.

Barkley, R.A. (2000). Genetics of childhood disorders: XVII. ADHD, Part 1: The executive functions and ADHD. *Journal of the American Academy of Child and Adolescent Psychiatry, 39*, 1064–1068.

Barkley, R.A., Edwards, G., Laneri, M., Fletcher, K., & Metevia, L. (2001). Executive functioning, temporal discounting, and sense of time in adolescents with Attention Deficit Hyperactivity Disorder (ADHD) and Oppositional Defiant Disorder (ODD). *Journal of Abnormal Child Psychology, 29*, 541–556.

Barkley, R.A., Fischer, M., Edelbrock, C.S., & Smallish, L. (1990). The adolescent outcome of hyperactive children diagnosed by research criteria, I: An 8-year prospective follow-up study. *Journal of the American Academy of Child and Adolescent Psychiatry, 29*, 546–557.

Barnhill, G. P. (2001). What's new in AS research: A synthesis of research conducted by the Asperger Syndrome Project. *Interventions in School and Clinic, 36*, 300–307.

Barnhill, G.P., Tapscott, K., Tebbenkamp, K., & Smith, B. (2002). The effectiveness of social skills intervention targeting nonverbal communication for adolescents with Asperger syndrome and related pervasive developmental delays. *Focus on Autism and Other Developmental Disabilities, 17*, 112–118.

Baron-Cohen, S., Joliffe, T., Mortimore, C., & Robertson, M. (1997). Another advanced test of theory of mind: Evidence from very high functioning adults with autism or Asperger's syndrome. *Journal of Child Psychology and Psychiatry, 38*, 813–822.

Baron-Cohen, S., Leslie, A.M., & Frith, U. (1985). Does the autistic child have a "theory of mind?" *Cognition, 21*, 37–46.

Baron-Cohen, S., Mortimore, C., Moriarty, J. et al. (1999). The prevalence of Gilles de la Tourette's syndrome in children and adolescents with autism. *Journal of Child Psychology and Psychiatry, 40*, 213–218.

Baron-Cohen, S., Tager-Flusberg, H., & Cohen, D.J. (Eds.) (2000). *Understanding other minds: Perspectives from developmental cognitive neuroscience.* Oxford: Oxford University Press.

Barrett, P.M., Shortt, A., & Healy, L. (2002). Do parent and child behaviours differentiate families whose children have obsessive-compulsive disorder from other clinic and non-clinic families? *Journal of Child Psychology and Psychiatry, 43,* 597–607.

Barry, T.D., Lyman, R.D., & Klinger, L.G. (2002). Academic underachievement and attention-deficit/hyperactivity disorder: The negative impact of symptom severity on school performance. *Journal of School Psychology, 40,* 259–283.

Barth, J.M., & Bastiani, A. (1997). A longitudinal study of emotion recognition and preschool children's social behavior. *Merrill-Palmer Quarterly, 43,* 107–128.

Barton, B., & North, K. (2004). Social skills of children with neurofibromatosis type 1. *Developmental Medicine and Child Neurology, 46,* 553–563.

Bates, J.E., Bayles, K., Bennett, D.S., Ridge, B., & Brown, M.M. (1991). Origins of externalizing behavior problems at eight years of age. In D.J. Pepler and K.H. Rubin (Eds.), *The development and treatment of childhood aggression* (pp. 93–120). Hillsdale, NJ: Erlbaum.

Bates, M., E., & Labouvie, E.W. (1995). Personality-environment constellations and alcohol use: A process-oriented study of intraindividual change during adolescence. *Psychology of Addictive Behaviors, 9,* 23–35.

Bates, L., Luster, T., & Vandenbelt, M. (2003). Factors related to social competence in elementary school among children of adolescent mothers. *Social Development, 12,* 107–124.

Baum, S., & Olenchak, F.R., & Owen, S.V. (1998). Gifted students with attention deficits: Fact and/or fiction? Or, can we see the forest for the trees? *Gifted Child Quarterly, 42,* 96–104.

Baum, S., & Owen, S.V. (1988). High-ability/learning-disabled students: How are they different? *Gifted Child Quarterly, 32,* 321–326.

Baum, S., Owen, S.V., & Dixon, J. (1991). *To be gifted and learning disabled: From definitions to practical intervention strategies.* Mansfield Center, CT: Creative Learning Press.

Baumeister, R.F., & Sommer, K.L. (1997). What do men want? Gender differences and two sphere of belongingness: Comment on Cross and Madson (1997). *Psychological Bulletin, 122,* 38–44.

Bauminger, N. (2002). The facilitation of social-emotional understanding and social interaction in high-functioning children with autism: Intervention outcomes. *Journal of Autism and Developmental Disorders, 32,* 283–298.

Bawden, H.N., Stokes, A., Camfield, C.S., Camfield, P.R., & Salisbury, S. (1998). Peer relationship problems in children with Tourette's disorder or Diabetes Mellitus. *Journal of Child Psychology and Psychiatry, 39,* 663–668.

Bayliss, D.M., & Roodenrys, S. (2000). Executive processing and attention deficit hyperactivity disorder: An application of the supervisory attentional system. *Developmental Neuropsychology, 17,* 161–180.

Bear, G.G., Juvonen, J., & McInerney, F. (1993). Self-perceptions and peer relations of boys with and without learning disabilities in an integrated setting: A longitudinal study. *Learning Disability Quarterly, 16,* 127–136.

Beardslee, W.R., Versage, E.M., & Gladstone, T.R.G. (1998). Children of affectively ill parents: A review of the past 10 years. *Journal of the American Academy of Child and Adolescent Psychiatry, 37,* 1134–1141.

Bebko, J.M., Wainwright, A., Brian, J.A., Coolbear, J., Landry, R., & Vallance, D.D. (1998). Social competence and peer relations in children with mental retardation: Models of the development of peer relations. *Journal on Developmental Disabilities, 6,* 1–31.

Becker, D.F., Doane, J.A., & Wexler, B.E. (1993). Effects of emotion on perceptual asymmetry in adolescent inpatients with attention-deficit hyperactivity disorder. *Journal of the American Academy of Child and Adolescent Psychiatry, 32*, 318–321.

Beeghly, M., Perry, B., & Cicchetti, D. (1989). Structural and affective dimensions of play development in young children with Down Syndrome. *International Journal of Behavioral Development, 12*, 257–277.

Befera, M., & Barkley, R.A. (1985). Hyperactive and normal boys and girls: Mother-child interaction, parent psychiatric status, and child psychopathology. *Journal of Child Psychology and Psychiatry, 26*, 439–452.

Begali, V. (1992). *Head injury in children and adolescents* (2nd edition). Brandon, VT: Clinical Psychology Publishing Company, Inc.

Bell, R.A. (1985). Conversational involvement and loneliness. *Communication Monographs, 52*, 218–235.

Bellack, A.S., Hersen, M., & Lamparski, D. (1979). Role-play tests for assessing social skills: Are they valid? Are they useful? *Journal of Consulting and Clinical Psychology, 47*, 335–342.

Bell-Dolan, D.J., Reaven, N.M., & Peterson, L. (1993). Depression and social functioning: A multidimensional study of the linkages. *Journal of Clinical Child Psychology, 22*, 306–315.

Bellmore, A.D., & Cillessen, A.H. (2003). Children's meta-perceptions and meta-accuracy of acceptance and rejection by same-sex and other-sex peers. *Personal Relationships, 10*, 217–233.

Belser, R.C., & Sudhalter, V. (1995). Arousal difficulties in males with fragile X syndrome: A preliminary report. *Developmental Brain Dysfunction, 8*, 252–269.

Bennetto, L., Pennington, B., & Rogers, S. (1996). Intact and impaired memory functions in autism. *Child Development, 67*, 1816–1835.

Bentall, R.P. (2005). Instability of psychological processes in psychosis: Studies of patients with bipolar disorder and patients with paranoid delusions. *Proceedings of the British Psychological Society, 73*, 137.

Benton, A. & Tranel, D. (1993). Visuoperceptual, visuospatial and visuoconstructive disorders. In K.M. Heilman and E. Valenstein (Eds.), *Clinical Neuropsychology* (pp. 215–278). New York: Oxford University Press.

Bentsgard, K., & Bohlin, G. (2001). Social inhibition and overfriendliness: Two-year follow-up and observational validation. *Journal of Clinical Child Psychology, 30*, 364–375.

Berch, D.B. (1996). Memory. In J. Rovet (Ed.), *Turner syndrome across the lifespan* (pp. 140–145). Toronto: Klein Graphics.

Bergin, D.A. (1989). Student goals for out-of-school learning activities. *Journal of Adolescent Research, 4*, 92–109.

Berk, L.E. (2002). *Infants, children, and adolescents* (4th ed.). Boston: Allyn & Bacon.

Berlin, L., Bohlin, G., Nyberg, L., & Janols, L-O. (2004). How well do measures of inhibition and other executive functions discriminate between children with ADHD and controls? *Child Neuropsychology, 10*, 1–13.

Berlin, L., Bohlin, G., & Rydell, A-M. (2003). Relations between inhibition, executive functioning, and ADHD symptoms: A longitudinal study from age 5 to 8 1/2 years. *Child Neuropsychology, 9*, 255–266.

Berndt, T.J., Hawkins, J.A., & Hoyle, S.G. (1986). Changes in friendship during a school year: Effects on children's and adolescnts' impressions of friendship and sharing with friends. *Child Development, 57*, 1284–1297.

Berthier, M.L. (1994). Foreign accent syndrome. *Neurology, 44*, 990–991.

Berthier, M.L., Bayes, A., & Tolosa, E.S. (1993). Magnetic resonance imaging in patients with concurrent Tourette's disorder and Asperger's syndrome. *Journal of the American Academy of Child and Adolescent Psychiatry, 32*, 633–639.

Berthier, M.L., Starkstein, S.E., & Leiguarda, R. (1990). Developmental cortical anomalies in Asperger's syndrome: Neuroradiological findings in two patients. *Journal of Neuropsychiatry and Clinical Neuroscience, 2,* 197–201.

Bessell, A.G. (2001). Children surviving cancer: Psychosocial adjustment, quality of life, and school experiences. *Exceptional Children, 67,* 345–359.

Bibby, P., Eikeseth, S., Martin, N.T., Mudford, O.C., & Reeves, D. (2001). Progress and outcomes for children with autism receiving parent-managed intensive interventions. *Research in Developmental Disabilities, 22,* 425–447.

Bickett, L.R., & Milich, R. (1990). First impressions formed of boys with learning disabilities and attention deficit disorder. *Journal of Learning Disabilities, 23,* 253–259.

Bickett, L.R., Milich, R., & Brown, R.T. (1996). Attributional styles of aggressive boys and their mothers. *Journal of Abnormal Child Psychology, 24,* 457–472.

Biederman, J., Faraone, S.V., & Chen, W.J. (1993). Social adjustment inventory for children and adolescents: Concurrent validity in ADHD children. *Journal of the American Academy of Child and Adolescent Psychiatry, 32,* 1059–1065.

Biederman, J., Milberger, S., Faraone, S.V., Guite, J., & Warburton, R. (1994). Associations between childhood asthma and ADHD: Issues of psychiatric comorbidity and familiality. *Journal of the American Academy of Child and Adolescent Psychiatry, 33,* 842–848.

Biederman, J., Newcome, J., & Sprich, S. (1991). Comorbidity of attention-deficit hyperactivity disorder with conduct, depressive, anxiety, and other disorders. *American Journal of Psychiatry, 48,* 564–577.

Biederman, J., Petty, C., Faraone, S.V., Henin, A., Hirshfeld-Becker, D., Pollack, M.H., de Figueriedo, S., Feeley, R., & Rosenbaum, J.F. (2006). Effects of parental anxiety disorders in children at high risk for panic disorder: A controlled study. *Journal of Affective Disorders, 94,* 191–197.

Biederman, J., Rosenbaum, J.F., Hirshfeld, D.R., Farone, S.V., Bolduc, E.A., Gusten, M., Meminger, S.R., Kagan, J., Snidman, N., & Reznick, J.S. (1990). Psychiatric correlates of behavioral inhibition in young children of parents with and without psychiatric disorders. *Archives of General Psychiatry, 47,* 21–26.

Bielecki, J., & Swender, S.L. (2004). The assessment of social functioning in individuals with mental retardation. *Behavior Modification, 28,* 694–708.

Bierman, K.L., & Furman, W. (1984). The effects of social skills training and peer involvement on the social adjustment of preadolescents. *Child Development, 55,* 151–162.

Bierman, K.L., Greenberg, M.T., & Conduct Problems Prevention Resarch Group (1996). Social skills training in the Fast Track program. In R. DeV. Peters and R.J. McMahon (Eds.), *Preventing childhood disorders, substance abuse, and delinquency* (pp. 65–89). Thousand Oaks, CA: Sage.

Bierman, K.L., & Welsh, J.A. (1997). Social relationship deficits. In E.J. Mash and L.G. Terdal (Eds.), *Assessment of childhood disorders* (pp. 328–365). New York: Guilford.

Bierman, K.L., & Welsh, J.A. (2000). Assessing social dysfunction: The contributions of laboratory and performance-based measures. *Journal of Clinical Child Psychology, 29,* 526–539.

Bird, H.R., Canino, G., Rubio-Stipec, M., Gould, M.S., Ribera, J., Sesman, M., Woodbury, M., Hertas-Goldman, S., Pagan, A., Sanchez-Lacay, A., & Moscoco, M. (1988). Estimates of the prevalence of childhood maladjustment in a community survey in Puerto Rico. *Archives of General Psychiatry, 45,* 1120–1126.

Black, B., & Hazen, N.L. (1990). Social status and patterns of communication in acquainted and unacquainted preschool children. *Developmental Psychology, 26,* 379–387.

Blair, C. (2002). School readiness: Integrating cognition and emotion in a neurobiological conceptualization of child functioning at school entry. *American Psychologist, 57,* 111–127.

Blair, C. (2003). Behavioral inhibition and behavioral activation in young children: Relations with self-regulation and adaptation to preschool in children attending Head Start. *Developmental Psychobiology, 42*, 301–311.

Blanz, B.J., Rensch-Riemann, B.S., Fritz-Sigmund, D.I., & Schmidt, M.H. (1993). IDDM is a risk factor for adolescent psychiatric disorders. *Diabetes Care, 16*, 1579–1587.

Bodenhausen, G.V., Sheppard, L.A., & Kramer, G.P. (1994). Negative affect and social judgment: The differential impact of anger and sadness. *European Journal of Social Psychology, 24*, 45–62.

Bohlin, G., Bengtsgard, K., & Anderson, K. (2000). Social inhibition and over-friendliness as related to socioemotional functioning in 7- and 8-year-old children. *Journal of Clinical Child Psychology, 29*, 414–423.

Boivin, M., Poulin, F., & Vitaro, F. (1994). Depressed mood and peer rejection in childhood. *Development and Psychopathology, 6*, 483–498.

Bolton, P.F., & Griffiths, P.D. (1997). Association of tuberous sclerosis of temporal lobes with autism and atypical autism. *Lancet, 349*, 392–395.

Bolton, P.F., Park, R.J., Higgins, J.N., Griffiths, P.D., & Pickles, A. (2002). Neuroepileptic determinants of autism spectrum disorders in tuberous sclerosis complex. *Brain, 125*, 1247–1255.

Booth, C.L. (1999). Beliefs about social skills among mothers of preschoolers with special needs. *Early Education and Development, 10*, 455–473.

Borod, J.C., Andelman, F., Obler, L.K., Tweedy, J.R., & Welkowitz, J. (1992). Right hemispheric specialization for the identification of emotional words and sentences: Evidence from stroke patients. *Neuropsychologia, 30*, 827–844.

Borthwick-Duffy, S.A., & Eyman, R.K. (1990). Who are the dually diagnosed? *American Journal on Mental Retardation, 94*, 586–595.

Bosacki, S.L. (2003). Psychological pragmatics in preadolescents: Sociomoral understanding, self-worth, and school behavior. *Journal of Youth and Adolescence, 32*, 141–155.

Bosacki, S.L., & Astington, J.W. (1999). Theory of mind in preadolescence: Relations between social understanding and social competence. *Social Development, 8*, 237–255.

Bowker, A., Bukowski, W.M., Hymel, S., & Sippola, S.K. (2000). Coping with daily hassles in the peer group during early adolescence: Variations as a function of peer experience. *Journal of Research on Adolescence, 10*, 211–243.

Bretherton, I. (1985). Attachment theory: Retrospect and prospect. *Monographs of the Society for Research in Child Development, 50*, 3–35.

Brody, G.H., & Flor, D.L. (1997). Maternal psychological functioning, family processes, and child adjustment in rural, single-parent, African-American families. *Developmental Psychology, 33*, 1000–1011.

Bronfenbrenner, U. (1986). Ecology of the family as a context for human development: Research perspectives. *Developmental Psychology, 22*, 723–742.

Bronson, M.G. (2000). *Self-regulation in early childhood.* New York: Guilford.

Bronson, M.G., Tivnan, T., & Seppanen, P.S. (1995). Relations between teacher and classroom activity variables and the classroom behavior of prekindergarten children in Chapter 1 funded programs. *Journal of Applied Developmental Psychology, 16*, 253–282.

Brotman, L.M., Gouley, K.K., Chesir-Teran, D., Dennis, T., & Klein, R.G. (2005). Prevention for preschoolers at high risk for conduct problems: Immediate outcomes on parenting practices and child social competence. *Journal of Clinical Child and Adolescent Psychology, 34*, 724–734.

Brown, J.R., Donelan-McCall, N., & Dunn, J. (1996). Why talk about mental states? The significance of children's conversations with friends, siblings, and mothers. *Child Development, 67*, 836–849.

Brown, R.T., & Ievers, C.E. (1999). Gilles de la Tourette Syndrome. In S. Goldstein and C.R. Reynolds (Eds.), *Handbook of Neurodevelopmental and Genetic Disorders* (pp-185–215). New York: Guilford Press.

Brown, W.T., Jenkins, E.C., Cohen, I.L., Fisch, G.S., Wolf-Schien, E.G., Gross, A., Waterhouse, L., Fein, D., Mason-Brothers, A., Ritvo, E., Rittenberg, B.A., Bentley, W., & Castells, S. (1986). Fragile X and autism: A multicenter survey. *American Journal of Medical Genetics, 23,* 341–352.

Brown, R.T., Sawyer, M.B., Antoniou, G., Toogood, I., Rice, M., Thompson, N., & Madan-Swain, A. (1996). A 3-year follow-up of the intellectual and academic functioning of children receiving central nervous system prophylactic chemotherapy for leukemia. *Journal of Developmental and Behavioral Pediatrics, 17,* 392–398.

Bruner, J.S. (1998). Routes to reference. *Pragmatics and Cognition, 6,* 209–227.

Bruun, R.D. (1988). The natural history of Tourette's syndrome. In D.J. Cohen, R.D. Bruun, and J.F. Leckman (Eds.), *Tourette's syndrome and tic disorders: Clinical understanding and treatment* (pp. 21–39). New York: Wiley.

Bryan, T. (1994). The social competence of students with learning disabilities over time: A response to Vaughn and Hogan. *Journal of Learning Disabilities, 27,* 304–309.

Bryan, T. (1997). Assessing the personal and social status of students with learning disabilities. *Learning Disabilities Research & Practice, 12,* 63–76.

Bryan, T., & Bryan, J.H. (1991). Some personal and social experiences of learning disabled children. In B.K. Keogh (Ed.), *Advances in special education* (Vol. 3, pp. 147–186). Greenwich, CT: JAI Press.

Bryant, B. (1995). The neighborhood walk: Sources of support in middle childhood. *Monographs of the Society for Research in Child Development, 50.*

Buchanan, L., Pauvlovic, J., & Rovet, J. (1998). A reexamination of the visuospatial definition of Turner syndrome: Contributions of working memory. *Developmental Psychology, 14,* 341–367.

Buhrmester, D., Caparo, L., Christensen, A., Gonzalez, L.S., & Hinshaw, S.P. (1992). Mothers and fathers interacting in dyads and triads with normal and hyperactive sons. *Developmental Psychology, 28,* 500–509.

Buhrmester, D., & Furman, W. (1986). The changing functions of friendships in childhood: A neo-Sullivanian perspective. In V.J. Derlega & B.A. Winstead (Eds.), *Friendship and social interaction* (pp. 41–62). New York: Springer-Verlag.

Buitelaar, J.K., & van der Wees, M. (1997). Are deficits in the decoding of affective cues and in mentalizing abilities independent? *Journal of Autism and Developmental Disorders, 27,* 539–556.

Bukowski, W.M., Sippola, L.K., & Hoza, B. (1999). Sam and other: Interdependency between participation in same- and other-sex friendships. *Journal of Youth and Adolescence, 28,* 439–459.

Burger, J.M. (1995). Individual differences in preference for solitude. *Journal of Research in Personality, 29,* 85–108.

Burks, B.S., Jensen, D.W., & Terman, L.M. (1930). *The promise of youth: Volume 3: Genetic studies of genius.* Stanford, CA: Stanford University Press.

Burleson, B.R., Applegate, J.L., Burke, J.A., Clark, R.A., Delia, J.G., & Kline, S.L. (1986). Communicative correlates of peer acceptance in childhood. *Communication Education, 35,* 343–361.

Burleson, B.R., Kinkel, A.W., Samter, W., & Weking, K.J. (1996). Men's and women's evaluations of communication skills in personal relationships: When sex differences make a difference—and when they don't. *Journal of Social and Personal Relationships, 12,* 201–224.

Buss, A.H., & Plomin, R. (1984). *Temperament: Early developing personality traits.* Hillsdale, NJ: Lawrence Erlbaum Associates, Publishers.

Bussin, R., & Burket, R.C. (1993). Anxiety and intrafamilial stress in children with hemophilia after the HIV crisis. *Journal of the American Academy of Child and Adolescent Psychiatry, 32*, 562–567.

Butz, A.M., & Alexander, C. (1993). Anxiety in children with asthma. *Journal of Asthma, 30*, 199–309.

Cairns, R.B., & Cairns, B.D. (1994). *Lifelines and risks: Pathways of youth in our times*. New York: Cambridge University Press.

Cairns, R.B., Cairns, B.D., Neckerman, H.J., Gest, D.C., & Gariepy, J.-L. (1988). Social networks and aggressive behavior: Peer support or peer rejection? *Developmental Psychology, 24*, 815–823.

Cairns, R.B., Cairns, B.D., Xie, H., Leung, M.-C., & Hearne, S. (1998). Paths across generations: Academic competence and aggressive behaviors in young mothers and their children. *Developmental Psychology, 34*, 1162–1174.

Cairns, R.B., Leung, M.-C., Gest, S.D., & Cairns, B.D. (1995). A brief method for assessing social development: Structure, reliability, stability, and developmental validity of the Interpersonal Competence Scale. *Behaviour Research and Therapy, 33*, 725–736.

Campbell, S.B. (1990). Hyperactivity in preschoolers: Correlates and prognostic implications. *Clinical Psychology Review, 5*, 502–524.

Campbell, S.B. (1994). Hard-to-manage preschool boys: Externalizing behavior, social competence, and family context at two-year follow-up. *Journal of Abnormal Child Psychology, 22*, 147–167.

Cantwell, D.P., & Baker, L. (1991). *Psychiatric and developmental disorders in children with communication disorder*. Washington, DC: American Psychiatric Press.

Capaldi, D.M., & Stoolmiller, M. (1999). Co-occurrence of conduct problems and depressive symptoms in early adolescent boys: III. Prediction to young-adult adjustment. *Development and Psychopathology, 11*, 59–84.

Caplan, R., Guthrie, D., & Komo, S. (2002). Social communication in pediatric epilepsy. *Journal of Child Psychology and Psychiatry and Allied Disciplines, 43*, 245–253.

Caplan, R., Siddarth, P., Gurbani, S., Hanson, R., Sankar, R., & Shields, W.D. (2005a). Depression and anxiety disorders in pediatric epilepsy. *Epilepsia, 46*, 720–730.

Caplan, R., Sagun, J., Siddarth, P., Gurbani, S., Koh, S., Gowrinathan, R., & Sankar, R. (2005b). Social competence in pediatric epilepsy: Insights into underlying mechanisms. *Epilepsy and Behavior, 6*, 218–228.

Capps, L., Kehres, J., & Sigman, M. (1998). Conversational abilities among children with autism and children with developmental delays. *Autism, 2*, 325–244.

Capps, L., Sigman, M., & Mundy, P. (1994). Attachment security in children with autism. *Development and Psychopathology, 6*, 249–261.

Carey, J.C., & McMahon, W.M. (1999). Neurobehavioral disorders and medical genetics: An overview. In S. Goldstein and C.R. Reynolds (Eds.), *Handbook of Neurodevelopmental and genetic disorders in children* (pp. 61–83). New York: Guilford.

Carlberg, C., & Kavale, K. (1980). The efficacy of special versus regular class placement for exceptional children: A meta-analysis. *Journal of Special Education, 14*, 25–52.

Carlson, C.I. (1987). Social interaction goals and strategies of children with learning disabilities. *Journal of Learning Disabilities, 20*, 306–311.

Carlson, C., Lahey, B.B., Frame, C.L., Walker, J., & Hynd, G.W. (1987). Sociometric status of clinic-referred children with attention deficit disorders with and without hyperactivity. *Journal of Abnormal Psychology, 15*, 537–547.

Carlson, S.M., & Moses, L.J. (2001). Individual differences in inhibitory control and children's theory of mind. *Child Development, 72*, 1032, 1053.

Carolyn, W.D. (1997). Attribtuion retraining: Implications for its integration into prescriptive social skills training. *School Psychology Review, 26*, 61–73.

Carpenter, M., Atkar, N., & Tomasello, M. (1998). 14- to 18-month old infants differentially imitate intentional and accidental actions. *Infant Behavior and Development, 21*, 315–330.

Carter, C., Meckes, L., Pritchard, L., Swensen, S., Wittman, P.P., & Belde, B. (2004). The friendship club: An after-school program for children with Asperger syndrome. *Family Community Health, 2*, 143–150.

Casanova, M.F., Buxhoeveden, D.P., Switala, A.E., & Roy, E. (2002). Minicolumnar pathology in autism. *Neurology, 58*, 428–432.

Caspi, A. (2000). Personality development across the life course. In N. Eisenberg (Ed.), & W. Damon (Series Ed.), *Handbook of child psychology, Vol. 3. Social, emotional and personality development* (pp. 311–388). New York: Wiley.

Caspi, A. (2000). The child is father of the man: Personality continuities from childhood to adulthood. *Journal of Personality and Social Psychology, 78*, 158–172.

Cassidy, J., & Asher, S.R. (1992). Loneliness and peer relations in young children. *Child Development, 63*, 350–365.

Cassidy, J., & Asher, S.R. (1992). Loneliness and peer relations in young children. *Child Development, 61*, 1101–1111.

Cassidy, J., Kirsh, S.J., Scolton, K.L., & Parke, R.D. (1996). Attachment and representations of peer relationships. *Developmental Psychology, 32*, 892–904.

Cassidy, J., & Parke, R.D. (1989, April). *Family expressiveness and children's social competence.* Symposium presented at the biennial meeting of the Society for Research in Child Development, Kansas City, MO.

Cassidy, K.W., Werner, R.S., Rourke, M., Zubernis, L.S., & Balarman, G. (2003). The relationship between psychological understanding and positive social behaviors. *Social Development, 12*, 198–221.

Castellanos, F.X. (2000, November). *ADHD or gifted: Is it either/or?* Paper presented at the annual meeting of the National Association for Gifted Children, Atlanta, GA.

Castelli, F., Frith, C., Happe, F., & Frith, U. (2002). Autism, Asperger's syndrome and brain mechanisms for the attribution of mental states to animated shapes. *Brain, 125*, 1839–1849.

Castelli, F., Happe, F., Frith, U., & Frith, C. (2000). Movement and mind: A functional imaging study of perception and interpretation of complx intentional movement patterns. *Neuroimage, 12*, 314–325.

Castles, E.E., & Glass, C.R. (1986). Empirical generation of measures of social competence for mentally retarded adults. *Behavioral Assessment, 8*, 319–330.

Cavell, T.A. (1990). Social adjustment, social perfomance, and social skills: A tricomponent model of social competence. *Journal of Clinical Child Psychology, 19*, 111–122.

Cavell, T.A., & Kelley, M.L. (1992). The measure of adolescent social performance: Development and initial validation. *Journal of Clinical Child Psychology, 21*, 107–114.

Cavell, T.A., Meehan, B.T., & Fiala, S.E. (2003). Assessing social competence in children and adolescents. In C.R. Reynolds & R.W. Kamphaus (eds.). *Handbook of psychological and educational assessment of children: Personality, behavior, and context* (pp. 433–454). New York: Guilford Press.

Chakrabarti, S., & Fombonne, E. (2001). Pervasive developmental disorders in preschool children. *Journal of the American Medical Association, 285*, 3093–3099.

Chang, E.C., & D'Zurilla, T.J. (1996). Relations between problem orientation and optimism, pessimism, and trait affectivity: A construct validation study. *Behaviour Research and Therapy, 34*, 185–194.

Chansky, T.C., & Kendall, P.C. (1997). Social expectancies and self-perceptions of children with anxiety disorders. *Journal of Anxiety Disorders, 11*, 347–363.

Chelune, G.J., Ferguson, W., Koon, R., & Dickey, T.O. (1986). Frontal lobe disinhibition in attention deficit disorder. *Child Psychiatry and Human Development, 16*, 221–234.

Chen, C., Greenberger, E., Lester, J., Dong, Q., & Guo, M. (1998). A cross-cultural study of family and peer correlates of adolescent misconduct. *Developmental Psychology, 34*, 770–781.

Chen, X., Rubin, K.H. (1994). Family conditions, parental acceptance and social competence and aggression in Chinese children. *Social Development, 3,* 269–290.

Childs, H.F., Schneider, H.G., & Dula, C.S. (2001). Adolescent adjustment: Maternal depression and social competence. *International Journal of Adolescence and Youth, 9*, 175–184.

Chow, D., & Skuy, M. (1999). Simultaneous and successive cognitive processing in children with nonverbal learning disabilities. *School Psychology International, 20*, 219–231.

Chu, L., & Powers, P.A. (1995). Synchrony in adolescence. *Adolescence, 30*, 1–7.

Church, C., Alisanski, S., & Amanullah, S. (2000). The social, behavioral, and academic experiences of children with Asperger syndrome. *Focus on Autism and Other Developmental Disorders, 1*, 12–20.

Ciarrochi, J., Scott, G., Deane, F.P., & Heaven, P.C.L. (2003). Relations between social and emotional competence and mental health: A construct validation study. *Personality and Individual Differences, 35*, 1947–1963.

Cicchetti, D. (1990). A historical perspective on the discipline of developmental psychopathology. In J. Rolf, A. Masten, D. Cicchetti, K. Neuchterlein, & S. Weintraub (Eds.), *Risk and protective factors in the development of psychopathology* (pp. 2–28). Cambridge: Cambridge U. Press.

Cicchetti, D. (1991). Fractures in the crystal: Developmental psychopathology and emergence of self. *Developmental Review, 11*, 271–287.

Cicchetti, D., & Beeghly, M. (1990). An organizational approach to the study of Down Syndrome: Contributions to an integrative theory of development

Cicchetti, D., & Toth, S.L. (1998). The development of depression in children and adolescence. *American Psychologist, 52*, 221–241.

Cillessen, A.H.N., & Bellmore, A.D. (2004). Social skills and interpersonal perception in early and middle childhood. In P.K. Smith & C.H. Hart (Eds.), *Blackwell Handbook of Childhood Social Development* (pp. 355–374). London: Blackwell Publishing.

Cillessen, A.H., & Bellmore, A.D. (1999). Accuracy of social self-perceptions and social competence in middle childhool. *Merrill-Palmer Quarterly, 54*, 650–676.

Cillessen, A.H.N., & Bukowski, W.M. (2000). Conceptualizing and measuring peer acceptance and rejection. In A.H.N. Cillessen and W.M. Bukowski (Eds.), *Recent advances in the measurement of acceptance and rejection in the peer system* (New Directions for Child and Adolescent Development Series No. 88, pp. 3–10). San Francisco: Jossey-Bass.

Ciesielkski, K.T., & Harris, R.J. (1997). Factors related to performance failure on executive tasks in autism. *Child Neuropsychology, 3*, 1–12.

Clark, C., Prior, M., & Kinsella, G. (2002). The relationship between executive function abilities, adaptive behaviour, and academic achievement in children with externalising behaviour problems. *Journal of Child Psychology and Psychiatry, 43*, 785–796.

Cochran, M., Larner, M., Riley, D., Gunnarson, L., & Henderson, C. (1990). *Extending families: The social networks of parents and their children.* New York: Cambridge University Press.

Cohen, I.L. (1995). Behavioral profiles of autistic and nonautistic fragile X males. *Developmental Brain Dysfunction, 8,* 252–269.

Cohen, R., Duncan, M., & Cohen, S.L. (1994). Classroom peer relations of children participating in a pull-out enrichment program. *Gifted Child Quarterly, 38,* 33–38.

Cohen, I.L., Fisch, G.S., Sudhalter, V., Wolf-Schien, E.G., Hanson, D., & Hagerman, R. (1988). Social gaze, social avoidance, and repetitive behavior in Fragile X males: A controlled study. *American Journal on Mental Retardation, 92,* 436–446.

Coie, J.D. (1990). Adapting intervention to the problems of aggressive and disruptive rejected children. In S.R. Asher and J.D. Coie (1990). *Peer rejection in childhood* (pp. 309–337). Cambridge: Cambridge University Press.

Coie, J.D., & Dodge, K.A. (1983). Continuities and changes in children's social status: A 5-year longitudinal study. *Merrill-Palmer Quarterly, 29,* 261–282.

Coie, J.D., & Dodge, K.A. (1998). Aggression and antisocial behavior. In W. Damon (Series Ed.) & N. Eisenberg (Vol. Ed.), Handbook of child psychology: Vol. 3. *Social, emotional and personality development* (pp. 234–321). New York: Wiley.

Coie, J.D., Dodge, K.A., & Kupersmidt, J.B. (1990). Peer group behavior and social status. In S.R. Asher & J.D. Coie (Eds.), *Peer rejection in childhood* (pp. 17–59). New York: Cambridge University Press.

Coie, J.D., & Krehbiel, G. (1984). Effects of academic tutoring on the social status of low-achieving, socially-rejected children. *Child Development, 55,* 1465–1478.

Colangelo, N., & Dettman, D.F. (1983). A review of research on parents and families of gifted children. *Exceptional Children, 50,* 20–27.

Cole, D.A., & Carpentieri, S. (1990). Social status and the comorbidity of child depression and conduct disorder. *Journal of Consulting and Clinical Psychology, 58,* 748–757.

Cole, D.A., Martin, J.M., Peeke, L.G., Seroczynski, A.D., & Hoffman, K. (1998). Are cognitive errors of underestimation predictive or reflective of depressive symptoms in children: A longitudinal study. *Journal of Abnormal Psychology, 107,* 481–496.

Cole, D.A., Martin, J.M., Powers, B., & Truglio, R. (1996). Modeling causal relations between academic and social competence and depression: A multitrait-multimethod longitudinal study of children. *Journal of Abnormal Psychology, 105,* 258–270.

Coleman, J.M., Angevine, McHamm, L., & Minnett, A.M. (1992). Similarities in social competence of learning disabled and low achieving elementary school children. *Journal of Learning Disabilities, 25,* 671–677.

Coleman, J.M., & Minnett, A.M. (1992). Learning disabilities and social competence: A social ecological perspective. *Exceptional Children, 59,* 234–247.

Colvin, C.R., Block J., & Funder, D.C. (1995). Overly positive self-evaluations and personality: Negative implications for mental health. *Journal of Personality and Social Psychology, 68,* 1152–1162.

Compas, B.E., Connor-Smith, J.K., Saltzman, H., Thomsen, A.H., & Wadsworth, M.E. (2001). Coping with stress during childhood and adolescence: Problems, progress, and potential in theory and research. *Psychological Bulletin, 127,* 87–127.

Conduct Problems Prevention Resarch Group (1992). A developmental and clinical model for the prevention of conduct disorder: The FAST Track Program. *Development and Psychopathology, 4,* 509–527.

Conduct Problems Prevention Resarch Group (1999a). Initial impact of the Fast Track prevention trial for conduct problems: I. The high-risk sample. *Journal of Consulting and Clinical Psychology, 67,* 631–647.

Conduct Problems Prevention Resarch Group (1999b). Initial impact of the Fast Track prevention trial for conduct problems: II. Classroom Effects. *Journal of Consulting and Clinical Psychology, 67,* 648–657.

Conduct Problems Prevention Resarch Group (2002). Evaluation of the first three years of the Fast Track prevention trial with children at high risk for adolescent conduct problems. *Journal of Abnormal Child Psychology, 30,* 19–35.

Conduct Problems Prevention Resarch Group (2004). The effects of the Fast Track Program on Serious Problem Outcomes at the end of elementary school. *Journal of Clinical Child and Adolescent Psychology, 33,* 650–661.

Conger, R.D., Patterson, G.R., & Ge, X. (1995). It takes two to replicate: A mediational model for the impact of parent's stress on adolescent adjustment. *Child Development, 66,* 80–97.

Conners, C.K. (1997). *The Conner's Rating Scales-Revised.* Toronto: Multi-Health Systems.

Connor, D.F., & Swanson, J.M. (1999). Clonidine and guanfacine in the treatment of children with ADHD and associated conditions. *Child and Adolescent Psychopharmocology News, 4,* 1–8.

Cooper, M.L., Shaver, P.R., & Collins, N.L. (1998). Attachment styles, emotion regulation, and adjustment in adolescence. Journal of Personality and *Social Psychology, 74,* 1380–1397.

Copeland, E.D., & Love, V.L. (1991). *Attention please! A comprehensive guide for successfully parenting children with attention deficit disorders and hyperactivity.* Atlanta, GA: Southeastern Psychological Institute Press.

Coplan, R.J. (2000). Assessing nonsocial play in early childhood: Conceptual and methodological approaches. In K. Gitlin-Weiner, A. Sandgrund, & C. Schaefer (Eds.), *Play diagnosis and assessment* (2nd ed., pp. 563–598). New York: Wiley.

Coplan, R.J., Gavinski-Molina, M.-H., Lagace-Seguin, D.G., & Wichmann, C. (2001). When girls versus boys play alone: Nonsocial play and adjustment in kindergarten. *Developmental Psychology, 37,* 464–474.

Coplan, R.J., & Prakash, K. (2003). Spending time with teacher: Characteristics of preschoolers who frequently elicit versus initiate interactions with teachers. *Early Childhood Research Quarterly, 18,* 143–158.

Coplan, R.J., & Rubin, K.H. (1998). Social play. In D.P. Fromberg & D. Bergen (Eds.), *Play from birth to twelve: Contexts, perspectives, and meanings* (pp. 368–377). New York: Garland.

Corbett, B.A. (2003). Video Modeling: A window into the world of autism. *The Behavior Analyst Today, 4,* 1–10.

Corbett, B., & Glidden, H. (2000). Processing affective stimuli in children with attention-deficit hyperactivity disorder. *Child Neuropsychology, 6,* 144–155.

Corkum, P.V., & Siegel, L.S. (1993). Is the continuous performance task a valuable research tool for use with children with attention-deficit hyperactivity disorder? *Journal of Child Psychology and Psychiatry, 34,* 1217–1239.

Corlett, M. (2002). *Visual perceptual processing errors in children with nonverbal learning disabilities (NVLD).* Unpublished dissertation, University of Texas at Austin.

Cornell, D. (2004). High ability students who are unpopular with their peers. In S.M. Reiss and S.M. Moon (Eds.) *Social/emotional issues, underachievement and counseling of gifted and talented students* (pp. 31–42). Thousand Oaks, CA: Corwin Press.

Cornell, D., & Grossberg, I.N. (1989). Parent use of the term 'gifted': Correlates with family environment and child adjustment. *Journal for the Education of the Gifted, 12,* 218–230.

Cornoldi, C. (1999). Imagery deficits in nonverbal learning disabilities. *Journal of Learning Disabilities, 32*, 48–60.

Cornoldi, C., Dalla Vechhia, R., & Tressoldi, P.E. (1995). Visuo-spatial working memory limitations in low visuo-spatial high verbal intelligence children. *Journal of Child Psychology and Psychiatry, 36*, 1053–1064.

Courchesne, E., Karns, C.M., Davis, H.R., Ziccardi, R., Carper, R.A., Tigue, Z.D., Chisum, H.J., Moses, P., Pierce, K., Lord, C., Lincoln, A.J., Pizzo, S., Schreibman, L., Haas, R.H., Akshoomoff, N.A., & Courchesne, R.Y. (2001). Unusual brain growth patterns in early life in patients with autistic disorder. An MRI study. *Neurology, 57*, 245–254.

Cousins, L.S., & Weiss, G. (1993). Parent training and social skills training for children with attention-deficit hyperactivity disorder: How can they be combined for greater effectiveness? *Canadian Journal of Psychiatry, 38*, 449–457.

Cramer, P. (2000). Defense mechanisms in psychology today: Further processes for adaptation. *American Psychologist, 55*, 637–646.

Creel, C.S., & Karnes, F.A. (1988). Parental expectancies and young gifted children. *Roeper Review, 11*, 48–50.

Cresci, M.B.M. (1989). Preparation for fatherhood: Dreams of transition. In J. Offerman-Zuckerberg (Ed.), *Gender in transition* (pp. 35–46). New York: Plenum Press.

Crick, N.R., & Dodge, K.A. (1994). A review and reformulation of social information-processing mechanisms in children's social adjustment. *Psychological Bulletin, 115*, 74–101.

Crick, N.R., & Dodge, K.A. (1996). Social information-processing mechanisms on reactive and proactive aggression. *Child Development, 67*, 993–1002.

Crick, N.R., & Ladd, G.W. (1993). Children's perceptions of their peer experiences: Attributions, loneliness, social anxiety, and social avoidance. *Developmental Psychology, 29*, 244–254.

Crnic, K., Friedrich, W.N., & Greenberg, M.T. (1983). Adaptation of families with mentally retarded children: A model of stress, coping and family ecology. *American Journal of Mental Deficiency, 88*, 125–138.

Crockenberg & Litman (1990).

D'Zurilla, T., Chang, E.C., Nottingham, E.J., & Faccini, L. (1998). Social problem-solving deficits and hopelessness, depression, and suicidal risk in college students and psychiatric inpatients. *Journal of Clinical Psychology, 54*, 1091–1107.

Dahlgren, S.O., & Gillberg, C. (1989). Symptoms in the first two years of life: a preliminary population study of infantile autism. *European Archives of Psychiatry and Neurological Science, 283*, 169–174.

Darber, S.L., & Benbow, C.P. (1990). Aspects of personality and peer relations of extremely talented adolescents. *Gifted child Quarterly, 34*, 10–15.

Dalton, E.J., Cate-Carter, T.D., Mundo, E., Parikh, S.V., & Kennedy, J.L. (2003). Suicide risk in bipolar patients: the role of co-morbid substance use disorders. *Bipolar Disorders, 5*, 58–61.

Damasio, A.R. (1994). *Descartes' error: Emotion, reason, and the human brain.* New York: Putnam.

Damasio, A.R. (2001). Emotion and the human brain. *Annals of the New York Academy of Sciences, 935*, 101–106.

Daniels, D., Miller, J.J., III, Billings, A.G., & Moos, R.H. (1986). Psychosocial functioning of siblings of children with rheumatic disease. *Journal of Pediatrics, 109*, 397–383.

Das, J.P. (1993). Neurocognitive approach to remediation: The PREP model. *Canadian Journal of School Psychology, 9*, 157–173.

Dauber, S.L., & Benbow, C.P. (1990). Aspects of personality and peer relations of extremely talented adolescents. *Gifted Child Quarterly, 34*, 10-15.

Davidson, R. (1994). Asymmetric brain function, affective style, and psychopathology: The role of experience and plasticity. *Development and Psychopathology, 6,* 741–758.

Davies, P.T., & Windle, M. (1997). Gender-specific pathways between maternal depressive symptoms, family discord, and adolescent outcomes. *Developmental Psychology, 33,* 657–668.

Davis, G.A., & Rimm, S.B. (1998). *Education of the gifted and talented* (4th ed.). Boston: Allyn & Bacon.

Daviss, W.B., Coon, H., Whitehead, P., Ryan, K., Burkley, M., & McMahon, W. (1995). Predicting diabetic control from competence, adherence, adjustment, and psychopathology. *Journal of the American Academy of Child and Adolescent Psychiatry, 34,* 1629–1636.

Dawson, G., Hill, D., Spencer, A., & Galpert, L. (1990). Affective exchanges between young autistic children and their mothers. *Journal of Abnormal Child Psychology, 18,* 335–345.

deHaan, M., Nelson, C.A., Gunnar, M.R., & Tout, K.A. (1998). Hemispheric differences in brain activity related to the recognition of emotional expressions by 5-year-old children. *Developmental Neuropsychology, 14,* 495–518.

Deasy-Spinetta, P., Spinetta, J.J., & Oxman, J.B. (1988). The relationship between learning deficits and social adaptation in children with leukemia. *Journal of Psychosocial Oncology, 6,* 109–121.

Delprato, D.J. (2001). Comparisons of discrete-trial and normalized behavioural language intervention for young children with autism. *Journal of Autism and Developmental Disorders, 31,* 315–325.

Denham, S.A. (1998). *Emotional development in young children.* New York: Guilford Press.

Denham, S.A., McKinley, M., Couchoud, E.A., & Holt, R. (1990). Emotional and behavioral predictors of peer status in young preschoolers. *Child Development, 61,* 1145–1152.

Denham, S., von Salisch, M., Olthof, T., Kochanoff, A., & Caverly, S. (2004). Emotional and social development in childhood. In P.K. Smith & C.H. Hart (Eds.), *Blackwell Handbook of Childhood Social Development* (pp. 307–328). London: Blackwell Publishing.

Dennis, M., Guger, S., Roncadin, C., Barnes, M., & Schachar, R. (2001). Attentional-inhibitory control and social-behavioral regulation after childhood closed head injury: Do biological, developmental, and recovery variables predict outcome? *Journal of the International Neuropsychological Society, 7,* 683–692.

Dennis, M., Lockyer, L., Lazenby, A.L., Donnelly, R.E., Wilkinson, M., & Schoonheyt, W. (1999). Intelligence patterns among children with high-functioning autism, phenylketonuria, and childhood head injury. *Journal of Autism and Developmental Disorders, 29,* 5–17.

Derryberry, D., & Rothbart, M.K. (1997). Reactive and effortful processes in the organization of temperament. *Development and Psychopathology, 9,* 633–652.

de Sonneville, L.M.J., & Njiokiktjien, C.H. (1988). Aspects of information processing: A computer-based approach to development and disorders. *Pediatric Behavioural Neurology, 2,* Amsterdam Suyi Publishers.

de Sonneville, L.M.J., Schmidt, E., Michel, U., & Batzler, U. (1990). Preliminary neuropsychological test results of the German Phenylketonuria Collaborative Study. *European Journal of Pediatrics, 149 (Suppl. 1),* S 39–S44.

Dettman, D.F., & Colangelo, N. (2004). A functional model for counseling parents of gifted students. In S.M. Reis and S.M. Moon (Eds.), *Social/emotional issues, underachievement, and counseling of gifted and talented students* (pp. 213–220). Thousand Oaks, CA: Corwin Press.

De Vries, B.B.A., Wiegers, A.M., Smits, A.P.T., Mohkamsing, S., Duivenvoorden, H.J., Fryns, J.-P., Curfs, L.M.G., Halley, D.J.J., Oostra, B.A., van den Ouweland, A.M.W., & Niermeijer, M.F. (1996). Mental status of females with an FMR1 gene full mutation. *American Journal of Human Genetics, 58*, 1025–1032.

DeWolfe, N.A., Byrne, J.M., & Bawden, H.N. (2000). ADHD in preschool children: Parent-rated psychosocial correlates. *Developmental Medicine and Child Neurology, 42*, 825–830.

Diamond, A. Prevor, M.B., Callender, G., & Druin, D.P. (1997). Prefrontal cortex cognitive deficits in children treated early and continuously for PKU. *Monographs of the Society for Research in Child Development, 62*, 1–208.

Diener, M.L., & Kim, D.-Y. (2003). Maternal and child predictors of preschool children's social competence. *Journal of Applied Developmental Psychology, 25*, 3–24.

Diener, M.L., & Milich, R. (1997). Effects of positive feedback on the social interactions of boys with attention deficit hyperactivity disorder: A test of the self-protective hypothesis. *Journal of Clinical Child Psychology, 26*, 256–265.

DiGirolamo, A.M., Quittner, A.L., Ackerman, V., & Stevens, J. (1997). Identification and assessment of ongoing stressors in adolescents with a chronic illness: An application of the behavior-analytic model. *Journal of Clinical Child Psychology, 26*, 53–66.

Dilts, C.V., Carey, J.C., Kircher, J.C., Hoffman, R.O., Creel, D., Ward, K., & Clark Leonard, C.O. (1996). Children and adolescents with neurofibromatosis 1: A behavioral phenotype. *Journal of Developmental Behavioral Pediatrics, 17*, 229–239.

Dishion, T. (1990). Peer context of troublesome behavior in children and adolescents. In P.E. Leone (Ed.), *Understanding troubled and troubling youth: A multidisciplinary perspective* (pp. 128–153). Beverly Hills, CA: Sage.

Dishion, T., Patterson, G.R., & Griesler, P.C. (1994). Peer adaptations in the development of antisocial behavior. In L.R. Huesmann (Ed.), *Aggressive behavior. Current perspectives* (pp. 61–96). New York: Plenum Press.

Dix, T., & Lochman, J.E. (1990). Social cognition and negative reactions to children: A comparison of mothers of aggressive and nonaggressive boys. *Journal of Social and Clinical Psychology, 9*, 418–438.

Dodge, K.A. (1986). A social information processing model of social competence in children. In M. Perlmutter (Ed.), *Minnesota Symposium on Child Psychology* (Vol. 18, pp. 77–125). Hillsdale, NJ: Erlbaum.

Dodge, K.A. (1993). *Social information processing and peer rejection factors in the development of behavior problems in children*. Paper presented at the biennial meeting of the Society for Research in Child Development.

Dodge, K.A., Coie, J.D., Petit, G.S., & Price, J.M. (1990). Peer status and aggression in boys' groups: Developmental and contextual analyses. *Child Development, 61*, 1289–1309.

Dodge, K.A., & Crick, N.R. (1990). Social information processing bases of aggressive behavior in children. *Personality and Social Psychology Bulletin, 16*, 8–22.

Dodge, K.A., & Feldman, E. (1990). Issues in social cognition and sociometric status. In S.R. Asher and J.D. Coie (Eds.), *Peer rejection in childhood* (pp. 119–155). Cambridge, UK: Cambridge University Press.

Dodge, K.A., & Frame, C.L.O. (1982). Social cognitive biases and deficits in aggressive boys. *Child Development, 53*, 620–635.

Dodge, K.A., Lansford, J.E., Salzer Burks, V., Bates, J.E., Pettit, G.S., Fontaine, R., & Price, J.M. (2003). Peer rejection and social information-processing factors in the development of aggressive behavior problems in children. *Child Development, 74*, 374–393.

Dodge, K.A., & Newman, J.P. (1981). Biased decision-making processes in aggressive boys. *Journal of Abnormal Psychology, 90,* 375–379.

Dodge, K.A., Pettit, G.S., Bates, J.E., & Valente, E. (1995). Social information-processing patterns partially mediate the effect of early physical abuse on later conduct problems. *Journal of Abnormal Psychology, 104,* 632–643.

Dodge, K.A., & Somberg, D.R. (1987). Hostile attributional biases among aggressive boys are exacerbated under conditions of threats to the self. *Child Development, 58,* 213–224.

Dodge, K.A., & Tomlin, A.M. (1987). Utilization of self-schemas as a mechanism of interpretational bias in aggressive children. *Social Cognition, 5,* 280–300.

Dole, S. (2000). The implications of the risk and resilience literature for gifted students with learning disabilities. *Roeper Review 23,* 91–96.

Dosen, A. & Gielen, J.J.M. (1990). Psychological characteristics of mentally retarded persons and the risk of depression. In A. Dosen & F.J. Menolascino (Eds.), *Depression in mentally retarded children and adults* (pp. 81–94). Netherlands: Logon Publications.

Downey, J., Ehrhardt, A., Guen, R., Bell, J., & Morishima, A. (1989). Psychopathology and social functioning in women with Turner syndrome. *Journal of Nervous and Mental Disease, 177,* 191–200.

Drew, A., Baird, G., Baron-Cohen, S., Cox, A., Slonims, V., Wheelwright, S., Swettenham, J., Berry, B., & Charman, T. (2002). A pilot randomized control trial fo a parent training intervention for preschool children with autism. Preliminary findings and methodological challenges. *European Child and Adolescent Psychiatry, 11,* 266–272.

Drotar, D., Doershak, C.F., Stern, R.C., Boat, T.F., Boyer, W., & Matthews, I. (1981). Psychological functioning of children with cystic fibrosis. *Pediatrics, 67,* 338–343.

Dubois, D.L., & Hirsch, G.J. (1993). School/nonschool friendship patterns in early adolescence. *Journal of Early Adolescence, 13,* 102–122.

Duncan, D., Matson, J.L., Bamburg, J.W., Cherry, K.E., & Buckley, T. (1999). The relationship of self injurious behavior and aggression to social skills in persons with severe and profound learning disability. *Research in Developmental Disabilities, 20,* 441–448.

Dyches, T.T., Wilder, L.K., & Obiakor, F.E. (2001). Autism: Multicultual perspectives. In T. Wahlberg, F. Obiakor, & S. Burkhardt (Eds). Educational and clinical interventions (pp. 151–177). Oxford, EK: Elsevier Science Ltd.

Dykens, E.M. (2003). The Williams syndrome behavioral phenotype: the 'whole person' is missing. *Current Opinion in Psychiatry, 16,* 523–528.

Dykens, E.M., & Cassidy, S.B. (1996). Prader-Willi syndrome: Genetic, behavioral, and treatment issues. *Child and Adolescent Psychiatric Clinics of North America, 5,* 913–927.

Dykens, E., Leckman, J.F., & Riddle, M. (1990). Intellectual, academic, and adaptive functioning of Tourette syndrome children with and without attention deficit hyperactive disorder. *Journal of Abnormal Child Psychology, 18,* 608–615.

Dykens, E.M., Rosner, B.A., & Ly, T.M. (2001). Drawings by individuals with Williams syndrome: Are people different from shapes? *American Journal of Mental Retardation, 106,* 94–107.

Dykens, E.M., Shah, B., Sagun, J., Beck, T., & King, B.Y. (2002). Maladaptive behavior and psychiatric disorders in persons with Down's syndrome. *Journal of Intellectual Disabilities Research, 46,* 484–492.

Dykman, B.M., Horowitz, L., Abramson, L.Y., & Usher, M. (1991). Schematic and situational determinants of depressed and non-depressed students' interpretation of feedback. *Journal of Abnormal Psychology, 100,* 45–55.

Dyson, L.L. (1993). Siblings of children with learning disabilities. In Z. Stoneman and P.W. Berman (Eds.) *The effects of mental retardation, disability, and illness on sibling relationships* (pp. 235–252). Baltimore, MD: Paul H. Brookes, Publishing

Dyson, L.L. (1999). The psychosocial functioning of school-age children who have siblings with developmental disabilities: Change and stability over time. *Journal of Applied Developmental Psychology, 20*, 253–271.

Dyson, L.L., Edgar, E., & Crnic, K. (1989). Psychological predictors of adjustment by siblings of developmentally disabled children. *American Journal of Mental Retardation, 94*, 292–302.

Eaton, Y.M., Mitchell, M.L., & Holley, J.M. (1991). Gender differences in the development of relationships during late adolescence. *Adolescence, 26*, 565–568.

Eccles, J.S., Midgley, C., Wigfield, A., Buchanan, C.M., Reuman, D., Flanagan, C., & Iver, D.M. (1993). Development during adolescence: The impact of stage-environment fit on young adolescents' experiences in schools and families. *American Psychologist, 48*, 90–101.

Edell, B.H., & Motta, R.W. (1989). The emotional adjustment of children with Tourette's syndrome. *Journal of Psychology, 123*, 1–57.

Edell-Fisher, B.H., & Motta, R.W. (1990). Tourette syndrome: Relation to children's and parents' self-concepts. *Psychological Reports, 66*, 539–545.

Edens, J.F., Cavell, T.A., & Hughes, J.N. (1999). The self-systems of aggressive children: A cluster-analytic investigation. *Journal of Child Psychology and Psychiatry, 40*, 441–454.

Ehlers, S., & Gillberg, C. (2003). The epidemiology of Asperger Syndrome: A total population study. Website for Asperger Syndrome Coalition of the U.S. *www.asperger./org/asperger/asperger_epidemiology.htm.*

Ehlers, S., Nyden, A., Gillberg, C., & Dahlgren Sandberg, A. (1997). Asperger syndrome, autism, and attention disorders: A comparative study of the cognitive profiles of 120 children. *Journal of Child Psychology and Psychiatry, 38*, 207–217.

Eikeseth, S., Smith, T., Jahr, E., & Eldevik, S. (2002). Intensive behavioral treatment at school for 4- to 7-year-old children with autism: A 1-year comparison controlled study. *Behaviour modification: Special Issue: Autism, Part 2, 26*, 49–68.

Einfeld, S.L., Tonge, B.J., & Florio, T. (1997). Behavioral and emotional disturbance in individuals with Williams syndrome. *American Journal of Mental Retardation, 102*, 45–53.

Einfeld, S.L., Tonge, B.J., Turner, G., Parmenter, T., & Smith, A. (1999). Longitudinal course of behavioural and emotional problems of young persons with Prader-Willi, Fragile X, Williams, and Down's syndromes. *Journal of Intellectual and Developmental Disability, 24*, 349–354.

Eisenberg, N., & Fabes, R. (1992). Emotion, regulation, and the development of social competence. In M.S. Clark (Ed.), *Emotion and social behavior: Review of personality and social psychology* (pp. 119–150). Newbury Park, CA: Sage.

Eisenberg, N., Fabes, R., Bernzweig, J., Karbon, M., Poulin, R., & Hanish, L. (1993). The relations of emotionality and regulation to preschoolers' social skills and sociometric status. *Child Development, 64*, 1418–1438.

Eisenberg, N., Fabes, R.A., Murphy, B., Karbon, M., Smith, M., & Maszk, P. (1996). The relations of children's dispositional empathy-related responding to their emotionality, regulation, and social functioning. *Developmental Psychology, 32*, 195–209.

Eisenberg, N.A., Fabes, R.A., Guthrie, I.K., & Reiser, M. (2000). Dispositional emotionality and regulation: Their role in predicting quality of social functioning. *Journal of Personality and Social Psychology, 78*, 136–157.

Eisenberg, N., Guthrie, I., Murphy, B.C., Shepard, S.A., Cumberland, A., & Carlo, G. (1999). Consistence and development of prosocial dispositions: A longitudinal study. *Child Development, 70*, 1360–1372.

Elsenberg, N., Murphy, B.C., & Shepard, S. (1997). The development of empathic accuracy. In W.J. Ickes (Ed.), *Empathic accuracy* (pp. 73–116). New York: Guilford Press.

Eisenmajer, R., Prior, M., & Leekam, S. (1996). A comparison of clinical symptoms in individuals diagnosed with autism and Asperger's syndrome. *Journal of the American Academy of Child and Adolescent Psychiatry, 35*, 1523–1531.

Elbaum, B. (2002). The self-concept of students with learning disabilities: A meta-analysis of comparisons among different placements. *Learning Disabilities, Research & Practice, 17*, 216–226.

Elias, M.J. (2004). The connection between social-emotional learning and learning disabilities: Implications for intervention. *Learning Disability Quarterly, 27*, 53–63.

Elliott, C. (1990). Differential Ability Scales. San Antonio, TX: *Psychological Corporation.*

Emery, R.E., Finchan, F.D., & Cummings, E.M. (1992). Parenting in context: Systemic thinking about parental conflict and its influence on children. *Journal of Consulting and Clinical Psychology, 60*, 909–912.

Epkins, C.C. (1998). Mother-and father-related competence, child-perceived competence and cognitive distortions: Unique relations with children's depressive symptoms. *Journal of Clinical Child Psychology, 27*, 442–451.

Erikson, E.H. (1980). *Identity and the life cycle* (2nd ed.). New York: Norton.

Erk, R.R. (1997). Multidimensional treatment of attention deficit disorder: A family oriented approach. *Journal of Mental Health Consulting, 19*, 3–23.

Ernst, M., Zametkin, A.J., Matochik, J.A., Pascualvaca, D., & Cohen, R.M. (1997). Reduced medial prefrontal dopaminergic activity in autistic children. *Lancet, 350*, 638–645.

Esser, G., Schmidt, M.H., & Woerner, W. (1990). Epidemiology and course of psychiatric disorders in school-age children: Results of a longitudinal study. *Journal of Child Psychology and Psychiatry, 31*, 243–263.

European Chromosome 16 Tuberous Sclerosis Consortium (1993). Identification and characterization of the tuberous sclerosis gene on chromosome 16. *Cell, 75*, 1305–1315.

Evans, I.M., Salisbury, C.L., Palombaro, M.M., Berryman, J., & Hollowood, T.M. (1992). Peer interactions and social acceptance of elementary-age children with severe disabilities in an inclusive school. *The Journal of the Association for Persons with Severe Handicaps, 17*, 205–212.

Evans, C.A., Stevens, M., Cushway, D., & Houghton, J. (1993). Sibling response to childhood cancer: A new approach. *Child: Care, Health and Development, 18*, 229–244.

Ewart, C.K., Taylor, C.B., Kraemer, H.C., & Agras, W.S. (1991). High blood pressure and marital discord: Not being nasty matters more than being nice. *Health Psychology, 10*, 155–163.

Ewing-Cobbs, L., Landry, S., Steubing, K., Prasad, M., & Leal, F. (2000). Social competence in young children with inflicted or noninflicted traumatic brain injury (TBI). *Journal of the International Neuropsychological Society, 6*, 226.

Fantuzzo, J., Coolahan, K., Mendez, J., McDermott, P., & Sutton-Smith, B. (1998). Contextually-relevant validation of peer play constructs with African American Head Start children: Penn Interactive Peer Play Scale. *Early Childhood Research Quarterly, 13*, 422–431.

Fantuzzo, J., McDermott, P.A., Holliday Manz, P., Hampton, V.R., & Alvarez Burdick, N. (1996). The Pictorial Scale of Perceived Competence and Social Acceptance: Does it work with low-income urban children? *Child Development, 67*, 1071–1084.

Farmer, T.W., Rodkin, P.C., Pearl, R., & Van Acker, R. (1999). Teacher-assessed behavioral configurations, peer-assessments, and self-concepts of elementary students with mild disabilities. *The Journal of Special Education, 33*, 66–80.

Farver, J., Kim, Y.K., & Lee, Y. (1995). Cultural differences in Korean- and Anglo-American preschoolers' social interaction and play behaviors. *Child Development, 66*, 1088–1099.

Faust, J., Rosenfeld, R.G., Wilson, D., Durham, L., & Vardopoulos, C.C. (1995). Prediction of depression in parents of Turner syndrome adolescents as a function of growth hormones, family conflict, and coping style. *Journal of Developmental and Physical Disabilities, 7*, 221–233.

Feehan, M., McGee, R., Williams, S.M., & Nada-Raja, S. (1995). Models of adolescent psychopathology: Childhood risk and the transition to adulthood. *Journal of the American Academy of Child and Adolescent Psychiatry, 34*, 670–680.

Feldman, D.H. (1986). Giftedness as a developmentalist sees it. In R.J. Sternberg and J.E. Davidson (Eds.), *Conceptions of giftedness* (pp. 285–305). Cambridge, MA: Cambridge University Press.

Fenzel, L.M. (2000). Prospective study of changes in global self-worth and strain during transition to middle school. *Journal of Early Adolescence, 20*, 93–116.

Fergusson, D.M., Lynskey, M.T., & Horwood, J.L. (1996). Origins of comorbidity between conduct and affective disorders. *Journal of the American Academy of Child and Adolescent Psychiatry, 35*, 451–460.

Ferro, T., Carlson, G.A., Grayson, P., & Klein, D.N. (1994). Depressive disorders: Distinctions in children. *Journal of the American Academy of Child and Adolescent Psychiatry, 33*, 664–670.

Field, T. (1997). The treatment of depressed mothers and their infants. In L. Murray and P. Cooper (Eds.), *Postpartum depression and child development* (pp. 221–236). New York: Guilford.

Finnie, V. & Russell, A. (1988). Preschool children's social status and their mothers' behavior and knowledge in the supervisory role. *Developmental Psychology, 24*, 789–801.

Fischer, M., Barkely, R.A., Edelbrock, C.S., & Smallish, L. (1993). The stability of dimensions of behavior in ADHD and normal children over an 8-year follow-up. *Journal of Abnormal Child Psychology, 21*, 315–337.

Fischer Fritz, M. (1990). A comparison of social interactions using a friendship awareness activity. *Education and Training in Mental Retardation, 25*, 352–359.

Flavell, J.H., Miller, P.H., & Miller, S.A. (1985). *Cognitive development* (3rd edition). New Jersey: Prentice-Hall.

Fleishner, J.E. (1994). Diagnosis and assessment of mathematics learning disabilities. In G.R. Lyon (Ed.), *Frames of reference for the assessment of learning disabilities: New views on measurement issues* (pp. 441–458). Baltimore, MD: Paul H. Brookes.

Fombonne, E. (2001). What is the prevalence of Asperger disorder? *Journal of Autism and Developmental Disorders, 31*, 363–364.

Fombonne, E. (2003a). The prevalence of autism. *Journal of the American Medical Association, 289*, 87–89.

Fombonne, E. (2003b). Epidemiological surveys of autism and other pervasive developmental disorders: An update. *Journal of Autism and Developmental Disorders, 33*, 365–382.

Fombonne, E., Simmons, H., Ford, T., Meltzer, H., & Goodman, R. (2001). Prevalence of pervasive developmental disorders in the British nationwide survey of child mental health. *Journal of the American Academy of Child and Adolescent Psychiatry, 40*, 820–827.

Fonzi, A., Schneider, B.H., Tani, F., & Tomada, G. (1997). Predicting children's friendship status from their dyadic interaction in structured situations of potential conflict. *Child Development, 68,* 496–506.

Ford, D.Y. (1994/95, Winter). Underachievement amoung gifted and non-gifted Black females: A study of perceptions. *The Journal of Secondary Gifted Education, 6,* 165–175.

Fordyce, D.J., Roueche, J.R., & Prigatano, G.P. (1983). Enhanced emotional reaction in chronic head trauma patients. *Journal of Neurology, Neurosurgery, & Psychiatry, 46,* 620–624.

Forehand, R., Neighbors, B., & Wierson, M. (1991). The transition of adolescence: The role of gender and stress in problem behavior and competence. *Journal of Child Psychology and Psychiatry, 32,* 929–937.

Forgas, J.P. (1995). Mood and judgment: The affect infusion model (AIM). *Psychological Bulletin, 117,* 39–66.

Forgatch, M., Patterson, G., & Skinner, M. (1988). A mediational model for the effect of divorce on antisocial behavior in boys. In E.M. Hetherington and J.D. Arasteh (Eds.), *Impact of divorce, single parent, and step-parenting on children* (pp. 135–154). Hillsdale, NJ: Lawrence Erlbaum Associates, Inc.

Forness, S.R., & Kavale, K.A. (1996). Treating social skill deficits in children with learning disabilities: A meta-analysis of the research. *Learning Disability Quarterly, 19,* 2–13.

Forness, S.R., Kavale, K.A., & San Miguel Bauman, S. (1998). The psychiatric comorbidity hypothesis revisited. *Learning Disability Quarterly, 21,* 203–206.

Foss, J.M. (1991). Nonverbal learning disabilities and remedial interventions. *Annals of Dyslexia, 41,* 128–140.

Franke, P., Maier, W., Iwers, B., Hautzinger, M., & Froster, U.G. (1996). Fragile X carrier females: Evidence for a distinct psychopathological phenotype? *American Journal of Medical Genetics, 64,* 334–339.

Freeman, J. (2001). *Gifted children grown up.* London: David Fulton Publishers.

Freeman, J. (2005). Permission to be gifted: How conceptions of giftedness can change lives. In R. Sternberg & J. Davidson (Eds.), *Conceptions of giftedness* (pp. 80–97). Cambridge, UK: Cambridge University Press.

Freeman, J. (2006). Giftedness in the Long Term. *Journal for the Education of the Gifted, 29,* 384–485.

Freeman, J.B., Garcia, A.M., Fucci, C., Karitani, M., Miller, L., & Leonard, H.L. (2003). Family-based treatment of early-onset obsessive-compulsive disorder. *Journal of Child and Adolescent Psychopharmacology, 13, Supplement 1,* S71-S80.

Frick, P. J., Lahey, B.H., Christ, M.A., Loeber, R., & Green, S. (1991). History of childhood behavior problems in biological relatives of boys with attention deficit hyperactivity disorder and conduct disorder. *Journal of Clinical Child Psychology, 18,* 114–120.

Friedman, S.R., Rapport, L.J., Lumley, M., Tzelepis, A., VanVoorhis, A., Stettner, L., & Kakaati, L. (2003). Aspects of social and emotional competence in adult Attention-Deficit/Hyperactivity Disorder. *Neuropsychology, 17,* 50–58.

Frith, U. (1989). *Autism: Explaining the enigma.* Oxford: Blackwell.

Frith, U., Happe, F., & Siddons, F. (1994). Autism and theory of mind in everyday life. *Social Development, 3,* 108–124.

Fydrich, T., Chambless, D.L., Perry, K.J., Buergener, F., & Beazley, M.B. (1998). Behavioral assessment of social performance: A rating system for social phobia. *Behaviour Research and Therapy, 36,* 995–1010.

Gable, S.L., & Shean, G.D. (2000). Perceived social competence and depression. *Journal of Social and Personal Relationships, 17,* 139–150.

Gagne, F. (2003). Transforming gifts into talents: The DGMT as a developmental theory. In N. Colangelo & G.A. Davis (Eds.), *Handbook of gifted education* (pp. 3–10). (3rd edition). Boston: Allyn & Bacon.

Galluci, N.R., Middleton, G., & Kline, A. (1999). Intellectually superior children and behavioral problems and competence. *Roeper Review, 22*, 18–21.

Gardner, H. (1999). *Intelligence reframed: Multiple intelligences for the 21st century.* New York: Basic Books.

Gardynik, U.M., & McDonald, L. (2005). Implications of risk and resilience in the life of the individual who is gifted/learning disabled. *Roeper Review, 27*, 1–16.

Garfield, J.L., Peterson, C.C., & Perry, T. (2001). Social cognition, language acquisition, and the development of the theory of mind. *Mind and Language, 16*, 494–541.

Garland, A.F., & Zigler, E. (1999). Emotional and behavioral problems among highly intellectually gifted youth. *Roeper Review, 22*, 41–44.

Garmezy, N., & Tellegen, A. (1984). Studies of stress-resistant children: Methods, variables, and preliminary findings. In F. Morrison, D. Keating, and C. Lord (Eds.), *Applied developmental psychology* (Vol. 1). New York: Academic Press.

Garrison, W., Biggs, D., & Williams, K. (1990). Temperament characteristics and clinical outcomes in young children with diabetes mellitus. *Journal of Child Psychology and Psychiatry, 31*, 1079–1088.

Gaub, M., & Carlson, C.L. (1997). Behavioral characteristics of DSM IV ADHD subtypes in a school-based population. *Journal of Abnormal Child Psychology, 25*, 103–111.

Gerdes, A.C., Hoza, B., & Pelham, W.E. (2003). Attention-deficit/hyperactivity disordered boys' relationship with their mothers and fathers: Child, mother, and father perceptions. *Development and Psychopathology, 15*, 363–382.

Geurts, H.M., Verte, S., Oosterlaan, J., Roeyers, H., & Sergeant, J.A. (2004). How specific are executive functioning deficits in attention deficit hyperactivity disorder and autism? *Journal of Child Psychology and Psychiatry, 45*, 836–854.

Ghaziuddin, M., Tsai, L.Y., & Ghaziuddin, N. (1992). Brief report: A comparison of the diagnostic criteria for Asperger syndrome. *Journal of Autism and Developmental Disorders, 22*, 643–649.

Gillberg, C. (1991). Outcome in autism and autistic-like conditions. *Journal of the American Academy of Child and Adolescent psychiatry, 30*, 375–382.

Gillberg, I.C., Gillberg, C, & Ahlsen, G. (1994). Autistic behavior and attention deficits in tuberous sclerosis: A population-based study. *Developmental Medicine and Child Neurology, 36*, 50–56.

Gladstone, T.R.G., Kaslow, N.J. (1995). Depression and attributions in children and adolescents: A meta-analytic review. *Journal of Abnormal Child Psychology, 23*, 597–606.

Glanville, D.N. & Nowicki, S. (2002). Facial expression recognition and social competences among African American elementary school children: An examination of ethnic differences. *Journal of Black Psychology, 28*, 318–329.

Glass, K. (2003). Nonverbal Learning Disabilities Unpublished dissertation. University of Texas at Austin.

Glass, K., Guli, L., & Semrud-Clikeman, M. (2000). The social competence intervention program for use with developmental disorders. *Journal of Psychotherapy in Independent Practice, 4*, 21–34.

Goetzel, R.Z., Hawkins, K., Ozminkowski, R.J., & Wang, S. (2003). The health and productivity cost burden of the "top 10" physical and mental health conditions affecting six large U.S. employers in 1999. *Journal of Occupation and Environmental Medicine, 45*, 5–14.

Goldberg, E., & Costa, L.D. (1981). Hemispheric differences in the acquisition and use of asymmetries in the brain. *Brain and Language, 14*, 144–173.

Goleman, D. (1995). *Emotional intelligence*. New York: Bantam.

Gomez, M.R. (1999). *Tuberous Sclerosis* (3rd edition). New York: Raven Press.

Goodman, S.H., Brogan, D., Lynch, M.E., & Fielding, B. (1993). Social and emotional competence in children of depressed mothers. *Child Development, 64*, 516–531.

Goodman, S.H., & Gotlib, I.H. (2002). *Children of depressed parents: Mechanisms of risk and implications for treatment.* American Psychological Association: Washington, DC.

Goodwin, R., & Lee, I. (1994). Taboo topics among Chinese and English friends: A cross-cultural comparison. *Journal of Cross-Cultural Psychology, 25*, 325–328.

Goodyer, I., Wright, C., & Althan, P. (1990). The friendships and recent life events of anxious and depressed school-age children. *British Journal of Psychiatry, 156*, 689–698.

Gordon, T. (2006). Parent Effectiveness Training. Solana Beach, CA: *Gordon Training International.*

Gorenstein, E.E., Mammato, C.A., & Sandy, J.M. (1989). Performance on inattentive-overactive children on selected measures of prefrontal-type function. *Journal of Clinical Psychology, 45*, 619–632.

Gosch, A., & Pankau, R. (1994). Social-emotional and behavioral adjustment in children with Williams-Beuren syndrome. *American Journal of Medical Genetics, 53*, 335–339.

Gotlib, I.H., Lewinsohn, P.M., Seeley, J.R., Rhode, P., & Redner, J. E. (1993). Negative cognitions and attributional style in depressed adolescents: An examination of stability and specificity. *Journal of Abnormal Psychology, 107*, 607–615.

Gottfried, A.W., Gottfried, A.E., Bathurst, K., & Guerin, D.W. (1994). *Gifted IQ: Early developmental aspects.* New York: Plenum.

Gottman, J.M. (1983). How children become friends. *Monographs of the Society for Research in Child Development, 48 (2, Serial no. 201).*

Gottman, J.M., Katz, L.F., & Hooven, C. (1997). *Meta-emotion: How families communicate emotionally.* Mahwah, NJ: Lawrence Erlbaum.

Goutz, K. (1987). Attention and social problem-solving as correlates of aggression in preschool males. *Journal of Abnormal Child Psychology, 15*, 181–197.

Gouze, J.R. (1987). Attention and social problem-solving as correlates of aggression in preschool males. *Journal of Abnormal Child Psychology, 15*, 181–197.

Gray, C., & Garand, J. (1993). Social stories: Improving responses of students with autism with accurate social information. *Focus on Autistic Behavior, 8*, 1–10.

Green, J. (1990). Is Asperger's a syndrome? *Developmental Medicine and Child Neurology, 32*, 743–747.

Green, L., Fein, D., Joy, S., & Waterhouse, L. (1995). Cognitive functioning in autism: An overview. In E. Schopler & G.B. Mesibov (Eds.), *Learning and cognition* (pp. 200–215). New York: Plenum Press.

Greenberg, H., Kazak, A., & Meadows, A. (1989). Psychological adjustment in 8–16 year old cancer survivors and their parents. *Journal of Pediatrics, 114*, 488–493.

Greenberg, M., & Kusche, C.A. (2006). Building social and emotional competence: the PATHS curriculum. In S.R. Jimerson and M. Furlong (Eds.), *Handbook of school violence and school safety: From research to practice* (pp. 395–412). Mahwah, NJ: Lawrence Erlbaum.

Greenberg, M., Speltz, M., & DeKlyen, M. (1993). The role of attachment in the early development of disruptive behavior problems. *Development and Psychopathology, 5*, 191–213.

Greene, R.W., & Biederman, J. (1999). Further validation of social impairment as a predictor of substance use disorders: Findings from a sample of siblings of boys with and without ADHD. *Journal of Clinical Child Psychology, 28,* 349–355,

Greene, R.W., Biederman, J., Faraone, S.V., Sienna, M., & Garcia-Jetton, J. (1997). Adolescent outcome of boys with attention-deficit/hyperactivity disorder and social disability: Results from a 4-year longitudinal follow-up study. *Journal of Consulting and Clinical Psychology, 65,* 758–767.

Gresham, F.M., & Elliott, S.N. (1990). *The Social Skills Rating System.* Circle Pines, MN: American Guidance Service.

Gresham, F.M., Lane, K.L., & Beebe-Frankenberger, M. (2005). Predictors of hyperactive-impulsive-inattention and conduct problems: A comparative follow-back investigation. *Psychology in the Schools, 42,* 721–736.

Gresham, F.M., & MacMillan, D.L. (1996). Learning disabilities, low achievement, and mild mental retardation: More alike than different? *Journal of Learning Disabilities, 29,* 570–582.

Gresham, F.M., & MacMillan, D.L. (1997). Social competence and affective characteristics of students with mild disabilities. *Review of Educational Research, 67,* 377–415.

Gresham, F.M., Sugai, G., & Horner, R.H. (2001). Interpreting outcomes of social skills training for students with high-incidence disabilities. *Exceptional Children, 67,* 331–344.

Grizenko, N., Papineau, D., & Sayegh, L. (1993). Effectiveness of a multimodal day treatment program for children with disruptive behavior problems. *Journal of the American Academy of Child and Adolescent Psychiatry, 32,* 127–134.

Grodzinsky, G.M., & Diamond, R. (1992). Frontal lobe functioning in boys with attention deficit hyperactivity disorder. *Developmental Neuropsychology, 8,* 427–445.

Grolnick, W.S., Kurowski, C.O., & Gurland, S.T. (1999). Family processes and the development of children's self-regulation. *Educational Psychologist, 34,* 3–14.

Grotpeter, J.K., & Crick, N.R. (1996). Relational aggression, overt aggression, and friendship. *Child Development, 67,* 2328–2338.

Gross, A.L., & Ballif, B. (1991). Children's understanding of emotion from facial expressions and situations: A review. *Developmental Review, 11,* 368–398.

Gross, J.J. (1998). Sharpening the focus: Emotion regulation, arousal, and social competence. *Psychological Inquiry, 9,* 287–290.

Gross, M.U.M. (1993). *Exceptionally gifted children.* London: Routledge.

Gross, M.U.M. (2001). From "play partner" to "sure shelter": what do gifted children seek from friendship? *GERRIC News,* 4–5.

Gross, M.U.M. (2002). Social and emotional issues for exceptionally intellectually gifted students. In M. Neihart, S.M. Reis, N.M. Robinson, & S.M. Moon (Eds.), *The social and emotional development of gifted children* (pp. 19–30). Waco, TX: Prufrock Press.

Gross-Tsur, V., Shalev, R.S., Manor, O., & Amir, N. (1995). Developmental right-hemisphere syndrome: Clinical spectum of the nonverbal learning disability. *Journal of Learning Disabilities, 28,* 80–86.

Guevremont, D.C., & Dumas, M.C. (1994). Peer relationship problems and disruptive behavior disorders. *Journal of Emotional and Behavioral Disorders, 2,* 164–175.

Guli, L. (2005). *The efficacy of the social competence intervention program.* Unpublished dissertation, University of Texas at Austin.

Guli, I.A., Semrud-Clikeman, M., Wilkinson, A. (2007). Use of Creative Drama as Intervention for Children with Social Competence Deficits. Manuscript submitted for publication.

Gunter, H.L., Ghaziuddin, M., & Ellis, H.D. (2002). Asperger Syndrome: Tests of right hemisphere functioning and interhemispheric communication. *Journal of Autism and Developmental Disorders, 32*, 263–281.

Guralnick, M.J. (1994). Social competence with peers: Outcome and process in early childhood special education. In P.L. Safford (Ed.), *Yearbook in early childhood education: Early childhood special education* (Vol. 5, pp. 47–71). New York: Teachers College Press.

Guralnick, M.J. (1998). The effectiveness of early intervention for vulnerable children: A developmental perspective. *American Journal on Mental Retardation, 102*, 319–345.

Guralnick, M.J. (1999). The nature and meaning of social integration for young children with mild developmental delays in inclusive settings. *Journal of Early Intervention, 22*, 70–86.

Guralnick, M.J., Connor, R.T., Neville, B., & Hammond, M.A. (2002). Mothers' perspectives of the peer-related social development of young children with developmental delays and communication disorders. *Early Education and Development, 13*, 59–80.

Guralnick, M.J., Gottman, J.M., & Hammond, M.A. (1996). Effects of social setting on the friendship formation of young children differing in developmental status. *Journal of Applied Developmental Psychology, 17*, 625–651.

Guralnick, M.J., & Groom, J.M. (1987). The peer relations of mildly delayed and nonhandicapped preschool children in mainstreamed playgroups. *Child Development, 58*, 1556–1572.

Guralnick, M.J., Hammond, M.A., & Connor, R.T. (2003). Subtypes of nonsocial play: Comparisons between young children with and without developmental delays. *American Journal of Mental Retardation, 108*, 347–362.

Guralnick, M.J., Paul-Brown, D., Groom, J.M., Booth, C.L., Hammond, M.A., Tupper, D.B., & Geltner, A. (1998). Conflict resolution patterns in preschool children with and without developmental delays in heterogeneous play groups. *Early Education and Development, 9*, 49–77.

Guralnick, M.J., & Neville, B. (1997). Designing early intervention programs to promote children's social competence. In M.J. Guralnick (Ed.), *The effectiveness of early intervention* (pp. 579–610). Baltimore: Brookes.

Guralnick, M.J., Neville, B., Connor, R.T., & Hammond, M. (2003). Family factors associated with the peer social competence of young children with mild delays. *American Journal on Mental Retardation, 108*, 272–287.

Guralnick, M.J., & Weinhouse, E.M. (1984). Peer-related social interactions of developmentally delayed young children: Development and characteristics. *Developmental Psychology, 20*, 815–827.

Gutstein, S.E., & Whitney, T. (2002). Asperger syndrome and the development of social competence. *Focus on Autism and Other Developmental Disabilities, 17*, 161–171.

Haager, D., & Vaughn, S. (1995). Parent, teacher, peer, and self-reports of the social competence of students with learning disabilities. *Journal of Learning Disabilities, 28*, 205–215.

Hackney, H. (1981). The gifted child, the family, and the school. *Gifted Child Quarterly, 25*, 51–54.

Hadwin, J., Baron-Cohen, S., Howlin, P., & Hill, K (1997). Does teaching theory of mind have an effect on the ability to develop conversation in children with autism? *Journal of Autism and Developmental Disorders, 27*, 519–537.

Hagerman, R.J. (1996). Physical and behavioral phenotype. In R.J. Hagerman and A.C. Cronister (Eds.), *Fragile X syndrome: Diagnosis treatment, and research* (2nd ed., pp. 3–87). Baltimore, MD: Johns Hopkins University Press.

Hagerman, R.J., & Lampe, M.E. (1999). Fragile X syndrome. In S. Goldstein and C.R. Reynolds (Eds.), *Handbook of Neurodevelopmental and genetic disorders in children* (pp. 298–316). New York: Guilford.

Hala, S. Hug, S., & Henderson, A. (2003). Executive function and false-belief understanding in preschool children: Two tasks are harder than one. *Journal of Cognition and Development, 4,* 275–298.

Halberstadt, A.G., Denham, S.A., & Dunsmore, J.C. (2001). Affective social competence. *Social Development, 10,* 79–119.

Hall, S., DeBernardis, M., & Reiss, A. (2006). Social escape behaviors in children with fragile X syndrome. *Journal of Autism and Developmental Disorders, 36,* 935–947.

Hall, S., Oliver, C., & Murphy, G. (2001). Self-injurious behavior in young children with Lesch-Nyhan syndrome. *Developmental Medicine and Child Neurology, 43,* 745–749.

Hamilton, E.B., Asarnow, J.R., & Tompson, M.C. (1996). Social, academic, and behavioral competence of depressed children: Relationship to diagnostic status and family interaction style. *Journal of Youth and Adolescence, 26,* 77–87.

Hammen, C., & Brennan, P.A. (2001). *Children of depressed parents: Mechanisms of risk and implications for treatment.* American Psychological Association: Washington, DC.

Hammen, C., Shih, J.H., & Brennan, P.A. (2004). Intergenerational transmission of depression: Test of an interpersonal stress model in a community sample. *Journal of Consulting and Clinical Psychology, 72,* 511–522.

Hamre, B.K., & Pianta, R.C. (2001). Early teacher-child relationships and the trajectory of children's school outcomes through eighth grade. *Child Development, 72,* 625–638.

Hamre-Nietupski, S. (1993). How much time should be spent on skill instructions and friendship development? Preferences of parents of students with moderate and severe/profound disabilities. *Education and training in mental retardation, 28,* 220–231.

Hansen, D.J., St. Lawrence, J.S., & Christoff, K.A. (1988). Conversational skills of inpatient conduct-disordered youths: Social validation of component behaviors and implications for skills training. *Behavior Modification, 12,* 424–444.

Hansen, R.L., & Hagerman, R.J. (2003). Contributions of pediatrics. In S. Ozonoff, S.J. Rogers, & R.L. Hendren (Eds.), *Autism spectrum disorders* (pp. 87–110). Washington, DC: American Psychiatric Publishing, Inc.

Hanson, C.L., Cigrang, J.A., Harris, M.A., Carle, D.L., Relyea, G., & Burghen, G.A. (1989). Coping styles in youths with insulin-dependent diabetes mellitus. *Journal of Consulting and Clinical Psychology, 57,* 644–651.

Hanson, C.L., Henggeler, S.W., & Burghen, G.A. (1987). Social competence and parental support as mediators of the link between stress and metabolic control in adolescents with insulin-dependent diabetes mellitus. *Journal of Consulting and Clinical Psychology, 55,* 529–533.

Happe, F.G., & Frith, U. (1996). The neuropsychology of autism. *Brain, 119,* 1377–1400.

Hardan, A.Y., Mishew, N.J., & Keshavan, M.S. (2000). Corpus callosum size in autism. *Neurology, 55,* 1033–1036.

Harrington, R., Fudge, H., Rutter, M., Pickles, A., & Hill, J. (1991). Adult outcomes of childhood and adolescent depression, II: Links with antisocial disorders. *Journal of the American Academy of Child and Adolescent Psychiatry, 30,* 434–439.

Hart, C.H., DeWolf, M., & Burts, D.C. (1993). Parental disciplinary strategies and preschoolers' play behavior in playground settings. In C.H. Hart (Ed.), *Children on playgrounds: Research perspectives and applications* (pp. 271–313). Albany NY: State University of New York Press.

Hart, C.H., Nelson, D.A., Robinson, C.C., Olsen, S.F., McNeilly-Choque, M.K., Porter, C.L., & McKee, T.R. (2000). Russian parenting styles and family processes: Linkages with subtypes of victimization and aggression. In K.A. Kerns, J.M. Contreras, & A.M. Neal-Barnett (Eds.), *Family and peers: Linking two social worlds* (pp. 47–84). Westport, CT: Praeger.

Hart, C.H., Newell, L.D., & Olsen, S.F. (2003). Parenting skills and social-communicative competence in childhood. In J.O. Greene & B.R. Burleson (Eds.). *Handbook of communication and social interaction skills* (pp. 753–797). Mahwah, NJ: Lawrence Erlbaum & Associates.

Hart, C.H., Olsen, S.F., Robinson, C., & Mandleco, B.L. (1997). The development of social and communicative competence in childhood: Review and a model of personal, familial, and extra familial processes. In B.R. Burleson (Ed.), *Communication yearbook, Vol. 20* (pp. 305–373). Thousand Oaks, CA: Sage.

Hartas, D., & Donahue, M.L. (1997). Conversational and social problem-solving skills in adolescents with learning disabilities. *Learning Disabilities Research & Practice, 12*, 213–220.

Harter, S. (1985). *Manual for the Self-Perception Profile for Children*. Denver, CO: University of Denver Press.

Harter, S. (1986). *Manual: Self-Perception Profile for Adolescents*. Denver, CO: University of Denver Press.

Harter, S., & Pike, R. (1984). The pictorial scale of perceived competence and social acceptance for young children. *Child Development, 55*, 1969–1982.

Hartup, W.W., French, D.C., Laursen, B., Johnston, M.K., & Ogawa, J.R. (1993). Conflict and friendship relations in middle childhood: Behavior in a closed-field situation. *Child Development, 64*, 445–454.

Hartup, W.W., Laursen, B., Stewart, M.A., & Eastenson, A. (1988). Conflict and friendship relations of young children. *Child Development, 59*, 1590–1600.

Haslett, B., & Samter, W. (1997). *Children communicating: The first five years*. Mahwah, NJ: Lawrence Erlbaum Associates.

Hawley, P.H. (2003). Prosocial and coercive configurations of resource control in early adolescence: A case for the well-adapted Machiavellian. *Merrill-Palmer Quarterly, 49*, 279–309.

Haznedar, M.M., Buchsbaum, M.S., Wei, T.C., Hoff, P.R., Cartwright, C., Bienstock, C.A., & Hollander, E. (2000). Limbic circuitry in patients with autism spectrum disorders studied with positron emission tomography and magnetic resonance imaging. *American Journal of Psychiatry, 157*, 1994–2201.

Heberlein, A.S., Adolphs, R., Pennebaker, J.W., & Tranel, D. (2003). Effects of *damage* to right-hemisphere brain structures on spontaneous emotional and social judgments. *Political Psychology, 24*, 705–726.

Hecht, H., Collier, M.J., & Ribeau, S.A. (1993). African-American communication: A comparative analysis of satisfying communication. *International Journal of Intercultural Relations, 8*, 135–151.

Hecht, M.L., Collier, M.J., & Ribeau, S.A. (1993). *African American communication*. Newbury Park, CA: Sage.

Hecht, H., & Wittchen, H. –U. (1988). The frequency of social dysfunction in a general population sample and in patients with mental disorders: A comparison using the social interview schedule (SIS). *Social Psychiatry and Psychiatric Epidemiology, 23*, 17–29.

Hechtman, L., Abikoff, H., Klein, R.G., Weiss, G., Respitz, C., Kouri, J., Blum, C., Greenfield, B., Etcovitch, J., Fleiss, K., & Pollack, S. (2004). Academic achievement and emotional status of children with ADHD treated with long-term methylphenidate and multimodal psychosocial treatment. *Journal of the American Academy of Child and Adolescent Psychiatry, 43,* 812–819.

Heinbaugh, H. (2006). Unpublished dissertation. University of Texas at Austin.

Henin, A., Biederman, J., Mick, E., Sachs, G.S., Hirshfeld-Becker, D.R., Siegel, R.S., McMurrich, S., Grandin, L., & Nierenberg, A.A. (2005). Psychopathology in the offspring of parents with bipolar disorder: A controlled study. *Biological Psychiatry, 58,* 554–561.

Henker, B., & Whalen, C.K. (1999). The child with attention-deficit/hyperactivity disorder in school and peer settings. In H.C. Quay & A.E. Hogan (Eds.), *Handbook of disruptive behavior disorders* (pp. 157–178). Dordrecht, Netherlands: Kluwer Academic Publishers.

Herbert, M.R. (1991). *Clinical child psychology: Social learning, development and behavior.* Chichester, England: Wiley.

Herbert, M.R., Harris, G.J., Adrien, K.T., Ziegler, D.A., Makris, N., Kennedy, D., Lange, N., Deutsch, C.K., Chabris, C.F., Bakardjiev, A., Hodgson, J., Takeoka, M., Tager-Flusberg, H., & Caviness, V.S. (2002). Abnormal symmetry in language association cortex in autism. *Annals of Neurology, 52,* 588–596.

Herbert, M.R., Ziegler, D.A., Deutsch, C.K., O'Brien, L.M., Lange, N., Bakardjiev, A., Hodgson, J., Adrien, K.T., Steele, S., Makris, N., Kennedy, D., Harris, G.J., & Caviness, V.S. (2003). Dissociations of cerebral cortex, subcortical and cerebral white matter volumes in autistic boys. *Brain, 126,* 1182–1192.

Herrmann, B.P., Whitman, S., Hughes, J.R., Melyn, M.M., & Dell, J. (1988). Multietiological determinants of psychopathology and social competence in children with epilepsy. *Epilepsy Research, 2,* 51–60.

Hess, U., Kappas, A., & Scherer, K.R. (1988). Multichannel communication of emotion: Synthetic signal production. In K.R. Scherer (Ed.), *Facets of emotion: Recent research* (pp. 161–183). Hillsdale, NJ: Lawrence Erlbaum Associates, Inc.

Hill, L.G., Lochman, J.E., Coie, J.D., Greenberg, M.T., & the Conduct Problems Prevention Research Group (2006). Effectiveness of early screening for externalizing problems: Issues of screening accuracy and utility. *Journal of Consulting and Clinical Psychology.*

Hirschfeld-Becker, D.R., Biederman, J., Henin, A., Faraone, S.V., Cayton, G.A., & Rosenbaum, J.F. (2006). Laboratory-observed behavioral disinhibition in the young offspring of parents with bipolar disorder: A high-risk pilot study. *American Journal of Psychiatry, 163,* 265–271.

Hock, E., & Schirtzinger, M.G. (1992). Maternal separation and anxiety: Its developmental course and relation to maternal mental health. *Child Development, 63,* 93–102.

Hollingworth, L.S. (1942). *Children above 180 IQ Stanford-Binet: Origin and development.* Yonkers on Hudson, NY: World book.

Holmes, C.S., Karlsson, J.A., & Thompson, R.G. (1985). Social and school competencies in children with short stature: Longitudinal patterns. *Developmental and Behavioral Pediatrics, 6,* 263–267.

Holyrod, J., & Baron-Cohen, S. (1993).

Hornig, M., & Lipkin, W.I. (2001). Infectious and immune factors in the pathogenesis of neurodevelopmental disorders :Epidemiology, hypotheses, and animal models. *Mental Retardation and Developmental Disabilities Research Review, 7,* 200–210.

Horwitz, W.A., & Kazak, A.E. (1990). Family adaptation to childhood cancer: Sibling and family systems variables. *Journal of Clinical Child Psychology, 19,* 221–228.

Horwitz, B., Rumsey, J.M., Grady, C.L., & Rapoport, S.I. (1998). The cerebral metabolic landscape in autism: Intercorrelations of regional glucose utilization. *Archives of Neurology, 45,* 749–755.

Howard, B., & Kendall, P.C. (1996a). Cognitive-behavioral family therapy for anxiety-disordered children: A multiple-baselines evaluation. *Cognitive Therapy and Research, 20,* 423–443.

Howard, B., & Kendall, P.C. (1996b). *Cognitive-behavioral family therapy for anxious children: Therapist manual.* Ardmore, PA: Workbook Publishing.

Howard, K.A., & Tryon, G.S. (2002). Depressive symptoms in and type of classroom placement for adolescents with LD. *Journal of Learning Disabilities, 35,* 185–190.

Howlin, P. (2000). Outcome in adult life for more able individuals with autism. *Journal of Child Psychology and Psychiatry, 39,* 307–322.

Howlin, P., & Goode, S. (1998). Outcome in adult life for people with autism and Asperger's syndrome. In F.R. Volkmar (Ed.), *Autism and pervasive developmentl disorders* (pp. 7–24). New York: Cambridge University Press.

Hoy, E., Sykes, D., Bill, J., Halliday, H., McClure, B., & Reid, M. (1992). The social competence of very low birthweight children: Teacher, peer and self-perceptions. *Journal of Abnormal Child Psychology, 20,* 123–150.

Hoza, B., Bukowski, W.M., & Beery, S. (2000). Assessing peer network and dyadic loneliness. *Journal of Clinical Child Psychology, 29,* 119–131.

Hoza, B., Gerdes, A.C., Hinshaw, S.P., Arnold, L.E., Pelham, W.E., Molina, B.S.G., Abikoff, H.B., Epstein, J.N., Greenhill, L.L., Hechtman, L., Odbert, C., Swanson, J.M., & Wigal, T. (2004). Self-perceptions of competence in children with ADHD and comparison children. *Journal of Consulting and Clinical Psychology, 72,* 382–391.

Hoza, B., Mrug, S., Pelham, W.E., Greiner, A.R., & Gnagy, E.M. (2003). A friendship intervention for children with attention-deficit/hyperactivity disorder: Preliminary findings. *Journal of Attention Disorders, 6,* 87–98.

Hoza, B., Pelham, W.E., Dobbs, J., Owens, J.S., & Pillow, D.R. (2002). Do boys with Attention-Deficit/Hyperactivity Disorder have positive illusory self-concepts? *Journal of Abnormal Psychology, 111,* 268–278.

Hoza, B., Pelham, W.E., Milich, R., Pillow, D., & McBride, K. (1993). The self-perceptions and attributions of attention deficit hyperactivity disordered and nonreferred boys. *Journal of Abnormal Child Psychology, 21,* 271–286.

Hoza, B., Pelham, W.E., Waschbusch, D.A., Kipp, H., & Owens, J.S. (2001). Academic task persistence of normally achieving ADHD and control boys: Performance, self-evaluations, and attributions. *Journal of Consulting and Clinical Psychology, 69,* 271–283.

Hubbard, J.A., & Newcomb, A.F. (1991). Initial dyadic peer interaction of attention-deficit/hyperactivity disorder and normal boys. *Journal of Abnormal Child Psychology, 19,* 179–195.

Hubka, G.B., Fulton, W.A., Shady, G.A., Champion, L.M., & Wand, R. (1988). Tourette syndrome: Impact on Canadian family functioning. *Neuroscience and Behavioral Reviews, 12,* 259–261.

Huessman, L.R., Eron, L.D. (1989). Individual differences and the trait of aggression. *European Journal of Personality, 3,* 95–106.

Huessman, L.R., & Guerra, N.G. (1997). Children's normative beliefs about aggression and aggressive behavior. *Journal of Personality and Social Psychology, 76,* 677–685.

Hughes, C. (1996). Control of action and thought: Normal development and dysfunction in autism: A research note. *Journal of Child Psychology and Psychiatry, 37,* 229–236.

Hughes, J.N., Cavell, T.A., & Grossman, P.B. (1997). A positive view of self: Risk or protection for aggressive children? *Development and Psychopathology, 9,* 75–94.

Hunt, A. (1993). Development, behaviour and seizures in 300 cases of tuberous sclerosis. *Journal of Intellectual Disability Research, 37,* 41–51.

Hunt, A., & Dennis, J. (1987). Psychiatric disorder among children with tuberous sclerosis. *Developmental Medicine and Child Neurology, 29*, 190–198.

Hupp, S.D.A., & Reitman, D. (1999). Improving sports skills and sportsmanship in children diagnosed with attention-deficit/ hyperactivity disorder. *Child and Family Behavior Therapy, 21*, 35–51.

Huson, S.M., & Hughes, R.A.C. (1994). *The neurofibromatosis: A pathogenetic and clinical overview.* London: Chapman & Hall.

Hwang, B., & Hughes, C. (2000). The effects of social interactive training on early social communicative skills of children with autism. *Journal of Autism and Developmental Disorders, 30*, 331–343.

Hyde, T.M., Aaronson, B.A., Randolph, C., Rickler, K.C., & Weinberger, D.R. (1992). Relationship of birth weight to the phenotypic expression of Gilles de la Tourette's syndrome in monozygotic twins. *Neurology, 42*, 652–658.

Hyde, T.M, & Weiberger, D.R. (1995). Tourette's syndrome: A model neuropsychiatric disorder. *Journal of the American Medical Association, 239*, 498–511.

Hyman, S.L., Shores, A., & North, K.N. (2005). The nature and frequency of cognitive deficits in children with neurofibromatosis type 1. *Neurology, 65*, 1037–1044.

Hymel, S., Bowker, A., & Woody, E. (1993). Aggressive versus *withdrawn,* unpopular children: Variations in peer and self-perceptions in multiple domains. *Child Development, 64*, 879–896.

Isley, S.L., O'Neil, R., Clatfelter, D., & Parke, R. D. (1999). Parent and child expressed affect and children's social competence: Modeling direct and indirect pathways. *Developmental Psychology, 35*, 547–560.

Jacobson, A.M., Hauser, S.T., Lavori, P., Wolfsdorf, J.I., Herskowitz, R.D., Milley, J.E., Bliss, R., Gelfand, E., Wertlieb, D., & Stein, J. (1990). Adherence among children and adolescents with insulin-dependent diabetes mellitus over a four-year longitudinal follow-up: I. The influence of patient coping and adjustment. *Journal of Pediatric Psychology, 15*, 511–526.

Janos, P.M., Marwood, K.A., & Robinson, N.M. (1985). Friendship patterns in highly intelligent children. *Roeper Review, 8*, 46–49.

Janos, P.M., Robinson, N.M., & Lunneborg, C.E. (1989). Markedly early entrance to college: A multi-year comparative study of academic performance and psychological adjustment. *Journal of Higher Education, 60*, 496–518.

Janusz, J.A., Kirkwood, M.W., Yeates, K.O., & Taylor, H.G. (2002). Social problem-solving skills in children with traumatic brain injury: Long-term outcomes and prediction of social competence. *Child Neuropsychology, 8*, 179–194.

Jenkins, J.R., Odom, S.L., & Speltz, M.L. (1989). Effects of social integration on preschool children with handicaps. *Exceptional Children, 55*, 420–428.

Johnson, D.J. (1987). Nonverbal learning disabilities. *Pediatric Annals, 16*, 133–141.

Johnson, D.J., & Blalock, J. (1987). *Adults with learning disabilities.* New York: Grune & Stratton.

Johnson, N.S., Saal, H.M., Lovell, A.M., & Schorry, E.K. (1999). Social and emotional problems in children with neurofibromatosis type 1: Evidence and proposed interventions. *Journal of Pediatrics, 134*, 767–772.

Johnston, C. (1996). Parent characteristics and parent-child interactions in families of nonproblem children and ADHD children with higher and lower levels of oppositional-defiant behavior. *Journal of Abnormal Child Psychology, 24*, 85–104.

Johnston, C. & Pelham, W.E. (1986). Teacher ratings predict peer ratings of aggression at 3-year follow-up in boys with attention deficit disorder with hyperactivity. *Journal of Consulting and Clinical Psychology, 54*, 571–572.

Joiner, T. (1999). A test of interpersonal theory of depression in youth psychiatric inpatients. *Journal of Abnormal Child Psychology, 3*, 77–85.

Joiner, T., & Coyne, J.C. (1999). *The interactional nature of depression*. Washington, DC: American Psychological Association.

Joiner, T., & Wagner, K.D. (1995). Attributional style and depression in children and adolescents: A meta-analytic view. *Clinical Psychology Review, 15,* 777–798.

Joinson, C., O'Callaghan, F.J., Osborne, J.P., Martyn, C., Harris, T., & Bolton, P.F. (2003). Learning disability and epilepsy in an epidemiological sample of individuals with tuberous sclerosis complex. *Psychological Medicine, 33,* 335–344.

Jones, D.C., (1992). Parental divorce, family conflict, and friendship networks. *Journal of Social and Personal Relationships, 9,* 219–235.

Jones, S.H., Tai, S., Evershed, K., Knowles, R., & Bentall, R. (2006). Early detection of bipolar disorder: A pilot familial high-risk study of parents with bipolar disorder and their adolescent children. *Bipolar Disorder, 8,* 362–372.

Joseph, J. (1979). *Joseph Pre-school and Primary Self-Concept Screening Test.* Wood Dale, IL: Stoelting.

Joseph, R.M., & Tager-Flusberg, H. (2004). The relationship of theory of mind and executive functions to symptom type and severity in children with autism. *Development and Psychopathology, 16,* 137–155.

Judd, L.L., & Akiskal, H.W. (2003). The prevalence and disability of bipolar spectrum disorders in the U.S. population: Re-analysis of the ECA database taking into account subthreshold cases. *Journal of Affective Disorders, 73,* 123–131.

Jurado, L.A.P., Peoples, R., Kaplan, P., Hamel, B.C.J., & Francke, U. (1996). Molecular definition of the chromosome 7 deletions in Williams syndrome and parent-of-origin effects on growth. *American Journal of Human Genetics, 59,* 781–792.

Kagan, J. (1994). *Galen's prophecy.* New York: Basic Books.

Kagan, J., Reznick, S.J., Clarke, C., Snidman, N., & Garcia-Coll, C. (1984). Behavioral inhibition toward the unfamiliar. *Child Development, 55,* 2212–2225.

Kagan, J., Reznick, S.J., & Gibbons, J. (1989). Inhibited and uninhibited types of children. *Child Development, 60,* 838–845.

Kane, P., & Garber, J. (2004). The relations among depression in fathers, children's psychopathology, and father-child conflict: A meta-analysis. *Clinical Psychology Review, 24,* 339–360.

Kashani, J.H., Beck, N.C., Hoeper, E.W., Fallahi, C., Corcoran, M.A., McAllister, J.A., Rosenberg, T.K., & Reid, J.C. (1987). Psychiatric disorders in a community sample of adolescents. *American Journal of Psychiatry, 144,* 584–589.

Kaufmann, F.A., & Castellanos, F.X. (2000). Attention-deficit/hyperactivity disorder in gifted students. In K.A. Heller, F.J. Monks, R.J. Sternberg, & R.F. Subotnik (Eds.), *International handbook of giftedness and talent* (2nd ed., pp. 621–632). Amsterdam: Elsevier.

Kaufmann, F.A., Castellanos, F.X. & Rotatori, A.F. (1986). Counseling the gifted child. In A.F. Rotatori, P.J. Gerber, & F.W. Litton (Eds.), *Counseling exceptional students* (pp. 232–251). New York: Human Sciences Press, Inc.

Kavale, K.A. (1984). Potential advantages of the meta-analysis technique for special education. *Journal of Special Education, 18,* 61–72.

Kavale, K.A., & Forness, S.R. (1995). Social skill deficits and training: A meta-analysis of the research in learning disabilities. *Advances in Learning and Behavioral Disabilities, 9,* 119–160.

Kavale, K.A., & Mostert, M.P. (2004). Social skills interventions for individuals with learning disabilities. *Learning Disability Quarterly, 27,* 31–42.

Kazak, A.E. (1994). Implications of survival: Pediatric oncology patients and their families. In D.J. Bearison and R.K. Mulhern (Eds.), *Pediatric pscyhooncology: Psychological perspectives on children with cancer.* New York: Oxford University Press.

Kazdin, A. (1987). *Conduct disorders in childhood and adolescence.* London: Sage.

Kazdin, A.E. (1987). *Treatment of antisocial behavior in children and adolescents.* Homewood, IL: Dorsey Press.

Keiley, M.K. (2002). Affect regulation and the gifted. In M. Neihart, S.M. Reis, N.M. Robinson, & S.M. Moon (Eds.), *The social and emotional development of gifted children* (pp. 41–50). Waco, TX: Prufrock Press.

Keirouz, K.S. (1990). Concerns of parents of gifted children: A research review. *Gifted Child Quarterly, 34,* 56–63.

Kellner, R., Houghton, S., & Graham, D. (2003). Peer-related personal experiences of children with attention-deficit/hyperactivity disorder with and without comorbid learning disabilities. *International Journal of Disability, Development, and Education, 50,* 119–136.

Kemper, T.L., & Bauman, M. (1998). Neuropathology of infantile autism. *Journal of Neuropathology and Experimental Neurology, 57,* 645–652.

Kempton, S., Vance, A., Maruff, P., Luk, E., Costin, J., & Pantelis, C. (1999). Executive function and attention deficit hyperactivity disorder: Stimulant medication and better executive function performance in children. *Psychological Medicine, 29,* 527–538.

Kendall, P.C., Panichelli-Mindel, S.M., Sugarman, A., & Callahn, S.A. (1997). Exposure to child anxiety: Theory, research, and practice. *Clinical Psychology: Science and Practice, 4,* 29–39.

Kendall, P.C., Stark, K.D., & Adam, T. (1990). Cognitive deficit or cognitive distortion in childhood depression. *Journal of Abnormal Child Psychology, 18,* 255–270.

Keogh, B.K., Garnier, H.E., Bernheimer, L.P., & Gallimore, R. (2000). Models of child-family interactions for children with developmental delays: Child-driven or transactional? *American Journal on Mental Retardation, 105,* 32–46.

Kerbeshian, J., Burd, L., & Fisher, F. (1990). Asperger's syndrome: To be or not to be? *British Journal of Psychiatry, 156,* 721–725.

Kerns, K.A., Cole, A.K., & Andrews, P.B. (1998). Attachment security, parent peer management practices, and peer relationships in preschoolers. *Merrill-Palmer Quarterly, 44,* 504–522.

Kerr, A. (2002). Rett syndrome: Recent progress and implications for research and clinical practice. *Journal of Child Psychology and Psychiatry, 43,* 277–287.

Kiesner, J. (2002). Depressive symptoms in early adolescence: Their relations with classroom problem behavior and peer status. *Journal of Research on Adolescence, 12,* 463–478.

Kiesner, J., Cainu, M., Poulin, F., & Bucci, M. (2002). Group identification in early adolescence: Its relation with peer adjustment and its moderator effect on peer influence. *Child Development, 73,* 196–208.

Kim, J.A., Szatmari, P., Bryson, S.E. et al. (2000). The prevalence of anxiety and mood problems among children with autism and Asperger Syndrome. *Autism, 4,* 117–132.

King, S.R. (1993). Agreement across self, peer, parent, and teacher versions of the MASP: A validation study. Unpublished manuscript. Cited in Cavell, T.A., Meehan, B.T., & Fiala, S.E. (2003). Assessing social competence in children and adolescents. In C.R. Reynolds & R.W. Kamphaus (eds.). *Handbook of psychological and educational assessment of children: Personality, behavior, and context* (pp. 433–454). New York: Guilford Press.

Klein, D.N., Depue, R.A., & Slater, J.F. (1985). Cyclothymia in the adolescent offspring of parents with bipolar affective disorder. *Journal of Abnormal Psychology, 94,* 115–127.

Klein, H.A. (1992). Temperament and self-esteem in late adolescence. *Adolescence, 27,* 689–695.

Klein, R.G., Abikoff, H., Hechtman, L., & Weiss, G. (2004). Design and rationale of controlled study of long-term methylphenidate and multimodal psychosocial treatment in children with ADHD. *Journal of the American Academy of Child and Adolescent Psychiatry, 43,* 792–801.

Klin, A., Jones, W., Schultz, R., & Volkmar, F.R. (2003). The Enactive Mind—from actions to cognition: Lessons from autism. Philosophical Transactions of the Royal Society. *Biological Sciences, 358,* 345–360.

Klin, A., Jones, W., Schultz, R., Volkmar, F., & Cohen, D. (2002). Defining and quantifying the social phenotype in autism. *American Journal of Psychiatry, 159,* 895–908.

Klin, A., & Volkmar, F.R. (1995). Autism and the pervasive developmental disorders. *Child and Adolescent Psychiatric Clinics of North America, 4,* 617–630.

Klin, A., & Volkmar, F.R. (1997). Asperger syndrome. In D. Cohen & F.R. Volkmar (Eds.), *Handbook of autism and pervasive developmental disorders* (2nd edition, pp. 94–112). New York: John Wiley & Sons.

Klin, A., Volkmar, F.R., Sparrow, S.S., Cichetti, D.V., & Rourke, B.P. (1995). Validity and neuorpsychological characterization of Asperger syndrome: Convergence with nonverbal learning disabilities syndrome. *Journal of Child Psychology and Psychiatry, 36,* 1127–1140.

Klingner, J.K., Vaughn, S., Schumm, J.S., Cohen, P., & Forgan, J.W. (1998). Inclusion or pull-out: Which do students prefer? *Journal of Learning Disabilities, 31,* 148–158.

Kloomak, S. & Cosden, M. (1994). Self-concept in children with learning disabilities: The relationship between global self-concept, academic "discounting," and nonacademic self-concept and perceived social support. *Learning Disability Quarterly, 17,* 140–153.

Klorman, R., Hazel-Fernandez, L.A., Shaywitz, S.E., Fletcher, J.M., Marchione, K.E., Holahan, J.M., Stueving, K.K., & Shaywitz, B.A. (1999). Executive functioning deficits in attention-deficit/hyperactivity disorder are independent of oppositional defiant disorder or reading disorder. *Journal of the American Academy of Child and Adolescent Psychiatry, 38,* 1148–1156.

Knowles, B., Bentall, R.P., Jones, S., & Tai, S. (2003). Coping with depression and fluctuations of self-esteem in relation to vulnerability to bipolar disorder. *Proceedings of the British Psychological Society, 11,* 291.

Konstantareas, M.M., & Homatidis, S. (1991). Effects of developmental disorder on parents: Theoretical and applied considerations. *Psychiatric Clinics of North America, 14,* 183–198.

Kopp, C. (1982). Antecedents of self-regulation: A developmental perspective. *Developmental Psychology, 18,* 199–214.

Kopp, C.B. (1990). The growth of self-monitoring among young children with Down Syndrome. In D. Cicchetti & M. Beeghly (Eds.), *Children with Down syndrome: A developmental perspective* (pp. 231–251). Cambridge: Cambridge University Press.

Kopp, C.B., Baker, B.I., & Brown, K.W. (1992). Social skills and their correlates: Preschoolers with developmental delays. *American Journal on Mental Retardation, 97,* 393–404.

Korkman, M., & Pesonen, A.E. (1994). A comparison of neuropsychological test profiles of children with attention deficit hyperactivity disorder and/or learning disorder. *Journal of Learning Disabilities, 37,* 383–392.

Kortlander, E., Kendall, P.C., & Panichelli-Mindel, S.M. (1997). Maternal beliefs about coping in clinically anxious children. *Journal of Anxiety Disorders, 11,* 297–315.

Kotler, J.C., & McMahon, R.J. (2002). Differentiating anxious, aggressive, and socially competent preschool children: Validation of the Social Cometpence and Behavior Evaluation-30 (parent version). *Behaviour Research and Therapy, 40*, 947–959.

Kovacs, M. (1979). *Children's Depression Inventory.* Pittsburgh, PA: Author.

Kovacs, M., & Beck, A.T. (1977). An empirical-clinical approach toward a definition of childhood depression. In J.G. Schulterbrandt & A. Raskin (Eds.), *Depression in childhood: Diagnosis, treatment, and conceptual models* (pp. 1–25). New York: Raven.

Kraus, J.F. (1995). Epidemiological features of brain injury in children: Occurrence, children at risk, causes and manner of injury, severity, and outcomes. In S.H. Broman and M.E. Michel (Eds.), *Traumatic head injury in children* (pp. 22–39). New York: Oxford University Press.

Krauss, M.W. (1993). Child-related and parenting stress: Similarities and differences between mothers and fathers of children with disabilities. *American Journal on Mental Retardation, 97*, 393–404.

Kucharska-Pietura, K., Phillips, M.L., Gernand, W., & David, A.S. (2003). Perception of emotion from faces and voices following unilateral brain damage. *Neuropsychologia, 41*, 1082–1090.

Kuhne, M., & Wiener, J. (2000). Stability of social status of children with and without learning disabilities. *Learning Disabilities Quarterly, 23*, 64–75.

Kupersmidt, J.B., Coie, J.D., & Dodge, K.A. (1990). Predicting disorder from peer social problems. In S.R. Asher & J.D. Coie (Eds.), *Peer rejection in childhood.* New York: Cambridge Press.

Kurdek, L.A., & Krile, D. (1982). A developmental analysis of the relation between peer acceptance and both interpersonal understanding and perceived social self-competence. *Child Development, 53*, 1485–1491.

Kurita, H. (1985). Infantile autism with speech loss before the age of thirty months. *Journal of the American Academy of Child Psychiatry, 24*, 191–196.

Ladd, G.W. (1981). Effectiveness of a social learning method for enhancing children's social interaction and peer acceptance. *Child Development, 52*, 171–178.

Ladd, G. W., & Emerson, E.S. (1984). Shared knowledge in children's friendships. *Developmental Psychology, 20*, 932–940.

Ladd, G.W. & Golter, B.S. (1988). Parents' management of preschooler's peer relations: Is it related to children's social competence? *Developmental Psychology, 14*, 109–117.

Ladd, G. W., & Hart, C.H. (1992). Creating informal play opportunitites: Are parents' and preschoolers' initiations related to children's competence with peers? *Developmental Psychology, 28*, 1179–1187.

Ladd, G. W., & Price, J. (1987). Predicting children's social and school adjustment following the transition from preschool to kindergarten. *Child Development, 58*, 1168–1189.

LaFreniere, P.J., & Dumas, J.E. (1996). Social competence and behavior evaluation in children ages 3 to 6 years: the short form (SCBE-30). *Psychological Assessment, 8*, 369–377.

LaFrance, E.B. (1995). Creative thinkiing differences in three groups of exceptional children as expresed through completion of figural forms. *Roeper Review. 17*, 248–252.

LaGreca, A.M., & Stone, W.L. (1990). Children with learning disabilites: The role of achievement in their social, personal and behavioral functioning. In H.L. Swanson and B. Keogh (Eds.), *Learning disabilities: Theoretical and research issues* (pp. 333–352). Hillsdale, NJ: Erlbaum.

Lahey, B.B., Loeber, R., Burke, J., Rathouz, P.J., & McBurnett, K. (2002). Waxing and waning in concert: Dynamic comorbidity of conduct disorder and other disruptive and emotional problems over 17 years among clinic-referred boys. *Journal of Abnormal Psychology, 111,* 556–557.

Lahey, B.B., Loeber, R., Quay, H.C., & Frick, P.J. (1992). Oppositional defiant and conduct disorders: Issues to be resolved for DSM-IV. *Journal of the American Academy of Child and Adolescent Psychiatry, 31,* 539–546.

Lahey, B.B., Loeber, R., Quay, H.C., Frick, P.J., & Grimm, J. (1984). Treatment and generalization effects of cognitive-behavioral and goal-setting interventions with aggressive boys. *Journal of Consulting and Clinical Psychology, 52,* 915–916.

Landry, S.H., & Chapieski, M.L. (1998). Joint attention and infant toy exploration: Effects of Down syndrome and prematurity. *Child Developoment, 60,* 103–118.

Landry, S.H., Garner, P.W., Pirie, D., & Swank, P.R. (1994). Effects of social context on mothers' requesting strategies on Down's Syndrome Children's Social Responsiveness. *Developmental Psychology, 30,* 293–302.

Lainhart, J.E., Oxonoff, S., & Cooh, H. (2002). Autism, regression, and the broader autism phenotype. *American Journal of Medical Genetics, 113,* 231–237.

Lainhart, J.E., Piven, J., Wzorek, M., Landa, R., Santangelo, S.L., Coon, H., & Folstein, S.E. (1997). Macrocephaly in children and adults with autism. *Journal of the American Academy of Child and Adolescent Psychiatry, 36,* 282–290.

Laird, R.D., Pettit, G.S., Mize, J., Brown, E.G., & Lindsey, E. (1994). Mother-child conversations about peers: Contributions to competence. *Family Relations, 43,* 425–432.

Laman, D.S., & Reiss, S. (1987). Social skill deficiencies associated with depressed mood in mentally retarded adults. *American Journal of Mental Deficiency, 92,* 224–229.

Landau, S., Milich, R., Diener, M.B. (1998). Peer relations of children with attention-deficit hyperactivity disorder. *Reading and Writing Quarterly, 14,* 83–106.

Landau, S., & Moore, L.A. (1991). Social skill deficits in children with attention-deficit/hyperactivity disorder. *School Psychology Review, 20,* 235–251.

Landsheer, H.A., Maassen, G.H., Bisschop, P., Adema, L. (1998). Can higher grades result in fewer friends? A re-examination of the relation between academic and social competence. *Adolescence, 33,* 185–192.

Laor, N., Wolmer, L., & Cicchetti, D.V. (2001). The Comprehensive Assessment of Defense Style: Measuring defense mechanisms in children and adolescents. *Journal of Nervous and Mental Disease, 189,* 360–368.

Lapadat, J.C. (1991). Pragmatic language skills of students with language and/or learning disabilities: A quantitative synthesis. *Journal of Learning Disabilities, 24,* 147–158.

Lawrence, V., Houghton, S., Tannock, R., Douglas, G., Durkin, K., & Whiting, K. (2002). ADHD outside the laboratory: Boys' executive function performance on tasks in videogame play and on a visit to the zoo. *Journal of Abnormal Child Psychology, 30,* 447–462.

Leal, D., Kearney, K., & Kearney, C. (1995). The world's youngest university graduate: Examining the unusual characteristics of profoundly gifted children. *Gifted Child Today, 18,* 26–31,41.

Leanh, N., & Frye, D. (1999). Children's theory of mind: Understanding of desire, belief, and emotion with social referents. *Social Development, 8,* 70–92.

Leaper, C. (1994). (Ed.) Exploring the consequences of gender segregation on social relationships. *Childhood gender segregation: Causes and consequences* (pp. 67–86). San Francisco: Jossey-Bass.

Leckman, J.F., Walker, D.E., Goodman, W.K., Pauls, D.L., & Cohen, D.J. (1994). "Just right" perceptions associated with compulsive behaviors in Tourette's syndrome. *American Journal of Psychiatry, 151*, 675–680.

LeCouteur, A., Bailey, A.J., & Goode, S. (1996). A broader phenotype of autism: the clinical spectrum in twins. *Journal of Child Psychology and Psychiatry, 37*, 785–801.

LeFrancois, G.R. (1995). *An introduction to child development* (8th ed.). Belmont, CA: Wadsworth.

Lempers, J.D., & Clarke-Lempers, D.S. (1992). Young, middle, and late adolescents comparisons of the functional importance of five significant relationships, *Journal of Youth and Adolescence, 21*, 54–96.

Lenane, M. (1989). Families and obsessive-compulsive disorder. In J.L. Rapoport (Ed.), *Obsessive-compulsive disorder in children and adolescents* (pp. 237–249). Washington, DC: American Psychiatric Association.

Lengua, L.L. (2002). The contribution of emotionality and self-regulation to the understanding of children's response to multiple risk. *Child Development, 73*, 144–161.

Lengua, L.L. (2003). Associations among emotionality, self-regulation, adjustment problems, and positive adjustment in middle childhood. *Applied Developmental Psychology, 24*, 595–618.

Lengua, L.L., West, S.G., & Sandler, I.N. (1998). Temperament as a predictor of symptomatology in children: Addressing contamination of measures. *Child Development, 69*, 164–181.

Lenhart, L.A., & Rabiner, D.L. (1995). An integrative approach to the study of social competence in adolescence. *Development and Psychopathology, 7*, 543–561.

Leroux, J.A., & Levitt-Perlman, M. (2000). The gifted child with attention deficit disorder: An identification and intervention challenge. *Roeper Review, 22*, 171–176.

Lewinsohn, P.M., Olino, T.M., & Klein, D.N. (2005). Psychosocial impairment in offspring of depressed parents. *Psychological Medicine, 35*, 1–11.

Lewis, J.C., Thomas, H.V., Murphy, K.C., & Sampson, J.R. (2004). Genotype and psychological phenotype in tuberous sclerosis. *Journal of Medical Genetics, 41*, 203–207.

Lezak, M. (1995). *Neuropsychological Assessment.* New York: Oxford University Press.

Liles, B.Z. (1993). Narrative discourse in children with language disorders and children with normal language: A critical review of the literature. *Journal of Speech and Hearing Research, 36*, 868–882.

Lincoln, A., Courchesne, E., Allen, M., Hanson, E., Ene, M. (1998). Neurobiology of Asperger syndrome: Seven case studies and quantitative magnetic resonance imaging findings. In E. Schopler, G.B. Mesibov, & L.J. Kunc (Eds.), *Asperger syndrome or high functioning autism?* (pp. 145–166). New York: Plenum Press.

Lindsey, E.W., & Colwell, M.J. (2003). Preschoolers' emotional competence: Links to pretend and physical play. *Child Study Journal, 33*, 39–52.

Liss, D.S., Waller, D.A., Kennard, B.D., McIntire, D., Capra, P., & Stephens, J. (1998). Psychiatric illness and family support in children and adolescents with diabetic ketoacidosis: A controlled study. *Journal of the American Academy of Child and Adolescent Psychiatry, 37*, 536–544.

Listernick, R., Darling, C., Greenwald, M., Strauss, L., & Charrow, J. (1995). Optic pathway tumors in children: the effect of neurofibromatosis 1 on clinical manifestations and natural history. *Journal of Pediatrics, 127*, 718–722.

Lochman, J.E., & Dodge, K.A. (1994). Social-cognitive processes of severly violent, moderately aggressive, and nonaggressive boys. *Journal of Consulting and Clinical Psychology, 62*, 366–374.

Lochman, J.E., Wayland, K.K., & White, K.J. (1993). Social goals: Relationship to adolescent adjustment and to social problem solving. *Journal of Abnormal Child Psychology, 21*, 135–151.

Lochman, J.E., & Wells, K.C. (2004). The Coping Power program for preadolescent aggressive boys and their parents: Outcome effects at the one-year follow-up. *Journal of Consulting and Clinical Psychology, 72*, 571–578.

Loeber, R. (1991). Antisocial behavior: More enduring than changeable? *Journal of the American Academy of Child and Adolescent Psychiatry, 30*, 393–397.

Logie, R.H. (1995). *Visuo-spatial working memory.* Hove, England: Erlbaum.

Lonigan, C.J., & Phillips, B.M. (2001). Temperamental influences on the development of anxiety disorders. In M.W. Vesey and M.R. Dadds (Eds.), *The developmental psychopathology of anxiety* (pp. 60–91). New York: Oxford University Press.

Lord, C., & Paul, R. (1997). Language and communication in autism. In D. Cohen & F. Volkmar (eds.), *Handbook of autism and pervasive developmental disorders* (2nd ed., pp. 195–225). New York: Wiley.

Lord, C., & McGee, J.P. (2001). *Educating children with autism.* Washington, DC: National Academy Press.

Lord, C., Schopler, E., & Revicki, D. (1982). Sex differences in autism. *Journal of Autism and Developmental Disorders, 12*, 317–330.

Lovaas, O.I. (1987). Behavioral treatment and normal educational and intellectual functioning in young autistic children. *Journal of Consulting and Clinical Psychology, 55*, 3–9.

Lloyd-Still (1983). *Textbook of Cystic Fibrosis.* Boston: Wright.

Luftig, R.L., & Nichols, M.L. (1990). Assessing the social status of gifted students by their age peers. *Gifted Child Quarterly, 34*, 111–115.

Luoma, I., Koivisto, A-M., & Tamminen, T. (2004). Fathers' and mothers' perceptions of their child and maternal depressive symptoms. *Nordic Journal of Psychiatry, 58*, 206–211.

Luoma, I., Tamminen, T., Kaukonen, P., Laippala, P., Puura, K., Salmelin, R., & Almquist, F. (2001). Longitudinal study of maternal depressive symptoms and child well-being. *Journal of the American Academy of Child and Adolescent Psychiatry, 40*, 1367–1374.

Luria, A.S. (1980). *Higher cortical functions of man.* New York: Plenum Press.

Lyon, G.R. (1994). Frames of reference for the assessment of learning disabilities: New views on measurement issues. Baltimore, MD: Paul H. Brookes.

Lyon, G.R. (1996a). Learning disabilities. *Special Education for Students with Disabilities, 6*, 54–76.

Lyon, G.R. (1996b). *Learning disabilities.* In E. Marsh and R.A. Barkely, (Eds.), Child psychopathology (pp. 390–434). New York: Guilford Press.

Maccoby, E.E., & Jacklin, C.N. (1987). Gender segregation in childhood. In H.W. Reese (Ed.), *Advances in child development and behavior* (Vol. 20, pp. 239–288). Orlando, FL: Academic Press.

Madan-Swain, A., Brown, R.T., Walco, G.A., Cherrick, I., Ievers, C.E., Conte, P.M., Vega, R., Bell, B., & Lauer, S.J. (1998). Cognitive, academic, and psychosocial late effects among children previously treated for acute lymphocytic leukemia receiving chemotherapy as CNS prophylaxis. *Journal of Pediatric Psychology, 23*, 333–340.

Maassen, G.H., Akkermans, W., & Van der Linden, J.L. (1996). Two-dimensional sociometric status determination with rating scales. *Small Group Research, 27*, 56–78.

Maassen, G.H., & Vershueren, K. (2005). A two-dimensional ratings-based procedure for sociometric status determination as an alternative to the Asher and Dodge system. *Merrill-Palmer Quarterly, 51*, 192–212.

Magill-Evans, J., Koning, C., Cameron-Sadava, A., & Manyk, K. (1996). *Child and adolescent social perception measure*. Alberta, Canada: Authors.

Malloy, T.E., Yarlas, A.S., Montvilo, R.K., Sugarman, D.B. (1996). Agreement and accuracy in children's interpersonal perceptions: A social relations analysis. *Journal of Personality and Social Psychology, 71*, 692–702.

Mannuzza, S., Gittelman, R., Konig, P.H., & Giampino, T.L. (1989). Hyperactive boys almost grown up: IV. Criminality and its relationship to psychiatric status. *Archives of General Psychiatry, 46*, 1073–1079.

Mannuzza, S., Klein, R.G., Bessler, A., Malloy, P., & LaPadula, M. (1993). Adult outcome of hyperactive boys. *Archives of General Psychiatry, 50*, 565–576.

Marfo, K. (1990). Maternal directiveness in interactions with mentally handicapped children: An analytical commentary. *Journal of Child Psychology and Psychiatry, 31*, 531–549.

Margalit, M. (1995). Social skills learning for students with learning disabilities and students with behavior disorders. *Educational Psychology, 15*, 445–457.

Margalit, M. (1998a). Sense of coherence and loneliness experience among kindergarten children with learning disabilities. *Journal of Learning Disabilities, 31*, 173–180.

Margalit, M. (1998b). Loneliness and coherence among preschool children with learning disabilities. *Journal of Learning Disabilities, 31*, 173–181.

Margalit, M., & Eysenck, S. (1990). Prediction of coherence in adolescence: Gender differences in social skills, personality, and family climate. *Journal of Research in Personality, 24*, 510–521.

Margalit, M., & Levin-Alyagon, M. (1994). Learning disability subtyping, loneliness, and classroom adjustment. *Learning Disability Quarterly, 17*, 297–310.

Martin, A., & Weiberg, J. (2003). Neural foundations for understanding social and mechanical concepts. *Cognitive Neuropsychology, 20*, 575–587.

Martinez, R., & Semrud-Clikeman, M. (2004). Emotional Adjustment of Young Adolescents with Different Learning Disability Subtypes. *Journal of Learning Disabilities, 37*. 411–420.

Masten, A.S., Coatsworth, J.D., Neemann, J., Gest, S.D., Tellegen, A., & Garmezy, N. (1995). The structure and coherence of competence from childhood through adolescence. *Child Development, 66*, 1635–1659.

Masten, A.S., Morison, P., & Pelligrini, D.S. (1985). A revised class play method of peer assessment. *Developmental Psychology, 21*, 523–533.

Maston, J.L., Smiroldo, B.B., & Bamburg, J.W. (1998). The relationship of social skills to psychopathology for individuals with severe or profound mental retardation. *Journal of Intellectual and Developmental Disability, 23*, 137–145.

Matson, J.L. (1994). *Autism in children and adults: Etiology, assessment, and intervention*. Pacific Grove, CA: Brooks/Cole.

Matson, J.L., Helsel, W.J., Bellack, A.S., & Senatore, V. (1983). Development of a rating scale to assess social skill deficits in mentally retarded adults. *Applied Research in Mental Retardation, 4*, 399–407.

Matson, J.L., Rotari, A.F., & Helsel, W.J. (1983). Development of a rating scale to measure social skills in children: The Matson Evaluation of Social Skills with Youngsters (MESSY). *Behaviour Research and Therapy, 21*, 335–340.

Matthews, K.A., Woodall, K.L., Kenyon, K., & Jacob, T. (1996). Negative family environment as a predictor of boys' future status on measures of hostile attitudes, interview behavior, and anger expression. *Health Psychology, 15*, 30–37.

Matthews, M., Eustace, C., Grad, G., Pelcovita, D., & Olson, M. (1985). A family systems perspective on Tourette's syndrome. *International Journal of Family Psychiatry, 6*, 53–66.

Mayeux, L., & Cillessen, A.H.N. (2003). Development of social problem solving in early childhood: Stability, change, and associations with social competence. *Journal of Genetic Psychology, 164*, 153–173.

Maziade, M., Cote, R., Bernier, H., Boutin, P., & Thivierge, J. (1989). Significance of extreme temperament in infancy for clinical status in preschool years I. *British Journal of Psychiatry, 14,* 535–543.

McBride, S., & Belsky, J. (1988). Characteristics, determinants, and consequences of maternal separation anxiety. *Developmental Psychology, 24,* 407–414.

McCallister, C., Nash, W.R., & Meckstroth, E. (1996). The social competence of gifted children: Experiments and experience. *Roeper Review, 18,* 273–276.

McCauley, E., Ross, J.L., Kushner, H., & Cutler, G. (1995). Self-esteem and behavior in girls with Turner syndrome. *Developmental and Behavioral Pediatrics, 16,* 82–88.

McCoy, J.K., Brody, G.H., & Stoneman, Z. (1994). A longitudinal analysis of sibling relationships as mediators of the link between family processes and youths' best friendships. *Family Relations, 43,* 400–408.

McCusker, C., Kennedy, P., Anderson, J., Hicks, E., & Harahan, D. (2002). Adjustment in children with intractable epilepsy: Importance of seizure duration and family factors. *Developmental Medicine and Child Neurology, 44,* 681–687.

McDowell, D.J., & Parke, R.D. (2000). Differential knowledge of display rules for positive and negative emotions: Influence for parents, influence on peers. *Social Development, 9,* 415–432.

McDowell, D.J., Parke, R.D., & Wang, S.J. (2003). Differences between mothers' and fathers' advice-giving style and content: relations with social competence and psychological functioning in middle childhood. *Merrill-Palmer Quarterly, 49,* 55–76.

McEachin, J.J., Smith, T., & Lovaas, O.I. (1993). Long-term outcome for children with autism who received early intensive behavioral treatment. *American Journal of Mental Retardation, 97,* 359–372.

McGee, G.G., Morrier, M.J., & Daly, T. (1999). An incidental teaching approach to early intervention for toddlers with autism. *Journal of the Association for Persons with Severe Handicaps, 24,* 133–146.

McGee, J.J., & Menolascino, F.J. (1990). Depression in persons with mental retardation: Toward an existential analysis. In A. Dosen and F.J. Menolascino (Eds.), *Depression in mentally retarded children and adults* (pp. 95–112). Netherlands: Logon Publications.

McGee, R. & Williams, S. (1991). Social competence in adolescence: Preliminary findings from a longitudinal study of New Zealand 15-year olds. *Psychiatry: Journal for the Study of Interpersonal Processes, 54,* 281–291.

McGough, J.J., Speier, P.L., & Cantwell, D.P. (1993). Obsessive-compulsive disorder in childhood and adolescence. *School Psychology Review, 22,* 1–10.

McHale, S.M., Dariotis, J.K., & Kauh, T.J. (2003). Social development and social relationships in middle childhood. In R. M. Lerner & M.A. Easterbrooks (Eds.), *Handbook of psychology: Developmental Psychology* (pp. 241–265). New York: John Wiley & Sons.

McKelvey, J.R., Lambert, R., Mottron, L., & Shevell, M.I. (1995). Right hemisphere dysfunction in Asperger's syndrome. *Journal of Child Neurology, 10,* 310–314.

McLaughlin-Cheng, E. (1998). Asperger syndrome and autism: A literature review and meta-analysis. *Focus on Autism and Other Developmental Disorders, 4,* 234–245.

McMahon, R.J., & Forehand, R. (1984). Parent training for the noncompliant child: Treatment outcome, generalization, and adjunctive therapy procedures. In R.F. Dangel and R.A. Polster (Eds.), *Parent training: Foundations of research and practice* (pp. 298–328). New York: Guilford Press.

McMahon, R.J., Slough, N., & the Conduct Problems Prevention Resarch Group (1996). Family-based intervention in the Fast Track Program. In R. DeV. Peters and R.J. McMahon (Eds.), *Preventing childhood disorders, substance use, and delinquency* (pp. 90–110). Thousand Oaks, CA: Sage.

Meadan, H., & Halle, J.W. (2004). Social perceptions of students with learning disabilities who differ in social status. *Learning Disabilities Research & Practice, 19*, 71–82.

Measelle, J.R., Ablow, J.C., Cowan, P.A., & Cowan, C.P. (1998). Assessing young children's views of their academic, social, and emotional lives: An evaluation of the self-perception scales of the Berkeley Puppet Interview. *Child Development, 69*, 1556–1576.

Medora, N., & Woodward, J.C. (1986). Loneliness among adolescent college students at a midwestern university. *Adolescence, 21*, 291–402.

Meichenbaum, D., Gnagy, B., Flammer, L., Molina, B., Pelham, W.E. (2001). *Why stop success? Exploration of long-term use of medication in a clinical ADHD sample from childhood through young adulthood.* Presented at the 8th Florida Conference on Child Health Psychology, Gainesville, FL.

Mendaglio, S. (1995). Sensitivity among gifted persons: A multi-faceted perspective. *Roeper Review, 17*, 169–172.

Menolascino, F. (1990). Mental retardation and the risk, nature and types of mental illness. In A. Dosen & F.J. Menolascino (Eds.), *Depression in mentally retarded children and adults* (pp. 11–34). Netherlands: Logon Publications.

Merrell, K.W., Gill, S.J., McFarland, J., & McFarland, T. (1996). Internalizing symptoms of gifted and non-gifted elementary-age students: A comparative validity study using the Internalizing Symptoms Scale for children. *Psychology in the Schools, 33*, 185–191.

Merrell, K.W., & Merz, J.M. (1992). The effect of service delivery model on the social-behavioral competence of learning disabled students. *British Columbia Journal of Special Education, 16*, 82–91.

Mervis, C.B., Klein, B.P., & Rothstein, M. (2001). Daptive behavior of 4- to 8-year-olds with Williams syndrome. *American Journal on Mental Retardation, 106*, 82–93.

Meyers, J.E., & Meyers, K.R. (1995). *The Meyers Scoring System for the Rey Complex Figure and the Recognition Trial: Professional Manual.* Odessa, FL: Psychological Assessment Resources.

Milich, R., & Dodge, K.A. (1984). Social information processing in child psychiatric populations. *Journal of Abnormal Child Psychology, 12*, 471–490.

Milich, R., & Landau, S. (1989). The role of social status variables in differentiating subgroups of hyperactive children. In L.M. Bloomingdale & J. Swanson (Eds.), *Advances in learning and behavioral disabilities* (Vol. 3, pp. 117–150). Greewich, CT: JAI Press.

Miller, L.C., Berg, J.H., & Archer, R.L. (1983). Openers: Individuals who elicit intimate self-disclosure. *Journal of Personality and Social Psychology, 44*, 1234–1244.

Miller, J., Leddy, M., Miolo, G., & Sedey, A. (1995). The development of early language skills in children with Down's syndrome. In L. Nadel and D. Rosenthal (Eds.), *Down's Syndrome: Living and learning in the community* (pp. 115–120). New York: Wiley-Liss.

Miller, J.N., & Ozonoff, S. (1997). Did Asperger's cases have Asperger disorder? *Journal of Child Psychology and Psychiatry, 38*, 247–251.

Mills, C.J. (1993). Personality, learning style, and cognitive style profiles of mathematically talented students. *European Journal for High Ability, 4*, 70–85.

Mink, I.T., & Nihira, K. (1986). Family life-styles and child behaviors: A study of direction of effects. *Developmental Psychology, 22*, 610–616.

Minner, S. (1990). Teacher evaluations of case descriptions of LD/gifted children. *Gifted Child Quarterly, 34*, 37–39.

Minshew, N.J., Goldstein, G., Taylor, H.G., & Siegel, D.J. (1994). Academic achievement in high functioning autistic individuals. *Journal of Clinical and Experimental Neuropsychology, 16*, 261–270.

Mize, J., & Pettit, G.S. (1997). Mothers' social coaching, mother-child relationship style, and children's peer competence: Is the medium the message? *Child Development, 68*, 312–322.

Mize, J., Pettit, G.S., & Brown, E.G. (1995). Mothers' supervision of their children's peer play: Relations with beliefs, perceptions, and knowledge. *Developmental Psychology, 31*, 311–324.

Mize, J., Pettit, G.S. Laird, R.D., & Lindsey, E. (1993, April). *Mothers' coaching of social skills and children's peer competence: Independent contributions of substance and style.* Paper presented at the biennial meeting of the Society for Research in Child Development, New Orleans, LA.

Moes, D.R. (1998). Integrating choice-making opportunities within teacher-assigned academic tasks to facilitate the performance of children with autism. *Journal of the Association for Persons with Severe Handicaps, 23*, 319–328.

Moffitt, T.E., (1993). The Neuropsychology of conduct disorder. *Development and Psychopathology, 5*, 135–151.

Moon, S. (2002). Gifted children with Attention-Deficit/Hyperactivity Disorder. In M. Neihart, S.M. Reis, N.M. Robinson, & S.M. Moon (Eds.), *The social and emotional development of gifted children* (pp. 193–201). Waco, TX: Prufrock Press.

Moon, S., Zentall, S., Grskovic, J., Hall, A., & Stormon-Spurgin, M. (2001). Emotional, social, and family characteristics of boys with AD/HD and giftedness: A comparative case study. *Journal for the Education of the Gifted, 24*, 207–247.

Moore, B., Ater, J., Needle, M., Slopis, J., & Copeland, D. (1994). Neuropsychological profile of children with neurofibromatosis, brain tumor, or both. *Journal of Child Neurology, 9*, 368–377.

Monsour, M. (1992). Meanings of intimacy in cross-and same-sex friendships. *Journal of Social and Personal Relationships, 9*, 277–295.

Morris, C.A., & Mervis, C.B. (1999). Williams Syndrome. In S. Goldstein and C.R. Reynolds (Eds.), *Handbook of Neurodevelopmental and genetic disorders in children* (pp. 555–590). New York: Guilford.

Morrison, G.M., & D'Incau, B. (1997). The web of zero-tolerance: Characteristics of students who are recommended for expulsion from school. *Education and Treatment of Children, 20*, 316–335.

Most, T., Al-Yagon, M., Turk-Kaspa, H., & Margalit, M. (2000). Phonological awareness, peer nominations, and social competence among kindergarten children at risk for developing learning disabilities. *International Journal of Disability, Development and Education, 47*, 89–105.

Most, T., & Greenbank, A. (2000). Auditory, visual, and auditory-visual perception of disabilities, and their relationships to social skills. *Learning Disabilities Research & Practice, 15*, 171–179.

Moulton, C., Coplan, R.J., & Mills, C. (1999). The Teaching Practices Observation Scale (TPOS): An observational taxonomy for assessing teacher-preschooler interactions during free play. *Canadian Journal of Research in Early Childhood Education, 8*, 19–30.

Mounts, N.S. (2000). Parental management of adolescent peer relationships: What are its effects on friend selection? In K.A. Kerns, J.M. Contreras, & A.M. Neal-Barnett (Eds.), *Family and peers: Linking two social worlds* (pp. 169–194). Westport, CT: Praeger.

MTA Cooperative Group (1999). A 14-monthy randomized clinical trial of treatment strategies for attention-deficit/hyperactivity disorder. *Archives of General Psychiatry, 56*, 1073–1086.

Mudford, O.C., Martin, N.T., Eikeseth, S., & Bibby, P. (2001). Parent-managed behavioral treatment for preschool children with autism: Some characteristics of UK programs. *Research in Developmental Disabilities: Special Issue, 22,* 173–182.

Muir-Broaddus, J.E., Rosenstein, L.D., Medina, D.E., & Soderberg, C. (2002). Neuropsychological test performance of children with ADHD relative to test norms and parent behavioral ratings. *Archives of Clinical Neuropsychology, 17,* 671–689.

Mulhern, R., Carpenteri, S., Shema, S., Stone, P., & Fairclough, D. (1993). Factors associated with social and behavioral problems among children recently diagnosed with brain tumors. *Journal of Pediatric Psychology, 18,* 339–350.

Mulhern, R.K., Wasserman, A.L., Friedman, A.G., & Fairclough, D. (1989). Social competence and behavioral adjustment of children who are long-term survivors of cancer. *Pediatrics, 83,* 18–25.

Mundy, P., Sigman, M., & Kasari, C. (1993). The theory of mind and joint-attention deficits in autism. In S. Cohen, H. Tager-Flusberg, & D. Cohen (Eds.), *Understanding other minds: Perspectives from autism* (pp. 181–203). Oxford, England: Oxford University Press.

Murphy, M., Bolton, P.F., Pickles, A., Fombonne, E., Piven, J., & Rutter, M. (2000). Personality traits of the relatives of autistic probands. *Psychological Medicine, 30,* 1411–1424.

Murphy, B.C., Shepard, S.A., Eisenberg, N., & Fabes, R.A. (2004). Concurrent and across time prediction of young adolescents' social functioning: The role of emotionality and regulation. *Social Development, 13,* 56–86.

Myklebust, H.R. (1975). *Progress in learning disabilities* (Vol. 3). New York: Grune & Stratton.

Nabuzoka, D., & Smith, P.K. (1993). Sociometric status and social behavior of children with and without learning disabilities. *Learning Disabilities Research & Practice, 10,* 91–101.

Nassau, J., & Drotar, D. (1997). Social competence among children with central nervous system-related chronic health conditions: A review. *Journal of Pediatric Psychology, 22,* 771–793.

National Heart, Lung, and Blood Institute. (1995). *Global strategy for asthma management and prevention.* NHBI/workshop report. March 1993. Publication Number 95–3659.

National Institutes of Health (NIH) Consensus Development Conference (1988). Neurofibromatosis: Conference statement. *Archives of Neurology, 45,* 575–578.

National Research Council (2001). *Educating young children with autism.* Washington, DC: National Academy Press.

Nelson, C.A., & Bosquet, M. (2000). Neurobiology of fetal and infant development: Implications for infant mental health. In C.H. Zeanah (Ed.), *Handbook of infant mental health* (pp. 37–59). New York: Guilford.

Nelson, K.B., Greather, J.K., Croen, L.A., Dambrosia, J.M., Dickens, B.F., Jeliffe, L.L., Hansen, R.L., & Phillips, T.M. (2001). Neuropeptides and neurotrophins in neonatal blood of children with autism or mental retardation. *Annals of Neurology, 49,* 597–606.

Nelson, K., Henseler, S., & Plesa, D. (2000). Entering a community of minds: "Theory of Mind" from a feminist standpoint. In P. Miller and E. Scholnick (Eds.), *Toward a Feminist Developmental Psychology* (pp. 61–84). New York: Routledge.

Newcomb, A.F., Bukowski, W.M., & Pattee, L. (1993). Children's peer relations: A meta-analytic review of popular, rejected, neglected, controversial and average sociometric status. *Psychological Bulletin, 113,* 99–128.

Newman, J.P., & Wallace, J.F. (1993). Diverse pathways to deficient self-regulation: Implications for disinhibitory psychopathology in children. *Clinical Psychology Review, 13,* 699–720.

Newton, J.S., Olson, D., Horner, R.H., & Ard, W.R. Jr. (1996). Social skills and the stability of social relationships between individuals with intellectual disabilities and other community members. *Research in Developmental Disabilities, 17,* 15–26.

Niehart, M. (2002). Gifted children and delinquency. In M. Neihart, S.M. Reis, N.M. Robinson, & S.M. Moon (Eds.), *The social and emotional development of gifted children* (pp. 103–112). Waco, TX: Prufrock Press.

Nieves, N. (1992). Childhood psychopathology and learning disabilities: Neuropsychological relationships. In J.E. Obrzut & G.W. Hynd (Eds.), *Neuropsychological foundations of learning disabilities* (pp. 113–145). San Diego: Academic Press.

Nigg, J.T. (2000). On inhibition/disinhibition in developmental psychopathology: Views from cognitive and personality psychology and a working inhibition taxonomy. *Psychological Bulletin, 126,* 220–246.

Nigg, J.T. (2001). Is ADHD a disinhibitory disorder? *Psychological Bulletin, 127,* 571–598.

Nigg, J.T., Blaskey, L.G., Huang-Pollock, C.L., & Rappley, M.D. (2002). Neuropsychological executive functions and DSM IV ADHD subtypes. *Journal of the American Academy of Child and Adolescent Psychiatry, 41,* 59–66

Nihira, K., Leland, H., & Lambert, N. (1993). *AAMD Adaptive Behavior Scale—Residential and Community* (2nd ed.). Austin, TX: Pro-Ed.

Nilsson, D.E., & Bradford, L.W. (1999). Neurofibromatosis. In S. Goldstein and C.R. Reynolds (Eds.), *Handbook of Neurodevelopmental and genetic disorders in children* (pp. 350–367). New York: Guilford.

Nixon, E. (2001). The social competence of children with Attention Deficit Hyperactivity Disorder: A review of the literature. *Child and Adolescent Mental Health, 6,* 172–180.

Njardvik, U., Matson, J.L., & Cherry, K.E. (1999). A comparison of social skills in adults with autistic disorder, pervasive developmental disorder not otherwise specified, and mental retardation. *Journal of Autism and Developmental Disorders, 19,* 41–55.

Njiokoktjien, C., de Rijke, W., & Jonkman, E.J. (2001). Children with nonverbal learning disabilities (NLD) coherence values in the resting state may reflect hypofunctional long distance connections in the right hemisphere. *Human Physiology, 27,* 523–528.

Nolan, S.A., Flynn, C., & Garber, J. (2003). Prospective relations between rejection and depression in young adolescents. *Journal of Personality and Social Psychology, 85,* 745–755.

Nolen-Hoeksema, S., & Girgus, J.S. (1995). Explanatory style and achievement, depression, and gender differences in childhood and early adolescence. In G.M. Buchana and M.E.P. Seligman (Eds.), *Explanatory style* (pp. 57–70). Hillsdale, NJ: Lawrence Erlbaum, Associates, Inc.

Nolen-Hoeksema, S., Girgus, J.S., & Seligman, M.E.P. (1986). Learned helplessness in children: A longitudinal study of depression, achievement, and explanatory style. *Journal of Personality and Social Psychology, 51,* 435–442.

Noll, R.B., Bukowski, W.M., Davies, W.H., Koontz, K., & Kulkarni, R. (1993). Adjustment in the peer system of children with cancer: A two-year follow-up study. *Journal of Pediatric Psychology, 18,* 351–364.

Noll, R., Gartstein, M., Vannatta, K., Correll, J., Bukowski, W. & Davies, W. (1999). Social, emotional, and behavioral functioning of children with cancer. *Pediatrics, 103,* 71–78.

Noll, R.B., MacLean, W.E., Whitt, J.K., Kaleita, T.A., Stehbens, J.A., Waskerwitz, M.J., Ruymann, F.B., & G.D. Hammond (1997). Behavioral adjustment and social functioning of long-term survivors of childhood leukemia: Parent and teacher reports. *Journal of Pediatric Psychology, 22,* 827–841.

Noom, M.J., Dekovic, M., & Meeus, W.H.J. (1999). Autonomy, attachment and psychosocial adjustment during adolescence: A double-edged sword? *Journal of Adolescence, 22,* 771–783.

Nowicki, S. (2002). *Diagnostic Analysis of Nonverbal Accuracy II.* Atlanta, GA: Dyssemia Incorporated.

Nowicki, S., & Carton, E. (1997). The relation of nonverbal processing ability of faces and voices and children's feelings of depression and competence. *The Journal of Genetic Psychology, 158,* 357–363.

Nowicki, S., & Mitchell, J. (1998). Accuracy in identifying affect in child and adolt faces and voices and social competence in preschool children. *Genetic, Social, & General Psychology Monographs, 124,* 39–59.

Nugent, S.A. (2000). Perfectionism: Its manifestations and classroom-based interventions. *Journal of Secondary Gifted Education, 11,* 215–221.

O'Donnell, D.A., Schultz, R.T., Scahill, L., Leckman, J.F., & Pauls, D.L. (2000). Social and emotional adjustment in children affected with Gilles de la Tourette's Syndrome: Associations with ADHD and family functioning. *Journal of Child Psychology and Psychiatry, 41,* 215–223.

Ohan, J.L., & Johnston, C. (2002). Are the performance overestimates given by boys with ADHD self-protective? *Journal of Clinical Child Psychology, 31,* 230–241.

O'Leary, K.D., & Emery, R.E. (1982). Marital discord and child behavior problems. In M.D. Levine and P. Satz (Eds.), *Middle childhood: Developmental variation and dysfunction* (pp. 345–364). New York: Academic Press.

Olenchak, F.R. (1994). Talent development: Accommodating the social and emotional needs of secondary gifted/learning-disabled students. *Journal of Secondary Gifted Education, 5,* 40–52.

Olenchak, F.R., & Reis, S.M. (2002). Gifted students with learning disabilities. In M. Neihart, S.M. Reis, N.M. Robinson, & S.M. Moon (Eds.), *The social and emotional development of gifted children* (pp. 177–191). Waco, TX: Prufrock Press.

Olenchak, F.R., & Renzulli, J.S. (2004). The effectiveness of the school-wide enrichment model of selected aspects of elementary school change. In C.A. Tomlinson and S.M. Reis (Eds.), *Differentiation of gifted and talented students* (pp. 17–37). Thousand Oaks, CA: Corwin Press.

Oliver, C., Murphy, G., Crayton, L., & Corbett, J. (1993). Self-injurious behavior in Rett syndrome: Interactions between features of Rett syndrome and operant conditioning. *Journal of Autism and Developmental Disorders, 23,* 91–109.

Olsen, S.F., Yang, C., Hart, C.H., Robinson, C.C., Wu, P., Nelson, D.A., Nelson, L.J., Jin, S., & Wo, J. (2002). Maternal psychological control and preschool children's behavioral outcomes in China, Russia, and the United States. In B.K. Barber (Ed.), *Intrusive parenting: How psychological control affects children and adolescents* (pp. 235–262). Washington, DC: American Psychological Association.

O'Neill, H.F., Jr., Allred, K., & Baker, E.L. (1997). Review of workforce readiness theoretical frameworks. In H.F. O'Neill, Jr. (Ed.), *Workforce readiness: Competencies and assessment* (pp. 229–254). Mahwah, NJ: Lawrence Erlbaum Associates.

O'Neill, R., Parke, R.D., & McDowell, D.J. (2001). Objective and subjective features of children's neighborhoods: Relations to parental regulatory strategies and children's social competence. *Journal of Applied Developmental Psychology, 22,* 135–155.

Orten, J.D., & Orten, J.L. (1992). Achievement among women with Turner's syndrome. *Families in Society: The Journal in Contemporary Human Services, 73,* 424–431.

Owens, J.S., & Hoza, B. (2003). The role of inattention and hyperactivity/ impulsivity in the positive illusory bias. *Journal of Consulting and Clinical Psychology, 71,* 680–691.

Ownsworth, T.L., McFarland, K.M., & Young, R. (2002). The investigation of factors underlying deficits in self-awareness and self-regulation. *Brain Injury, 16,* 291–309.

Ozonoff, S., & Cathcart, K. (1998). Effectiveness of a home program intervention for young children with autism. *Journal of Autism and Developmental Disorders, 28,* 25–32.

Ozonoff, S., & Jensen, J. (1999). Brief report: Specific executive function profiles in three neurodevelopmental disorders. *Journal of Autism and Developmental Disorders, 29,* 171–177.

Ozonoff, S., & McEvoy, R.E. (1994). A longitudinal study of executive function and theory of mind development in autism. *Development and Psychopathology, 6,* 415–431.

Ozonoff, S., & Miller, J.N. (1995). Teaching theory of mind: A new approach to social skills training for individuals with autism. *Journal of Autism and Developmental Disorders, 25,* 415–433.

Ozonoff, S. & Rogers, S.J. (2003). From Kanner to the millennium: Scientific advances that have shaped clinical practice. In S. Ozonoff, S.J. Rogers, & R.L. Hendren (Eds.), *Autism spectrum disorders* (pp. 3–36). Washington, DC: American Psychiatric Publishing, Inc.

Ozonoff, S., Pennington, B.F., & Rogers, S. (1991). Executive function deficits in high-functioning autistic individuals: Relationship to Theory of Mind. *Journal of Child Psychology and Psychiatry, 32,* 101–105.

Pakaslahti, L. (2000). Children's and adolescents' aggressive behavior in context: The development and application of aggressive problem-solving strategies. *Aggression and Violent Behavior, 5,* 467–490.

Pakaslahti, L., Asplund-Peltola, R.-L., & Keltikangas-Jarvinen, L. (1996). Parents' social problem-solving strategies in families with aggressive and non-aggressive boys. *Aggressive Behavior, 22,* 345–356.

Pakaslahti, L., & Keltikangas-Jarvinen, L. (1996). The relationship between aggressive problem-solving strategies, and aggressive behavior in 14 year-old adolescents. *European Journal of Personality, 10,* 365–378.

Pakaslahti, L., Spoof, I., Asplund-Peltola, R.-L., & Keltikangas-Jarvinen, L. (1998). Parents' social problem-solving strategies in families with aggressive and non-aggressive girls. *Aggressive Behavior, 24,* 37–51.

Palacios, E., & Semrud-Clikeman, M. (2005). Delinquency, hyperactivity, and phonological awareness: A comparison of adolescents with ODD and ADHD. *Applied Neuropsychology, 12,* 94–105.

Panella, D., & Henggeler, S.W. (1986). Peer interactions of conduct-disordered, anxious-withdrawn, and well-adjusted black adolescents. *Journal of Abnormal Child Psychology, 14,* 1–11.

Papero, P.H., Prigatano, G.P., Snyder, H.M., & Johnson, D.L. (1993). Children's adaptive behavioural competence after head injury. *Neuropsychological Rehabilitation, 3,* 321–340.

Papini, D.R., Sebby, R.A., & Clark, S. (1989). Affective quality of family relations and adolescent identity exploration. *Adolescence, 24,* 457–466.

Parke, R.D., & O'Neill, R. (1997). The influence of significant others on learning about relationships. In S. Duck (Ed.), *The handbook of personal relationships,* 2nd ed. (pp. 29–60). New York: Wiley.

Parke, R.D., Simpkins, S.D., McDowell, D.J., Kim, M., Killian, C., Dennis, J., Flyr, M.L., Wild, M., & Rah, Y. (2004). Relative contributions of families and peers to children's social development. In P.K. Smith & C.H. Hart (Eds.), *Blackwell Handbook of Childhood Social Development* (pp. 156–177). London: Blackwell Publishing.

Parker, J.G. (1983). *Parental overprotection: A risk factor in psychosocial development*. New York: Grune & Stratton.

Parker, J.G., & Asher, S.R. (1993). Friendship and friendship quality in middle childhood: Links with peer group acceptance and feelings of loneliness and social dissatisfaction. *Developmental Psychology, 29*, 611–621.

Parker, J.G., & Gottman, J.M. (1989). Social and emotional development in a relational context: Friendship interaction from early childhood to adolescence. In T.J. Berndt & G.W. Ladd (Eds.), *Peer relationships in child development* (pp. 95–131). New York: Wiley.

Parker, J.G., & Seal, J. (1996). Forming, losing, renewing, and replacing friendships: Applying temporal parameters to the assessment of children's friendship experiences. *Child Development, 67*, 2248–2268.

Patterson, C.J., Kupersmidt, J.B., & Griesler, P.C. (1990). Children's perceptions of self and relationships with others as a function of sociometric status. *Child Development, 61*, 1335–1349.

Patterson, G.R. (1986). Performance models for antisocial boys. *American Psychologist, 41*, 432–444.

Patterson, G.R., & Capaldi, D.M. (1990). A mediational model for boys' depressed mood. In J.Rolf, A.S. Masten, D. Cicchetti, K.H. Nuechterlein, & S. Weintraub (Eds.), *Risk and protective factors in the development of psychopathology* (pp. 141–163). New York: Cambridge University Press.

Patterson, G.R., & Chamberlain, P. (1988). Treatment process: A problem at three levels. In L.C. Wynne (Ed.), *The state of art in family therapy research: Controversies and recommendations* (pp. 189–223). Springfield, IL: Charles G. Thomas.

Patterson, G.R., & Stouthamer-Loeber, M. (1984). The correlation of family management and delinquency. *Child Development, 55*, 1299–1307.

Patterson, J., Pryor, J., & Field, J. (1995). Adolescent attachment to parents and friends in relation to aspects of self-esteem. *Journal of Youth and Adolescence, 24*, 365–380.

Patterson, G.R., Reid, J.B., & Dishion, T.J. (1992). *Antisocial boys*. Eugene, OR: Castalia.

Patterson, G.R., Vaden, N.A., Griesler, P.C., & Kupersmidt, J.B. (1991). Income level, gender, ethnicity, and household composition as predictors of children's peer companionship outside of school. *Journal of Applied Developmental Psychology, 12*, 447–465.

Pavlidis, K., McCauley, E., & Sybert, V.P. (1995). Psychosocial and sexual functioning in women with Turner syndrome. *Clinical Genetics, 47*, 85–89.

Pavri, S., & Monda-Amaya, L. (2000). Loneliness and students with learning disabilities in inclusive classrooms: Self-perceptions, coping strategies, and preferred interventions. *Learning Disabilities Research & Practice, 15*, 22–33.

Pelham, W.E., & Bender, M.E. (1982). Behavior therapy, behavioral assessment and psychostimulant medication in the treatment of attention deficit disorders: An interactive approach. In L.M. Bloomingdale and J. Swanson (Eds.), *Advances in learning and behavioral disabilities: A research annual* (pp. 365–436). Greenwich, CT: JAI Press.

Pellegrini, A.D., Kato, K., Blatchfor, P., & Baines, E. (2002). A short-term longitudinal study of children's playground games across the first year of school:

Implications for social competence and adjustment to school. *American Educational Research Journal, 39*, 991–1015.

Pellegrini, D.S. (1985). Social cognition and competence in middle childhood. *Child Development, 56*, 253–264.

Pennington, B.F. (1991). *Diagnosing learning disorders: A psychological framework.* New York: Guilford Press.

Pennington, B.F., & Ozonoff, S. (1996). Executive function and developmental psychopathology. *Journal of Child Psychology and Psychiatry, 37*, 51–87.

Perrin, E.C., Ramsey, B.K., & Sandler, H.M. (1987). Competent kids: Children and adolescents with a chronic illness. *Child: Care, Health, and Development, 13*, 13–32.

Perrin, E.C. Stein, R.E., & Drotar, D. (1991). Cautions in using the Child Behaviour Checklist: Observations based on research about children with a chronic illness. *Journal of Pediatric Psychology, 16*, 411–421.

Peterson, B.S., Leckman, J.F., & Cohen, D.J. (1995). Tourette's : A genetically predisposed and environmentally specified developmental psychopathology. In D. Cicchetti and D.J. Cohen (Eds.), *Manual of developmental psychology* (pp. 213–242). New York: Wiley.

Peterson, C. (2000). The future of optimism. *American Psychologist, 55*, 44–55.

Petti, V.L., Voelker, S.L., Shore, D.L., & Hayman-Abello, S.E. (2003). Perception of nonverbal emotion cues by children with nonverbal learning disabilities. *Journal of Developmental and Physical Disabilities, 15*, 23–36.

Pettit, G.S., & Harrist, A.W. (1993). Children's aggressive and social unskilled playground behavior with peers: Origins in early family relations. In C. Hart (Ed.), *Children on playgrounds: Research perspectives and applications* (pp. 240–270). Albany, NY: State University of New York Press.

Pettit, G.S., Laird, R.D., Bates, J.C., & Dodge, K.A. (1997). Patters of after-school care in middle childhood: Risk factors and developmental outcomes. *Merrill-Palmer Quarterly, 43*, 515–530.

Pfiffner, L.J., & Barkley, R.A. (1990). Educational placement and classroom management. In R.A. Barkley, *Attention-deficit hyperactivity disorder: A handbook for diagnosis and treatment* (pp. 498–539). New York: Guilford Press.

Pfiffner, L.J., Calzada, E., & McBurnett, K. (2000). Interventions to enhance social competence. *Child and Adolescent Psychiatric Clinics of North America, 9*, 689–709.

Phelan, T.W. (1993). *Surviving your adolescents: How to manage and let go of your 3–18 year olds.* Glen Ellyn, IL: Child Management.

Philip, R., & Turk, J. (2006). Neurofibromatosis and attentional deficits: An illustrative example of the common association of medical causes with behavioural syndromes, implications for general child mental health services. *Child and Adolescent Mental Health, 11*, 89–93.

Phillips, A.T., Wellman, H.M., & Spelke, E.S. (2002). Infants' ability to connect gaze and emotional expression to intentional action. Cognition, 85, 53–78.

Phillips, D. (1984). The illusion of incompetence among academically competent children. *Child Development, 55*, 2000–2016.

Pianta, R.C. (1998). *Enhancing relationships between children and teachers.* Washington, DC: American Psychological Association.

Pianta, R.C., Steinberg, M., & Rollins, K.B. (1995). The first two years of school: Teacher-child relationships and deflections in children's classroom adjustment. *Development and Psychopathology, 7*, 295–312.

Piacentini, J., Bergman, R.L., Keller, M., & McCracken, J. (2003). Functional impairment in children and adolescents with obsessive-compulsive disorder. *Journal of Child and Adolescent Psychopharmacology, 13 supplement*, S61-S69.

Piers, E.V. (1984). *Revised manual for the Piers-Harris Children's Self-Concept Scale.* Nashville, TN: Counselor Recordings and Tests.

Platt, J.J. & Spivack, G. (1975). Unidimensionality of the Means-Ends Problem-Solving (MEPS) procedure. *Journal of Clinical Psychology, 31,* 15–16.

Porges, S.W. (1998). Love: An emergent property of the mammalian autonomic nervous system. *Psychoneuroendocrinology, 23,* 837–861.

Povey, S., Burley, M.W., Attwood, J., Benham, F., Hunt, D., Jeremiah, S.J., Franklin, D., Gillett, G., Malas, S., Robson, E.B., Tippett, P., Edwards, J.H., Kwiatkowski, D.J., Super, M., Mueller, R., Fryer, A., Clarke, A., Webb, D., & Osborne, J. (1994). Two loci for tuberous sclerosis: One on 9q34 and one on 16p13. *Annals of Human Genetics, 58,* 107–127.

Powell, M.P., & Schulte, T. (1999). Turner syndrome. In S. Goldstein and C.R. Reynolds (Eds.), *Handbook of Neurodevelopmental and genetic disorders in children* (pp. 277–297). New York: Guilford.

Prasad, M., Ewing-Cobbs, L., Landry, S., & Kramer, L. (2000). Premorbid child characteristics and recovery from traumatic brain injury in infants and preschoolers. *Journal of the International Neuropsychological Society, 6,* 226.

Prater, M.A., Serna, L., & Nakamura, K.K. (1999). Impact of peer teaching on the acquisition of social skills by adolescents with learning disabilities. *Education and Treatment of Children, 22,* 19–36.

Prinstein, M.J., & La Greca, A.M. (1999). Links between mothers' and children's social competence and associations with maternal adjustment. *Journal of Clinical Child Psychology, 28,* 197–210.

Przeworski, A., Sacks, M., Hamlin, C., Zoellner, L., Nelson, A., Foa, E.B., & March, J. (1999, March). *Family interactions in OCD-relevant and irrelevant situations.* Paper presented at the 33rd Annual Convention of the Association for Advancement of Behavior Therapy, Toronto, Canada.

Puig-Antich, J., Lukens, E., Davies, M., Goetz, D., Brennan-Quattrock, J., & Todak, G. (1985). Psychosocial functioning in prepubertal major depressive disorders: I. Interpersonal relationships during the depressive episode. *Archives of General Psychiatry, 42,* 500–507.

Pumariega, A.J., Brieger, D., Pearson, D., Dreyer, C., & Seilheimer, D.K. (1990). Behavioral symptoms in cystic fibrosis vs. neurological patients. *Psychosomatics, 31,* 405–409.

Putallaz, M. (1987). Maternal behavior and sociometric status. *Child Development, 58,* 324–340.

Putallaz, M., & Sheppard, B.H. (1990). Social status and children's orientation to limited resources. *Child Development, 61,* 2022–2027.

Putallaz, M., & Wasserman, A. (1990). Children's entry behavior. In S.R. Asher & J.D. Coie (Eds.), *Peer rejection in childhood* (pp. 60–89). New York: Cambridge University Press.

Quay, H. (1993). The psychobiology of undersocialized aggressive conduct disorder: A theoretical perspective. *Development and Psychopathology, 5,* 165–180.

Radke-Yarrow, M., Nottlemann, E., Martinez, P., Fox, M.B., & Belmont, F. (1992). Young children of affectively ill parents: A longitudinal study of psycho-social development. *Journal of the American Academy of Child and Adolescent Psychiatry, 31,* 68–77.

Raffaelli, M., & Duckett, E. (1989). "We're just talking . . .": Conversations in early adolescence. *Journal of Youth and Adolescence, 18,* 567–582.

Randolph, J.J., & Dykman, B.M. (1990). Perceptions of parenting and depression-proneness in the offspring: dysfunctional attitudes as a mediating mechanism. *Cognitive Therapy and Research, 22,* 377–400.

Rapport, L.J., Friedman, S., Tzelepis, A., & VanVoorhis, A. (2002). Experienced emotion and affect recognition in adult attention-deficit hyperactivity disorder. *Neuropsychology, 16,* 102–110.

Raznahan, A., Joinson, C., O'Callaghn, F., Osborne, J.P., & Bolton, P.F. (2006). Psychopathology in tuberous sclerosis: An overview and findings in a population-based sample of adults with tuberous sclerosis. *Journal of Intellectual Disability Research, 50,* 561–569.

Reichert, E.S. (1985). The state of the art of identification of gifted students in the United States. *Gifted Education International, 3,* 47–51.

Reichert, E.S. (1987). Rampart problems and promising practices in the identification of disadvantaged gifted students. Gifted Child Quarterly *31,* 149–154.

Reid, J.B., Taplin, P., & Loeber, R. (1981). A social interactional approach to the treatment of abusive families. In R. Stewart (Ed.), *Violent behavior: Social learning approaches to prediction management and treatment.* New York: Brunner/Mazel.

Reijntjes, A., Stegge, H., & Terwogt, M.M. (2006). Children's coping with peer rejection: The role of depressive symptoms, social competence, and gender. *Infant and Child Development, 15,* 89–107.

Reis, S.M., Neu, T.W., & McGuire, J.M. (1995). *Talents in two places: Case studies of high ability students with learning disabilities who have achieved* (Research Monograph 95113). Storrs: National Research Center on the Gifted and Talented, The University of Connecticut.

Reis, S.M., Neu, T.W., & McGuire, J.M. (1997). Case studies of high-ability students with learning disabilities who have achieved. *Exceptional Children, 63,* 463–479.

Renouf, A.G., Kovacs, M., & Mukerji, P. (1997). Relationship of depressive, conduct, and comorbid disorders and social functioning in childhood. *Journal of the American Academy of Child and Adolescent Psychiatry, 36,* 998–1004.

Renwick, S., & Emler, N. (1991). The relationship between social skills deficits and juvenile delinquency. *British Journal of Clinical Psychology, 30,* 61–71.

Renzulli, J.S. (2000). *A practical system for identifying gifted and talented students* (http://www.sp.uconn.edu/~nrcgt/sem/semart04.html).

Reynolds, C.R., & Kamphaus, R.W. (2005). *Behavior Assessment System for children II (BASC).* Circle Pines, MN: American Guidance Service.

Reynolds, C.R., & Richmond, B.O. (1978). What I think and feel: A revised measure of children's manifest anxiety. *Journal of Abnormal Child Psychology, 6,* 271–280.

Reynolds, W.M. (1996). *Reynolds Adolescent Depression Scale.* Odessa, FL: Psychological Assessment Resources.

Reiff, H.B., & Gerber, P.J. (1990). Cognitive correlates of social perception in students with learning disabilities. *Journal of Learning Disabilities, 23,* 260–262.

Rice, K.G. (1990). Attachment in adolescence: A narrative and meta-analytic review. *Journal of Youth and Adolescence, 19,* 511–538.

Rimland, B. (1990). Sound sensitivity in autism. *Autism Research Review International, 4,* 1–6.

Rimm, S. (2002). Peer pressures and social acceptance of gifted students. In Neihart, M., Reis, S.M., Robinson, N.M., & Moon, S.M. (Eds.), *The social and emotional development of gifted children* (pp. 13–18). Waco, TX: Prufrock Press.

Rimm, S., Rimm-Kauffman, S., & Rimm, I. (1999). *See Jane win: The Rimm report on how 1,000 girls became successful women.* New York: Crown.

Ritvo, E.R., Freeman, B.J., Pingree, C., Mason-Brothers, A., Jorde, L., Jenson, W.R., McMahon, W.M., Petersen, P.B., No, A., & Ritvo, A. (1989). The UCLA-University of Utah epidemiological survey of autism: Prevalence. *American Journal of Psychiatry, 146,* 194–199.

Roberts, R.J., & Pennington, B.F. (1996). An interactive framework for examining prefrontal cognitive processes. *Developmental Neuropsychology, 12,* 105–126.

Robertson, L.M., Harding, M.S., & Morrison, G.M. (1998). A comparison of risk and resilience indicators among Latino/a students: Differences between students identified as at-risk, learning disabled, speech impaired and not at-risk. *Education & Treatment of Children, 21*, 333–354.

Robinson, N. (2002). Introduction. In Neihart, M., Reis, S.M., Robinson, N.M., & Moon, S.M. (Eds.), *The social and emotional development of gifted children* (pp. xi–xxiv). Waco, TX: Prufrock Press.

Robinson, M.M., Lanzi, R.G., Weinberg, R.A., Ramey, S.L., & Ramey, C.T. (2004). Family factors associated with high academic competence in former head start children at third grade. In S.M. Reis and S.M. Moon (Eds.) *Social/emotional issues, underachievement and counseling of gifted and talented students* (pp. 83–104). Thousand Oaks, CA: Corwin Press.

Rodkin,, P.C., Farmer, T.W., Pearl, R., & VanAcker, R. (2000). Heterogeneity of popular boys: Antiscocial and prosocial configurations. *Developmental Psychology, 36*, 14–24.

Rojas, D.C., Bawn, S.D., Benkers, T.L., Reite, M.L., & Rogers, S.J. (2002). Smaller left hemisphere planum temporale in adults with autistic disorder. *Neuroscience Letters, 328*, 237–240.

Rogers, S.J., Ozonoff, S., & Maslin-Cole, C. (1991). A comparative study of attachment behavior in children with autism and children with other disorders of behavior and development. *Journal of the American Academy of Child and Adolescent Psychiatry, 30*, 433–438.

Roscoe, B., & Skomski, G.G. (1989). Loneliness among late adolescents. *Adolescence, 24*, 947–955.

Rose, A., & Asher, S. (1999). Children's goals and strategies in response to conflicts within a friendship. *Developmental Psychology, 35*, 69–79.

Rosenthal, M., & Bond, M.R. (1990). Behavioral and psychiatric sequelae. In M. Rosenthal, M. Bond, E.R. Griffith, and J.D. Miller (Eds.), *Rehabilitation of the adult and child with traumatic brain injury* (pp. 179–192). Philadelphia: Davis Company.

Rosner, B.A., Hodapp, R.M., Fidler, D.J., Sagun, J.N., & Dykens, E.M. (2004). Social competence in persons with Prader-Willi, Williams, and Down's Syndromes. *Journal of Applied Research in Individual Disabilities, 17*, 209–217.

Rothbart, M.K. (1989). Temperament in childhood: A framework. In G. Kohnstamm, J. Bates, & M.K. Rothbart (Eds.), *Handbook of temperament in childhood* (pp. 59–73). New York: Wiley.

Rothbart, M.K., & Ahadi, S.A. (1994). Temperament and the development of personality. *Journal of Abnormal Psychology, 103*, 55–66.

Rothbart, M.K., Ahadi, S.A., & Evans, D.E. (2000). Temperament and personality: Origins and outcomes. *Journal of Personality and Social Psychology, 78*, 122–135.

Rothbart, M.K., Ahadi, S.A., & Hershey, K. (1994). Temperament and personality: Origins and outcomes. *Journal of Personality and Social Psychology, 78*, 122–135.

Rothbart, M.K., & Bates, J. (1998). Temperament. In W. Damon (Series Ed.), & N. Eisenberg, (Vol. Ed.), *Handbook of child psychology, Vol. 3, Social, emotional, and personality development* (pp. 105–176). New York: Wiley.

Rothbart, M.K., Derryberry, D., & Posner, M.I. (1994). A psychobiological approach to the development of temperament. In J.E. Bates & T.D. Wachs (Eds.), *Temperament: Individual differences at the interface of biology and behavior* (pp. 83–116). Washington, DC: American Psychological Association.

Rourke, B.P. (1988). The syndrome of nonverbal learning disabilities: Developmental manifestations in neurologic disease, disorder, and dysfunction. *Clinical Neuropsychologist, 2*, 293–330.

Rourke, B.P. (1995). Syndrome of nonverbal learning disabilities: *Neurodevelopmental manifestations*. New York: Guilford Press.

Rourke, B.P., Ahmad, S.A., Collins, D.W., Hayman-Abello, B.A., Hayman-Abello, S.E., & Warriner, E.M. (2002). Child clinical/pediatric neuropsychology: Some recent advances. *Annual Review of Psychology, 53*, 309–39.

Rourke, B.P., & Fuerst, D.R. (1992). Psychosocial dimensions of learning disabilities subtypes: Neuropsychological studies in the Windsor laboratory. *School Psychology Review, 21*, 361–374.

Rourke, B.P., & Fuerst, D.R. (1995). *Syndrome of nonverbal learning disabilities: Manifestations of neurological disease, disorder, and dysfunction*. New York: Guilford Press.

Rourke, B.P., Young, G.C., & Leenaars, A.A. (1989). A childhood learning disability that predisposes those afflicted to adolescent and adult depression and suicide risk. *Journal of Learning Disabilities, 22*, 169–174.

Rousseau, F., Morel, M.-L., Rouillard, P., Khandjian, E.W., & Morgan, K. (1996). Surprisingly low prevalence of FMR1 premutation among males from the general population. *American Journal of Genetics, 59 (Suppl.)*, 1069.

Rousseau, F., Roukllard, P., Morel, M.-L., Khandjian, E.W., & Morgan, K. (1995). Prevlanece of carriers of permutation-sized alleles of the FMR1 gene—and implications for the population genetics of the fragile X syndrome. *American Journal of Human Genetics, 57*, 1006–1018.

Rovet, J.F. (1990). The cognitive and neuropsychological characteristics of children with Turner syndrome. In D. Berch and B. Bender (Eds.), *Sex chromosome abnormalities and human behavior: Psychological studies* (pp. 38–77). Boulder, CO: Westview Press.

Rovet, J.F. (1993). The psychoeducational characteristics of children with Turner syndrome. *Journal of Learning Disabilities, 26*, 333–341.

Rovet, J.F. (1995). Turner syndrome. In B. P. Rourke (Ed.), Syndrome of nonverbal learning disabilities: *Neurodevelopmental manifestations* (pp. 351–371). New York: Guilford Press.

Rovet, J.F., & Ehrlich, R. (1988). Effect of temperament on metabolic control in children with diabetes mellitus. *Diabetes Care, 11*, 77–81.

Rovet, J.F., & Ireland, L. (1994). The behavioral phenotype of children with Turner syndrome. *Journal of Pediatric Psychology, 19*, 779–790.

Rubin, K.H. (1993). The Waterloo Longitudinal Project: Correlates and consequences of social withdrawal from childhood to adolescence. In K.H. Rubin & J.B. Asendorpf (Eds.), *Social cognition and communication*. Hillsdale, NJ: Lawrence Erlbaum Associates, Inc.

Rubin, K.H., & Burgess, K.B. (2001). Social withdrawal and anxiety. In M.W. Vasey & M.R. Dadds (Eds.), *The developmental psychopathology of anxiety* (pp. 407–434). London: Oxford University Press.

Rubin, K.H., Bukowski, W., & Parker, J. (1998). Peer interaction, relationships, and groups. In W. Damon (Series Ed.) & N. Eisenberg (Vol. Ed.), *Handbook of Child Psychology: Vol. 3, Social, emotional, and personality development* (pp. 619–700). New York: Wiley.

Rubin, K.H., Chen, X., McDougall, P., & Bowker, A. (1995). The Waterloo Longitudinal Project: Predicting internalizing and externalizing problems in adolescence. *Development and Psychopathology, 7*, 751–764.

Rubin, K.H., & Mills, R.S.L. (1990). Maternal beliefs about adaptive and maladaptive social behaviors in normal, aggressive, and withdrawn preschoolers. *Journal of Abnormal Child Psychology, 18*, 419–435.

Rudolph, K.D., & Clark, A.G. (2001). Conceptions of relationships in children with depressive and aggressive symptoms: Social-cognitive distortion or reality? *Journal of Abnormal Child Psychology, 29*, 41–56.

Rudolph, K.D., Hammen, C., & Burge, D. (1994). Interpersonal functioning and depressive symptoms in childhood: Addressing the issues of specificity and comorbidity. *Journal of Abnormal Child Psychology, 22,* 355–371.

Rudolph, K.D., Hammen, C., & Burge, D. (1997). A cognitive-interpersonal approach to depressive symptoms in preadolescent children. *Journal of Abnormal Child Psychology, 25,* 33–45.

Rumsey, J.M. (1992). Neuropsychological studies of high-level autism. In E. Schopler and G.B. Mesibov (Eds.), *High-functioning individuals with autism* (pp. 41–64). New York: Plenum Press.

Russell, A.T. (1985). The mentally retarded, emotionally disturbed child and adolescent. In M. Sigman (Ed.), *Children with emotional disorders and developmental disabilities* (pp. 3–21). London: Grune & Stratton.

Russell, A.T., & Finnie, V. (1990). Preschool children's social status and maternal instructions to assist group entry. *Developmental Psychology, 26,* 603–611.

Russell, J., Jarrold, C., & Hood, B. (1999). Two intact executive capacities in children with autism: Implicatons for the core executive dysfunctions in the disorder. *Journal of Autism and Developmental Disorders, 29,* 103–112.

Russell, G., & Russell, A. (1987). Mother-child and father-child relationships in middle childhood. *Child Development, 58,* 1573–1585.

Rutter. M. (1984). Autistic children growing up. *Developmental Medicine and Child Neurology, 26,* 122–129.

Ryan, R.M., & Lynch, J.H. (1989). Emoitonal autonomy versus detachment: Revisiting the vicissitudes of adolescence and young adulthood. *Child Development, 60,* 340–356.

Rydell, A-M., Berlin, L., & Bohlin, G. (2003). Emotionality, emotion regulation, and adaptation among 5- to 8-year-old children. *Emotion, 3,* 30–47.

Saarni, C. (1999). *The development of emotional competence.* New York: Guilford Press.

Sale, P., & Carey, D.M. (1995). The sociometric status of students with disabilities in a full-inclusion school. *Exceptional Children, 62,* 6–19.

Samenow, S. (1998). *Before it's too late: Why some kids get into trouble—and what parents can do about it.* New York: Random House.

Sameroff, A.J. (1975). Transactional models in early social relations. *Human Development, 8,* 56–79.

Sameroff, A.J., Bartko, W.T., Baldwin, A., Baldwin, C., & Seifer, R. (1998). Family and social influences on the development of child competence. In M. Lewis & C. Feiring (Eds.), *Child and families at risk* (pp. 161–185). Hillsdale, NJ: Erlbaum.

Sameroff, A.J., & Chandler, M.J. (1975). Reproductive risk and the continuum of caretaking casualty. In F.D. Horowitz, M. Hetherington, S. Scarr-Salapatek, and G. Siegel (Eds.), *Review of child development research* (Vol. 4, pp. 187–244). Chicago: University of Chicago Press.

Samter, W. (2003). Friendship interaction skills across the life span. In J.O. Greene & B.R. Burleson (Eds.). *Handbook of communication and social interaction skills* (pp. 637–684). Mahwah, NJ: Lawrence Erlbaum & Associates.

Samter, W., Whaley, B.R., Mortenson, S.T., & Burleson, B.R. (1997). Ethnicity and emotional support in same-sex friendship: A comparison of Asian-Americans, African-Americans, and Euro-Americans. *Personal Relationships, 4,* 413–430.

Sandstrom, M.J., & Cramer, P. (2003). Defense mechanisms and psychological adjustment in childhood. *Journal of Nervous and Mental Disease, 191,* 487–495.

Sandstrom, M.J., & Schanberg, L.E. (2004). Brief report: Peer rejection, social behavior, and psychological adjustment in children with juvenile rhematic disease. *Journal of Pediatric Psychology, 29,* 29–34.

Sarimski, K. (1997). Behavioral phenotypes and family stress in three mental retardation syndromes. *European Journal of Child and Adolescent Psychiatry, 6,* 26–31.

Sarris, A., Winefield, H.R., & Cooper, C. (2000). Behaviour problems in adolescence: A comparison of juvenile offenders and adolescents referred to a mental health service. *Australian Journal of Psychology, 52,* 17–22.

Sattler, J.M. (2003). Assessment of Children: *Cognitive Applications.* San Diego, CA: Jerome M. Sattler, Publisher, Inc.

Sayler, M.F., & Brookshire, W.K. (2004). Social, emotional and behavioral adjustment of accelerated students, students in gifted classes, and regular students in eighth grade. In S.M. Reiss and S.M. Moon (2004). *Social/emotional issues, underachievement, and counseling of gifted students* (pp. 9–20). Thousand Oaks, CA: Corwin Press.

Schaie, K.W. (2005). What can we learn from longitudinal studies of adult development? *Research in Human Development. 2,* 133–158.

Schafer, V., & Semrud-Clikeman, M. (submitted). Neuropsychological functioning in subgroups of children with and without social perception deficits and/or hyperactivity/impulsivity.

Schapiro, N.A. (2005). Bipolar disorders in children and adolescents. *Journal of Pediatric Health Care, 19,* 131–141.

Schmidt, E., Rupp, A., Burgard, P., & Pietz, J. (1992). Information processing in early treated phenylketonuria. *Journal of Clinical and Experimental Neuropsychology, 14,* 388–395.

Schmidt, E., Rupp, A., Burgard, P., Pietz, J., Weglage, J., & de Sonneville, L.M.J. (1994). Sustained attention in adult phenylketonuria: the influence of the concurrent phenylalanine-blood-level. *Journal of Clinical and Experimental Neuropsychology, 16,* 681–688.

Schmidt, M. (2000). Social integration of students with learning disabilities. *Developmental Disabilities, 28,* 19–26.

Schultz, R.T., Grelotti, D.J., Kllin, A., Levitan, E., Cantey, T., Skudlarski, P., Gore, J.C., Volkmar, F.R., & Cohen, D.J. (2001). *An fMRI study of face recognition, facial expression detection, and social judgment in autism spectrum conditions.* International Meeting for Autism Research, San Diego, CA.

Schultz, R.T., Romanski, L., & Tsatsanis, K. (2000). Neurofunctional models of autistic disorder and Asperger's syndrome: Clues from neuroimaging. In A. Klin, F.R. Volkmar, & S.S. Sparrow (Eds.), *Asperger's syndrome* (pp. 19–209). New York: Plenum Press.

Schwartz, G., & Merten, D. (1967). The language of adolescence: An anthropological approach to the youth culture. *American Journal of Sociology, 72,* 453–468.

Schwartz, A.J., Kaslow, N.J., Seeley, J., & Lewinsohn, P. (2000). Psychological, cognitive, and interpersonal correlates of attributional change in adolescents. *Journal of Clinical Child Psychology, 29,* 188–198.

Seeley, K.R. (1984). Giftedness and juvenile delinquency in perspective. *Journal for the Education of the Gifted, 8,* 59–72.

Segrin, C. (1990). A meta-analytic review of social skill deficits in depression. *Communication Monographs, 57,* 292–308.

Segrin, C. (1998). The impact of assessment procedures on the relationship between paper and pencil and behavioral indicators of social skill. Journal of *Nonverbal Behavior, 22,* 229–251.

Segrin, C., & Flora, J. (2000). Poor social skills are a vulnerability factor in the development of prosocial problems. *Human Communication Research, 26,* 489–514.

Segrin, C., & Abramson, L.Y. (1994). Negative reactions to depressive behaviors: A communication theories analysis. *Journal of Abnormal Psychology, 103*, 655–668.

Seidman, L.J., Biederman, J., Faraone, S.V., Milberger, S., Seiverd, K., Benedict, K., Bernstein, J.H., Weber, W., & Ouellette, C. (1996). Toward defining a neuropsychology of ADHD: Performance of children and adolescents from a large clinical referred sample. *Journal of Consulting and Clinical Psychology, 65*, 150–160.

Semrud-Clikeman, M. (2000). Social aspects of neuropsychological disorders. In V.L. Schwean and D.H. Saklofske (Eds.), *Psychosocial correlates of exceptionality*. New York, NY: Plenum Press.

Semrud-Clikeman, M. (2001). *Traumatic Brain Injury in Children and Adolescents: Assessment and Intervention*. New York: Guilford.

Semrud-Clikeman, M. (2003). Executive functioning in NVLD. Perspectives

Semrud-Clikeman, M. (2004). *Social competence*. Paper presented at the annual conference of the American Psychological Association.

Semrud-Clikeman, M. (2006). Neuropsychological aspects for evaluating learning disabilities. *Journal of Learning Disabilities. 38*, 563–568.

Semrud-Clikeman, M., Biederman, J., Sprich-Buckminister, S., Lehman, B.K., Faraone, S.V., & Norman, D. (1992). Comobidity between ADDH and learning disability: A review and report in a clinically referred sample. *Journal of the American Academy of Child and Adolescent Psychiatry, 31*, 439–448.

Semrud-Clikeman, M., & Glass, K. (submitted). Comprehension of humour in children with nonverbal learning disabilities, verbal learning disabilities, and without learning disabilities.

Semrud-Clikeman, M., Harrington, K., Parkle, N., Clinton, A., & Connor, R. (1999). Innovative interventions with children with attentional difficultiesin the shool setting. *Journal of Learning Disabilities, 32*, 581–590.

Semrud-Clikeman, M., & Hynd, G.W. (1990). Right hemispheric dysfunction in nonverbal learning disabilities: Social, academic, and adaptive function in adults and children. *Psychological Bulletin, 107*, 196–207.

Semrud-Clikeman, M., Guli, L., & Bennett, L.S. (2003). Assessment of childhood depression. In C.R. Reynolds and R. Kamphaus (Eds.), *Handbook of psychological and educational assessment of children* (2nd edition). New York: Guilford.

Semrud-Clikeman, M., & Schaefer, V. (2000). Social competence in developmental disorders. *Journal of Psychotherapy in independent Practice, 4*, 3–20.

Semrud-Clikeman, M., Steingard, R., Filipek, P.A., Bekken, K., Biederman, J., & Renshaw, P. (2000). Neuroanatomical-neuropsychological correlates of ADHD. *Journal of the American Academy of Child and Adolescent Psychiatry, 39*, 477–484.

Semrud-Clikeman, M., Kamphaus, R., & Teeter, P.A. (1997). Behavioral and personality assessment in neuropsychology. In C.R. Reynolds (Ed.). *Handbook of clinical child neuropsychology* (2nd edition; pp. 320–341). New York: Plenum Press.

Semrud-Clikeman, M. & Wical, B. (1999). Components of attention and memory in complex-partial epilepsy in children with and without ADHD. *Epilepsia, 40, 211–215*.

Shah, F., & Morgan, S.B. (1996). Teachers' ratings of social competence of children with high versus low levels of depressive symptoms. *Journal of School Psychology, 34*, 337–349.

Shapiro, A.K., & Shapiro, E.S. (1988). Signs, symptoms, and clinical course. In D.J. Cohen, R.D. Bruun, & J.F. Leckman (Eds.), *Tourette's syndrome and tic disorders: Clinical understanding and treatment* (pp. 127–193). New York: Wiley.

Shapiro, T., Sherman, M., Calamari, G., & Koch, D. (1987). Attachment in autism and other developmental disorders. *Journal of the American Academy of Child and Adolescent Psychiatry, 26,* 480–484.

Shavinina, L.V., & Ferrari, M. (2004). *Beyond knowledge: Extracognitive aspects of developing high ability.* Mahwah, NJ: Erlbaum.

Shaw, D.S., & Emery, R.E. (1988). Chronic family adversity and school-age children's adjustment. *Journal of the American Academy of Child and Adolescent Psychiatry, 27,* 200–206.

Shaywitz, S.E., Fletcher, J., & Shaywitz, B.A. (1994). Issues in the definition and classification of attention deficit disorder. *Topics in Language Disorders, 14,* 1–25.

Sheridan, S.M., & Dee, C.C. (1996). A multimethod intervention for social skills deficits in children with ADHD and their parents. *School Psychology Review, 25,* 57–77.

Sherman, S. (1996). Epidemiology. In R.J. Hagerman and A.C. Cronister (Eds.), *Fragile X syndrome: Diagnosis, treatment, and research* (2nd ed., pp. 165–192). Baltimore, MD: Johns Hopkins University Press.

Shewchuk, R.M., Johnson, M.O., & Elliott, T.R. (2000). Self-appraised social problem solving abilities, emotional reactions, and actual problem solving performance. *Behaviour Research and Therapy, 38,* 727–740.

Shirk, S.R., Boergers, J., Eason, A., & Van Horn, M. (1998). Dysphoric interpersonal schemata and preadolescents' sensitization to negative events. *Journal of Clinical Child Psychology, 27,* 54–68.

Shucard, D.W., Shucard, J.L., Clpper, R.R., & Schacter, M. (1992). Electrophysiological and neuropsychological indices of cognitive processing deficits in Turner syndrome. *Developmental Neuropsychology, 8,* 299–323.

Siegel, D.J. (1998). Evaluation of high-functioning autism. In G. Goldstein, P.D. Nussbaum, and S.R. Beers (Eds.), *Neuropsychology* (pp. 109–134). New York: Plenum Press.

Sigman, M. D., Kasari, C., Kwon, J., Yirmiya, N. (1992). Responses to the negative emotions of others by autistic, mentally retarded, and normal children. *Child Development, 63,* 796–807.

Siller, M., & Sigman, M. (2002). The behaviors of parents of children with autism predict the subsequent development of their children's communication. *Journal of Autism and Developmental Disorders, 32,* 77–89.

Silva, R.R., Munoz, D.M., Barickman, J., & Friedhoff, A.J. (1995). Environmental factors and related fluctuation of symptoms in children and adolescents with Tourette's disorder. *Journal of Child Psychology and Psychiatry, 36,* 305–312.

Silverman, L.K. (2002). Asynchronous development. In M. Neihart, S.M. Reis, N.M. Robinson, & S.M. Moon (Eds.), *The social and emotional development of gifted children* (pp. 31–40). Waco, TX: Prufrock Press.

Simmons, R.J., Corey, M., Cowen, L., Keenan, N., Robertson, J., & Levison, H. (1987). Behavioral adjustment of latency age children with cystic fibrosis. *Psychosomatic Medicine, 49,* 291–301.

Singh, S.D., Ellis, C.R., Winton, A.S., Singh, N.N., Leung, J.P., & Oswald, D.P. (1998). Recognition of facial expressions of emotion by children with attention-deficit hyperactivity disorder. *Behavior Modification, 22,* 128–142.

Siqueland, L., Kendall, P.C., & Steinberg, L. (1996). Perceived family environments and observed family interaction styles. *Journal of Clinical Child Psychology, 25,* 225–237.

Sisterhern, S.H., & Gerber, P.J. (1989). Auditory, visual and multisensory nonverbal social perception in adolescents with and without learning disabilities. *Journal of Learning Disabilities, 22,* 245–249.

Skuse, D. (1987). Annotation: The psychological consequences of being small. *Journal of Child Psychology and Psychiatry, 28,* 641–650.

Slaby, G.R., & Guerra, N.G. (1988). Cognitive mediators of aggression in adolescent offenders: 1. Assessment. *Developmental Psychology, 24,* 580–588.

Slany, S.F., Wilkie, A.O.M., Hirst, M.C., Charlton, R., McKinley, M., Pointon, J., Christodoulou, Z., Huson, S.M., & Davies, K.E. (1995). DNA testing for fragile X syndrome in schools for learning difficulties. *Archives of Diseases in Childhood, 72*, 33–37.

Smalley, S.L. (1998). Autism and tuberous sclerosis. *Journal of Autism and Developmental Disorders, 28*, 407–414.

Smari, J., Petursdottir, G., & Porsteinsdottir, V. (2001). Social anxiety and depression in adolescents in relation to perceived competence and situational appraisal. *Journal of Adolescence, 24*, 199–207.

Smith B.H., Pelham, W.E., Evans, S., Gnagy E., Molina, B., Bukstein, O., Greener, A., Myak, C., Presnell M., & Willoughby, M. (1998). Dosage effects of methylphenidate on the social behavior of adolescents diagnosed with ADHD. *Experimental and Clinical Psychophamacology, 6*, 187–204.

Smith, D.E., & Tegano, D.W. (1992). Relationship of scores on two personality measures: Creativity and self-image. *Psychological Reports, 71*, 43–50.

Smith, P.K., & Delfosse, P. (1980). Accuracy of reporting own and others' companions in young children. *British Journal of Social and Clinical Psychology, 19*, 337–338.

Smith, T., Buch, G.A., & Gamby, T.E. (2000a). Parent-directed, intensive early intervention for children with pervasive developmental disorder. *Research in Developmental Disabilities, 21*, 297–309.

Smith, T., Groen, A.D., Wynn, J.W. (2000b). Randomized trial of intensive early intervention for children with pervasive developmental disorder. *American Journal of Mental Retardation, 105*, 269–285.

Smollar, J. & Youniss, J. (1982). Social development through friendship. In K.H. Rubin & H.S. Ross (Eds.), *Peer relationships and social skills in childhood* (pp. 277–298). New York: Springer-Verlag.

Snidman, N., Kagan, J., Riordan, L., & Shannon, D. (1995). Cardiac function and behavioral reactivity in infancy. *Psychophysiology, 31*, 199–207.

Snow, M.E., Hertzig, M.E., & Shapiro, T. (1987). Expression of emotion in young autistic children. *Journal of the American Academy of Child and Adolescent Psychiatry, 26*, 836–838.

Sobel, H.M. (1998). *Effect of visibility of neurofibromatosis and social skill on adolescents' social support.* Dissertation Abstracts Internation: Section B, 58.

Sparrow, S., Cicchetti, D.V., & Balla, D.A. (2005). *Vineland Adaptive Behavior Scales II.* Circle Pines, MN: AGS.

Speltz, M.L., DeKlyen, M., & Greenberg, M.T. (1999). Attachment in boys with early onset conduct problems. *Development and Psychopathology, 11*, 269–285.

Spitzberg, B.H. (2003). Methods of interpersonal skill assessment. In J.O. Greene and B.R. Burleson (Eds.), *Handbook of Communication and Social Interaction Skills* (pp. 93–134). Mahwah, NJ: Lawrence Erlbaum Associates, Inc.

Sprouse, C.A., Hall, C.W., Webster, R.E., & Bolen, L.M. (1998). Social perception in students with learning disabilities and attention-deficit/ hyperactivity disorder. *Journal of Nonverbal Behavior, 22*, 125–134.

Sroufe, L.A. (1982). Issues of temperament and attachment. *American Journal of Orthopsychiatry, 52*, 743–746.

Sroufe, L.A., Carlson, E., & Shulman, S. (1993). The development of individuals in relationships. In D.C. Funder, R.D. Parke, C. Tomlinson-Keasey, & K. Widaman (Eds.), *Studying lives through time: Approaches to personality and development.* Washington, DC: American Psychological Association.

Sroufe, L.A., Fox, N.E., & Pancake, V.R. (1983). Attachment and dependency in developmental perspective. *Child Development, 54*, 1615–1627.

Stainback, S., & Stainback, W. (1996). *Inclusion: A guide for educators.* Baltimore, MD: Brookes.

Stanovich, K.E., & Siegel, L.S. (1994). Phenotypic performance profile of children with reading disabilities: A regression-based test of the phonological-core variable-difference model. *Journal of Educational Psychology, 86*, 24–53.

Stehbens, J., Kaleita, T., Noll, R.B., MacLean, W., O'Brien, R., & Hammond, D. (1991). CNS prophylaxis of pediatric leukemia: What are the long-term neurological, neuropsychological, and behavioral effects? *Neuropsychology Review, 2*, 147–177.

Steinhausen, H.C., Von Gontrad, A. & Spohr, H.L. (2002). Behavioral phenotypes in four mental retardation syndromes: Fetal alcohol syndrome, Prader-Willi syndrome, fragile X syndrome, and tuberosis sclerosis. *American Journal of Medical Genetics, 111*, 381–387.

Stemerdink, B.A. (1996). *Early and continuously treated phenylketonuria: An experimental neuropsychological approach.* Amsterdam: Academisch Proefschrift.

Stemerdink, B.A., van der Meere, J.J., van der Molen, M.W., Kalverboer, A.F., Hendrikx, M.M.T., Huisamn, J., van der Schot, L.W.A., Slijper, F.M.E., van Spronsen, F.J., & Verkerk, P.H. (1995). Information processing in patients with early and continuously-treated phenylketonuria. *European Journal of Pediatrics, 154*, 739–746.

Sternberg, R.J., & Zhang, L. (1995). What do we mean by giftedness? A pentagonal implicit theory. *Gifted Child Quarterly, 39*, 88–94.

Stetketee, G. (1997). Disability and family burden in obsessive-compulsive disorder. *Canadian Journal of Psychiatry, 42*, 919–928.

Stifter, C.A., Coulehan, C., & Fish, M. (1993). Linking employment to attachment: The mediating effects of maternal separation anxiety and interactive behavior. *Child Development, 64*, 1451–1460.

Stocker, C.M. (1994). Children's perceptions of relationships with siblings, friends, and mothers: Compensatory processes and links with psychological adjustment. *Journal of Child Psychology and Psychiatry and Allied Disciplines, 35*, 1447–1459.

Stone, W.L., & LaGreca, A.M. (1984). Comprehension of nonverbal communication: A reexamination of the social competence of learning disabled children. *Journal of Abnormal Child Psychology, 12*, 505–518.

Stone, W.L., & LaGreca, A.M. (1990). The social status of children with learning disabilities: A re-examination. *Journal of Learning Disabilities, 23*, 32–37.

Strain, P.S., & Hoyson, M. (2000). The need for longitudinal, intensive social skill intervention: LEAP follow-up outcomes for children with autism. Topics in Early Childhood Special Education: Special Issue: Early childhood special education in a *new* century: *Voices from the past, visions for our future, part, 2, 20*, 116–122.

Strain, P.S., Odom, S.L., & McConnell, S. (1984). Promoting social reciprocity of exceptional children: Identification, target behavior, and intervention. *Remedial and Special Education, 5*, 21–28.

Strain, P.S., & Schwartz, I. (2001). ABA and the development of meaningful social relations for young children with autism. *Focus on Autism and Other Developmental Disabilities: Special Issue, 16*, 120–128.

Strang, J.D., & Rourke, B.P. (1985). Arthmetic disability subtypes: The neuropsychological significance of specific arithmetical impairment in children. In B.P. Rourke (Ed.), *Neuropsychology of learning disabilities* (pp. 167–183). New york: Guilford Press.

Strauss, C.C., Lease, C., Kazdin, A.E., Dulcan, M.K., & Last, C.G. (1989). Multimethod assessment of social competence of children with anxiety disorders. *Journal of Clinical Child Psychology, 18*, 184–189.

Strully, J.L., & Strully, C. (1993). That which binds us: Friendship as a safe harbor in a storm. In A.N. Amado (Ed.), *Friendships and community connections between people with and without developmental disabilities* (pp. 213–225). Baltimore, MD: Brookes.

Subotnik, R., Kassan, L., Summers, E., & Wasser, A. (1993). *Genius revisited: High IQ children grow up.* Norwood, NJ: Ablex.

Sugai, G., & Chanter, C. (1989). The effects of training students with learning and behavior disorders to modify the behaviors of their peers. *Education and Treatment of Children, 12,* 134–151.

Sukholdolsky, D.G., do Rosario-Campos, M.C., Scahill, L., Kastovich, L., Pauls, D.L., Peterson, B.S., King, R.A., Lombroso, P.J., Findley, D.B., & Leckman, J.F. (2005). Adaptive, emotional, and family functioning of children with obsessive-compulsive disorder and comorbid Attention Deficit Hyperactivity Disorder. *American Journal of Psychiatry, 162,* 1125–1132.

Swaiman, K., & Dyken, P.R. (1999). Degenerative diseases primarily of grey matter. In K. Swaiman and S. Ashwal (Eds.), *Pediatric neurology* (pp. 833–848). St. Louis, MO: Mosby.

Symons, D.K., & Clark, S.E. (2000). A longitudinal study of mother-child relationships and theory of mind in the preschool period. *Social Development, 9,* 3–23.

Szatmari, P. (1992). The validity of autistic spectrum disorders: A literature review. *Journal of Autism and Developmental Disorders, 22,* 583–600.

Szatmari, P., Archer, L., Fishman, S., & Streiner. D.L. (1995). Asperger's syndrome and autism: Differences in behavior, cognition, and adaptive functioning. *Journal of the American Academy of child and Adolescent Psychiatry, 34,* 1662–1671.

Szatmari, P., Bryon, S.E., Boyle, M.H., Steiner, D.L., & Duku, E. (2003). Predictors of outcome among high functioning children with autism and Asperger syndrome. *Journal of Child Psychology and Psychiatry, 44,* 520–528.

Tager-Flusberg, H. (1999). A psychological approach to understanding the social and language impairments in autism. *International Review of Psychiatry, 11,* 325–334.

Tanguay, J.P., & Fischer, K.W. (1995). *Self-concious emotions: The psychology of shame, guilt, embarrassment, and pride.* New York: Guilford Press.

Tavorima, J., Kastner, I., Slater, P., & Watt, S. (1976). Chronically ill children: A psychological and emotionally deviant population. *Journal of Abnormal Child Psychology, 4,* 99–110.

Taylor, S.E., & Brown, J.D. (1988). Illusion and well being: A social psychological perspective on mental health. *Psychological Bulletin, 103,* 193–210.

Teeter, P.A. (1998). *Interventions for ADHD: Treatment in Developmental Context.* New York: Guilford Press.

Teeter, P.A., & Semrud-Clikeman, M. (1997). *Child Neuropsychology.* Boston: Allyn & Bacon.

Temple, C.M., & Carney, R.A. (1993). Intellectual functioning of children with Turner syndrome: A comparison of behavioural phenotypes. *Developmental Medicine and Child Neurology, 35,* 691–698.

Temple, C.M., & Carney, R.A. (1995). Patterns of spatial functioning in Turner's syndrome. *Cortex, 31,* 109–118.

Terman, L.M. (1925–1929). *Genetic studies of genius* (Vols. 1–5). Stanford, CA: Stanford University Press.

Terrasier, J-C. (1985). Dyssynchrony-uneven development. In J. Freeman (Ed.), *The psychology of gifted children* (pp. 265–274). New York: Wiley.

Thiemann, K.S., & Goldstein, H. (2001). Social stories, written text cues, and video feedback: Effects on social communication of children with autism. *Journal of Applied Behavioral Analysis, 34,* 425–446.

Thomas, A., & Chess, S. (1977). *Temperament and development.* New York: Brunner/Mazel.

Thorell, L.B., Bohlin, G., & Rydell, A.M. (2004). Two types of inhibitory control: Predictive relations to social functioning. *International Journal of Behavioral Development, 28*, 193–203.

Thorne, B. (1986). Girls and boys together, but mostly apart: Gender arrangements in elementary school. In W.W. Hartup & Z. Rubin (Eds.), *Relationships and development* (pp. 167–184). Hillsdale, NJ: Lawrence Erlbaum Associates.

Ting-Toomey, S. (1986). Conflict management styles in black and white subjective cultures. In Y. Kim (Ed.), *Current studies in interethnic communication* (pp. 75–88). Newbury Park, CA: Sage.

Tomarken, A.J., Davidson, R.J., Wheeler, R.E., & Kinney, L. (1992). Psychometric properties of resting anterior EEG asymmetry: Temporal stability and internal consistency. *Psychophysiology, 29*, 576–592.

Tomchin, E.M., Callahan, C.M., Sowa, C.J., & May, K.M. (1996). Coping and self-concept: Adjustment patterns in gifted adolescents. *Journal of Secondary Gifted Education, 8*, 16–27.

Toupin, J., Dery, M., Pauze, R., Fortin, L., & Mercier, H. (1997). Social, psychological and neuropsychological correlates of conduct disorder in children and adolescents. In A. Raine, P.A. Brennan, D.P. Farrington, and A. Sarnoff (Eds.), *Biosocial bases of violence* (pp. 309–311). New York: Plenum Press.

Tremblay, R.E., Pagani-Kurtz, L., Masse, L.C., Vitaro, F., & Pihl, R.O. (1995). A bi-modal preventive intervention for disruptive kindergarten boys: Its impact through mid-adolescence. *Journal of Consulting and Clinical Psychology, 63*, 560–568.

Treuting, J.J., & Hinshaw, S.P. (2001). Depression and self-esteem in boys with attention-deficit/hyperactivity disorder: Associations with comorbid aggression and explanatory attributional mechanisms. *Journal of Abnormal Child Psychology, 29*, 23–39.

Trost, G. (2000). Prediction of excellence in school, university, and work. In K.A. Heller, F.J. Monks, R. Sternberg, & R. Subotnik (Eds.), *International handbook of research and development of giftedness and talent* (pp. 317–327). Oxford: Pergamon Press.

Tsatsanis, K.D. (2003). Outcome research in Asperger syndrome and autism. *Child and Adolescent Psychiatric Clinics of North America, 12*, 47–63.

Tuchman, R.F. & Rapin, I. (1997). Regression in pervasive developmental disorders: Seizure and epileptiform electroencephalogram correlates. *Pediatrics, 99*, 560–566.

Tur-Kaspa, H. (2002). Social cognition in learning disabilities. In B.Y. Wong and M. Donahue (Eds.), *The social dimensions of learning disabilities* (pp. 11–32). Hillsdale, NJ: Lawrence Erlbaum Associates.

Tur-Kaspa, H. (2004). Social-information-processing skills of kindergarten children with developmental learning disabilities. *Learning Disabilities Research & Practice, 19*, 3–11.

Tur-Kaspa, H., & Bryan, T. (1994). Social information-processing skills of students with learning disabilities. *Learning Disabilities Research & Practice, 9*, 12–23.

Tur-Kaspa, H., Margalit, M., & Most, T. (1999). Reciprocal friendship, reciprocal rejection, and socio-emotional adjustment: The social experiences of children with learning disorders over a one-year period. *European Journal of Special Needs Education, 14*, 37–48.

Tutty, S., Gephart, H., & Wurzbacher, K. (2003). Enhancing behavioral and social skill functioning in children newly diagnosed with attention-deficit hyperactivity disorder in a pediatric setting. *Journal of Developmental and Behavioral Pediatrics, 24*, 51–58.

Udvari, S.J., & Rubin, K.H. (1996). Gifted and non-selected children's perceptions of academic achievement, academic effort, and athleticism. *Gifted Child Quarterly, 40,* 311–319.

Udwin, O., & Yule, W. (1990). Expressive language of children with Williams syndrome. *American Journal of Medical Genetics Supplement, 6,* 108–114.

Valderhaug, R., & Ivarsson, T. (2005). Functional impairment in clinical samples of Norwegian and Swedish children and adolescents with obsessive-compulsive disorder. *European Child and Adolescent Psychiatry, 14,* 164–173.

Vallance, D.D., Cummings, R.L., & Humphries, T. (1998). Mediators of the risk for problem behavior in children with language learning disabilities. *Journal of Learning Disabilities, 31,* 160–172.

Vallance, D.D., & Wintre, M.G. (1997). Discourse processes underlying social competence in children with language learning disabilities. *Development and Psychopathology, 9,* 95–108.

van Ijzendoorn, M.J. (1997). Attachment, emergent morality, and aggression: Toward a developmental socioemotional model of antisocial behavior. *International Journal of Behavioral Development, 21,* 703–727.

Van Tassel-Baska, J., Olszewski-Kulbilius, P., & Kulieke, M. (1994). A study of self-concept and social support in advantaged and disadvantaged seventh and eighth grade gifted students. *Roeper Review, 16,* 186–191.

Varni, J.W. Blout, R.L., & Quiggins, D.L. (1998). Oncologic disorders. In R.T. Ammerman and J.V. Campo (Eds.), *Handbook of pediatric psychology and psychiatry* (pp. 313–346). Needham Heights, MA: Allyn & Bacon.

Varni, J.W., Katz, E.R., Colegrove, R., & Dolgin, M. (1994). Perceived stress and adjustment of long-term survivors of childhood cancer. *Journal of Psychosocial Oncology, 12,* 1–16.

Varni, J.W., Katz, E.R., Seid, M., Quiggins, D.J.L., & Friedman-Bender, A. (1998). The pediatric cancer Quality of Life Inventory-32 (PCQL-32). *Cancer, 82,* 1184–1196.

Vaughn, S.R., Elbaum, B.E., & Schumm, J.S. (1996). The effects of inclusion on the social functioning of students with learning disabilities. *Journal of Learning Disabilities, 29,* 598–608.

Vaughn, S.R. & Haager, D. (1994). Social competence as a multifaceted construct: How do students with learning disabilities fare? *Learning Disability Quarterly, 17,* 253–266.

Vaughn, S.R., Haager, D., Hogan, A., & Kouzekanani, K. (1992). Self-concept and peer acceptance in students with learning disabilities: A four- to five-year prospective study. *Journal of Educational Psychology, 84,* 43–50.

Vaughn, S., & Hogan, A. (1994). The social competence of students with learning disabilities over time: A within-individuals examination. *Journal of Learning Disabilities, 27,* 292–303.

Vaughn, S.R., Hogan, A., Kouzekanani, K., & Shapiro, S. (1990). Peer acceptance, self-perceptions, and social skills of LD students prior to identification. *Journal of Educational Psychology, 82,* 101–106.

Vaughn, S.R., McIntosh, R., Schumm, J.S., Haager, D., & Callwood, D. (1993). Social status, peer acceptance, and reciprocal friendships revisited. *Learning Disabilities, Research & Practice, 8,* 82–88.

Veld, B.P., & Fidler, G.S. (2002). *The Lifestyle Performance Model: A model for engaging the power of occupation.* Thorofare, NJ: Slack Inc.

Venter, A., Lord, C., & Schopler, E. (1992). A follow-up study of high-functioning autistic children. *Journal of Child Psychology and Psychiatry, 33,* 489–507.

Vernberg, E.M. (1990). Psychological adjustment and experiences with peers during early adolescence: Reciprocal, incidental, or unidirectional relationships? *Journal of Abnormal Child Psychology, 18,* 187–198.

Vespi, L., & Yewchuck, C. (1992). A phenomenological study of the social/emotional characteristics of gifted learning-disabled children. *Journal for the Education of the Gifted, 16*, 55–72.

Vila, G., Nollet-Clemencon, C., Vera, M., Robert, J.J., de Blic, J., Jouvent, R., Mouren-Simeoni, M.C., & Scheinmann, P. (1999). Prevalence of DSM IV disorders in children and adolescents with asthma versus diabetes. *Canadian Journal of Psychiatry, 44*, 1–13.

Vila, G., Nollet-Clemencon, C., Vera, M., Robert, J.J., de Blic, J., Mouren-Simeoni, M.C., & Scheinmann, P. (2000). Prevalence of DSM IV anxiety and affective disorders in a pediatric population of asthmatic children and adolescents. *Journal of Affective Disorders, 58*, 223–231.

Vliestra, A.G. (1981). Full-versus half-day preschool attendance: Effects in young children as assessed by teacher-ratings and behavioral observations. *Child Development, 52*, 603–610.

Voeller, K.K.S. (1986). Right hemisphere deficit syndrome in children. *American Journal of Psychiatry, 143*, 1004–1009.

Voeller, K.K.S. (1994). Techniques for measuring social competence in children. In G.R. Lyon (Ed.), *Frames of reference for the assessment of learning disabilities: New views on measurement issues* (pp. 523–554). Baltimore: Paul H. Brookes Publishing Company.

Voeller, K.K.S. (1995). Clinical neurologic aspects of the right-hemisphere deficit syndrome. *Journal of Child Neurology, 10*, S16-S22.

Vogel, J.J., Bowers, C.A., & Vogel, D.S. (2003). Cerebral lateralization of spatial abilities: A meta-analysis. *Brain and Cognition, 52*, 197–204.

Volkmar, F.R., Klin, A., & Pauls, D. (1998). Nosological and genetic aspects of Asperger Syndrome. *Journal of Autism and Developmental Disorders,* (2nd. Edition, pp. 47–59). New York: Wiley.

Volkmar, F.R., Klin, A., Schultz, R., Marano. W.D., Sparrow, S., & Cohen, D.J. (1996). Asperger's syndrome. *Journal of the American Academy of Child and Adolescent Psychiatry, 35*, 118–123.

Volkmar, F.R., Klin, A., Siegal, B., Szatmari, P., Lord, C., Campbell, M., Freeman, B.J., Cicchetti, D.V., Rutter, M., Kline, W., Buitelaar, J., Hattab, Y., Fombonne, E., Fuentes, J., Werry, J., Stone, W., Kerbeshian, J., Hoshino, Y., Bregman, J., Loveland, K., Szymanski, L., & Towbin, K. (1994). Field trial for autistic disorder in DSM IV. *American Journal of Psychiatry, 151*, 1361–1367.

Volkmar, F.R., Lord, C., Bailey, A., Schultz, R.T., & Klin, A. (2004). Autism and pervasive developmental disorders. *Journal of Child Psychology and Psychiatry, 45*, 135–170.

Volkmar, F.R., & Nelson, D.S. (1990). Seizure disorders in autism. *Journal of the American Academy of Child and Adolescent Psychiatry, 151*, 1361–1367.

Volkmar, F.R., Stier, D.M., & Cohen, D.J. (1985). Age of recognition of pervasive developmental disorder. *American Journal of Psychiatry, 142*, 1450–1452.

Volling, B.L., Youngblade, L.M., & Belsky, J. (1997). Young children's social relationships with sibling and friends. *American Journal of Orthopsychiatry, 67*, 102–111.

Vriezen, E.R. (2000). Cognitive and behavioral sequelae of very mild head injury in children. *Journal of the International Neuropsychological Society, 6*, 131.

Vygotsky, L.S. (1978). *Mind in Society: The development of higher psychological processes.* Cambridge, MA: MIT Press.

Vygotsky, L.S. (1986). *Thought and language.* Cambrtdge. MA: MIT Press.

Wahler, R.G., & Dumas, J.E. (1984). Changing the observational coding styles of insular and noninsular mothers: A step toward maintenance of parent training effects. In R.F. Dangel and R.A. Polster (Eds.), *Parent training: Foundations of research and practice* (pp. 379–416). New York: Guilford Press.

Waisbren, S.E. (1999). Phenylketonuria. In S. Goldstein and C.R. Reynolds (Eds.), *Handbook of neurodevelopmental and genetic disorders* (pp. 433–458). New York: Guilford

Waldron, K.A., Saphire, D.G., & Rosenblum, S.A. (1987). Learning disabilities and giftedness: Identification based on self-concept, behavior, and academic patterns. *Journal of Learning Disabilities, 20*, 422–427.

Walker, H., Stiller, B., Severson, H.H., Feil, E.G., Golly, A. (1998). First step to success: Intervening at the point of school entry to prevent antisocial behavior patterns. *Psychology in the Schools, 35*, 259–269.

Wals, M., Hillegers, M.H., Reichart, C.G., Ormel, J., Nolen, W.A., & Verhulst, F.C. (2001). Prevalence of psychopathology in children of a bipolar parent. *Journal of the American Academy of Child and Adolescent Psychiatry, 40*, 1094–1102.

Wang, R., He, Y., Liu, L. (2002). Social competence and related factors in primary school students. *Chinese Mental Health Journal, 16*, 791–793.

Wang, Y.K., Samos, C.H., Peoples, R., Perez-Jurado, L.A., Nusse, R., & Francke, U. (1997). A novel human homologue of the *Drosphila* frizzed wnt receptor gene binds wingless protein and is in the Williams syndrome deletion at 7q11.23. *Human Molecular Genetics, 6*, 465–472.

Warschausky, S., Cohen, E.H., Parker, J.G., Levendosky, A.A., & Okun, A. (1997). Social problem-solving skills of children with traumatic brain injury. *Pediatric Rehabilitation, 1*, 77–81.

Waschbusch, D.A. (2002). A meta-analytic examination of comorbid hyperactive-impulsive-attention problems and conduct problems. *Psychological Bulletin, 128*, 118–150.

Wassink T.H., Piven, J., & Vieland, V.J. (2001). Evidence supporting WNT2 as an autism susceptibility gene. *American Journal of Medical Genetics, 105*, 406–413.

Waters, E., & Sroufe, L. A. (1983). Social competence as a developmental construct. *Developmental Review. 3*, 79–97.

Webster-Stratton, C. (1984). Randomized trial of two parent-training programs for families with conduct disordered children. *Journal of Consulting and Clinical Psychology, 52*, 666–678.

Webster-Stratton, C. (1990). Stress: A potential disruptor of parent perceptions and family interactions. *Journal of Clinical Child Psychology, 19*, 302–312.

Webster-Stratton, C. (1993). Strategies for helping early school-aged children with oppositional defiant and conduct disorders: The importance of home-school partnerships. *School Psychology Review, 22*, 1–22.

Webster-Stratton, C., & Hammond, M. (1990). Predictors of treatment outcome in parent training for families with conduct problem children. *Behavior Therapy, 21*, 319–327.

Webster-Stratton, C., & Lindsay, D.W. (1999). Social competence and conduct problems in young children: Issues in Assessment. *Journal of Clinical Child Psychology, 28*, 25–43.

Webster-Sratton, C., & Spitzer, A. (1991). Reliability and validity of a parent Daily Discipline Inventory, DDI. *Behavior Assessment, 13*, 221–239.

Weckerly, J. (2002). Pediatric bipolar mood disorder. *Journal of Developmental and Behavioral Pediatrics, 23*, 42–56.

Weinfield, N.S., Ogawa, J.R. & Sroufe, L.A. (1997). Early attachment as a pathway to adolescent peer competence. *Journal of Research on Adolescence, 7*, 241–265.

Weintraub, S., & Mesulam, M-M. (1998). Visual hemispatial inattention: Stimulus parameters and exploratory strategies. *Journal of Neurology, Neurosurgery, and Psychiatry, 51*, 1481–1488.

Weiss, E. (1984). Learning-disabled children's understanding of social interactions of peers. *Journal of Learning Disabilities, 17*, 612–615.

Weiss, G. & Hechtman, L. (1993). *Hyperactive children grown up (2nd ed.):* ADHD in children, adolescents, and adults. New York: Guilford Press.

Weiss, M.J., & Harris, S.L. (2001). Teaching social skills to people with autism. *Behavior Modification, 25*, 785–802.

Weissberg-Benchell, J., & Glasgow, A. (1997). The role of temperament in children with insulin-dependent diabetes mellitus. *Journal of Pediatric Psychology, 22*, 795–809.

Weisse, D.F. (1990). Gifted adolescents and suicide. *School Counselor, 37*, 351–358.

Weissman, M.M., Warner, V., & Wickmaratne, P.J. (1999). Grandparents, parents, and grandchildren at high risk for depression: A three-generational study. *Journal of the American Academy of Child and Adolescent Psychology, 28*, 289–296.

Wellman, H.M., Cross, D., & Watson, J. (2001). Meta-analysis of theory of mind development: the truth about false belief. *Child Development, 72*, 655–684.

Wellman, H.M., & Liu, D. (2004). Scaling of theory of mind tasks. *Child Development, 75*, 523–541.

Wellman, H.M., Phillips, A.T., Dunphy-Lelii, S., & LaLonde, N. (2004). Infant social attention predicts preschool social cognition. *Developmental Science, 7*, 283–288.

Wesh, J.A., & Bireman, K.L. (2003). using the clinical interview to assess children's interpersonal reasoning and emotional understanding. In C.R. Reynolds, & R.W. Kamphaus (Eds.) *Handbook of Psychological and Educational Assessment of children* (2nd edition, pp. 219–234). New York: Guilford Press.

Welsh, J., Domitrovich, C.E., Bierman, K.L., & Lang, J. (2003). Promoting safe schools and healthy students in rural Pennsylvania. *Psychology in the Schools, 40*, 457–472.

Wenar, C. (1994). *Developmental psychopathology: From infancy through adolescence.* New York: McGraw Hill.

Wender, P. (1987). *The hyperactive child, adolescent, and adult.* New York: Oxford University Press.

Wentzel, K.R. (1994). Relations of social goal pursuit to social acceptance, classroom behavior, and perceived social support. *Journal of Educational Psychology, 86*, 173–182.

Wentzel, K.R., & Caldwell, K.C. (1997). Friendships, peer acceptance, and group membership: Relations to academic achievement in middle school. *Child Development, 68*, 1198–1209.

Wentzel, K.R., & Feldman, S.S. (1996). Relations of cohesion and power in family dyads to social and emotional adjustment. *Journal of Research on Adolescence, 6*, 225–244.

Wentzel, K.R., & McNamara, C.C. (1999). Interpersonal relationships, emotional distress, and prosocial behavior in middle school. *Journal of Early Adolescence, 19*, 114–125.

Wenz-Gross, M., & Siperstein, G.N. (1997). Importance of social support in the adjustment of children with learning problems. *Exceptional Children, 63*, 183–193.

Wetherby, A.M., & Prutting, C.A. (1984). Profiles of communicative and cognitive-social abilities in autistic children. *Journal of Speech and Hearing Research, 27*, 364–377.

Whalen, C.K., Henker, B., & Granger, D.A. (1990). Social judgment process in hyperactive boys: Effects of methylphenidate and comparisons with normal peers. *Journal of Abnormal Child Psychology, 18*, 297–316.

Whalen, C.K., & Schreibman, L. (2002). Joint attention training for children with autism using behavior modification procedures. *Journal of Child Psychology and Psychiatry, 44*, 456–468.

Wheeler, J., & Carlson, C.L. (1994). The social functioning of children with ADD with hyperactivity and ADD without hyperactivity: A comparison of their peer relations and social deficits. *Journal of Emotional and Behavioral Disorders, 2*, 2–13.

White, J., Moffit, T., Earls, F., & Robins, L. (1990). Preschool predictors of persistent conduct disorder and delinquency. *Criminology, 28*, 443–454.

Wiener, J. (2002). Friendship and social adjustment of children with learning disabilities. In B.Y.L. Wong and M.L. Donahue (Eds.), *The social dimensions of learning disabilities: Essays in honor of Tanis Bryan* (pp. 93–114). Mahway, NJ: Erlbaum.

Wiener, J., & Harris, P.J. (1997). Evaluation of an individualized context-based social skills training program for children with learning disabilities. *Learning Disabilities, Research & Practice, 12*, 40–53.

Wiener, J., Harris, P.J., & Shirer, C. (1990). Achievement and social-behavioral correlates of peer status in LD children. *Learning Disabilities Quarterly, 13*, 114–127.

Wiener, J., & Schneider, B. (2002). A multisource exploration of friendship patterns of children with and without learning disabilities. *Journal of Abnormal Child Psychology, 30*, 127–141.

Wiener, J., & Tardiff, C.Y. (2004). Social and emotional functioning of children with learning disabilities: Does special education placement make a difference? *Learning Disabilities, Research & Practice, 19*, 20–32.

Wiig, E.H., & Secord, W. (1989). *Test of Language Competence—Expanded Edition: Administration manual.* San Antonio, TX: Psychological Corporation.

Wilkinson, A.D., Schaefer, V.A., & Semrud-Clikeman, M. (2002). *Visual-motor and visual-perceptual abilities of children and adolescents with NVLD and ADHD.* Paper presented at the annual convention of the American Psychological Association, Chicago, IL.

Williams, J.K. (1995). Parenting a daughter with precocious puberty or Turner syndrome. *Journal of Pediatric Health Care, 9*, 109–114.

Williams, J., Sharp, G., & Bates, S. (1996). Academic achievement and the behavioral ratings of children with absence and complex partial epilepsy. *Educational Treatment of Children, 19*, 143–152.

Wilson, B.J. (1999). Entry behavior and emotion regulation abilities of developmentally delayed boys. *Developmental Psychology, 35*, 214–223.

Windecker-Nelson, E., Melson, G.F., & Moon, S.M. (1997). Intellectually gifted preschoolers' perceived competence: Relations to maternal attitudes, concerns, and support. *Gifted Child Quarterly, 41*, 133–144.

Wing, L. (1980). Childhood autism and social class: A question of selection? *British Journal of Psychiatry, 137*, 410–417.

Wing, L. (2000). Past and future research on Asperger Syndrome. In A. Klin, S.S. Sparrow, & F.R. Volkmar (Eds.), *Asperger Syndrome* (pp. 418–432). New York: Guilford Press.

Wolfberg, P.J., & Schuler, A.L. (1999). Fostering peer interaction, imaginative play and spontaneous language in children with autism. *Child Language Teaching and Therapy, 15*, 41–52.

Wolmer, L., Laor, N., & Cicchetti, D.V. (2001). Validation of the Comprehensive Assessment of Defense Style (CADS): Mothers' and children's responses to the stresses of missile attacks. *Journal of Nervous and Mental Disease, 189*, 369–376.

Wolraich, M.L., Hannah, J.N., Pinnock, T.Y., Baumaertel, A., & Brown, J. (1996). Comparison of diagnostic criteria for attention-deficit hyperactivity disorder in a county-wide sample. *Journal of the American Academy of Child and Adolescent Psychiatry, 35*, 319–324.

Wood, F., Felton, R., Flowers, L., & Naylor, C. (1991). Neurobehavioral definition of dyslexia. In D.D. Duane and D.B. Gray (Eds.), *The reading brain: The biological basis of dyslexia* (pp. 1–26). Parkton, MD: York Press.

Woods, S.P., Weinborn, M., Ball, J.D., Tiller-Nevin, S., & Pickett, T.C. (2000). Periventricular leukomalacia (PVL): An identical twin case study illustration of white matter dysfunction and nonverbal learning disability (NLD). *Child Neuropsychology, 6*, 274–285.

Woolfolk, A. (2004). *Educational Psychology* (9th ed.). Boston: Allyn & Bacon

World Health Organization (1993). *The ICD-10 Classification of Mental and Behavioural Disorders: Diagnostic Criteria for Research.* Geneva: World Health Organization.

Worling, D.E., Humphries, T., & Tannock, R. (1999). Spatial and emotional aspects of language inferencing in nonverbal learning disabilities. *Brain and Language, 70*, 220–239.

Wozniak, J., Biederman, J., Faraone, S.V. et al. (1997). Mania in children with pervasive developmental disorder revisted. *Journal of the American Academy of Child and Adolescent Psychiatry, 36*, 1552–1559.

Yirmiya, N., Erel, O., Shaked, M., & Solomonica-Levi, D. (1998). Meta-analyses comparing theory of mind abilities of individuals with autism, individuals with mental retardation, and normal developing individuals. *Psychological Bulletin, 124*, 282–307.

Ylvilsaker, M. (1993). Communication outcome in children and adolescents with traumatic brain injury. *Neuropsychological Rehabilitation, 3*, 367–387.

Ylvilsaker, M., Turkstra, L.S., & Coelho, C. (2005). Behavioral and social interventions for individuals with traumatic brain injury: A summary of the research with clinical implications. *Seminars in Speech and Language, 26*, 256–267.

Zakriski, A.L., Jacobs, M., & Coie, J.D. (1997). Coping with childhood peer rejection. In S.A. Wolchik, and I.N. Sandler (Eds.), *Handbook of children's coping: Linking theory and intervention* (pp. 97–123). New York: Plenum.

Zaroff, C.M., & Isaacs, K. (2005). Neurocutaneous syndromes: Behavioral features. *Epilepsy and Behavior, 7*, 133–142.

Zentall, S. S., Moon, S.M., Hall, A.M., & Grskovic, J.A. (2001). Learning and motivational characteristics of boys with AD/HD and/or giftedness. *Exceptional Children, 67*, 499–519.

Zhou, Q., Eisenberg, N., Losoy, S.H., Fabes, R.A., Reiser, M., Guthrie, I.K., Muprhy, B.C., Cumberland, A.J., & Shepard, S.A. (2002). The relations of parental warmth and positive expressiveness to children's empathy-related responding and social functioning: A longitudinal study. *Child Development, 73*, 893–915.

Zhu, Y., Leung, K.M., Liu, P-Z., Zhou, M., & Su, L-Y. (2005). Cormorbid behavioural problems in Tourette's syndrome are positively correlated with the severity of tic symptoms. *Australian and New Zealand Journal of Psychiatry, 40*, 67–73.

Zigler, E., & Burack, J.A. (1989). Personality development and the dually diagnosed person. *Research in Developmental Disabilities, 10*, 225–240.

Zoccolillo, M., Pickles, A., Quinton, D., & Rutter, M. (1992). The outcome of conduct disorder: Implications for defining adult personality disorder and conduct disorder. *Psychological Medicine, 22*, 971–976.

Zsolani, A. (2002). Relationship between children's social competence, learning motivation, and school achievement. *Educational Psychology, 22*, 317–330.

Zygmunt, L., Larson, M.S., & Tilson, G. P. (1994). Disability awareness training and social networking. In M.S. Moon (Ed.), *Making school and community recreation fun for everyone* (pp. 209–226). Baltimore, MD: Paul H. Brookes Publishing Co.

Index

Printed in the United States
83435LV00001B/117-140/A

9 780387 713656